WITHDRAWN

GOD AND THE SOCIAL PROCESS

THE UNIVERSITY OF CHICAGO PRESS
CHICAGO, ILLINOIS

—

THE BAKER & TAYLOR COMPANY
NEW YORK

THE CAMBRIDGE UNIVERSITY PRESS
LONDON

THE MARUZEN-KABUSHIKI-KAISHA
TOKYO, OSAKA, KYOTO, FUKUOKA, SENDAI

THE COMMERCIAL PRESS, LIMITED
SHANGHAI

GOD AND
THE SOCIAL PROCESS

A STUDY IN HEBREW HISTORY

By LOUIS WALLIS

Author of "Sociological Study of the Bible"

THE UNIVERSITY OF CHICAGO PRESS
CHICAGO · ILLINOIS

TO THE MEMORY OF
JOSEPH FELS
LOVER OF HUMANITY
PROMOTER OF DEMOCRACY

PREFACE

Hebrew history has meaning because it is known to bear some special relation to the idea of God which prevails in modern society. If it lacked this particular significance, it would get no more attention than do the histories of many other peoples now forgotten amid the dust of antiquity. But there are wide differences of opinion about the exact nature of the relationship between ancient Israel and the idea of God now professed in church and synagogue. We may think of Hebrew history as an epoch of supernaturalism, different in kind from the experience of other nations; or we may look at it from the standpoint of modern higher criticism, taking the so-called "miracles" at a discount; or again, by an illogical operation of the intellect, we may apply the term "history" to gentile nations alone, and thus ignore ancient Hebrew life entirely. As a matter of fact, whether we realize it or not, our attitude toward the subject is a more or less accurate index of the cultural stage in which we find ourselves. This fact was expressed in a striking way by the late Professor Albion W. Small, of the University of Chicago, who organized and for many years directed the Department of Sociology in that institution. Writing in 1905, he said:

Every one of us was taught to believe that certain representatives of the Hebrew race had different means of communicating with God from those that are available today. We consequently accepted a version of Hebrew history which made out of it a fantastic tradition that only began to take on the semblance of reality within the recollection of living men [*General Sociology* (1905), p. 483].

Since Hebrew history is connected in a special way with religion, and since religion is now passing through a crisis, it would not be strange to find that the crisis affects our idea of the history. The standard theological doctrines and religious atti-

tudes of the past are now so modified or challenged by the rapid
progress of scientific research in physics, biology, psychology,
and history that our educational system has not yet evolved an
adequate technique for procedure in this field. The scientific interpretation of Hebrew history gives a fascinating approach to
the religious problem of today; and while the pedagogical value
of this approach is not generally seen, it will certainly be recognized in the near future.

That our educational system should make scientific access to
Hebrew history more difficult than to Greek and Roman history
is both anomalous and illogical. The present work undertakes
to deal with that anomaly in a form serviceable both to the general reader and to the college student. The history of any nation is a double process, consisting (1) of *transactions*, or events,
which can be described in objective terms, and (2) of *ideas*
which are correlated with the events. The older, ecclesiastical
interpretation of Hebrew history approached the subject mainly
in view of ideas; whereas the newer, scientific treatment of the
subject seeks to relate the events to the ideas in terms of cause
and effect.

A preliminary treatment of this problem was undertaken
many years ago, beginning in 1902. Articles were published in
the *American Journal of Sociology* and the *American Journal of
Theology;* after which a volume, *Sociological Study of the Bible,*
was issued in 1912 by the University of Chicago Press. This
work has been frequently reprinted, reaching a wide circulation;
and although listed as a textbook in the *Catalogue* of the University Press, and used in schools, it is also intended for general
reading. Its aims are to suggest a new method of handling the
documents, or "sources," of Hebrew history, and to show the
relation of the Bible to social development. In reviewing the
book Professor Ernst Troeltsch, of Berlin University, and leader
of the "religious history" school in Germany, wrote: "This is
the path which theological research must follow if the history of

religious ethics is to be understood. This is one of the most suggestive and instructive books that have come into my hands in many a day" (*Theologische Literaturzeitung*, July 19, 1913). Professor Henry Preserved Smith, of Union Theological Seminary, New York, wrote: "The book will have great value as a contribution to a really historical understanding of the Bible. The argument is well sustained." Professor John E. McFadyen, of Free Church College, Glasgow, Scotland, wrote: " 'Sociological Study of the Bible' throws a fresh and brilliant light on the rise of the social problem in Israel." Professors George F. Moore, Benjamin W. Bacon, Crawford H. Toy, George A. Barton, Lewis B. Paton, Ira M. Price, Henry T. Fowler, J. M. P. Smith, and other Old Testament specialists co-operated in ways which the writer has never had opportunity fully to acknowledge.

The present volume undertakes to apply more concretely the method of the earlier book, and to show how the scriptural sources relate themselves to Hebrew history as an element in the cultural basis of modern society and as a discipline ranking with Greek and Roman studies. The history of Israel was not an episode in a corner; it was part of a widespread evolution which took place in the ancient oriental world. That vast and busy arena of human life was already old when the Hebrew state was born in Palestine; and Israel's distinctive idea of God arose at a period when civilization was falling into decay through much the same causes now at work in modern society. The oriental middle class, lying between the enslaved proletariat below and a small but powerful group of landed nobles above, was being gradually crushed out in all countries. This element in Egypt found very little voice; but in the Tigro-Euphrates Valley it was influential enough to inspire the Code of Hammurabi, which protected the weaker section of the property class against the more powerful; while among the Hebrews, the crushing-out of the peasantry was connected with the very forces which gave rise to ethical monotheism. But when the belief in one God had actually become established, it was divorced from the economic and social conditions that gave rise to it; so that monotheism took the form of an abstract idea in the Jewish synagogue and the Christian church, impeding the efforts of scientific scholarship to recover the facts of Hebrew history.

The subject is beset by two chief difficulties which were formidable thirty years ago, but which are now in the way of being overcome. The first relates to the higher criticism of the Bible as developed in the eighteenth and nineteenth centuries, from Astruc and De Wette to Wellhausen. The work of these critical investigators, in brief, was to take the ancient, orthodox formula, "The Law and the Prophets," and reverse it so as to read *"The Prophets* and the Law"—viewing Hebrew history as an evolution in which the prophets came before the Law instead of after it, leading the way upward out of paganism into ethical monotheism. The pioneers of modern biblical research conducted their work hampered by the fire of orthodoxy; and the conditions under which they were compelled to toil produced in them a strong apologetic tendency to outrun achievement by demonstrating that the new investigations and results were compatible with established religion. The critics found themselves in an atmosphere which tended to prevent them from realizing that their work was not so much a new interpretation of Hebrew history as it was a new theory of the biblical documents, which left the history unexplained. Wellhausen himself, writing in 1909, thirty years after the publication of his epoch-making work, *Geschichte Israels,* declared that he could not show how the distinctive ideas of Israel are correlated with the objective process of Hebrew history in terms of cause and effect ("Israelitisch-jüdische Religion," *Kultur der Gegenwart* [1909], Teil I, p. 15). A similar statement was made by Professor Francis Brown, of the Union Theological Seminary, New York, who said that we cannot show how the later and more developed Yahweh was differentiated from the earlier and more primitive Yahweh (*Old*

Testament and Semitic Studies in Honor of William Rainey Harper [1908], p. xxx). Such being the case, Wellhausen's remarkable volume, *Geschichte Israels* ("History of Israel"), was given this title prematurely. For Hebrew history has meaning through its identification with the idea of God; and any book which treats that history without explaining the central idea of God in terms of cause and effect is at best dealing with only the raw materials of the subject. This observation applies to such works as the following: Stade, *Geschichte des Volkes Israel* (1881–88); Kittel, *Geschichte der Hebräer* (1882–92); Klosterman, *Geschichte des Volkes Israel* (1896); Kent, *History of the Hebrew People* (1896–1900); Cornill, *History of the People of Israel* (1898); Guthe, *Geschichte des Volkes Israel* (1899); H. P. Smith, *Old Testament History* (1903). These works, and others in the same class, are based upon thoroughly respectable scholarship; and yet their treatment of the central problem leads to such declarations as those of Professors Francis Brown and Wellhausen cited above. The shortcomings of biblical higher criticism with reference to the interpretation of Hebrew history arise from the technical consideration that the new source-view itself (i.e., "The Prophets and the Law") took form prior to the development of sociological and economic scholarship which has occurred in the last fifty years. As a consequence, Hebrew studies have remained in the stage of prolegomena, while the field of general history has been transformed. Society throughout the globe, in all ages of the world, has come within the purview of the evolutionist—except that which anciently occupied the eastern highlands of the Mediterranean, and which has been held in spiritual quarantine. Meanwhile, biblical higher criticism, continuing to hold its ground by sheer force of merit, has tended to become a kind of modernist orthodoxy whose point is clear to scientific scholarship, while its real value is not known to the intelligent public.

The other difficulty to which we refer is concerned with the

alleged "atheistic" tendencies of the newer biblical interpretation. Orthodox writers have claimed that the higher criticism is
"naturalistic," and has a tendency to destroy belief in the idea
of God as the outcome of "supernatural revelation." That critical scholarship tends to assimilate with evolutionary modes of
thought is undeniable. Thus, Professor Kuenen, of Leiden University, Holland, wrote as follows: "It is the supposition of a
natural development alone which accounts for all the phenomena" (*Prophets and Prophecy in Israel* [1877], p. 585). But with
biblical critics, natural development is only a "supposition"
which is devoid of concrete content, and has no power to account for the phenomena of Hebrew religion. Moreover, the distinction between the so-called "natural" and the so-called "supernatural" is itself based upon a pure assumption which illog-
ically cuts the universe in two. Orthodox opponents of higher
criticism declare that an evolutionary interpretation of Hebrew
religion is "atheistic" because it seems to exclude God from Hebrew history. But against this objection the counterclaim arises
that no matter how radical may be an explanation of Hebrew
history in terms of evolution, we cannot assume that it is necessarily incompatible with the idea of divine Providence imma-
nent *in the process*. A scientific interpreter of Hebrew history is
bound to explain the development of Israel without apologetic
preoccupation; but no possible measure of success in this field
can discredit the claims of theistic belief. Theism, on the one
hand, and science, on the other hand, represent lines of thought
which are not mutually destructive and exclusive; they are simply *two different lines of interest* whose metaphysical relations we
are not able to demonstrate, just as we cannot show the nexus
between consciousness and the body. Thus, Principal George
Adam Smith, of Aberdeen University, Scotland, speaking as a
pure scientist, says that "the god of early Israel was a tribal
god," and that the Israelites "did not deny the reality of other
gods" (*Modern Criticism and the Preaching of the Old Testament*

[1901], pp. 128, 129). But, on the other hand, speaking as a theistic believer, the same authority says: "Behind that national deity of Israel, and through the obscure and vain imaginations the early nation had of him, there were present the Character and Will of God himself, using the people's low thoughts and symbols to express himself to them, lifting them always a little higher" (*Biblical World*, 1896, pp. 100, 101). Religious faith is independent of scientific results which may be reached in the field of Hebrew study or any other department of learning. The scientific scholar can have no quarrel with belief in a God who uses Hebrew history and world-history for divine ends; and since the human spirit can work within the terms of natural laws which condition our bodily existence, there is no ground for saying that a higher personality is not active within the terms of what we call "natural development." The long evolution which resulted in the appearance of man upon the earth, and which has continued its course through the stupendous march of human history from the Stone Age until now, is a tragic drama which loses all point and purpose if, in the background, there be no central Will imparting ultimate intelligibility to the vast process. And as man becomes more and more aware of his place in the cosmos, he will be forced either to rest upon the view that the universe is the home of God or to become increasingly conscious of alienation within the limits of his own thought.

These considerations, however, can have no influence upon scientific research, which must move independently within its own orbit. The physicist, the chemist, the biologist, and the astronomer will continue to explain complex phenomena in terms of simpler facts, linking their premises and conclusions together in terms of cause and effect, and conducting all research upon purely "naturalistic" grounds. And, in the same way, the historian writing about Greece, Rome, England, America, or any other gentile people is not supposed to weave theological demonstrations into his narrative. As a historian, he has no concern with the merits of theological questions. Likewise, it is clear that the intelligent public has been for some time approaching this position with reference to Hebrew history. The writer's experience in connection with *Sociological Study of the Bible* has led to the conviction that there is now a distinct place not merely among professional scholars, but outside the academic field, for what may be called a purely secular treatise on Hebrew history, interpreting the evolution of Hebrew religion from a new standpoint, within the terms of causes and effects intelligible at once to the general reader and to the college student.

But the problem of Hebrew history is involved with human emotions and faith to such an extent that every author who enters this field should bear in mind that he is dealing with a national experience which uniquely symbolizes moral and spiritual values. Any book written from the standpoint of this volume is sure to reach the hands of young people and others who are in revolt against the standard forms of religious and ethical doctrine; and therefore the considerations outlined above should be carefully held in view by general readers, teachers, and students. And when the book is used as a text, the instructor should have an opening session dealing with the topics raised in this Preface. Hebrew history can be made highly profitable not only as a scientific discipline but as giving emphasis to moral and spiritual values in a way which is not secured through any other form of study.

KEW GARDENS
LONG ISLAND, NEW YORK

ACKNOWLEDGMENTS

It is hoped that no name is omitted from the following list of those who, up to the time of final proof, have read the manuscript of this book: Professor George Aaron Barton, the University of Pennsylvania; Professor W. C. Bower, the University of Chicago; Rabbi Baruch Braunstein, Counselor to Jewish Students, Columbia University, New York City; Rev. Dr. Harry Emerson Fosdick, Riverside Church, New York City;

Professor Kemper Fullerton, Oberlin College; Professor William C. Graham, the University of Chicago; Professor Mordecai Kaplan, Jewish Theological Seminary, New York City; Rev. Dr. Albert A. Madsen, the First Congregational Church, Gloucester, Massachusetts; Professor Shailer Mathews, the University of Chicago; Bishop Francis J. McConnell, New York City; Professor Samuel A. B. Mercer, Trinity College, Toronto, Canada; Rabbi Louis I. Newman, Temple Rodeph Sholom, New York City; Professor Ismar Peritz, Syracuse University; Professor Ira M. Price, the University of Chicago; Professor Edward A. Ross, Wisconsin University; Professor Ovid R. Sellers, the Presbyterian Theological Seminary, Chicago; Principal George Adam Smith, Aberdeen University, Scotland; Professor Shalom Spiegel, the Jewish Institute of Religion, New York City; Professor Herbert L. Willett, the University of Chicago.

ADDITIONAL: Professor Harry E. Barnes, Smith College, Northampton, Massachusetts; Professor Loring W. Batten, the General Theological Seminary, New York City; Professor Raymond F. Bellamy, Florida State College for Women, Tallahassee, Florida; Professor George L. Robinson, the Presbyterian Theological Seminary, Chicago; Professor Ellsworth Faris, the University of Chicago; Rabbi Leo M. Franklin, Temple Beth El, Detroit, Michigan; Professor Theodore G. Soares, California Institute of Technology, Pasadena, California; Professor Willoughby C. Allen, Oxford University, England; Professor John F. Stenning, Oxford University, England; Professor Stanley A. Cook, Cambridge University, England; Professor William H. DuBose, the University of the South, Sewanee, Tennessee.

Omission of a name is due either to non-receipt of word, or to some unavoidable oversight; but in any case the writer is grateful to all who have read or commented upon the manuscript.

CONTENTS

xvii

CHAPTER I

INTRODUCTION

Heritage of modern civilization from Rome, Greece, and Israel not yet welded into unity.—Modern civilization rests upon three distinct lines of cultural development, arising from the law and politics of Rome, the philosophy, science, and art of Greece, and the ethical monotheism of Israel. But this complicated heritage has never been organized into spiritual unity. Greek and Roman subjects are taught in our high schools and colleges by means of well-arranged courses based upon the results of scientific research in those fields; and accordingly a knowledge of what scholarship has done to explain the *north-Mediterranean* culture is considered to be a mark of intelligence and refinement. But our educational system does not afford equal freedom to acquire the results of scientific research into *east-Mediterranean* culture, the subject being clouded by an atmosphere of prejudice, myth, and miracle. The schools each year pour forth armies of young people who have become familiar with modern methods in geology, astronomy, physics, biology, sociology, economics, and general history, but whose training has denied them opportunity for frank discussion of the circumstances and events through which ethical monotheism arose.

Forces opposing scientific study of Hebrew history should be respected.—The blockade against the scientific study of Hebrew history is of such a complex nature that a large volume could be devoted to its causes and manifestations. Religion is always involved with what are known as "conservative" social forces, even in pagan countries. These forces, among Christians and Jews, have been identified with a system of ideas called "orthodoxy," the object of which is to conserve moral and spiritual values in human life. And therefore anyone who comes into this field should realize that the opposition to scientific study of Hebrew history is not to be viewed as merely irrational. On the contrary, it calls for the respect of the scientific investigator who, though disagreeing with the intellectual standpoint of orthodoxy, can learn much about conservatism, as a legitimate social force, through study of its manifestations today.

Orthodox formula of Hebrew history: "The Law and the Prophets."—Orthodox theology declares that the idea of one true God was revealed amid portents of thunder and lightning upon a flaming mountain located in the desert of Arabia. Elaborate instructions for the ritual practice of monotheism, together with solemn and repeated warnings against the worship of "other gods," are believed to have been given upon this mountain by divine command, being recorded in five books, known as "The Law" (or, in Hebrew, *The Torah*). The Law is believed to have been carried into the land of Canaan by exactly twelve tribes, constituting a fully organized nation called "Israel." But instead of observing the Law, the Hebrew people are said to have ignored it straight along through their history for many hundreds of years until the Babylonian Exile: "Neither have our kings, our princes, our priests, nor our fathers, kept thy Law, nor hearkened unto thy commandments" (Neh. 9:34).

The alleged rejection of the Law is believed to account for the appearance of remarkable men called "prophets" (or *nebiim*), who are said to have known the contents of the Law, and who denounced the worship of heathen gods, predicting the downfall of the Hebrew nation. According to the orthodox view, the prophets were champions, or defenders, of a religion *founded long before their time by supernatural decree;* and, consequently, they have been regarded as occupying a much lower level of importance than the Law itself. Orthodox tradition, therefore, approaches Hebrew history in view of the conventional formula, "*The Law* and the Prophets."

Orthodox view declared by modern scholarship to be _post-eventum_ interpretation of Hebrew history.—That the ortho-dox view of Hebrew history is an _interpretation_ which acquired currency during the Babylonian Exile, after the fall of the He-brew state, is the conclusion reached through careful research by scientific scholars, and now accepted in the leading universities and theological seminaries of Europe and America. The He-brew Bible proves to have been written on long rolls of parch-ment by scribes who did two things: first of all, they copied a large amount of matter from ancient sources, far older than the Bible itself, quoting some of these early sources by name; and then, in the second place, they interspersed their own comments and explanations here and there throughout the copied or quoted matter. But since quotation marks were not used when the Old Testament was written, care is necessary in order to discriminate between the earlier, copied writings and the com-ments or observations of the compilers. The Old Testament therefore carries within its own structure the proof of its com-position by writers who were not contemporary with the events described.

New Formula of Hebrew history: "The Prophets and the Law."—That the prophets, instead of being mere imitators, were constructive leaders in a great historical, evolutionary movement which began amid heathenism, progressed upward into ethical monotheism, and then issued finally in the writing of the Law is another conclusion reached by critical investiga-tors. According to this view, the correct formula of Hebrew his-tory and biblical literature is not "The Law and the Prophets" but _"The Prophets_ and the Law"; and, therefore, the monothe-istic religion which underlies Judaism and Christianity is the product not of Mount Sinai but of Palestine.

Criticism thus challenges the claim of orthodoxy as an au-thentic version of Hebrew history. It asserts that the Law con-tains much material which is earlier than the Law itself; but claims that there are no traces of the Law's existence, *in its present form*, during the long period covered by the historical books of Judges, Samuel, and Kings, and the prophetical books of Amos, Hosea, Micah, Isaiah, Jeremiah, and Ezekiel. Critical scholarship, therefore, declares that the conventional arrangement of the Bible (with the Law in the *forefront*, and the other books coming after) is at variance with ascertainable facts, and is thus contrary to the real course of Hebrew history.

Hebrew history takes new form against background of biblical higher criticism.—The older, orthodox view of Hebrew history depended upon the Book of Joshua for its idea of the Israelite invasion of Canaan. In that book Israel has the form of a single, united army which exterminates the earlier population, and then divides the soil of Palestine by lot among twelve Hebrew tribes. But the higher criticism shows that the documents composing Joshua are a continuation of the Pentateuch, or Law, and that we must go to the Book of Judges for a more trustworthy introduction to Hebrew history. In Judges we see no united army of Israel overpowering the land, but merely a scattered and uncertain movement of separate clans, or tribes, each fighting independently on its own behalf, settling the *open hill-country*, and reducing a part of the older, Amorite population to slavery, *but leaving a large fraction of the Amorites in possession of twenty or more strong walled cities with suburban villages*, and then, at a later time, intermarrying with these inhabitants of the land. The Hebrew people therefore emerge into history not as a fully organized and "linebred" race, but as a gradually evolving nation, which arises out of a "melting pot" through the coalescence of clans from the Arabian desert with Amorite "city-states." This apparently new view, however, is not peculiar to the higher critics. It is in the Bible; but it was never understood until criticism gave us a truer idea of the biblical documents, or sources.

Criticism also helps us to understand that the notorious worship of many gods by the Hebrew people was not a lapse, or de-

fection, from an earlier, and metaphysically higher, faith revealed at Sinai, but that it merely exemplifies the polytheistic
heathenism *of all ancient and primitive races*. Yahweh thus appears at first as one among many gods whom the Hebrews worshiped as real beings. The original cult of Yahweh was brought
into Canaan from the desert by the clans of Israel, which also
had family gods, or domestic divinities, known as *teraphim*,
shaped like human beings; and when the newcomers intermar-
ried with the older inhabitants, the gods of the Amorites were
taken over as provincial divinities under the name of *Baal* (pl.
Baalim). Thus, the new Hebrew nation, originating at the point
of contact between Israelites and Amorites, developed a "pantheon," or collection of gods, consisting of (1) domestic deities,
or teraphim; (2) provincial deities, or Baalim; (3) the national
deity,Yahweh; and (4) such other gods as Chemosh of the Moabites, whose worship was brought in by King Solomon; the
Baal of Sidon, brought in by King Ahab; and the totem divinities mentioned by Ezekiel (chap. 8).

**Biblical criticism offers no explanation of religious develop-
ment.**—While the higher critics agree upon the foregoing historical outline, as well as upon many other details which need
not be mentioned here, biblical scholarship has never united
upon a consistent explanation of the developmental process by
which, in the absence of the Law as a miraculous driving force,
the Hebrew people were impelled upward from polytheism into
ethical monotheism. In other words, if the *Law* was not the
starting-point of prophecy, the Wellhausen critics, according to
their leader, have not explained how *prophecy* came to be the
starting-point of the Law. Since this consideration has been
treated in the Preface, it need not be further enlarged upon here.

**Scope of historical research broadens, leaving biblical criti-
cism in presociological stage.**—While biblical critics were preoccupied by the arduous labor of bringing the documentary
view of the Hebrew Bible into its modern form, historical re-

search in general, outside the Hebrew field, was gradually entering a new stage. Investigators were learning to go below the surface of events, and explain historical phenomena in terms of economic interests, social-group relationships, and class conflict within the limits of groups. The new methods had come into full use by the beginning of the present century; but biblical scholars were still at work analyzing the documents and reconstructing Hebrew history upon the tacit assumption that higher criticism was practically a self-contained circle of ideas unrelated to the general progress of scientific research outside the biblical domain.

Sociological interpretation of Hebrew history begins with commonplace facts.—Approaching Hebrew history from the sociological standpoint, we begin with certain familiar facts, preparatory to the correlation of these facts in a new perspective. Thus, for instance, we need to bear carefully in mind that ethical monotheism had no official status at any time during the life of the whole Hebrew nation before the Babylonian Exile; and that a long struggle took place in the pre-Exilic period, which led gradually up to the definitive establishment of monotheism in the single tribe of Judah after the Exile. The struggle was based upon the rivalries of two distinct groups, or lines of prophets, both claiming divine inspiration. One group stood for the *prevailing* social system; while the other contended for *social readjustment*, urging a limited, national monotheism *as a means toward that end*. The prophets of social readjustment were acclaimed *after* the Babylonian Exile as the precursors and founders of Jewish metaphysical monotheism; *but their posthumous triumph was achieved only through the segregation of religion and its divorce from social reform.*

The interpretation of Hebrew history in the light of these facts does not assume that the ideas of the reforming prophets were practicable. Nor, again, does it imply that ecclesiastical monotheism, divorced from social readjustment, has been, or is now, of no human advantage. Historical science is realistic; and history shows that ethical monotheism, even though segregated in church and synagogue, has been of tremendous effect in emancipating civilization from heathenism, securing moral and spiritual values, and promoting civil order.

Biblical monotheism by-product of utopian struggle to legalize migratory clan-ethics in territorial society.—The rise of biblical monotheism, as an exceptional cult amidst the ancient pagan world, is analogous to the rise of the human brain in the process of biological evolution. The brain of man, viewed from the purely scientific standpoint, is a by-product of the struggle for existence among the anthropoid species. The term "by-product," however, simply refers to the objective process by which man has appeared upon the scene. The biological scientist, as such, cannot say that the creation of the human race by this method is accidental; for in last analysis the resident force of the cosmos itself is what gives rise to the human brain and the human race; and if a biological scientist calls humanity an "accident," he goes beyond his province into a realm where, as a biologist, he has no entry. Science in general describes *processes* in terms that symbolize realities and forces lying beyond the ken of science; and the increasing recognition of this truth in recent years has done much to soften and abate the so-called "war" between science and religion.

The foregoing explanation is preliminary to the further statement, which might be otherwise misunderstood, that biblical monotheism is a *by-product* of a utopian struggle to impose migratory clan-ethics upon a territorial state. This formula will not prove to be so difficult as it looks; and by enlarging upon it we shall go farther into the subject. The Hebrew people took form through an unparalleled evolutionary process. While there was nothing unusual in the mere fact of assimilation between Israelites and Amorites, and while all the great peoples of the world have developed through the coalescence of earlier stocks, yet the ancient Palestinian "melting pot" operated according to a wholly unique logic. The Hebrew nation arose through the establishment of a desert-born cult as the symbol and rallying-point of a *state* which acknowledged local gods representing commercialism. While this fact is more or less known to biblical scholars, its implications have not been clearly perceived; and therefore its consequences have not definitely influenced the critical exposition of Hebrew history.

After the Hebrew nation took form in Canaan, it consisted primarily of an upper class, with a right wing resting on the walled cities and a left wing based on villages in the open country. A member of the upper class was called a *baal*, i.e., an owner, or proprietor, of land, houses, cattle, etc. The plural of baal is *baalim;* and the Hebrew aristocracy as a whole comprised all the individuals who were known by this collective term. Below the baalim was an inferior social class consisting of slaves, or *abadim*, together with landless aliens, or strangers, called *gerim*, who were hired laborers.

In this two-class nation the only individuals having full and complete legal standing before the courts were the baalim (*Ephraimite source:* Exod. 24:14, "If any *baal* have a law-suit"). Financial transactions were viewed as normally involving *only* the baalim (*Deuteronomic source:* Deut. 15:2, "Every *baal* that lends anything to his neighbor, etc."). In course of time the upper social class began to contract upon itself; the wealthier baalim engrossed the land; while the poorer and less fortunate baalim, deprived of their ancestral soil by legal processes, dropped out of the aristocracy into the lower, enslaved class of *abadim*. In justification of this economic development, the right wing of the aristocracy appealed to the veritable and undoubted usages of ancient Amorite law, guaranteed by the local gods of Canaan, the *Baalim;* and accordingly the conservative wing of the upper class applied the term "Baal" to Yahweh, seeking to worship the deity of Israel as a Canaanite god. But, on the other hand, the poorer Hebrew baalim raised the cry that land should not be put into the category of things to be sold, exchanged, or mortgaged, and that the soil should always rightfully continue in possession of the domestic social groups composing the state. For the validation of this claim, the small proprietors pointed to the customs and usages which had prevailed for generations among "them of old time" in the premonarchic period, when the royal state had not yet arisen, and when as yet the Amorite cities had not been absorbed into the social structure of the monarchy. These customs were authenticated by the primitive "justice," or *mishpat*, of Yahweh as a tribal deity of the wilderness, where all nomads in a kindred group have a right to the resources of nature.

The struggle first came to a head in *Ephraim*, the northern kingdom of Israel, which, through civil war, fell under the dictatorship of a military adventurer, *Omri*. This monarch (who was opposed by a large part of Israel under Tibni) built his capital, Samaria, upon a transaction in real estate contravening the mishpat-ideas of the "left-wing" aristocracy; and in due time the prejudices of the socially backward clans broke into flame when Ahab, the son of Omri, following in his father's footsteps, excited the horror of the peasant Naboth by proposing to make the ancestral soil of this conservative rustic an item of sale or exchange.

The critical school, following the lead of Wellhausen, have wrongly treated the struggle between Baalism and Yahwism as a war between opposed conceptions of the fertilizing power in the realm of nature (Wellhausen, *Prolegomena* [1885], pp. 96–98, 447). In other words, the local Baalim of Canaan, which the Hebrew nation inherited from the Amorite side of its descent, have been viewed simply as gods of good crops. That the issue displayed itself only upon this ground has been taken for granted under the influence of the prophet Hosea, in whose book the people of Israel are made to say, "I will go after my lovers [the

Baalim] that give me my bread and my water, my wool and my flax, mine oil and my drink"; to which Hosea replies in the name of Yahweh, "She [Israel] did not know that I [Yahweh] gave her the corn, and the wine, and the oil" (Hos. 2:5, 8).

But in Hosea's book the Baal-question is treated on the ground of the prophet's personal experience (chaps. 1 ff.); and while the idea of natural fertility was expressed by the Amorite cults, it should never have been generalized in this form as the exclusive characteristic of Baalism in the great Hebrew struggle. For the term "baal" denotes the Semitic proprietor in settled civilization; and long before the appearance of Israel on the soil of Palestine, this term had also come to signify the local gods of Canaan, *viewed as authenticating and validating the whole range of economic and social relationships in territorial civilization.* In other words, while the Baalim were undoubtedly worshiped as gods of good crops, their main function was to guarantee and legitimate the commercialistic régime of private property in land, slaves, cattle, merchandise, etc., which, during pre-Hebrew times, had come to a center in walled cities located on the oriental trade routes. *All contracts were legalized by oaths in the name of Baal;* while under this régime land came within the category of sale and exchange, and was the basis of mortgage-security foreclosed by legal process when the debtor failed to pay interest or principal.

On the other hand, the tribal nomad, not only among Semites but everywhere in the world, cannot comprehend the mysteries of territorial, commercialistic civilization, which he despises and looks down upon as beneath his moral and social dignity. The truly and completely nomadic social group has no class distinctions of rich and poor; for the clan, or tribe, in order to survive amid the precarious conditions of the open wilderness, *must maintain equalitarian relationships* as a condition of preserving the morale of the group in the struggle for existence. Any desert tribe, if powerful enough, will enslave the inhabitants of some oasis, forcing the settled aliens to relinquish a large part of the crops at every harvest. But this procedure is entirely consistent with nomadic social morality, which relates, in the first instance, only to the tribe or clan *itself*, and not to alien social groups. Thus, the Arab tribe, *within its own limits*, is a pure communism, or socialism, based on the ideal of justice and brotherhood as between its members. Accordingly, the tribes of the Arabian wilderness are pictured as follows by an English physician who lived and traveled with them and knew their ways of thought:

The nomad tribes we have seen to be commonwealths of brethren. *They divide each other's losses. The malicious subtlety of interest [on money] is foreign to the brotherly dealing of the nomad tribesmen.* Their justice is such that, in the opinion of the next governed countries, the Arabs of the wilderness are the justest of mortals. Seldom the judges and elders err, in these small societies of kindred, where the life of every tribesman lies open from his infancy and his state is to all men well known [Doughty, *Arabia Deserta*, I, 249, 318, 345 (italics ours)].

While the Hebrew state was coming into existence at the point of contact between Israelites from the desert and the older, Amorite "inhabitants of the land," the original social usages of the parent-races continued to prevail side by side. The *peasant aristocracy*, living in the villages of the hill country and out toward the Arabian desert, were strongly influenced by the social ethics of the wilderness, according to which the resources of nature are viewed as the inalienable right of kindred groups; while, on the other hand, the inhabitants of the *walled cities* tended to retain the commercialistic usages and laws of territorial society. The term "Israel" continued to designate the Hebrew nation merely because the incoming tribes under that name had actually furnished the political framework of the state, symbolized by the name "Yahweh." *Thus, the two parentraces disappeared within the mass of the new Hebrew nation; but their contrasted legalistic standpoints remained as distinctions at-*

*taching to social classes within the state; so that Baalism and Yah-
wism floated along together in the turbid stream of national history.*

The following chapters will show that the Hebrew struggle
began amid confusion and took form very slowly. Its roots go
back into the "pre-prophetic" age; and it does not come out
upon clear ground even when we reach the epoch of literary
prophecy. Thus, three important Judean prophets make no reference to Baalism and show a naïve outlook on the history. According to Amos, the Amorites had been destroyed, *root and
branch*, by the might of Yahweh (Amos 2:9). In place of the
Amorites, Israel had been planted as one plants a choice vine
(Isa. 5:2). And in this homogenous nation, of "line-bred" ancestry, the wealthier proprietors wickedly coveted and seized
the fields of their less fortunate neighbors (Mic. 2:2). *These
three Judean prophets took the view that the Hebrew nation had
simply broken away from its archaic moral moorings in the primitive customs, or "mishpat," of tribal justice.* Only one of them
uses the term "baal"—the city-prophet Isaiah; and even then
with reference only to a human being, the owner of cattle (Isa.
1:3).

The fundamental issue of clan-ethics, or mishpat, was gradually brought into explicit relation with Baalism through the
work of four outstanding *Ephraimite* prophets, who were identified with a section of the country where the mixture of Israel
with the Amorites was more thorough—Elijah, Elisha, Hosea,
and Jeremiah. The last-named has been wrongly classified as a
Judean, but was from the tribal district of Benjamin, by tradition the younger branch of the house of Joseph through Rachel.
This prophet alone refers to Rachel (Jer. 31:15); and to him
Ephraim is the "first-born" of Yahweh (31:9). The repeated
references to the Baalim in Hosea, as already pointed out, are
colored by that prophet's personal experience. But an advance
over Hosea is made by Jeremiah, who, though indebted to him,
is a clearer thinker. Baalism, in the mind of Jeremiah, is not
simply the cult of good crops; and he would never think of mak-

ing Israel say, "I will go after my lovers, who give me my food, etc." According to this prophet, Baalism stands for the whole gamut of social and economic relationships contravening the older, tribal mishpat; and, in consequence, Jeremiah's denunciation of Baalism, unlike the restricted usage of Hosea, extends over the prevailing social maladjustment whereby the wealthier members of the Hebrew aristocracy reduce the less fortunate, left-wing baalim into the lower, enslaved class. The emphasis upon Baalism is carried to the logical issue of defining it as an explicit symbol of opposition to the mishpat of Yahweh. Jeremiah refers to the Baalim frequently by name, but often merely as "other gods"; and the keynote of his platform is clearly struck in the opening chapter of his book: Yahweh will utter his mishpat against the people in regard to *all* their wickedness in forsaking him and following other gods (Jer. 1:16). The exposition of aristocratic mishpat goes clear through Jeremiah's work into the final siege of Jerusalem, when, speaking in the name of Yahweh, he demands the release of every slave *that is a Hebrew or an Hebrewess, that no man should make slaves of them* (Jer. 34:6-9).

The struggle for justice and the struggle against other gods, instead of being two separate movements, *are logically one and the same;* and thus the issue of Baalism raises the central problem of Hebrew history. The baalistic master-class divides into a right and left wing over the dispute about the relationship which rightly should exist between the members of the aristocracy. The poorer baalim, who have dropped into the slave class and lost their family property, contend that there should always be an open channel whereby the enslaved Israelite may reascend into the upper class, and regain "his possession"; so that he and his descendants may enjoy forever "the inheritance of their fathers." But, on the other hand, the wealthier baalim contend, with equal positiveness and sincerity, that the mere fact of Hebrew descent carries with it no legal guaranty of one's economic and social status.

Viewing the evolution of Israel in this light, we can see that the argument between tribalism and commercialism could never possibly have reached a definite and satisfactory conclusion. It was not a straight, clear-cut, yes-or-no issue; for both sides were partly right and partly wrong. And even if such prophets as Jeremiah had prevailed, they would only have succeeded in establishing a tribal, aristocratic socialism, based on human slavery and land monopoly, but ignoring the larger questions of social justice. The significance of Hebrew history, therefore, ultimately resides not in the merits of a social program but in the fact that a *social struggle took place*. The struggle itself pertains to the essence of the situation. And not only so; but we shall be impressed by the fact that its continual *frustration* was likewise necessary to that progress of thought which, moving upward through higher and higher planes, reached its outcome in synagogue and church. Without a slowly rising idealism, checkmated by the challenging pressure of real conditions, the career of ancient Israel would have been like the histories of many little undistinguished peoples which, living to themselves, have contributed nothing to the world's culture. It is in the light of these considerations, which can only be adumbrated by way of introduction, that Hebrew monotheism stands out as the "by-product" of an evolutionary process beginning on the level of primitive ethics and sociology. *The concentration of property in the grasp of the wealthier baalim acquired such powerful momentum that the struggle for justice, or "mishpat," was lost before the great Hebrew prophets arrived upon the stage of history; so that by the time of Amos the nation was like a basket of summer fruit, outwardly fair, but inwardly rotten and hopeless* (Amos 8:1–2).

Social evolution, complicated with economic forces, moves upward into a realm of higher spiritual values.—Social evolution involves economic facts and forces which cannot be isolated from their historical setting, or context. Food, clothing, and shelter are endlessly required by the physical body in which the human soul, or personality, is installed. This relation between man and his material environment is always presupposed, or implied, by the term "social process." Economic facts, therefore, cannot be dissected out from human life; and hence it follows that the so-called "economic man," of the older political economy, is a pure fiction.

Approaching Hebrew history and religion from the sociological standpoint, then, we cannot escape the constraint of these materialistic forces. The invasion of "the land flowing with milk and honey" was obviously economic in its impulse; while the land itself was regarded as an "inheritance" given to Israel by Yahweh; the phenomena of early Hebrew prophecy, in the days of Deborah, Samuel, and Saul, turned around the cult of Yahweh as guaranteeing continual possession of the land against the claims of Amorites, Philistines, and other foes; and by the time of Elijah the Tishbite and Zedekiah ben Chenaanah, the movement of Hebrew prophecy bifurcated: one school supporting the older idea that Yahweh was bound to guarantee Israel in perpetual occupancy of its land under any and all circumstances; while the other school advanced the novel doctrine that if the wealthier *baalim* engrossed the land for themselves, "adding house to house and field to field," Israel would be evicted from Palestine and thus debarred altogether from its land. *But the newer type of prophecy left the older school behind, rising gradually through higher and higher ethical planes into a realm of spiritual truths and values transcending the original economic and social experiences at the basis of Hebrew history. The long materialistic struggle was necessary as a discipline leading up to realization of the fact that "man shall not live by bread alone"* (Deut. 8:3). *Thus, the deeper concerns of religion were liberated from the secular process which gave rise to prophecy.*

The foregoing statement gives the general sense in which the present work seeks to deal with Hebrew history; it handles economic and social data as material entering into the evolution of monotheism; its method is that of pure science; and it does not find in the Bible any concrete program of social reform applicable to modern conditions.

Orthodox theology has interpreted the religion of the Bible as if it were a celestial product thrust into the stream of human history from a non-terrestrial source; while, on the other hand, modern critical scholarship has been slow to recognize that the Hebrew drama was enacted by flesh-and-blood men whose feet were on *terra firma;* and thus even the non-orthodox interpreters have regarded the evolution of Hebrew monotheism as if it were the work of disincarnate spirits functioning apart from commonplace human motives. In other words, as Professor W. C. Graham well says: "Higher criticism has devitalised much of the Biblical literature by failing to bring it into relation with the social process out of which it arose."

Accordingly, the overspiritualization of Hebrew history makes imperative a new and strong emphasis upon social and economic realities if the religion of the Bible is to be understood in terms of modern science. To isolate or ignore materialistic data while considering the moral and spiritual problems of Hebrew history is like trying to explain the human personality, or soul, without reference to the body and its physical environment. The proper attitude, then, for the scientific investigator of Hebrew history and the Bible is frankly and squarely to face the so-called "secular" facts as the original condition and starting-point of a process which, beginning on the levels of paganism, issued at length on the high ground of ethical monotheism.

Mishpat-struggle did not apply ready-made philosophy to Palestine.—It should be observed that the Hebrew struggle for mishpat in Canaan was not based upon any systematic outline of social justice, imported from the desert and applied to the conditions of settled life. No such proposition is put forward in this book; nor was any similar claim advanced in its predecessor, *Sociological Study of the Bible.* Yet the statement has been publicly made that the writer "assumes a pagan Israel coming into Palestine with an ideal *Mishpat*, or body of judicial decisions, ample for all social emergencies, while the long settled and cultured peoples of Palestine had none" (Godbey, *The Lost Tribes a Myth: Suggestions towards Rewriting Hebrew History*, pp. 750–51).

The Hebrew sense of social justice, or *mishpat*, as manifested in Palestine, was primarily a concrete, unwritten, uncodified feeling of *clan-equalitarianism* reminiscent of the desert, and expressing itself within the terms of Canaanite experience (cf. chap. v, pp. 54–55). But after the passage out of nomadism into territorialism, and the rise of a landed aristocracy imposed upon a mass of *alien slaves*, the logic of *mishpat* reappears in the claim that all members of the Hebrew aristocracy have a legal and moral right to a place in the upper social stratum. An important corollary of this doctrine is that if any of the poorer members of the free, aristocratic element fall into the lower class of alien bondservants, they must be retrieved and re-established in their former status. The newer sense of social justice began to take form about the time of Elijah; it slowly became definite in the various codes—E, D, and H—and in the preaching of the higher prophets who carried on after the ninth century; finding statement at the downfall of the Jewish kingdom, in the demand of Jeremiah for the elevation of *Hebrews* from the mass of non-Hebrew aliens which composed the bulk of the lower class (Jer., 34; cf. Deut., chap. 15).

Anticritics oppose imaginary theory of "Wellhausen evolution."—That the critical source theory of the Old Testament is a definite philosophy of religious evolution and a finished edifice of scriptural interpretation has been frequently taken for granted by anticritics. This error underlies attacks on the critical hypothesis by Robertson, in *Early Religion of Israel* (1889), and Orr, in *Problem of the Old Testament* (1906). It is voiced by Albright, in *Archaeology of Palestine* (1932), who speaks of "the picture of the *evolution* of Israelite religion drawn by Wellhausen," and who declares that Professor Driver, of Oxford, "together with all the other members and friends of the Wellhausen school, adopted false premises for his analysis of the *historical evolution* of Mosaic religion" (pp. 162, 176 [italics ours]). The mistake, of course, lies in assuming that the critical school (symbolized by the name of Wellhausen) were exploiting a definitive theory of religious evolution, when, as a matter of fact, they had no such theory, and were engaged only in laying the foundations of an edifice whose real nature *the critical school itself did not fully comprehend*.

Nevertheless, up to the period of the World War, biblical higher critics in general *felt* themselves to be setting forth a closed and final system of scriptural interpretation. Thus, Professor W. R. Smith spoke of Wellhausen and Kuenen as investigators whose acumen and research had left nothing of importance to be done for the historical study of the Old Testament! (*Religion of the Semites*, Pref.). That Wellhausen, however, admitted his inability even to formulate a theory of religious evolution, we have observed above. Yet the critical school as a whole had a sense of the finality of its work, and succeeded in giving this impression to scholars like Robertson, Orr, Albright, and others, whose activities were in cognate fields, and who were not themselves biblical critics.

The real position, then, is that the critical view of the Old Testament is misapprehended from different standpoints by defenders and opponents. The advocates of higher criticism have generally imagined themselves to be in possession of a complete scriptural philosophy; while detractors have taken criticism at the critics' estimate; and neither group has envisaged the underlying problem.

CHAPTER II

HEBREW HISTORY AND LEGEND

Hebrew history in Palestine gives pattern for legends about prehistoric times.—In using the Bible as a collection of "sources" for the study of Hebrew history, an important consideration to bear in mind is that the *development of the nation in Palestine gives a pattern, or ground plan, whereon are woven the striking Hebrew legends about earlier ages, before the dawn of written history.* Instead of being mere unsubstantial myths, which must be ruled out at the beginning, these legends prove to be full of significance when considered in relation to events recorded in the books of Judges, Samuel, Kings, and the Prophets. This consideration applies with special force to Genesis; for a careful study of that book not only elicits material which is clearly formed on the pattern of later events; but Genesis also includes material which enables us to round out more vividly the picture of Hebrew evolution after the settlement of Israel in Canaan.

Certain legends in Genesis woven on pattern of historic relations between Israelites and Edomites.—That the Israelites and Edomites were descended from two brothers, Jacob and Esau, is affirmed by stories in the Book of Genesis which very clearly undertake to account for actual, historic relations between the two peoples in the time of the Hebrew monarchy, long after the dim, early period covered by Genesis. The Edomites, as we know from the books of Samuel and Kings, were located in the wilderness to the *south* of Canaan; and thither, after the establishment of the united Hebrew monarchy, King David sent his army, and "put garrisons throughout all Edom; and all they of Edom became David's slaves" (II Sam. 8:14). But a

19

century or so later, "Edom revolted from under the hand of Judah *unto this day*" (II Kings 8:22).

Before turning directly to the legends about the respective ancestors of Israel and Edom, it is instructive to consider a passage in Genesis which gives a list of Edomite kings with the statement that "these are the kings that ruled in the land of Edom *before there reigned any king over the children of Israel*" (Gen. 36:31). The Book of Genesis, therefore, comes to us through the hands of a writer, or a school of writers, who knew about the Hebrew kingdom. And therefore Genesis, which seems to be the earliest book in the Bible, *originated from authors who lived more than one thousand years later than the patriarchal period to which the stories of Jacob and Esau refer.*

Bearing in mind the enslavement of Edom to Israel in the time of David, and its final emancipation through revolt, it is easy to see that the stories about Jacob and Esau are attempts of the legend-building faculty to justify and explain the historical relations which existed between these two neighboring Semitic peoples after the rise of the Hebrew monarchy. To this end, five attempts are made from five different points of view, as follows:

1. One story alleges that the warfare between Israel and Edom began so vigorously during the prenatal existence of Jacob and Esau that when Rebekah, their mother, became conscious of it, she "inquired of Yahweh," who replied that two nations were within her, and that two different kinds of people were destined to proceed from her, *whereof the elder should serve the younger* (Gen. 25:21–23). This phase of the legend therefore derives the conquest of Edom from a *prediction* by the tribal deity of Israel; and, accordingly, David's enslavement of Edom is justified as a matter of "divine right."

2. The relation of Israel to Edom is further set forth by the alleged manner in which the births of Jacob and Esau took place. *Esau,* being delivered *first,* was therefore the *elder;* and

afterward came his brother, whose hand took hold on Esau's heel (or *aqeb*). Therefore the younger is said to have been called *Ya'aqob*, "one who grasps by the heel," "one who supplants" (Gen. 25:24–26). Not content with basing David's conquest of Edom upon a prediction by the tribal god, the legend thus gives an *additional* explanation of the superiority of Israel over Edom, as being involved in the physical circumstances of their ancestral origin.

3. The third element in the Jacob-Esau legend is the best known of all, relating to the purchase of the elder brother's "birthright" by the younger. The point of the story is that the Edomites did not deserve the status of freemen because they sprang from an ancestor who "despised his birthright," and sold his expectancy for "a mess of pottage" (Gen. 25:29–34).

4. The fourth validation of Israel's ascendancy over Edom is furnished by the story of how Jacob, with the help of his mother, tricked his father Isaac into giving him the mystical "Blessing" which, of right, should have gone to Esau the *first-born*. A formal blessing, or benediction, by a patriarch was held in ancient times to be an objective reality, with materialistic and magical power, which, when actually bestowed, must expend itself upon the person to whom it was given. Thus, the power of Isaac's blessing, obtained through trickery, was absorbed by the younger son, Jacob, when otherwise it would have gone in due course to the elder son, Esau (Gen. 27:1 ff.).

5. The fifth alleged validation of David's assault upon Edom is found in the makeshift blessing which Isaac imparted to Esau after the discovery that Jacob had secured by wile the magic prize belonging of right only to the first-born. Isaac is made to say definitely to Esau, *"Thou shalt serve thy brother."* But the historical outlook of the legend at this point, as viewing the accomplished fact of Edomite revolt (*supra*), is revealed by the postscript, wherein Isaac says, "And it shall come to pass, when thou shalt have the rule, that thou shalt break his yoke from off

thy neck" (Gen. 27:39–40). Here, then, the date for the compilation of Genesis moves onward far beyond the time of David into the period of the two kingdoms.

All peoples in early times had a fondness for evolving tales to explain the actual, historic circumstances *in which they found themselves upon coming to collective consciousness as organized groups;* and these interesting stories took settled form in folklore, supplying welcome topics for conversation at the fireside, in the market place, and wherever men assembled. The case of Edom and Israel is an excellent illustration of the folklore process, and also helps us to understand the nature of the documents, or sources, which we must use in our study of Hebrew history as related to the idea of God. Here were two nations of recognized kindred origin, descended from the same Arabian desert-ancestry, and living in the same general part of the world as neighbors. The one, Edom, achieved nationality under the rule of kings "before there reigned any king over the children of Israel"; and therefore Edom was the older organized group, i.e., the "elder brother." Yet, by the evidence of plain fact, which all could perceive, the *older* nation was compelled by hard fate to occupy the *poorer* country south of Palestine; while the *younger* nation, Israel, possessed a land "flowing with milk and honey."

But the Jacob-Esau legend not only dealt with the territorial fortunes of Israel and Edom; it sought also to vindicate the rightfulness of the *tribute* which flowed in from the conquered Edomites to the victorious Hebrews: "The elder shall serve the younger." "And David put garrisons throughout all Edom; and all they of Edom became David's slaves." No nation or individual has ever experienced any difficulty in finding reasons to justify an income regularly received through tribute or special privilege. Thus, many grounds were given for the reduction of Negroes and Indians to slavery by the American people; and there has never been a lack of ethical, cultural, and legal reasons to justify British landlords in drawing ground rent from the conquered Irish, even when such rent was paid by the exportation of potatoes from Ireland in time of actual famine.

Edom's tribute, which was paid to Israel in the days of David and his successors, must have been of no small importance among the factors which went to upbuild the fabric of Hebrew prosperity; and one can imagine the satisfaction with which the stories of Jacob and Esau were told when caravans arrived from the south bearing the products of Edomite labor. The legend of the two brethren, the sons of Isaac, acquired great prestige among the Hebrew people, as pointing to Israelite superiority over Edom and as validating the relationship of master and slave; while in due time it obtained a secure place in the literature of Jewish and Christian revelation.

But one may be justified in doubting whether the Edomites themselves were favorably impressed by the legend of the two brothers; and, indeed, the final revolt of Edom "from under the hand of Judah until this day" might lend plausibility to the deduction that these neighbors of Israel are to be counted among the first higher critics; for if the Edomites had been impressed by the orthodox divine validation of their own slavery, they would not have dared to rebel against Israel; and in view of their successful revolt, the prediction placed in the mouth of Isaac, "Thou shalt break his yoke from thy neck," has the nature of a face-saving clause added by some later Hebrew scribe. Only as we approach Hebrew history from the standpoint of these human considerations does it begin to acquire significance and interest for the modern student.

Genesis legends also reflect rise of Ephraim to supremacy in Israel.—While the Jacob-Esau stories grew up around the relations between Israel and a people *outside its own borders*, the Book of Genesis also contains even more material which follows the pattern of Hebrew history *within the land of Canaan itself*. This phase of the subject is illustrated very instructively by the fortunes of *Manasseh* and *Ephraim*, two tribes, which, at a very early period, held the central highlands north of Jerusalem. The Ephraimites, having been at first only one among the tribes of Israel, *absorbed* the Manassites, and impressed the name of Ephraim upon the *entire territory north of Jerusalem;* so that their part of the land became known as the "house" or "kingdom" of Ephraim. Northern Israel is called "Ephraim" thirty-seven times in the book of the prophet Hosea. But, on the other hand, Hosea's Judean contemporary, Amos, prefers to call that part of Israel by the name of "Joseph," and this term is also used in I Kings, where we read that Solomon put Jeroboam "over all the labor of the house of Joseph" (I Kings 11:28).

This remarkable use of the terms "Joseph" and "Ephraim" in application to the northern kingdom of Israel required, of course, to be explained by an appropriate evolution of legend. Accordingly, we find in Genesis that *Joseph* was a prehistoric patriarch who had two sons, the elder being *Manasseh* and the younger being *Ephraim*. These boys are taken by Joseph to their grandfather, *Jacob*, in order to receive the patriarchal "blessing"; and at this point in the legend we begin to realize that the stage has been set for another "birthright" story, in which, again, the *elder* brother is to be superseded by the *younger*. The boys are presented to Jacob in such wise that the elder son, Manasseh, is at the *right* hand of the patriarch, in the position appropriate for absorbing the greater blessing, while Ephraim stands at the *left*. But in imparting the magical formula, *Jacob's arms are crossed*, so that his right hand, instead of resting upon the elder brother, is placed upon the head of Ephraim the younger. When Joseph, the father of the two boys, objects to this unusual procedure, Jacob replies that he is aware of what he is doing, and goes on to bless Ephraim the younger above Manasseh the elder (Gen. 48:13–20).

Not only did the house of Joseph, or Ephraim, rise to ascendancy in the highlands north of Jerusalem, and fix its name upon all that region; but by the time of King Ahab, Ephraim overshadowed the tiny state of Judah; and thus the Josephite aristocracy became the chief power in Israel (II Kings, chaps. 8 and 11). Following the suggestion of this fact, the *Ephraimite* document embodied in Genesis makes Joseph dream that he and his brothers, the sons of Jacob, were binding sheaves in a harvest field when the sheaf of Joseph stood upright while the sheaves of his brethren came and bowed down to the sheaf of Joseph. Moreover, in another dream, Joseph beheld the sun, moon, and eleven stars making obeisance to him—the interpretation being that his father, mother, and brethren should acknowledge him as ruler (Gen. 37:5–10 [E document]).

Book of Genesis in relation to Hebrew history.—The foregoing illustrations prove how remarkably certain parts of Genesis correspond with the actual course of Hebrew development after the tribes of Israel had settled in Canaan, as recorded in the books of Judges, Samuel, and Kings. Our purpose in this connection is not to make a detailed comparison of Genesis with other biblical writings, but only to show, in a preliminary way, how this book, standing in the forefront of the Hebrew Bible, is to be employed as we approach the intricate and fascinating subject of Hebrew history. And as the investigation proceeds, we shall not only find other startling parallels between the legends and the actual history of Israel in the land of Canaan; but at certain points where the books of Judges, Samuel, Kings, and the prophets are obscure, we shall discover that Genesis helps to fill out the body of the narrative and throw light on situations otherwise dark.

We have already seen in chapter i that the Judaic school of prophets—Amos, Micah, and Isaiah—looked at Hebrew history from a standpoint inconsistent with the facts (p. 12); and we shall be more and more impressed by the consideration that biblical monotheism can be fully explained only through the *Ephraimite* prophets—Elijah, Hosea, and Jeremiah—as viewed in relation to the "Ephraimite" document of the Law. We must not, of course, belittle the final importance of Judah in the perspective as a whole; for ultimately the southern remnant of the Hebrew people carried the whole burden of Israel. But for the time being we must focus our attention upon the central highlands of Canaan, to the *north* of Jerusalem, where the house of Joseph took form, *and where Hebrew history began.*

CHAPTER III
EARLY HEBREW SOURCES

"Song of Deborah" early document showing location of tribes.—One of the most ancient sources giving us a glimpse of Israel in Palestine is a document called the "Song of Deborah." This important material is found in the fifth chapter of Judges; and it refers to a great battle with the Amorite "inhabitants of the land," which took place at a very early period after the settlement of Israel in Canaan, when the older population of the country was not as yet reconciled to the presence of the newcomers. *Six* tribes are praised as having taken part in the action—*Ephraim, Machir, Benjamin, Naphtali, Issachar, and Zebulun.* But, on the other hand, *four* tribes are condemned as "slackers" for having kept out of the fight—*Dan, Asher, Gilead, and Reuben;* while at the same time certain tribes which we should suppose ought to have been spoken of in *some* way, either for praise or for blame, are conspicuous by their total absence—*Judah, Simeon, Levi, and Gad.*

Thus, where the conventional orthodox theory entitles us to assume thirteen or fourteen tribes able to enter the action, less than *half* that number took part in a battle which decided the fate of Israel. Not only so, but a strange effect is produced by the absence of the four tribes, the apathy of the four others, and the use of such unfamiliar tribal designations as "Machir" and "Gilead." Evidently we are in the midst of conditions which, to some extent at least, collide with ordinary ideas about early Hebrew history; and if we are to make the right start in following out the evolution of Israel with reference to the idea of God, we must examine the sources carefully at this point.

27

Clans of Simeon and Levi broken up at a still earlier period.
—Here, again, the Book of Genesis comes to our aid by pictur-
ing an earlier period, before the actual settlement of the tribes in
Canaan, when "Jacob," or "Israel," invaded the country in the
form of small groups or clans. According to this legend, the sons
of Jacob made a solemn treaty with the Amorite walled city of
Shechem; and this treaty was broken by the two tribes of Simeon and Levi, which are *said* to have slain all the men of Shechem,
taken the women captive, seized the movable property, and
wiped out the city. This terrible conduct was bitterly reproved
by public opinion, in words attributed to Jacob as follows: "Ye
have troubled me, to bring me into bad odor *among the inhabitants of the land;* and I, being few in number, they shall gather
themselves together against me and slay me" (Gen. 34:30).
The story is, of course, a legend of the archaic period in personal
form, like the stories about Edom, Joseph, Manasseh, and
Ephraim, already noticed; and the condemnation of the two
brother-tribes is carried out to its logical issue in the poetical
piece called the "Blessing of Jacob," in still another part of
Genesis:

Simeon and Levi are brethren. Instruments of cruelty are in their
habitations. O my soul, come not thou into their council! Unto their assembly, mine honor, be not thou united! For in their anger they slew
men; and in their self-will they mutilated oxen. Cursed be their anger, for
it was fierce; and their wrath, for it was cruel. *I will divide them in Jacob
and scatter them in Israel* [Gen. 49:5–7].

So far as the tribes of Levi and Simeon are concerned, the so-
called "Blessing of Jacob" is really a curse, darkly hinting Amorite revenge, by which these two groups were put out of existence
as organized kindreds. And this is the reason why the Song of
Deborah contains no mention of Simeon or Levi, in praise or
blame. There were no such tribes in existence after the Israelite
settlement upon the soil of Canaan. The apparently inconsistent records of early Hebrew times, therefore, begin to yield an

underlying logic. Since the legends were built up in the first instance from the standpoint of the Josephites, or Ephraimites (i.e., sons of the favorite wife Rachel), the tribes of Simeon and Levi, therefore, were derived from the hated wife, Leah.

Absence of Judah from Deborah Song due to nonexistence in early period.—While Simeon and Levi are omitted from the Song of Deborah because of their annihilation, the tribe of Judah is absent from the poem and from the great battle because no large tribal group under that name, holding the territory of southern Canaan, had yet come into existence. The whole situation of Judah, with reference to its late organization as a full-fledged kindred group and its geographical isolation from Ephraim, compromises the historicity of all sources identified with the south, i.e., the J document in the Torah; the prophets Amos, Micah, and Isaiah, who looked at the evolution of the Hebrew people out of true focus; the D, or Deuteronomic, document of the Torah; and, most of all, the Jewish document, par excellence, consisting of the narrative and legalistic matter identified by critics under the symbol "P," denoting the priestly, or ecclesiastical, school of writers.

How far is Hebrew Bible true to Hebrew history?—A natural question, then, is: If we owe the Hebrew Bible in its present form to *Judaic* editors and compilers, how can we hope to extract from it any true and consistent information about Hebrew history in general? The Judaic writers were identified with *southern* Palestine; and if they were unable justly to visualize the Hebrew past, which was mostly *northern*, their limitations would seem, at first glance, to debar us from the facts we wish to know. The Old Testament as it now stands is, indeed, Judaic; the tribe of Judah becoming ultimately the sole surviving representative of Israel and the only channel by which ethical monotheism reached the gentile world. But these considerations, although impressive, are overshadowed by others more cogent and compelling. In the first place, Judah was al-

ways proud of the Ephraimite heroes who figure in Hebrew annals, and would not wish them to be ignored. Take, for instance, the Book of Judges. How much of that book would be
left if we omitted the stories about Ehud, Deborah, Barak,
Jael, Gideon, Jephthah, Manoah, Samson, Micah, and the
Danites? Practically all of Judges relates to the *non-Judaic*, or
Ephraimite, country which lies north of Jerusalem. And in the
same way, on turning to the books of Samuel, which come next
after Judges, we again find that most of the outstanding characters are connected with Ephraim, such as Eli, Elkanah, Hannah, Samuel, Hophni, Phineas, Joel, Abiah, Kish, Saul, Jonathan, Abner, etc. Only *one* Judahite family appears, namely,
the house of David at Bethlehem. The narrative about Nabal
does not refer to Judah, but to the *Kenizzite* clan of Caleb,
which at that time controlled a large part of the region later
known as Judah (I Sam. 25:3; Num. 32:12; Judg. 3:9). The
Kenizzites are reckoned among the *pre-Hebrew* inhabitants of
Canaan, descended from Kenaz, the grandson of *Esau*, and were
therefore *Edomites* (Gen. 36:10–11; 15:19). The Judahite house
of David held the center of the Hebrew stage for only about
eighty years; and at the end of that brief period the bulk of the
Hebrew nation, lying *north* of Jerusalem, broke away from the
southern dynasty, and formed the kingdom of Ephraim, which
yielded most of the leading biblical characters during the remainder of the history, such as Jeroboam, Ahijah, Omri, Tibni,
Ahab, Elijah, Elisha, Jehu, Jehonadab the Rechabite, Naboth
the Jezreelite, Micaiah the son of Imlah, Hosea, and Jeremiah.

Looking at Hebrew history as a whole, then, we can easily see
that it is more Ephraimite than Judaic. Nevertheless, the destruction of the kingdom of Ephraim by the *Assyrians*, in 721
B.C., had the effect of suddenly concentrating the current of Hebrew history into Judah; and thereafter the prophets and scribes
of that region acquired the habit of looking at the national past
from their own limited, provincial standpoint, this tendency to-

ward Jewish concentration being heightened by the Babylonian Exile, which uprooted the more active Judaic elements from their native soil. The distortion of Hebrew perspective in Jewish minds is therefore natural; *but, even so, the Judean redactors and compilers who finally brought the Hebrew Bible together, and interspersed their own comments, could not venture upon any serious mutilation of the original Ephraimite sources without wholly obscuring Judah's* raison d'être *as the survivor of Israel and the bearer of ethical monotheism.*

This important phase of the subject will be taken up more fully as we proceed. And, in the meanwhile, the significance of the omission of Judah, Simeon, and Levi from the Deborah Song has been considered in sufficient detail to give us a clearer view of the biblical sources, and to supply a background for closer study of that vivid composition dealing with early Hebrew history in Canaan.

CHAPTER IV

EARLY TRIBES IN CANAAN

In early "Judges" period Amorites hold walled cities while Israelites occupy part of highlands.—The early period of Hebrew history which comes before us in the Song of Deborah is concerned with the hill-country north of Jerusalem, lying between the river Jordan on the east and the Mediterranean Sea on the west. The city of Jerusalem at that time, in common with about a score of other Amorite strongholds, was not yet in the hands of the Israelite newcomers, and was destined to continue as an independent Amorite city all through the period covered by Judges and I Samuel; while the Israelites were clan villagers, dwelling in the open country, and having no fortified places. The Amorites in the meantime possessed not only the fortified cities of Canaan, such as Jerusalem, but they also held a large part of the agricultural territory just outside their walls.

Outstanding importance attaches to Josephite, or Ephraimite, group in central highlands.—The Song of Deborah takes its point of departure from three tribes—Machir, Ephraim, and Benjamin—of which the first immediately attracts notice as having an unusual name (Judg. 5:14). "Machir," as a *tribal* designation, occurs nowhere else in the historical or prophetic writings. But if we consult the Ephraimite document, or section, with which the Book of Genesis ends, we find that *Machir* figures as the first and *only* son of Manasseh, and is put on a level with Manasseh's brother Ephraim, precisely as in the Deborah Song (Gen. 50:15-26). Machir, therefore, belongs to the powerful aggregate of clans developing in the central hill-country under the generic name "house of Joseph."

The other tribal term figuring in close relation to Machir and

Ephraim is *Benjamin;* and upon recurring to Genesis, we find that Benjamin is reckoned as the brother of Joseph through the maternity of *Rachel,* who has *only* these two sons and is the favorite wife of Jacob (Gen. 30:22–24; 35:16–18). Accordingly, the historical narratives recognize Benjamin as "Josephite"; for after the defeat of Absalom's revolt against David, a thousand men of Benjamin present themselves before the returning monarch, as he comes back over Jordan, saying that they are the first of all the house of Joseph to meet the king (II Sam. 19:16–20).

Josephites, or Ephraimites, the central stock and main trunk of Israel.—Not only do the stories in Genesis reveal the house of Joseph as descended from the favorite wife of Jacob, but these legends paint the superiority of the Josephites in such resplendent colors that all the remaining tribes of Israel are said to originate either from an *unloved* wife, Leah, who was forced upon Jacob by deceit, or from *slave-girls,* Bilhah and Zilpah (Gen., chaps. 29 and 30). In other words, the legends favor the Josephite group as against the remainder of Israel; from which the conclusion emerges that the house of Joseph, or Ephraim, was the original heart, or core, of Israel, and was able to build the legends in its own interest *by reason of its geographical and ethnic preponderance in Hebrew history.* In other words, we now discover that the legends do for the Joseph-group *within* Israel what the legends also do for the Israel-group as a *whole* when contrasted with *alien,* or foreign, social groups like *Edom (supra,* p. 24). The Edomites, located south of Israel, were supposed to have descended from Esau, who, as we have seen, labored under many disadvantages and inferiorities; while the Moabites and Ammonites, on the *eastern* frontier across the Jordan, were said to be the result of incest (Gen. 19:30–38).

Deborah-battle fought by Josephites co-operating with directly adjacent northern groups, Naphtali, Issachar, and Zebulun.—It is instructive to note that in the great battle against the Amorites, the house of Joseph had the co-operation of only *three* other tribal groups, whose origins were inferior. Two of these, Issachar and Zebulun, are said to have sprung from the hated wife, Leah, who actually *hired* Jacob to beget Issachar (Heb. *sachar*, "hire" [Gen. 30:16–18]). The third co-operating tribe, Naphtali, was counted as born of the slave-girl Bilhah. These three groups lay directly *north* of the Josephites. And therefore the allied elements taking part in the battle (i.e., the Josephites plus Issachar, Zebulun, and Naphtali) *constituted a north-and-south mass overlying central Canaan.*

"Slacker tribes" on four extremities of central north-and-south mass.—We have seen that the Deborah Song (Judg., chap. 5) goes on to denounce *four* other tribes, which took no part in the fight. One of these, *Reuben*, is counted among the sons of hated Leah, and is addressed in bitter sarcasm: "Why abodest thou among the sheepfolds? To hear the bleatings of the flocks?" Another is *Dan*, son of the slave-girl Bilhah, and held up to scorn by the question, "Why did Dan remain in ships?" Another, called *Asher*, born of the slave-girl Zilpah, is ironically described thus: "Asher continued on the seashore, and abode in his breaches." The remaining slacker, called *Gilead*, is mentioned in the words, "Gilead abode beyond Jordan." But there is no tribe regularly designated by the name "Gilead"; and we find a clue to its identity when we read that in the time of Saul certain Hebrews went over Jordan to the land of *Gad* and Gilead (I Sam. 13:7). Gad is derived by legend from the slave-girl Zilpah (Gen. 30:10–11).

It is important now to notice that the four "slacker" groups, condemned for non-participation in the battle, were located on the four extremities of the central north-and-south mass. Reuben was across Jordan on the *southeast;* Gilead (or Gad) was over Jordan on the *northeast;* Asher was on the *northwest;* while Dan was on the *southwest*, not having, as yet, reached its final, characteristic position in the farthest *north* of Israel.

Summary of early tribal situation in Canaan.—The general situation of the tribes at the time of the Deborah-battle, therefore, sums up as follows:

TRIBES IN DEBORAH-BATTLE AN AGGRE- GATE MASS LYING NORTH AND SOUTH IN CENTRAL CANAAN

Three Rachel-tribes......................	Machir Ephraim Benjamin
Two Leah-tribes..........................	Issachar Zebulun
One slave-girl tribe.........................	Naphtali

SLACKER-TRIBES LYING ON EXTREMITIES OF CENTRAL MASS

One Leah-tribe............................	Reuben
Three slave-girl tribes....................	Dan Asher Gilead [or Gad]

TRIBES WHOLLY UNNOTICED

Three Leah tribes.......................	Judah Simeon Levi

CHAPTER V

HEBREW TRIBAL EVOLUTION

Working hypothesis of tribal evolution helpful to clear outlook on Hebrew history.—The house of Joseph, or Ephraim, now stands out as the foundation stock of Israel. This part of the nation, located in the central highlands north of Jerusalem, had *legend-building power* strong enough to impress itself upon the mind of the future, as derived from the favorite wife of Jacob, while assigning humbler origins to the remainder of the tribes, as born either from an unloved wife or from slave-girls. But the J document in the Torah, although unable to deface tradition seriously, shows an inclination to tamper with Ephraimite legends. For instance, in the story of Joseph and his brethren, the J strand puts Judah in the forefront (Gen. 37:26, 27); whereas the Ephraimite strand of the narrative puts the *northerner* Reuben to the fore as the would-be savior of Joseph (Gen. 37:22). According to the Ephraimite source, Benjamin was born in *Ephraim* (Gen. 35:16–19); but the P document says that Benjamin's birth was in *Paddan-aram of Mesopotamia* (35:22b–26). In the J legend, the patriarch Judah is pictured as the spokesman and captain of his brothers when they go down to Egypt. (Gen. 43:3, 8; 44:14, 16, 18; 46:28). These and similar phenomena in the various documents make it necessary for us to clear up, as far as possible, the relationship of the tribes in the order of time and place. This will help us to get a more distinct idea of Israel's development when the actual progress of Hebrew history comes before us.

Josephites arrive in central highlands after break-up of earlier invasion.—The legend that the clans of Simeon and Levi were destroyed near Schechem suggests that an advance expeditionary movement was undertaken by a fraction of the Israelite stock before the main body of Josephites arrived in the hill-country of central Canaan west of Jordan. The east-Jordan region was the halting-place, and for a long time the home, of primitive Israel after leaving the Arabian desert; and as numbers increased, the more adventurous elements (later known as Levi and Simeon) broke westward across the river, being destroyed in the highlands. Then later on, profiting by the experience of these hardy forerunners, a larger and stronger group advanced over Jordan, and went up into the central highlands to the point where we actually find it in the Song of Deborah under the name of *Machir*. This clan-group, Machir, spreading itself out as an aristocracy imposed upon Amorite slaves, became the organizing fascicle of the Hebrew nation as a *territorial state*, and therefore the legend-building factor which impressed its point of view upon the consciousness of the mingled people known as "Israel."

From the standpoint of the *west-Jordan* settlers, the main fragment left behind on the *eastern* side of the river would seem the *older;* and therefore in time it became known as the firstborn, identified under the tribal name of Reuben, the etymology of which is not clear. Reuben, we recall, was one of the "slackers" denounced by Deborah as unwilling to help the house of Joseph against the Amorites. But we can easily see that the population of the older, east-Jordan settlements would be very slow to take the long journey across the river and up into the central highlands on behalf of an abstract Israelite patriotism; for if a strong body of Reubenites had temporarily joined the *west*-Jordan group, their own lands, houses, and families in the *east*-Jordan country would have been exposed at once to attack and conquest by the neighboring *Moabites*, who were a much more dangerous foe to "Reuben" than the far-away Amorites. And even though the Reubenites had justice on their side when sitting by the sheepfolds and listening to the call of their flocks, it was not *they*, on the frontier, but the house of *Joseph*, in the central highlands, which had the strategic nation-forming and legend-building position. Consequently, the legends which at length became standard Hebrew tradition bore hard upon the "first-born." Not only was Reuben denounced in historical actuality by Deborah, but a story became current that the ancestor of the tribe had violated one of the slave-girls of Jacob (Gen. 35:22), for which he was chided sharply in the patriarchal "Blessing" (Gen. 49:3–4); and later on the Ephraimite document blackened the two sons of Reuben (Dathan and Abiram) as terrible sinners, abhorred by all Israel, and swallowed up alive in the earth (Num. 16:1*b*, 25–34).

Considerations very similar to those which kept the Reubenites out of the Deborah-battle restrained the other "tribes" which are denounced as having failed to answer the war call. "Gilead" not only showed neutrality at this time in "abiding beyond the Jordan," but later on the men of that region were consistently hostile to the Manassites and Ephraimites (Judg. 8:4–17; 12:1–6); and only at the end of the Judges period were they won over to the Rachel tribes by Saul the Benjaminite (I Sam., chap. 11; 31:11–13). At the same time, the Danites, on the southwest, were preoccupied by Philistine pressure, and were not of the full Israelite blood, being derived by legend from the slave-girl Bilhah; while the Asherites, on the northwest, were compromised with the native Amorite population, and were of such diluted blood as to be reckoned, like Dan, from a slave-mother.

The tribe of Machir, being established more and more firmly in the central highlands, increased its numbers, and became known by the alternative name of *Manasseh*. Part of the Manassites went back over Jordan, and, settling north of the Reubenites, became the aristocracy of Gilead, alienated from the central body, as we have seen, until the time of Saul. But another part, pressing slowly westward to the Mediterranean, gave rise to the *younger* tribe, Ephraim. That the names Joseph and

Ephraim are from Hebrew roots meaning "increase" and "fruit-fulness" may have pertinence in this connection. That the younger tribe, Ephraim, eventually overshadowed the Manas-sites, or Machirites, and impressed its name on the whole country north of Jerusalem, has been already observed.

House of Joseph, spreading south, gives rise to youngest group, Ben Yemen (Son of the South), or Benjamin.—Emerging now into clearer light, we can see the fruitful stock of Joseph pushing gradually down from the central highlands into territory which, although still north of Jerusalem, is nevertheless to the *south* of Ephraim. Here a new Rachel-group, or tribe, takes form under the name of Ben Yemen (Son of the South), or *Benjamin*. And, accordingly, the legends of Genesis describe Rachel, the beloved wife of Jacob and mother of Joseph, as giving birth to her younger son, Benjamin, *at precisely this point, in what was then the extreme south of Israel*. Benjamin was the tribe of *Saul*, who comes before us as an Ephraimite peasant in search of lost animals which were the property of his father Kish. Describing Saul's journey, the Hebrew text says, "He passed through *eretz yimini*" (I Sam. 9:4). The Hebrew *eretz yimini* should be rendered in English as "land of the south" or "southland." But it is wrongly given as "land of the Benjamin-ites" by the King James and Revised versions and also in the Jewish Publication Society's Bible.

The grave of Rachel, the Ephraimite mother, was first located by tradition in territory pertaining to the house of Joseph, where it is referred to by the Ephraimite prophet Samuel after anointing Saul as king: "When thou art departed from me to-day, thou shalt find two men *by Rachel's sepulchre in the border of Benjamin at Zelzah*" (I. Sam. 10:2). And the Benjaminite prophet Jeremiah, centuries later, imagines Rachel in her Ephraimite tomb, near Samuel's village of Ramah, weeping for the lost tribes of Ephraim, and refusing to be comforted (Jer. 31:15).

But in spite of this clear, unambiguous tradition, according

to which the legendary Rachel dies and is buried in the territory
of Joseph, or Ephraim, the narrative in Genesis has been twice
corrupted by Judahite "glosses," which undertake to transfer
the grave of Rachel from the hill-country of Ephraim *north* of
Jerusalem, to the village of Bethlehem-Judah, *south* of Jerusalem (Gen. 35:19; 48:7). And since the Book of Genesis occupies
a position in the forefront of the Hebrew Bible, the Jewish
glosses have determined the later traditional site of the tomb,
and have obscured the *original*, early tradition represented by
the books of Samuel and Jeremiah, which were written *before*
Genesis. Accordingly, one may see today, alongside the road
near Bethlehem in the hills of Judah, a structure called the
"tomb of Rachel." This mausoleum perhaps contained the body
of some Islamic notable, now forgotten; but otherwise it represents only a Judaic distortion of the early Ephraimite legend.

**Further Ephraimite expansion southward fixes outpost at
Bethlehem, which becomes point of departure for new tribal
evolution.**—The rise of a new tribe in southern Palestine is reflected in the Judaic document of Genesis, which depicts the
legendary patriarch *Judah* as withdrawing from his brethren,
the sons of Israel, directly after the outrage upon Joseph, as
though Judah were too good for continued association with the
family (Gen., chap. 38). He is described as "going down" from
his brethren to a *foreign* friend, Hirah the Adullamite. He takes
to wife a *Canaanite* woman, Shuah, by whom he has three sons
—Er, Onan, and Shelah. And being separated from the house
of Israel, Judah also betroths his first-born son to another
Canaanite woman, Tamar. This woman, being left a widow,
disguises herself as a *kedeshah*, or "sacred" prostitute, and becomes the mother of twin boys by seducing the patriarch Judah
himself. One of these twins, Pharez, is reckoned the progenitor
of the *Bethlehemite* family which, in the ninth and tenth generations, gave rise to Jesse and David, respectively (Ruth 4:12,
18 ff.).

The historical reality back of this ethnic legend is the actual association of David ben Jesse, of Bethlehem, with the foreign Adullamites, who granted him the protection of their fortress (not "cave"), which lay west of Bethlehem (I Sam. 22:1 f.–3 and first sentence of vs. 4 are interpolated). After staying at Adullam for a time, David was advised to depart and go "into the land of Judah." Since Adullam, to the west of Bethlehem, was thus *non-Judaic* territory; and since Jerusalem, a little to the north of David's home village, was even yet an *Amorite* walled city; while, at the same time, Hebron, to the south of Bethlehem, was possessed by the clan of Caleb the *Kenizzite-Edomite*, it follows that in the early days of David the term "land of Judah" was applied to a very small district, amounting to little more than the village of Bethlehem and environs. The Canaanite feminine name, Tamar, associated above with the patriarch Judah, appears *only* in David's family, being borne by his daughter and his granddaughter (II Sam. 13:1; 14:27).

We now begin to see why no tribe of Judah is mentioned in the Ephraimite Song of Deborah. If such a tribe had existed in Deborah's time, it would have been able to answer the Ephraimite battle-summons more easily than the far-away Reubenites east of Jordan; but the Reubenites were denounced as blameworthy for not coming over and participating in the fight, whereas there is no reference whatever to Judah. And not until a time long after Deborah can we discern a small Judahite community at Bethlehem, as narrated in the appendix to the Book of Judges (chaps. 17 f.; the original, or "Deuteronomic," Book of Judges began with 2:6 of the *present* book by that name, and extended *through* chap. 16, of which more later).

The actual origin of a small community at Bethlehem, in the late Judges period, is best explained as a further southward movement of the central Israelite mass which had previously given rise to the tribe of Benjamin. But there was a vital difference between the two cases. For Benjamin, being merely an extension of the Ephraimite mass, was of pure Josephite, or Israelite, blood, and was therefore brought under the maternity of Rachel, the favorite wife of Jacob; whereas, on the other hand, the community at Bethlehem was no tribe to begin with, but only a small emigrant group of Ephraimites, who either founded or conquered the village, and became a local aristocracy, or clan-group, known as a *mishpachah* (I Sam. 20:6). This little enclave of pioneers eventually produced an organizing genius in the person of David ben Jesse, who became friendly with the Adullamites, west of Bethlehem, and who married into the foreign clan of Caleb (I Sam. 25:2–42). From the vantage-point thus won, David brought into a single organization the Bethlehemites, Adullamites, Calebites, Jerachmeelites, and Kenites— all of which, with the exception of the aristocracy at Bethlehem, were not Israelite in blood. And since David was a "Judahite," this designation (whatever it may have meant previously) was now extended to cover *all* the southern part of Canaan, exclusive of the still Amorite Jerusalem, which was not at first in the coalition. The later career of David (after accepting the crown of Ephraim and occupying Jerusalem as his capital) obscures the important fact that his original kingship was *only* in the south, with his headquarters for seven years at the Calebite city of *Hebron*, which thus became the capital of the new kingdom and tribe of Judah (II Sam., chap. 2).

Meanwhile a second Ephraimite outpost is fixed at Beersheba, still farther south.—The southward expansion of Ephraim which, before David's time, produced Benjamin and then Bethlehem continued its course in the same direction, avoiding the Calebite Hebron, veering westward of the Jerachmeelites and Kenites, and setting up a new outpost at *Beersheba* in the extreme south of the "Negeb." Here the sons of the Ephraimite prophet Samuel became judges, or *shophetim* (I Sam. 8:2); and as late as the time of Amos, Beersheba was connected in some special way with Ephraim (Amos 5:5; 8:14).

Its foundation is "authenticated" by the Ephraimite document as having been made by Abraham (Gen. 21:22–24, 27, 31).

Judah's legendary origin from the hated wife Leah intelligible.—In view of the foregoing consideration, the familiarity of the Ephraimite prophet Samuel with the elders of Bethlehem would have more significance than hitherto realized. Samuel's early preference for David would, in Saul's eyes, take on the appearance of a conspiracy with renegade southern Ephraimites against the hegemony of Benjamin, the tribe of Saul; and the memory of the break between Samuel and Saul would be a dramatic factor in the complicated antipathy between Judah and Ephraim. The actual tribe of Judah, being built up of so many non-Israelite, foreign elements, could not claim purity of blood from Jacob and Rachel, as Benjamin did; and so this tribe was allowed by Ephraimite tradition to have come from the hated Leah, along with Levi and Simeon, whose individual fragments took refuge with the emigrants at Bethlehem and Beersheba. After the legend of Levi's annihilation as a tribe in Genesis, the first appearance of Levites in the historical books is found in the appendix to Judges, where they have the character of wandering priests, or *cohanim*, who make a livelihood by manipulating the sacred dice, "Urim and Thummim." They maintain their ecclesiastical position as priests of the local altars, or *bamoth*, until the Babylonian captivity, after which, as we shall see later, the prophet Ezekiel and the Jewish "Priestly Code" degrade them to the level of *porters* in the sanctuary.

With Judah thus explained, Book of Judges becomes more serviceable as early Hebrew source.—Looking at Judah, then, as a late product of tribal development in southern Canaan, we are now at length in a position to use the Book of Judges more freely. The original book of that name, as incidentally observed above, commences with 2:6, and extends *through* chapter 16, forming what critics call "the early Deuteronomic Book of Judges." Examining this part of the work, we find that 2:6 begins by depicting a certain Joshua ben Nun as an *Ephraimite hero*, who directs Israel in taking possession of the central Canaanite highlands north of Jerusalem. Then the text goes on to say that the people of Israel served Yahweh *"all the days of Joshua"*; after which the narrative goes on to speak of the *death* of Joshua, and his burial "in his inheritance in the *hill-country of Ephraim"* (Judg. 2:6–9; cf. Josh. 19:49b–50). Its compilation at a relatively advanced period of Hebrew history is indicated by the term "hill-country of Ephraim" (*har Ephraim*), which entered the common speech only after that tribe had impressed its name on the whole region to the north of Jerusalem. The compiler, being a "Deuteronomist," was therefore a Judaic scribe who lived about the time of King Josiah in Jerusalem, long after *northern* Israel had been carried away by the Assyrians. He was not only compelled to show that the original conquest of Canaan by Israel was an *Ephraimite* movement into the central highlands north of Jerusalem, under charge of an Ephraimite leader, Joshua; but in searching the ancient records and folk tales about early ages before the Hebrew monarchy, he was embarrassed by discovering that all the stories were about *northern*, and therefore non-Judaic, leaders, such as Deborah, Gideon, Samson, etc. And so, before presenting the story of Ehud, the *Benjaminite*, who belonged to a *Rachel* tribe, the compiler tried to find some *Judaic* hero whom he could put in the forefront as the first judge and savior of "all Israel." But, naturally enough, he could unearth no Judaic hero because there was no tribe of Judah in the early period. And so he resorted to the Kenizzite, or Edomite, clan of Caleb, which, as we have seen, combined with other elements in south Palestine to make up the Kingdom of Judah under David. Here the compiler found what he supposed would serve as a *Jewish* judge in the person of "Othniel ben Kenaz, Caleb's younger brother." Having thus discovered in the *south* a leader prepared to save the country, the Judaic scribe then goes on to imagine the *entire land of*

Canaan conquered and subdued by a powerful enemy from beyond the *northern* frontier, "Cushanrishathaim, king of Mesopotamia." The scribe then brings the Kenizzite up from Judah to defeat the Mesopotamian king, and thus, in imagination, makes Othniel the first leader and savior of all the children of Israel after the settlement in Canaan (Judg. 3:1–10). The stories about the northern heroes reveal a genuine folk-tale development, with vivid touches and lifelike details; and they relate only to limited sections of Israel. But the narrative about Othniel is entirely in the language of the Deuteronomist, lacking color, and presenting the Kenizzite as a deliverer of "all Israel." These contrasts with the tales about other judges, and the obvious endeavor to find the premier judge in the south, betray the editor's anxiety to overcome the preponderance of Ephraimite material in his treatise.

Still later scribe prefixes introduction attempting further to demonstrate superiority of Judah over Ephraim (Judg. 1:1— 2:5).—Not satisfied with what the Deuteronomic compiler of Judges had thus accomplished on behalf of Judah, a new editor took the material in hand, seeking to adapt it still more to Jewish interests. He prefixed a remarkable introduction, emphasizing that while the house of Joseph took only the central highlands and were unable to reduce the Amorite walled cities, the tribe of Judah had, *from the first*, a position of greater power. Consequently, at the very beginning and forefront of the present expanded Book of Judges, we find an exultant picture of *all Israel* gathered together and putting the question to Yahweh, "Who shall *first* go up for us against the Canaanites, to fight against them?" To which the answer of Yahweh is, *"Judah shall go up. Behold, I have delivered the land into his hand"* (Judg. 1:1 f.). Accordingly, the tribe of Judah is pictured as advancing out of the Jordan Valley ahead of all Israel, slaughtering ten thousand Canaanites, conquering Jerusalem, smiting the city with the edge of the sword, and setting it on fire. Thus, at the very time when the house of Joseph, or Ephraim, could only take certain restricted parts of the hill-country, and was unable to reduce any of the Amorite walled cities, the tribe of Judah is described as promptly taking the fortified city of Jerusalem and victoriously establishing its power over all southern Canaan.

But, as we have already seen, Jerusalem (or "Jebus") actually remained an Amorite city all through the long period covered by the books of Judges and I Samuel. It was not taken until the various non-Israelite elements of southern Canaan were first organized into the Kingdom of Judah by David, who afterward captured Jerusalem without setting the city on fire and without massacring its Amorite population (II Sam. 5:4 f.). A good picture of the historical situation resulting from David's capture of the city is found in an old reliable Hebrew source quoted in the Book of Joshua as follows: "As for the Jebusites, the inhabitants of Jerusalem, *the children of Judah could not drive them out; but the Jebusites live with the children of Judah at Jerusalem unto this day*" (Josh. 15:63).

Another instance of this late editor's method is found in the first clause of his introduction, which he has placed before the earlier, Deuteronomic Book of Judges: "Now it came to pass *after the death of Joshua*, etc." (Judg. 1:1 f.). According to this account, the invasion of Canaan took place when Joshua had already passed away. But we have observed that in the *earlier* edition of Judges, the Ephraimite hero Joshua directs the house of Joseph in taking possession of the central highlands, and then lives for a long time after the Ephraimites are established in Canaan, being finally buried in his Ephraimite estate (Judg. 2:6 f.). If the reader has not already noticed the remarkable contrast between these passages, he will get a fuller sense of the documents by carefully comparing the two sections of Judges, observing that the one assumes the Israelite settlement in Canaan to have been achieved only after Joshua had left the scene

(Judg. 1:1 f.), whereas the other contemplates Joshua as living many years to watch the settling of Israel in its new home (Judg. 2:6 f.).

Hebrew Bible compiled from unofficial sources before age of scientific historical criticism.—In view of these literary phenomena it may be asked why the Hebrew writers did not scrutinize their productions with greater care, so as to give a more harmonious account of the national development. But we must bear in mind that such work was impossible under the conditions of those days. The documents which finally became the Bible were prepared by many different writers, who lived at various places and in successive ages, when there was no scientific sense of history and none of our modern feeling about literary "property"; so that a scribe who compiled a roll of writing out of earlier documents and folk tales, or who came into possession of a roll compiled by somebody else, felt free to interpolate comments and additions. The material which we now call "Bible," or "Scripture," was not at first regarded as Bible while it was going through the long process of compilation whereby its present shape was reached. The Bible is based upon ancient folk tales, legends, and historical narratives which no longer survive in their pre-biblical form. This earlier material was *private and unofficial;* and even when it was copied into the rolls which later on became parts of the Bible, these rolls had likewise the same private character for many centuries. Thus, a large mass of partly conflicting matter was gradually accumulated by Hebrew scribes; and when the resulting rolls were officially adopted by state and ecclesiastical authorities, the task of re-editing the matter was not only too great, but no scribe had the technical equipment for such an undertaking; and even if he had possessed the scientific knowledge, he would not have been permitted to use it in modifying what had now become official, sacred literature.

Jewish coloring of Hebrew Bible natural under circumstances.—While the Bible was yet in process of going through its preliminary, unofficial evolution, the Hebrew people suddenly encountered the tremendous catastrophe in which the *Ephraimites* (the greater part of the nation) were largely carried away, leaving Judah alone in the south as a tiny remnant. Thus, it was the Jewish portion of Israel which eventually assumed the burden of literary and religious development, and which brought the claims of ethical monotheism before the world at large. Such being the case, it is not strange, but natural, as already pointed out, that the Hebrew Bible, in its completed form, should be strongly colored at certain points by the mentality of Jewish writers who copied the ancient documents into new rolls and made what they felt were fitting additions to the Ephraimite sources inherited from earlier days. For after the destruction of Ephraim, Judah began its long and strange career as a detached Israelite fragment in a world of more or less hostile and unsympathetic gentiles, or *goyim;* and this peculiar condition had the effect not only of increasing Judah's absolute importance in the long run, but also of artificially coloring the vanished past and overemphasizing Judah as a factor in early Hebrew history. To the Jew after the Assyrian destruction of Ephraim, and especially in the Babylonian deportation of his own tribe, the pre-Exilic Hebrew epoch was gradually transformed into an age of magic, wherein Judah *must* have existed from the beginning as a full-fledged tribe whose place in Israel had been *always* commensurate with the Jew's final significance as the bearer of monotheism and keeper of the sacred scrolls. In the light of all these considerations, then, it is easy to see why the Deuteronomic editor of Judges was so desirous to find a Jewish hero as premier judge of all Israel; why he was unsuccessful in the search, being compelled to make mechanical use of an alien Kenizzite, whom he placed as a lay figure at the head of Israel's deliverers; why another editor prefixed an introduc-

tion saying that Joshua, the leader of Ephraim, passed away
before the Israelite invasion of Canaan, when the older and immediately following section declares that Joshua not only accompanied the Ephraimites into central Canaan, but lived a
long time thereafter; why Jerusalem is said to have been captured and burned with fire long before it was *really* taken; and
why the tribe of Judah is described as advancing into Canaan
first, ahead of all Israel, and slaying ten thousand Canaanites, at
a time when Judah was not yet in existence as a tribal organization. These phenomena illustrate, on a large scale, the growth
of legends patterned upon real experience, in which a later-de-
veloped situation is projected into the past. And they also show
us that the actual course of Hebrew history proceeds at first
without reference to Judah, and revolves primarily around the
house of Joseph, or Ephraim, in the central highlands of Canaan
to the north of Jerusalem.

**Deuteronomic Book of Judges compiled within editorial
"framework" describing repeated "sale" of Israel by Yahweh.**—Looking closely now at the original Book of Judges
(2:6 through chap. 16), we find that it is a collection of stories
about individual tribes and heroes engaged in fighting the Canaanites, Moabites, Midianites, Ammonites, and Philistines.
The Deuteronomic editor who compiled the book has copied
various interesting tales out of earlier documents, and linked
them together into a kind of treatise by prefixing and interject-
ing observations of his own, wherein he repeatedly says, in
substance, "The children of Israel did evil in worshiping the
Baalim, the gods of the Amorites; and therefore Yahweh was an-
gry, and 'sold' them into the hands of their enemies." In other
words, wherever the Deuteronomist can find an ancient folk
tale or narrative in which Israel is attacked or oppressed by
some enemy, he takes this misfortune to be an evidence of divine
displeasure which caused Yahweh to make temporary "sale" of
Israel as a punishment for the sin of worshiping "other gods."

But when we carefully examine the tales thus used, we find that they are not, in themselves, of a nature which would lead a modern scientific historian to give them the interpretation suggested by the Deuteronomic *editor*. The philosophy of the "framework," which artificially binds the hero stories together, does not agree with the fact basis of the tales which the compiler has copied so diligently from older sources. The compiler is, indeed, quarrying material out of ancient narratives for the homiletical purpose of demonstrating to his *contemporaries* the evil results of polytheism.

Manassites in Gideon's time, and Joseph in Genesis, alike "sold" to Midianites, or Ishmaelites.—Turning to the editorial framework, we find the Israelites described seven times as being "sold," or "given," into the hands of enemies (Judg. 2:14 [twice]; 3:8; 4:2; 6:1; 10:7; 13:1; cf. I Sam. 12:9). The Hebrew term for "sell" is *makar;* and with this term before us, we find a striking correspondence between the actual fortunes of the oldest Josephite group (Manasseh) and of the legendary hero Joseph himself. The tribal designation "Manasseh," the eldest "son" of Joseph, is equated with "Machir" in Genesis (50:23, pronounced *makeer*, past tense of "sell"); while in the Song of Deborah, as we have seen, Machir stands for Manasseh. According to the Manassite hero tale of Gideon, the children of Israel are actually "sold" into the hands of Midianites, or Ishmaelites; and the weight of oppression, falling upon the oldest group in the house of Joseph, rouses Gideon to action (Judg., chaps. 6–8); while in the legends of Genesis, Joseph is *makeer*, or "sold," to Midianites or Ishmaelites (Gen. 37:27, 28, 36). We are thus in touch with one phase of the actual history which produced the legends common to the "Ephraimite" and "Yahwistic" documents (JE) lying at the foundation of the Law, or Torah.

Josephite, or Ephraimite, nucleus of Israel in Goshen, outlying province of Egypt.—The original "Egyptian" tradition of

Israel turned wholly around a small Josephite, or Ephraimite, stock. Joseph only was there in the first form of the legend (Gen. chaps. 37, 39, 40, 41). Moreover, according to the older (JE) strata in the books of the Law, Israel was never in the Nile country proper, but only in the extreme northeastern province of *Goshen*, which lies nearest to Canaan (Gen. 46:28, 34; 47:4, 6, 27; Exod. 8:22; 9:26). This region is a natural resort for nomadic Arabian clans during famine periods; and there is nothing historically unreasonable in the supposition that a small group, which later served as the organizing nucleus of the Hebrew nation, was actually at one time in Goshen. The remaining "sons of Jacob," including Benjamin, who was born after Joseph, are mechanically imported into Egypt later, so as to fill out the legend according to the national history in Canaan. The region of Palestine first appropriated by the Josephites had been previously under the rule of Egypt; and accordingly Joseph's two sons, Manasseh and Ephraim, are derived from an Egyptian mother (Gen. 41:45, 50–52). But while we can find in the daylight of history, so to speak, the impulses which patterned the legend of Judah upon actual experience in Canaan and Babylon, the roots of the earlier legend of Israel in Egypt are obscured by a fantastic and complex evolution of ideas much harder to pierce and interpret concretely.

Israelites enter covenant relation with foreign tribe when leaving Goshen.—The climax of the Song of Deborah celebrates the exploit of a *non*-Ephraimite woman, "Jael, the wife of Heber the Kenite," who, after the great battle, slew the fugitive Amorite general, Sisera (Judg. 5:24 f.). Following along through the Ephraimite history, we find that when the Josephite king, Saul, was about to attack certain enemies of Israel, he became aware that the *Kenites* were in the vicinity of his foes. "And Saul said unto the Kenites, Go, depart, get you down from among the Amalekites, lest I destroy you with them; *for ye showed kindness to all the children of Israel when they came up*

out of Egypt. So the Kenites departed from among the Amalekites" (I Sam. 15:6). These friendly aliens were also favored by
David, who sent gifts to them (I Sam. 30:29).

Nearly all tribes in the desert places of the world are hostile
to each other on account of scanty food supply; and they fight
over the possession of wells and fertile spots. But sometimes
two or more tribes in a given district make a friendly covenant
of co-operation against common foes. Thus, the nomads in the
wilderness to the south of Canaan were always more or less conscious of the hostile and mighty empire enthroned on the Nile,
whose armed forces marched along the coast into Palestine or
penetrated the wilderness to chastise the nomad clans and
guard the mines owned by Egypt in the region of Mount Sinai.

It is not strange, therefore, to find in the Ephraimite and
Judahite sources a tradition of amity between Israel and a foreign tribe in the southern wilderness at the time the Josephite
nucleus was in Goshen. And the friendship (or *hesed*) which
arose between Israel and the Kenites was tenacious enough to
be preserved in the racial memory for centuries. Connections
of this kind never happen of themselves impersonally. They are
always brought about by the activities of leading men on both
sides, who start the covenant relationship through appropriate
formalities. The Kenite personage mentioned in this case is
called "Jethro the *cohen*" (priest) by the Ephraimite document
(Exod. 3:1; 4:18; 18:5, 12); but other names are also applied to
him or to members of his family (Judg. 4:11; Exod. 2:18). The
Israelite leader is called, in Hebrew, *Mosheh*, or, in the Greek
form, "Moses"; and he is said to have married Zipporah, one of
the daughters of Jethro the Kenite priest. It is very instructive
to notice that although the Jews in post-Exilic times were
strongly against marriage with foreign women, the pre-Exilic
Hebrew narratives and legends are full of assimilation and intermarriage between Israel and other peoples.

Worship of Yahweh acquired by Israelites in wilderness.— According to the Ephraimite source, Jethro, the leader of the Kenites, was a priest of Yahweh at a time when Israel was even yet serving *other gods;* and this document therefore speaks of "the gods which your fathers served on the other side of the [Euphrates] river and in Egypt" (Josh. 24:2, 14). Accordingly, the E document avoids the name "Yahweh" in Genesis, and also in Exodus *until the point is reached where Israel entered into covenant with the Kenites* (Exod. 3:13–15).

But, on the other hand, the Judahite source takes the worship of Yahweh for granted from the early days of mankind, in the same way that it assumes the existence of Judah as a full-fledged tribe from the beginning of Israel's history. Thus, the forefathers are described as worshiping in the name of Yahweh; and even Gentiles are spoken of as calling upon this name at the beginning of human history in the days of Adam (Gen. 4:26).

An attempt is made to account for this discrepancy by the *latest* Jewish document, the P source, which explains that even though the Israelites and their forefathers did not know the actual *name* "Yahweh" until the days of the exodus from Goshen, the patriarchs really worshiped this deity in earlier times under the name "El Shaddai," an untranslatable term, which is rendered, without due warrant, "God Almighty" (Exod. 6:3).

The Jewish "Priestly" document then goes on, in the books of Exodus, Leviticus, and Numbers (as we shall see more fully later) to give an elaborate, ecclesiastical treatise on Israel in the wilderness, emphasizing and exalting the tribe of Judah at the expense of Ephraim; thus achieving what the scribes considered to be a satisfactory balance for their own branch of Israel in the Hebrew Bible, and compensating, as they supposed, for the lack of Jewish matter in Hebrew history after the settlement of Israel in Canaan.

Exodus period gets importance when viewed from standpoint of Yahweh-Baal struggle in Canaan.—The conclusion will already have begun to be evident that Hebrew history in the land of Canaan must be interpreted mainly from the standpoint of developments after the arrival of the house of Joseph in the central highlands of Ephraim. We must, indeed, regard with even more seriousness than the Wellhausen school itself the displacement of the orthodox formula, "The Law and the Prophets," by the critical formula, *"The Prophets and the Law."* For as our investigation of Hebrew history proceeds, we shall realize with more and more distinctness that the great campaign of "insurgent" prophecy derived its chief impulse, not from any peculiar institutions or ideas discovered or established in the wilderness, but from the very special and hitherto little-understood situation *at the basis of Israel's development in Palestine.*

The higher criticism shows that the various documents of the Law did *not* come into existence before the settlement of Israel in Canaan; and it therefore spreads these writings out through various periods in the Canaanite and Babylonian history of Israel. And while no historian can deny that a kernel of objective reality lies under the imposing tradition of Egypt and the Exodus, the fact remains that many critical scholars reveal an "orthodox" tendency to read back too much into the wilderness experience of Israel prior to the settlement in Palestine. This tendency is correlated with the fact that Hebrew evolution in Canaan has been regarded, by conventional higher criticism, from a subjective standpoint which does not adequately take into account the peculiar sociological and economic factors of the situation *in Palestine.* The human mind is always restlessly in search of causal factors; and if a cause is not at once apparent in the closer and more immediate circumstances before us, we seek it in remote or far-off times and conditions. And such being the case, critics feel themselves under pressure to retreat upon the hazy past in order to find some peculiar driving-force, or some extraordinary and exclusive impulse, for the admittedly peculiar development which took place in Hebrew history after the arrival of Israel from the wilderness. That a covenant relationship arose in the wilderness between Yahweh and Israel was believed alike by the insurgent prophets and by their *enemies*, the reactionaries; but this idea was at first liquid and fluctuating. And when the pressure of economic centralization began to be felt, the insurgents and their foes built up competing views of the common tradition; whereupon each party sought to enforce its own platform as final and official. The struggle practically resulted in the success of the reactionaries, who stood for the *baalization* of Yahweh. But at the critical moment, *the walls of Jerusalem were crashed by the battering rams of Nebuchadnezzar;* and the insurgent party rose victorious under the Ephraimite prophet Jeremiah.

The problem of economic centralization has appeared over and over again during the course of human history; and it is now pressing upon the entire modern world. As a mere economic matter, therefore, it was not in any way peculiar to Israel; and if the social development of the Hebrew people had not placed a god of wilderness-mishpat, or clan-justice, in a position of political superiority over and above territorial gods (the Amorite Baalim) which represented the usages of a settled community long fixed on trade routes—if this peculiar social evolution had not occurred in the centuries prior to Elijah, no struggle between Yahweh and Baal would have been possible, and the problem of economic centralization could have come to nothing distinctive in Israel.

In the campaign against Amorite Baalism, the insurgent prophets did not invoke any unusual institution or peculiar ideal established in the dim past; they merely pointed back to the mishpat of the desert-clan as against the "civilized" view of legality current in Canaan and symbolized by the local gods which the Hebrews inherited from the Amorites. The insurgent prophets undertook the *humanly impossible task* of preventing the evolution of Yahweh into a god identical psychologically with the Baalim, but physically more powerful. The rich and influential elements of the nation, therefore, believed in a materialistic Yahweh, who had delivered Israel out of Egypt, and who was to be worshiped by sacrifice and burnt-offering as a magnified Baal. They were, consequently, "stiff-necked"; and they remained unconvinced by the mishpat-argument.

That any system of sacrifice and offering had been given to Israel in the desert is denied by Jeremiah, the last and greatest of the prophets (Jer. 7:22); and his argument in this connection would have no point whatever if, at any time in the wilderness, Israel had been given a system of ritual institutions for the worship of Yahweh. This Ephraimite insurgent declared that Jerusalem was a wholly evil city (Jer. 5:1–2); and he charged that the Jewish writers wielded lying pens which wrote falsehood (Jer. 8:8). Jeremiah was evidently opposed, in principle, to a large part of what later became orthodox in the Mosaic tradition, and which attained its ultimate form long after his day in the P document. He agrees with his predecessor, the Judahite Amos, who asks, in the name of Yahweh, "Did ye bring sacrifices and offerings unto me in the wilderness, O house of Israel?" (Amos 5:25). It is thus clear that the complex traditions which finally became authoritative and *official* among the Jews were still fluctuating in the time of Jeremiah; and this prophet has in mind a simple tradition harmonizing with the basic Ephraimite view that Israel's bond with Yahweh dates from the Exodus, when the name was first used in Israel (Jer., chap. 2).

Hence, up to the very end of his ministry, Jeremiah's gospel of Yahweh is built upon the conventional usages of the primitive nomadic, non-territorial clan, according to which the members of a given social group have mutual responsibilities, and should *never* permit the less fortunate "brethren" to fall permanently into the lower, enslaved social class (the *abadim*). And thus, amid all the uproar of Nebuchadnezzar's final attack on Jerusalem, which resulted in the destruction of the city, we see Jeremiah's ethical standpoint asserting itself in the arraignment which he levels at the richer baalim, the wealthier members of the Hebrew aristocracy: "Every man should let his man-slave and his woman-slave, *being an Hebrew or an Hebrewess*, go free; that none should serve himself of them,—*of a Jew his brother*" (Jer. 34:9).

Following the clue thus given by the Ephraimite prophet, we now turn to the movement of invasion and conquest by which the house of Joseph arose in the central highlands of Canaan.

CHAPTER VI

PRIMITIVE AGE OF MISHPAT

Mishpat-idea comes from wilderness.—The foregoing study shows that the Hebrew nation evolved at the point of contact between Amorite society on the Mediterranean seaboard and certain tribes, or clans, from the wilderness of Arabia. Hebrew history, therefore, is like the intermingling of two rivers which meet and flow onward in a single current, each river making its own contribution to the new stream. Only as we learn to hold this fact in full view, with all its implications, can we understand the historical problem of Israel. Accordingly, the conventional idea that the wandering tribes of the wilderness were the one, *original* Israel is very misleading; for only a *part* of the Hebrew nation's ancestry was of immediate origin from the desert.

Furthermore, the experiences of the ancestors in the wilderness, or *midbar*, were much simpler than the orthodox theory proclaims. Our actual *knowledge* of pre-Canaanite Hebrew history is very slender: The wilderness forefathers of Israel, in common with all nomadic folk, had the mishpat-idea that the *source of life* (i.e., land, water, etc.) is communal and not rightly commercial (i.e., not to be disposed of by private persons through sale or exchange). And while this idea, *later on*, took special form, or emphasis, through the work of the insurgent prophets, long after the settlement in Canaan, there is no evidence that it was in the least peculiar to the desert ancestors of Israel at the start. And not only does the mishpat-idea go back to a common root among all nomads; but it invariably occurs in association with some local, or tribal, cult, fetish, or divinity. That is, it never stands as an abstract philosophy, independent of ritual. Accordingly, the desert ancestors of the Hebrew peo-

ple expressed the mishpat-idea through the cult of *Yahweh*—
taken over by friendly contact with another social group in the
wilderness. And, like all such deities, Yahweh was necessarily
viewed as a war-god, who protected his followers against their
enemies.

These exceedingly primitive thoughts are in the background
of the E and J documents at the basis of the "Law"; they can
be read between the lines of the literary prophets, from Amos
onward; and they underlie the original "source-narratives"
which the Deuteronomic school worked up into the books of
Judges, Samuel, and Kings. From the *pre-Canaanite epoch*,
then, we can scarcely extract anything more than these very
simple notions: Yahweh a god of mishpat as the norm of
group life; Yahweh a war-god; and Yahweh a god of the Joseph-
group, or of Israel, through some helpful experience in the
wilderness.

**Torah-documents not authoritative history of wilderness
period.**—The E and J sources in the books of the Law are
farther from the times which they profess to describe than we of
today are from the Pilgrim fathers who journeyed across the
Atlantic Ocean to America in 1620. Moreover, they were combined at certain points into a single narrative, JE, by a later
hand; after which they were mingled with a great deal of matter
by the Deuteronomic scribes, D, who lived at the very end of
Hebrew history in Judah; and then, later still, the J-E-D combination was blended with a vast amount of *priestly* writings, P,
by scribes who flourished in the Babylonian Exile. The object of
the earliest, or Ephraimite, document was to express the rising
popular protest (950–850 B.C.) against the Ephraimite Baalistic
régime, which finally came to a head after the time of King
Omri, and which found its first great figure in the prophet *Elijah*.
It is based on a fluctuating, unofficial tradition; and instead of
being a definitive *history* of the wilderness epoch, it is an insurgent prophetic pamphlet, addressed to its own times, projecting

the ideas of a heretical sect into the dim past, and viewing the
pre-Canaanite age from an *ex parte* standpoint.

We cannot absolutely deny the existence of a Mosheh, or
Moses, who promoted contact between the Josephite group and
the friendly Kenites; but the *traditional* Moses of the E document is an early Ephraimite, or Josephite, prophet, or *nabi*,
whose picture is drawn by the same school which gave us the
portraits of Elijah and Elisha, identified with the slaughter of
Baal-priests and the massacre of Ahab's Baal-worshiping family
(I Kings 18:40; II Kings 9:1-9). The ideals which animate
these early prophetic leaders of revolt in Ephraim also inspire
the artistry which created the figure of Moses, who issues the
sanguinary decree, "Slay ye every one his men that were joined
unto Baal-peor" (Num. 25:4-5; cf. Exod. 32:26-27). The story
of escape from Egyptian chariots, which were lost in the sea,
was written by Josephite scribes looking back into the archaic
past through the refracting medium of the actual, historic Deborah-battle, when the chariots of Sisera were lost in the waters
of Megiddo (Exod., chap. 14; cf. Judg., chap. 5). The so-called
"Song of Moses," in Exodus, chapter 15, is far later than the
Deborah Song. The Mosaic legend, as it appears in document
E, thus gives a literary background for Hebrew insurgent
prophecy, which began, as we must always remember, in *Ephraim* and not in Judah; the traditional Moses being morally on a
par with Elijah and Elisha, but ethically *below* the level of later
prophets, such as Amos, Hosea, and Isaiah; while the still further magnified Moses of the P document, as we shall see in due
time, is impossible. We believe that the situation is correctly
envisaged by Professor George A. Barton, of the University of
Pennsylvania, in his book, *Semitic and Hamitic Origins* (1934),
page 350:

Moses was the intermediary by whom the primitive, anthropological
cult of Yahweh entered the stream of Hebrew tradition; and then, cen-

turies later, an ethical movement was intiated in the time of Elijah, which at length came to full fruitage in the literary prophets.

Joseph-story an Ephraimite prophetic parable, not Hebrew history in Egypt.—The linguistic stamp of Ephraim is evident in the story of Joseph: "Behold this *baal* of dreams cometh" (Gen. 37:19; the term in J would be *adon*). And when we take the story as an Ephraimite parable applying to conditions in the ninth and eighth centuries B.C., its meaning begins to come out clearly into relief. Joseph was sold into bondage for silver (Gen. 37:28); and likewise, after the reign of Omri, the poorer baalim of Ephraim were sold into slavery for silver—"*the affliction of Joseph*" (Amos. 2:6; 6:6; 8:6). The richer baalim, on the right wing of the Hebrew aristocracy, were adding house to house and field to field; while the poorer baalim on the left wing (the mass of peasant proprietors) were transformed into slaves of the wealthy. The nation, *considered as the family of Jacob*, was disintegrating. The claims of kinship as a social principle uniting *all* the free citizens of the upper class, rich and poor, were systematically denied. It was a time of profound social stress, characterized not only by economic problems, but by sexual corruption: "A man and his father go in unto the same maid" (Amos 2:7). The sacred prostitutes of Baal (the *kedeshoth*) were openly plying their trade (Hos. 4:14). And against this dark background the authors of the Ephraimite document painted a vividly contrasting picture of *Joseph*, the ancestor of the north, who was a hero on three counts: (1) he stood above sexual temptation; (2) he acknowledged the brotherly claims of the entire kindred group, in that he nourished *all his father's house;* and (3) he set up a national "planned economy," *based on a program of social justice which guaranteed peasant-possession of the soil with 80 per cent of its annual produce.*

The later Jewish non-Ephraimite scribe has redacted and mixed the Ephraimite and Judaic documents of Genesis in a way at first confusing, but which presently becomes clear. The original chief of the brethren is the *northern* patriarch Reuben, the "first-born," who proposes merely to *conceal* Joseph in a pit, with the secret intention of restoring him later to Jacob (Gen. 37:22 [E]). But in the J document the leader is *Judah*, who proposes that the ancestor of the house of Ephraim be sold into *slavery*, thus revealing the ancient prejudice of the southern kingdom against the northern monarchy (vss. 26–27). No Egyptologist has ever found any trace of a Hebrew dictatorship in the empire of the Nile.

Primitive ancestral group leaves Goshen for oasis of Kadesh.—That an Egyptian tradition was ultimately impressed upon the Hebrew people of later history by a small group which, like other Arab tribes, pastured its flocks for a time in the land of Goshen (not Egypt proper), has been already admitted (chap. v, p. 51). But this group may not have been identified at *that* time by the names Joseph, Jacob, or Israel, which may possibly have been acquired *after* the desert group invaded and settled the central highlands of Canaan. The Ephraimite document says that the group which left Goshen (not Egypt) carried with them only the bones of their ancestor *Joseph* (Exod. 13: 19 [E]). On the other hand, in the interests of southern prestige, the Judaic, or J, document contains an account of the funeral of Jacob (Gen. 50:1–11, 14), wherein, at verses 12–13, P, the latest school of Jewish writers, inserts a passage locating the grave of Jacob at *Hebron* in central Judah (cave of Machpelah; cf. also Gen. 23:19). Thus, not only is the grave of Rachel, the Ephraimite mother, transferred from Zelzah in the north to Bethlehem in Judah (chap. v, p. 39), but the legendary ancestor of the entire Hebrew nation is also given a Jewish interment at the center of the southern highlands.

The nomads, according to one source, J, were able to pass through a marsh called "Sea of Reeds (*Yam Suph*) because the ground was dried off by a wind which blew for many hours:

"And Yahweh caused the sea to go back by a strong east wind all that night" (Exod. 14:21b). But the later, Priestly document has Mosheh lift his hand, causing the sea to part and make a wall on either side: "And Mosheh stretched out his hand over the sea, and made the sea dry, and the waters were divided; and the B'nae Israel went into the midst of the sea upon the dry ground; and the waters were a wall unto them on their right hand, and on their left" (Exod. 14:21a, c, 22). And even as the chariots of Sisera floundered and were lost at Megiddo in the waters of Kishon, so the Egyptian chariots perish at the Yam Suph. But while Sisera fled from the wreck of the Amorite host, this must be outdone by the later legend, which declares that not so much as *one* of the enemy remained alive (Exod. 14:28).

The simpler, primitive sense which underlies the complex and highly miraculous account of the Exodus is that the group which came out of Goshen (not Egypt) went directly across the desert and made their headquarters at a large oasis known as "Kadesh," to the *south* of Canaan and *west* of Edom. A summary of the route is given as follows in the Book of Judges: "Israel came up from Egypt and walked through the wilderness unto Yam Suph, and came to Kadesh" (11:16). The nomads could hardly have numbered more than a thousand souls at this time; and even such a small group would have taxed the capacity of Kadesh, the site of which has been probably identified as the modern "Ain Kadis," fifty miles below the southern frontier of Canaan.

Oasis of Kadesh known also as "En Mishpat."—A significant alternative name for Kadesh is given in Genesis: *"En Mishpat,* the same is Kadesh" (Gen. 14:7). The meaning of this term is "Fountain of Justice" or "Well of Justice"—an appropriate symbol for the headquarters of a desert group which was to impress the mishpat tradition upon the future history of Canaan. The Genesis passage quoted above is the only case in the Bible where the strategic and highly important Hebrew

word "mishpat" is actually trans*literated* instead of being interpreted or translated. The term occurs again and again in the
Hebrew text of the Bible, and is variously translated as "judgment," "ordinance," "that which is lawful," etc., but more truly
and finely by the American Revised and the American Jewish
versions as "justice."

The other name of the oasis, *Kadesh*, means "holy place" or
"sanctuary"; and it comes from a Semitic root indicating isolation, or a state of being *set apart*. Kadesh, then, would have the
character of a primitive, Arabian holy place, where the social
customs, or mishpat, of wilderness clans were declared by elders
and priests in the name of a local divinity whom the Joseph-
group worshiped here as "Yahweh." The identification of Yahweh with mishpat is the underlying theme of all the insurgent
prophets. "Yahweh is a god of mishpat" (Isa. 30:18). "What
does Yahweh require but to do mishpat?" (Mic. 6:8). This key-
term occurs with impressiveness and frequency in the Hebrew
text; and its profound significance in relation to the entire problem of Hebrew history is only now beginning to emerge from the
clouds of controversy that have obscured the Bible for thousands
of years. Vast and laborious efforts have been wasted in discussion of alleged miracles and in attempting to sustain the literal
authority of documents written many centuries after the Exodus; while at the same time the basic social and ethical facts have
been either ignored or misunderstood. But these fundamental
facts are the measuring rods which alone should be employed in
the study of Hebrew history.

**Desert ancestors leave En Mishpat and invade Gilead, east
of Jordan.**—How long the primitive ancestral group made use
of En Mishpat or Kadesh as headquarters in the desert we cannot say. That they remained here continuously between the
time of their exodus from Goshen and their entrance into Canaan is the earlier and simpler form of tradition represented by
the interwoven J and E sources. Natural increase of numbers,

combined perhaps with hostile pressure from wilderness clans, would be enough to explain the migration which at length took the primitive Israel-group away from this friendly oasis. According to the Book of Judges, they passed around through the desert, and approached Canaan from the east, where they found a small Amorite kingdom barring the way in the land of *Gilead*. Defeating these Amorites, the Israel-group established itself east of Jordan (Judg. 11:18–22).

Gilead is a region, even today, for shepherds and cattlemen, without possibilities for trade or manufacture (cf. Num. 32:1–4). Here the invaders planted themselves firmly in small tent villages. Their southern border touched *Moab;* and their eastern frontier touched *Ammon*. The Moabites and Ammonites were later alleged by Hebrew mythology to be the product of incest between Lot and his daughters (Gen. 19:30–38); while the Book of Deuteronomy says, "An Ammonite or Moabite shall not enter into the congregation of Yahweh. . . . . Thou shalt not seek their peace nor their prosperity all thy days forever" (23:3–6).

Our survey having now carried us to the threshold of Hebrew history in Canaan, it is well for us to look at the biblical documents from a still broader standpoint, in their bearing upon Israel as a group *amid other nations*.

Hebrew myths give normal, primitive expression of hostility between social groups.—It now becomes even clearer than before that Hebrew myths give primitive expression to various degrees of social-group hostility. This fact is consistent with the social psychology of all nations, and may be advantageously enlarged upon here. *Israel, instead of being an old nation, was in fact one of the latest Semitic peoples to achieve nationality.* Viewing Israel as a new group arising among gentile nations, the Hebrew mythology seeks to provide a morally *righteous* point of origin for Israel, the burden-bearer of ethical monotheism to less instructed peoples. Accordingly, three non-Israelite patri-

archs are called into existence in the dim, prehistoric age, namely, *Enoch*, *Noah*, and *Abram*, each of whom "walked with God"
(Gen. 5:24; 6:9; 17:1). All these passages occur in the late
Priestly document, which takes the expression "walking with
God" from earlier *prophetic* sources. The three God-fearing
gentile patriarchs are described as a kind of spiritual aristocracy
from whom, by honorable descent in the direct line, come the
Hebrew people; while other nations originate in less creditable
ways. And not only is this principle imagined as operating to
distinguish Israel from the rest of the world; but, as we have
already seen, it is illustrated by the *interior group-economy* of the
Hebrew people themselves. For the house of Joseph is at first
the dominant legend-building power in the nation, taking chief
credit to itself and assigning less honorable positions and origins
to the other sections of Israel; while after the downfall and ob-
literation of the northern Ephraimite or Josephite kingdom, the
scribes of Judah finally undertake to exploit all previous Hebrew tradition in the southern, or Jewish interest. Thus, at the
very moment when the "Law," or Torah, is deprived of supernatural infallibility, it acquires a new and interesting character
as the authentic deposit of documents coming from various
periods and originating in successive stages of Hebrew evolution. These facts will help us to make even fuller use of the Law
as a collection of sources bearing upon the study of Hebrew history after the settlement in Canaan.

Consolidation of ancestral group in Gilead.—So far as the
actual process of events is concerned, the scene is even yet
largely obscured in darkness. How long the invaders from En
Mishpat continued, as a whole, to remain in Gilead before moving westward across the Jordan into Canaan proper we cannot
say. Possibly the more adventuresome elements, later called
Simeon and Levi, with another clan Dinah, may have migrated
over the river and up into the central highlands, where they had
trouble with the Amorite city of Shechem and perished as or-

ganized groups (chap. iii, p. 28). On this view, the main body would have continued in Gilead for some time while their numbers were augmenting by natural increase and through alliance with other clans in that region. A period of rest and growth would seem normal after the exertion of invading the country, destroying the Amorite kingdom of Sihon, and settling down to peaceful occupancy. Gilead never found a place in the main stream of Hebrew history; and it was a kind of halfway point in the transition from desert nomadism to the agricultural and commercial existence of central Canaan. For this very reason it was admirably fitted to strengthen the primitive Israel-group in the usages of mishpat, and to generate hostility against the baalistic, Amorite régime which they were to challenge on the other side of Jordan. From this region at a much later time, indeed, was to come the first great prophetic figure in the campaign to overthrow Baalism: *"And Elijah was among the inhabitants of Gilead"* (I Kings 17:1).

CHAPTER VII

PEASANT ARISTOCRACY AND MISHPAT

Israelite names used in pre-Hebrew Canaan during Egyptian suzerainty.—In the pre-Hebrew epoch, the land of Canaan was controlled at various times by Egypt, Babylon, and the Hittites from Asia Minor. An inscription from the time of Merneptha reads: "Israel is laid waste; its corn is destroyed." Other sources also indicate that the names "Israel," "Jacob," and "Asher" were used in Canaan during the pre-Hebrew era. Thus a tradition of bondage to Egypt might already have become current among the Amorites west of Jordan, to be carried along in the psychology of Palestine after the invaders from Gilead had superimposed themselves upon the older inhabitants through gradual conquest. We know that the Normans, invading England, were unable to give their name to the country, but were compelled by the logic of circumstances to build a state in the name of the conquered English. The Normans were thus transformed into Englishmen; and they became the new aristocracy under whom the nation was organized. Something of this kind may have taken place when the primitive group from Gilead and Kadesh finally swarmed westward across the Jordan. Only by a narrow margin did they and their successors transform Canaan into Israel; and by a similar narrow margin they might themselves have sunk into the mass of the earlier inhabitants, disappearing from history. The so-called "conquest of Canaan" brought into existence a "melting-pot" which remolded and fused the ideas and cultures of the older and newer inhabitants, and, indeed, almost obliterated the name Yahweh under the term "Baal."

Baalism and harlotry of Amorites known to Gilead-group.— A certain empirical knowledge of the social system prevailing west of Jordan was naturally acquired in various ways by the Gilead-group after their settlement east of the river. That the Amorite inhabitants were called "baalim," or proprietors; that they worshiped gods under the name of Baal; that the land system was commercialized and contrary to the idea of mishpat; that slavery existed; and that sexual corruption was practiced as an element of the Baal cult—such facts would hardly escape the knowledge of the would-be conquerors. A great deal of this information could be collected by the work of spies; and according to the JE narrative, emissaries were sent over the river to explore the land. Making their way by stealth into the walled city of Jericho, they obtained lodging at the house of a harlot, who directed them up into the central hill-country (Josh., chap. 2 [JE]). Ascending the highlands, the spies found themselves in the midst of a region which was to become the headquarters of the house of Joseph and the stronghold of Hebrew nationality.

Gilead-group seizes agricultural territory with few fortified cities.—For a clear understanding of Hebrew history, it is important that we realize at the very start the exact nature of the movement by which the central highlands of Canaan became identified with the house of Joseph, because the facts, although accessible, have been befogged by the misapprehensions and prejudices of southern scribes. This part of the country was mostly agricultural, and to a smaller extent pastoral. Its pre-Hebrew, or Amorite, inhabitants lived in many small villages, the most important of which was *Luz*, or *Bethel*, identified with the name *Jacob* (Gen. 28:18–19). There were only *two* fortified cities of importance—*Jericho*, down in the hot, stifling valley of the Jordan, three thousand feet below the central hill-country, and *Shechem*, in the highlands, between Mount Ebal and Mount Gerizim, on a trade route running clear across Canaan. To gain full possession of the central highlands a *long struggle* took place.

The *beginning* of the movement was the destruction of Jericho, as mentioned by the Ephraimite, or E, source in the words of Joshua: "The *baalim* of Jericho fought against you; and I delivered them into your hand" (Josh. 24:11). That this place was taken, and its aristocratic proprietors effectually disposed of, there is no reason to doubt. But the J writer has filled the narrative with incredible miraculous details (Josh., chap. 6). The city occupied a vulnerable position, and has been taken time and again at different periods by successive besiegers. The invaders from Gilead could not afford to leave it unreduced in their rear; but the place had no great importance, and lay in ruins for centuries until the time of King Ahab (I Kings 16:34). The struggle for possession of the central hill-country came to an end many years later with the fall of Shechem and the massacre of its baalim by the Manassite branch of Joseph (Judg., chap. 9, where "baalim" of the city are mentioned sixteen times in the Hebrew text). Thus the older Amorite proprietary of central Canaan were annihilated by certain kinship groups which, in some way, came to be known as "the house of Joseph."

The important consideration which calls for special notice at this point is that after the destruction of Shechem, the original and proper territory of Joseph, or Ephraim, was clear of Amorite walled cities. *In other words, most of the fortified cities of Canaan were not in the Josephite hill-country, but lay beyond its borders; and for the time being they did not come within the scope of Hebrew history.* Their names (twenty-three in number) will be listed here as giving emphasis to the point in view: Jerusalem, Gibeon, Aijalon, Shaalbim, Gezer, Beth-shemesh, Taanach, Ibleam, Megiddo, Beth-shan, Nahalol, Kitron, Aphik, Rehob, Helbah, Acco, Ahlab, Achzib, Dor, Beth-anath, Heres, Hazor, Laish.

Ephraimite document in touch with military tradition viewing Jacob as warrior equivalent to Joseph.—The traditional "Blessing of Jacob," in Genesis, chapter 49, is a late and amorphous collection of material based upon the "orthodox" view that Jacob was a peaceful emigrant with twelve individual "sons." But the *real* blessing, i.e., the tradition based upon earlier Hebrew history, is found in the preceding chapter (48): "And Israel said unto Joseph, I have given thee one portion above thy brethren, *which I took out of the hand of the Amorite with my sword and with my bow*" (Gen. 48:21-22). The central highlands, identified with the house of Joseph, were, indeed, the only territory which the original "Jacob" could bequeath to later ages. In other words, the hill-country of Ephraim was the only conquest effected by the ancestral group at the basis of Hebrew tradition. This fact explains why the "Blessing of Jacob" in Genesis, chapter 49, and the "Blessing of Moses," in Deuteronomy, chapter 33, assume that Joseph has the central hill-country, *while the only tribes receiving land are Zebulun and Naphtali, which earned a place by co-operating with the Josephites in the Deborah battle* (see chaps. iii and iv, *supra*).

In view of the foregoing considerations, we can realize even more clearly how the final Judaic editors of Judges have redacted the book so as to obscure the real historic place of the Josephites. This is accomplished by putting the nonexistent tribe of Judah at the forefront of the invasion (see chap. v, pp. 44 ff.), and then saying casually, "And the house of Joseph, they *also* went up, etc." (Judg. 1:22). The intention of the compiler is made still plainer by his literary treatment of the unconquered Amorite cities which lay beyond the frontiers of Joseph. Thus, *Jerusalem*, which was not conquered until hundreds of years later by David, is alleged to have been promptly taken and set on fire by the house of Judah (Judg. 1:8). And then, with this fictitious achievement in the background, the editor mentions five Amorite cities (*Taanach, Megiddo, Ibleam, Dor, and Gezer*), and makes the purely gratuitous observation that the Joseph tribes (Manasseh and Ephraim) did *not* drive out the inhabitants of these places (Judg. 1:27-29). Thus, by putting irrelevance in contrast with preceding fiction, he makes heroic a tribe which was not then organized.

Conquest necessarily affects land tenure.—Reverting again to the subject of conquest, we need to examine more closely the fact that hostile invasion and settlement of a country *always* bring disturbance of land titles. And not merely does conquest involve *transfer* of land; but when the newcomers are in a stage of social evolution which varies from that prevailing in the conquered country, the soil passes under a tenure which differs from that of its previous holders. Thus, *Roman Britain* was to some extent based upon a system of private landed property; but the coming of the Anglo-Saxon tribes out of the German forests brought a reversion to a more primitive, communistic tenure; and later on the Norman conquest involved a tendency back toward the Roman jurisprudence; while at the same time the modification of land titles in Germany, through the influence of Roman law, tended to enslave the peasantry under the rule of "junkerdom." The American Indians had no knowledge of absolute private property in the soil; and when settlers from England imagined themselves, in all good faith, to be purchasing land from the aborigines, the Indians had no idea that they were actually parting with their birthright in their native country. All wars of American Indians and Europeans arose directly or indirectly out of the land question. Thus, to take but one example, six hundred Indians, protected by a stockade in eastern Connecticut, had to be slaughtered to the last man by prayerful Puritans before land titles in that territory were secure. The Indians believed in a Great Spirit who gives water, air, sunshine, and soil for human use; and these children of nature had no conception of land as absolute private property. A similar problem was encountered by English settlers in Australia, when buying land from the aborigines of that country; for after the English had, as they supposed, concluded a given real estate transaction by payment of the agreed price, the natives would later on return with new-born babes, demanding that every child coming into the world *after* the sale should also be paid for his divinely given right, or share, in the land.

Thus we see that when two varying social groups are brought into contact upon the same territory, the land tenure is transformed in one direction or another, according to circumstances which differ at various times and places. Such considerations have not been properly taken into account by historians of the Hebrew people.

Josephite conquest a social revolution.—When the invaders from Gilead established themselves in the central hill-country of Canaan, a large amount of land was wrested from the grip of Amorite baalim and brought into the possession of new owners, untouched by the commercialism of territorial civilization, and powerfully swayed by the usages and ideas of wilderness nomads. The newcomers, like the insurgent prophets who sprang from them, felt the deep resentment of the Beduin against a city-dominated régime which enthrones a small upper class of wealthy nobles in the seats of power, while forcing the multitude into that servile and hopeless poverty which characterizes the Orient. The whole system of territorial society is condemned in the Bible as "the iniquity of the *Amorite*" (Gen. 15:6). The conquest of central Canaan, therefore, brought with it, *in that part of the country*, an economic revolution.

Not only so; but the rise of the house of Joseph, as a mishpat group, was an open challenge to the remaining Amorite aristocrats in the twenty-three unconquered cities of the land. For, by the influence of example, the spread of mishpat ideas among the enslaved Canaanite peasantry, lying beyond the frontiers of Joseph, could not fail to infect the whole country with the leaven of revolt and the desire to secure liberation from tyrannical, baalistic overlords. And thus the upper class in the still independent parts of Canaan was potentially threatened with direct physical overthrow by the mere presence of the house of Joseph in the central highlands.

Without giving careful consideration to these facts, we cannot understand Hebrew history as an objective process taking place in the actual affairs of real human beings. The conquest of the central highlands planted the seeds of that insurgent prophecy which appeared, centuries later, in the person of Elijah the Gileadite. But if the new settlers had been expelled, or even subjugated, by the military force of the remaining Amorites, the fateful moment would have passed; the little nucleus of power would have been dissipated which at length formed a Hebrew national government, lifting Yahweh to political superiority over the local Baal divinities of Palestine; and no broad platform would have been erected whereon the mishpat idea could be enduringly generalized in opposition to "the iniquity of the Amorite."

Yahweh or Baal, then.—The great question, therefore, which overhung the confusing welter of racial groups in Canaan at that time was whether a national state would eventually be organized under the name of *Israel*, in allegiance to a deity of mishpat called "Yahweh"; or whether Canaan as a whole should fall back into the grasp of its Baal-worshiping tyrants, who still had great power, and whose headquarters were in the twenty-three unconquered cities lying *beyond* the frontiers of the Josephite hill-country. And so far as outward appearances gave any indication, the prospects were uncertain, with the chances against the house of Joseph and against Yahweh. The margin of probability was narrow in any event; and the tide might be turned in one direction or the other—for Baalism or for Mishpat.

Conditions desperate by time of Deborah.—Naturally, the house of Joseph, as an isolated group threatened by fierce enemies, found itself in growing difficulties. Its numbers were multiplying rapidly through normal increase, which is reflected in the legendary "Blessing of Jacob": "*Let them grow into a multitude in the midst of the land*" (Gen. 48:16). The Machirites, the original stock of Joseph, had already given rise to Ephraim, on the western slope, and to Benjamin at the south; so that the need for more territory was pressing. "And the children of Joseph said, the hill-country is not enough for us. *But all the Canaanites that dwell in the land of the Valley have chariots of iron*" (Josh. 17:16 [J source]). In other words, the Amorites interposed a blockade against further expansion.

New policy forced upon house of Joseph.—What now could be done? The only hope was in a policy of co-operation with *non*-Josephite elements against the baalistic lords who, in other parts of the country, held the masses in bondage. And, fortunately, an opening toward the accomplishment of this purpose lay close at hand, immediately *north of the Josephite frontier*, in a lower section of territory called the Plain, or Valley, of Esdraelon, where the peasantry of a district known as "Issachar" were in galling bondage under the Amorite yoke. Their condition comes out with startling clearness in the later "Blessing of Jacob," as follows: "Issachar is a strong ass crouching down between the sheep-folds. And he saw a resting-place, that it was good, and the land, that it was pleasant; *and he bowed his shoulder, and became a slave under taskwork*" (Gen. 49: 14–15).

Campaign against Amorites inspired by prophetess Deborah.—The key to the situation, then, was furnished by the enslaved inhabitants of Issachar. If that province could be roused against the Amorite lords, the movement of social unrest would naturally extend farther north beyond the Valley, or Plain, and up into the hill districts known as *Naphtali* and *Zebulun*. The inspiring impulse came from the highlands of Ephraim, and found voice in the enthusiastic prophecies of Deborah. "She dwelt under the palm tree of Deborah between Ramah and Bethel in the hill country of Ephraim. And the children of Is-

rael came up to her for *mishpat*" (Judg. 4:5). But the actual
organizing genius of the situation lived among the oppressed inhabitants of Issachar, and was known by the sobriquet *Barak*,
or "Lightning," because he acted with quick decision. This remarkable man was exhorted by Deborah to *"lead captivity captive"* (Judg. 5:12). About forty thousand fighting men were
available (vs. 8); and from this potential army Barak secretly
prepared a force of *ten thousand*, ready to assemble on short notice. His agents kept off the main-traveled roads and used by-
paths; and so quietly did they work that scarcely a shield or
spear was visible to betray the progress of military preparation.
The army thus organized was chosen from the house of Joseph
(i.e., Machir, Ephraim, Benjamin); while the recruits from beyond the central highlands were furnished by the province of
Issachar in the Valley, and by the peasantry of Naphtali and
Zebulun in the hills of Galilee to the north (Judg. 5:14-15,
18).

Amorites prepare to make Canaan safe for Baalism.—That
a mass movement of such proportions, based upon social-revolu-
tionary idealism, should continue in secrecy without being discovered was impossible. And therefore the Amorite lords, headed by *Sisera*, were now making ready hundreds of iron chariots,
horsemen, and footmen for the coming struggle. They hoped
not only to crush forever the radical house of Joseph, but also to
quell the disaffected native peasantry who appeared to be on
the verge of going over wholesale into alliance with the Yahweh-
group which held the central highlands. The Amorite headquarters were at a place called "Harosheth hagoyim," or "Harosheth of the gentiles" (Judg. 4:2). This was a hill in the western
part of Esdraelon, rising above the Kishon River at a spot where
even today are found the remains of strong fortifications. Here
the army of Baal was being mobilized for action; and the outlook for Israel was dark. The powerful military equipment of
the foe, as we have seen, was greatly dreaded by the highlanders:

"And the children of Joseph said, the Canaanites that live in the valley have iron chariots." But it was now impossible to turn back from the conflict, which must be fought through to a finish, come what may.

The Deborah-battle.—Finding that the Amorites were gathering in the western part of the Plain, Barak sent out a call for his peasant-army; and a host of ten thousand men assembled upon the lower slopes of Mount Tabor, in a strategic position overlooking the lowland, where they could observe signs of activity in the far-away camp of the foe.

Soon great masses of Amorite infantry and cavalry, *with nine hundred chariots of iron*, were put into motion. But as the glittering host of Baal came on along the river Kishon, dark thunderclouds began to roll up from the Mediterranean Sea— as later in the time of Elijah, when King Ahab drove his chariot furiously, to escape the coming rain (I Kings 18:44–45). Chariots operate under a handicap in wet weather, and must have dry ground if they are to do effective work. Yet the advancing Amorites could not pause now; for they were already in full motion, hoping to do battle before the storm could break.

In the meanwhile, the host of Barak had come sweeping down from Tabor into the Plain, and was moving straight on to meet the chariots, cavalry and footmen of Sisera, when suddenly a *drenching rain* turned the lowland soil into mud. *"The clouds dropped water!"* exclaims Deborah. *"The stars in their courses fought against Sisera"* (Judg. 5:4, 20). The Amorite chariots began to lurch and skid; and presently the frightened horses were out of control. *"Then were the horse-hoofs broken by the plungings —the plungings of their mighty ones"* (vs. 22). The river Kishon quickly overflowed its banks, transforming the plain into a morass; while the highland followers of Barak, rushing into the midst of the enemy, cut down the demoralized foe right and left, sending the infantry headlong, while the chariots of Baal were driven into the flooded stream: *"The river Kishon swept them away—that ancient river, the river Kishon! O my soul, thou hast trodden down strength!"* (vs. 21).

Deborah-battle has peculiar effect upon evolution of Hebrew nationalism.—This important action, the significance of which is not generally understood, marked a very dramatic turning-point in Hebrew evolution. The prestige of Yahweh as a god of battle was immensely increased. But, on the other hand, the Josephites and their allies in other parts of the land were not professional soldiers; they had no regular army; and their valiant but crude militia quickly melted away; so that in consequence the twenty-three fortified cities of Canaan outside the central highlands remained intact. Yet the power of the Amorite aristocracy was reduced; and never again did they rally to subjugate the worshipers of Yahweh. For now the village population of Canaan had learned that by standing together against the Amorite baalistic proprietors they need not bow their necks in slavery to the walled cities; and therefore a spirit of independence was abroad. The less important communities north of Esdraelon acquired a new standing through association with the house of Joseph; and thus the Deborah-battle created an atmosphere for the growth of legends about inferior "tribes," or "children," of Jacob.

Legend of purest Hebrew blood based upon political center of nationality.—The legend that the house of Joseph had in its veins the purest Hebrew blood, while the other tribes were born of slave mothers or from a hated wife, merely indicates that the hill-country of Ephraim was the focus of the nationalizing movement and the foundation upon which Hebrew government and religion were built up. The scribes of Judah, who gave us the Hebrew Scriptures, were never wholly able to accept this obstinate fact. The situation is tersely expressed by the Ephraimite prophet Jeremiah when he speaks for Yahweh saying, "I am a father to Israel; *and Ephraim is my firstborn*" (Jer. 31:9). This passage does not agree with the genealogical scheme which

at length became standard mythology of Israel; but nevertheless it is *practically* true; because the "firstborn" Reuben fragment, which was left behind in Gilead, refused to co-operate in
the Deborah-battle; and the burden of nation-building was actually borne by the house of Ephraim; so that even the intensely
Judaic author of the late book known as "Chronicles" is compelled to say of Reuben, *"His birthright was given unto the sons of
Joseph"* (I Chron. 5:1).

Nationalist movement very slow and irregular in progress.
—Lack of co-operation between different parts of the country
shows the real character of the national evolution. There was
no abstract idealism at work, and no disinterested love of Yahweh. The inhabitants of each locality moved when their own
immediate interests were believed to be affected, and even then
only when action seemed possible or expedient. A nationalistic
impulse was undoubtedly gathering force; but it was very slow
in taking decisive, definite form; and there is no little justification for the writer of the appendix to Judges when he says, "In
those days there was no king in Israel; and every man did that
which was right in his own eyes" (Judg. 17:6).

Moreover, there is one sense in which the Deuteronomic editor of Judges correctly explains the conditions of those days.
For in the degree that more and more groups, or "tribes," acted
in harmonious co-operation under the mishpat ideal symbolized
by the term "Yahweh," they triumphed over the Amorite aristocracy as well as over enemies from outside of Canaan; while,
on the other hand, failure to co-operate under a common allegiance resulted in confusion and anarchy. Through the murky
haze of the Judges period, therefore, an impersonal movement
of nationalism, typified by the cult of Yahweh, was gradually
unfolding; and the interest of the reader can be focalized around
this fact. *A double process of integration, both religious and political, gives a point of view from which the events and heroes of the
early age can be tested.*

Ephraim and Benjamin co-operate against Moabites.—
Another hero mentioned in the early period is *Ehud ben Gera*,
of the Josephite tribe of Benjamin. His exploits are dealt with
in the Book of Judges on the assumption that they preceded the
Deborah-battle; but we shall presently see grounds for placing
Ehud later. The southeast corner of Benjamin brought the inhabitants of that region closely in touch with *Moab*, which is
said to have oppressed "all Israel" in the days of Ehud. The
Deuteronomic introduction to the story of this leader is in Judg.
3:12–14 and the first sentence of verse 15, ending with the word
"lefthanded." In the tale itself, Ehud conveys *tribute* from
"Israel" into the land of Moab; assassinates the king of that
east-Jordan country; and then, escaping, he makes his way
home, blows a trumpet in the hills of Ephraim, and leads the
people to victory over Moab (vss. 27–28). Intertribal co-operation here is only between two groups; none of the other tribes
are noticed; nor is there any sense of Moabite oppression as extending beyond the immediate vicinity of southern Ephraim.

The reason for placing Ehud's exploits after the time of Deborah is very simple. The tribe of Reuben, which was denounced
for lack of national feeling by the Deborah Song, has now vanished; else it would necessarily appear in the tale of Ehud. The
military operations of the Benjaminite chief were conducted on
the territory of Reuben against the Moabites, who were enemies
of the "firstborn" tribe, which, if it had existed at that time,
would have gone into action along with Ephraim and Benjamin
as a matter of self-defense. The omission of Reuben, therefore,
carries Ehud on into the times after Deborah.

**Nationalizing process advanced by Manassite hero Gideon
ben Joash.**—The next phase in the growth of Hebrew nationalism relates to Gideon, of the Josephite tribe Manasseh. The
material concerning him begins with Judges, chapter 6, in which
the first half-dozen verses are by the editor; then follows a kind
of "prophetic" introduction, in 6:7–10; after which comes the

tale of Gideon, commencing at verse 11, running through the rest of chapter 6 and all of chapters 7 and 8, except the last three verses of chapter 8, which are editorial. The actual narrative about Gideon is composed of ancient stories which already reveal the influence of miracle and legend, and which are woven together arbitrarily and inconsistently by the compiler.

The Manassite hero's chief exploit was the defeat of nomadic *Midianites*, who came out of the desert and invaded the east-central highlands. These enemies were pursued by Gideon at the head of three hundred men whom he called into action from his own tribe. When chasing the foe, he went through Gilead; but the inhabitants of Succoth and Penuel in that region refused help, and showed as much lack of national feeling as they did when Deborah held them up to scorn (Judg. 8:4–17; cf. 5:17). On the other hand, the Ephraimites chided Gideon for not calling them to battle (8:1). The legend about the three hundred men being supernaturally chosen out of thirty-two thousand by command of Yahweh is a later, theological decoration.

A number of tribal names are mentioned in the Gideon stories; but it is noticeable that *Issachar*, which would naturally come in for attention, has dropped out of the reckoning. This enslaved community, which figured in the Deborah conflict, has vanished from Hebrew history; and, being thus out of the way, it could safely be made the victim of a legend that Jacob was hired by his unloved wife to beget Issachar, the imaginary tribal ancestor (Gen. 30:16–18).

In consequence of Gideon's military and executive talents, a proposition was made that he assume authority under the title of king (*melek*), and that his power be transmitted by hereditary succession. He is said to have rejected this offer; but the story nevertheless makes him follow a line of policy looking toward royal state; for just as all kings at that day provided houses of public worship, so Gideon took the golden spoil of the defeated foe and had it cast into an image, or *ephod*, which was placed in a sanctuary at his home town of Ophrah as a rallying-point for the religious devotion of the Josephites.

Amorite city of Shechem appears abruptly in Book of Judges.—The story of Gideon brings abruptly into view the Amorite walled city of Shechem, which remained as yet unconquered in the very heart of the Ephraimite highlands, between Mount Ebal and Mount Gerizim, on a trade route running across Canaan. This place, along with the villages of the open country, was indebted to Gideon for having driven away the Midianite invaders (Judg. 9:17). And, accordingly, a woman of Shechem was given to the Manassite chieftain, by way of state marriage, as a kind of secondary wife or concubine. Remaining with her own kindred, she gave birth to *Abimelek*, the son of Gideon; and it is with relation to this woman that the city of Shechem suddenly appears in the Book of Judges.

Shechemite baalim seek to enslave house of Joseph.—Some years after the death of Gideon, the baalim of Shechem used the ambition of Abimelek in a plot against the house of Joseph. Taking funds from the public treasury in the temple of Baal, they gave money to this half-Amorite, half-Josephite adventurer. He then proceeded to hire a band of gangsters, who, in approved modern style, went out to the village of Ophrah and murdered the sons of Gideon, "three score and ten persons upon one stone" (Judg. 9:5). The bloody affair being satisfactorily concluded, Abimelek was chosen *king*, not by his Josephite relatives in the country, but "*by all the baalim of Shechem*," after which he ruled, not merely over this Amorite city, but "*over Israel*" (Judg. 9:1–6, 22). And thus we see that the baalim of Shechem undertook, as far as lay in their power, to reverse the advancing Israelite conquest of Canaan, and fasten their yoke upon the rural population whose ancestors had invaded the land in the days of Joshua.

Shechem destroyed and inhabitants massacred by Josephite clansmen.—But the plans of the Amorite baalim of Shechem to subjugate the rural population did not work out successfully. The clansmen of the surrounding hills were sons of conquerors from the desert. The peculiar circumstances of the Josephite invasion had made the highlands of Ephraim an enclave of primitive mishpat within a country which was as yet largely ruled by baalism. The Hebrew highlanders cherished an already lengthening tradition of liberty whose perspective extended clear back to the wilderness, where men are poor but free. Their spiritual inheritance from the past was identified with heroic struggles led by Joshua, Deborah, Barak, Ehud, and Gideon, which were a living memory. For under these leaders the house of Joseph had successfully challenged Amorite baalism; seized a large part of the central hill-country; and reduced the soil of that region to the tenure of mishpat. *In the light of these considerations, we can begin to realize how Shechem, as a dark citadel of baalism, would be more and more viewed as a blot upon the escutcheon of Israel.* Unlike the twenty-three walled cities of Canaan which lay beyond the central highlands, *this* metropolis was an alien within the very midst of the house of Joseph—an enemy stronghold in the very heart of the district which had been taken from the Amorite by the sword and bow of Jacob. And as the clans of Ephraim and Manasseh grew into "a multitude in the midst of the earth," and felt the need for more territory, this Amorite city, whose baalim were so quick to subsidize murder, became increasingly hateful to the Israelite highlanders. Thus, whatever may have been the *superficial occasion* for dispute, the fact is that the Shechemites actually broke with Abimelek their tool; whereupon this half-blood son of Gideon went over to his relatives in the house of Joseph, and called into action the peasantry of Ephraim, who, in a revolutionary uprising, destroyed the city and slew the entire population, *"about a thousand men and women"* (Judg. 9:44–49; in the Hebrew text of this chapter, the term "baal" is applied to the Amorite aristocracy of Shechem sixteen times, but its implications and connotations are lost in modern Bibles). *Thus we see that the conquest of central Canaan, which began decades before with the slaughter of Jericho's baalim, was now at length completed by the destruction of Shechem, the great citadel of baalism in the house of Joseph.*

Double tradition of Shechem arises from peculiar circumstances of conquest.—The chaotic state of Hebrew history in the Judges period gave rise to a *double tradition* about the mythical ancestor *Jacob*, which the compilers of the Bible could never harmonize. *On the one hand*, the patriarch was a military hero, personifying the Joseph group as an invading horde, wresting the central hill-country from the hand of the Amorite by force (Gen. 48:22). This phase of the patriarch's activity found expression in the work of Joshua, Barak, Deborah, Ehud, Gideon, and a heroic multitude, unknown to history, by whose valor the central highlands were seized and whose power maintained possession in that rude, stern age of the world.

But on the *contrary*, after the invaders had settled upon the soil, they became shepherds and farmers, dwelling peacefully in "the tents of Jacob." And then, as they grew in multitude, they became increasingly conscious of the rich territory still held by the Amorite baalim of Shechem. But, unfortunately, the house of Joseph was now at peace with this ancient stronghold of Canaan; and in a time of *peace*, there was no way of acquiring land from the proprietary of Shechem save through *purchase*. And this phase of the development became the starting-point of *another* tradition about Jacob, according to which he was a quiet man, dwelling in tents, who came peacefully to Shechem and was on good terms with its aristocracy, *just as the Josephites were for a long time.* This phase of the history is covered by the peculiar document (neither J nor E) commencing with Gen. 33:18:

And Jacob came peacefully to the city of Shechem in the land of Canaan. And he purchased land from the children of Hamor, Shechem's father, for a hundred pieces of money. . . . . And Hamor went out unto Jacob to commune with him, ... saying, Make ye marriages with us. Give your daughters unto us; and take our daughters unto you. And ye shall dwell with us; and the land shall be before you. Dwell and trade ye therein; and *get you possessions therein.* . . . . And Hamor and Shechem his son came unto the gate of their city, and communed with the men of their city, saying, these men [of Jacob] are peaceable with us. Therefore, let them dwell in the land, and trade therein; for the land, behold, is large enough for them [Gen. 33:18–19; 34:6, 9, 10, 20, 21].

The lords of Shechem appear in this document as having jurisdiction over a large part of central Canaan. They can give or withhold permission to settle in the country; and they can then sell real estate to the newcomers. This interesting source throws a valuable sidelight on conditions in the Judges period. The story of Abimelek itself deals only with external, surface events in a complicated situation whose merits wholly escaped the compilers and scribes of later times. There could be no lasting peace in the Judges period between a clannish hill folk, inspired by the mishpat idea of landholding, and city aristocrats who recognized only the commercial, baalistic tenure.

Under circumstances of this kind, the purchase of land from the Amorite baalim by the newer population in the hills would not provide a ground of conciliatory adjustment between the two races, any more than buying out the absentee English landlords of Ireland could convert the Irish into friends of England. For such transactions always bind the new purchasers to the older proprietary through payments which take on the form of rent and bring with them a sense of bondage. Thus, the narrative quoted above goes on to put the following words in the mouths of the Shechemite landlords, when proposing to admit the sons of Jacob to the franchise of the locality: *"Shall not their cattle and their substance and every beast of theirs be ours?"* (Gen. 34:23). By such means, the country dwellers within the jurisdiction of all ancient cities were subjugated; thus the commonalty of Greece became slaves to the eupatrids; while the plebeians of Italy were brought under the rule of patrician landlords. In such cases the landlord class not only exercises property rights over the soil; but, at the same time, it is also the *government*, wielding the power of taxation; so that it rules through the use of two legal weapons, which are supplemented upon occasion by physical violence, as when the Shechemites, in murdering the seventy sons of Gideon, destroyed the nascent royal family of the house of Joseph, and sought thus to intrench themselves in their ancient pre-Hebrew authority.

Moreover, the purchase of Shechemite real estate by the house of Joseph would not only raise difficulties between the newer settlers and the older inhabitants, but it would come into collision with a growing dogma of divine right in the soil of central Canaan, which had been given to Jacob in a vision of Yahweh at *Beth-el*, south of Shechem (Gen. 28:10–19 [JE]). Since Yahweh *gave* the land, why should any purchase price, or ground rental, be paid to the Shechemite baalim for that which the house of Joseph really owned? According to this logic, the Shechemites had no legal standing in Canaan whatever; and if their claims could be impeached by their total extermination, *then all of central Canaan would at length be consecrated to mishpat*. And, therefore, whatever may have been the superficial merits of the quarrel between Abimelek and his former allies the Amorite baalim, the underlying facts of the situation made the tragedy of Shechem inevitable; and the city was consequently annihilated. In these facts we shall find the germ of insurgent prophecy and the key to all Hebrew history: *"They are not grieved for the affliction of Joseph. I will deliver up the city and all that is therein"* (Amos 6:6–8, *passim*). *"Run ye to and fro through the streets of Jerusalem, and see now, and know, and seek in the broad places thereof, if ye can find a man, if there be any that executeth mishpat"* (Ephraimite prophet, in denunciation of Judah [Jer. 5:1]).

House of Joseph gives proto-Deuteronomic form to early Hebrew history.—The fate of Shechem exercises an irresistible attraction upon the compiler of Judges because he finds here the suggestions, rudiments, or beginnings of that *later* theory on which no peace *ever* should have been made with the Amorites; no marriages *ever* contracted with them; and according to which *all* the inhabitants of the land should have been "utterly destroyed" by the invaders. The simplest form of this theory, or dogma, occurs in the Ephraimite document about the time of Elijah: "He that sacrificeth unto any god save Yahweh shall be utterly destroyed" (Exod. 22:20). It becomes fully explicit in the Book of Deuteronomy, which was composed in dependence upon Ephraimite sources about the time of King Josiah: "Thou shalt smite them and utterly destroy them. Thou shalt make no covenant [*berith*] with them, nor show mercy unto them. Neither shall thou make marriages with them. Thy daughter thou shalt not give unto his son; nor his daughter shalt thou take unto thy son" (Deut. 7:2–3).

But the old narratives about Gideon, Shechem, and Abimelek, which the editor of Judges combines in his book, fail to yield the explicit *formula* dear to the heart of the Deuteronomist. These ancient stories afford only raw material. Gideon, instead of remaining clear from domestic relationship with the older inhabitants of Canaan, actually *marries* an Amorite woman of Shechem. The Josephites, instead of making no covenant, or *berith*, with the baalim of the city, became involved in the worship of Baal-*berith* (Judg. 8:33; cf. 9:4). Moreover, a covenant between the new settlers and the Shechemites is directly witnessed by the wholesale circumcision of the latter (Gen. 34:24). These traditions from the past bore evidence to stubborn realities which could not be expurgated by the Deuteronomic editors of the Bible without making the ancient source-narratives unintelligible. But in spite of the perversity of these old stories, their fascination could not be resisted. And hence the compiler of Judges fails to reconcile their contradictory features, fumbling the material in his own "framework" of editorial observations and in his treatment of the stories themselves. Gideon and Abimelek fell far short of the Deuteronomic ideal. *Nevertheless, Gideon demolished an altar of Baal at Ophrah, together with a "grove" (asherah), or wooden pole, standing by it* (Judg. 6:25–28); *while Abimelek and his three companies of Josephites acted like pious Deuteronomists in wiping out the Amorites of Shechem and razing their city to the ground.*

Thus, in spite of the confused and halting way in which the authors of Judges and other biblical books treated their "sources," and in spite of the unscientific methods by which the E, J, D, P, and other documents are assembled, *we now begin to realize that the Josephite conquest of central Canaan, starting with the destruction of Jericho and concluding with the downfall of Shechem, was a Deuteronomic movement in the germ; taking place long before Deuteronomy itself was written or even conceived; and foreshadowing in miniature the program which that strategic book of the Law holds up as an ideal for the conquest of all Canaan by the imaginary hosts of Israelite invaders;* BUT WHICH, AS A MATTER OF REAL HISTORY, WAS NEVER FULLY CARRIED OUT.

In these highly significant facts, then, we find the palpable suggestions out of which came what is, in many respects, the most important and central book of the Law, *with its well-known curses and blessings on the two Shechemite mountains, Ebal and Gerizim* (Deut. 11:29; 27:4, 12, 13). Deuteronomy is, in spirit, a *northern*, or Ephraimite, work, which has come to us through the hands and authorship of Judaic, or southern, writers, who think it would have been well if, like Jericho and Shechem, the remaining Amorite walled cities which lay outside the frontiers of Joseph could have been utterly destroyed at the very start, instead of being left independent, and then at length assimilated, *as they actually were*, within the composite structure of the Hebrew nation.

Conquest of central hill-country generalized by orthodox tradition to include entire land of Canaan.—Critical investigators of Hebrew history have often dwelt with justice upon the gross inaccuracy of the orthodox claim that *all* Canaan was conquered by the united tribes of Israel; that the Amorites were completely exterminated; and that the soil was thereupon divided by lot among the victorious invaders. This claim is, of course, without the bounds of truth; for the conquest was partial. But, on the other hand, if we take the house of Joseph as forming the original body of the nation "Israel," we shall see that the idea of complete conquest was, in reality, a *phase* of the veritable "proto-Deuteronomic" history which the Josephites transacted in the central highlands. For the movement which began with the destruction of Jericho in the time of Joshua, and came to an end with the downfall of Shechem in the days of Abimelek, rounded out the title of the house of Joseph to central Canaan, *thus constituting, on a small scale, a complete conquest which was later generalized by tradition to include and embrace the entire land.*

Accordingly, the point of departure for tradition is the undoubtedly historic fate of Jericho in the Jordan Valley, which furnishes a dramatic introduction to the Ephraimite story of conquest beginning in Joshua, chapter 6. Reviewing the campaign, Joshua is made to say, in the latter part of the book attributed to him, "The *baalim* of Jericho fought against you; and I delivered them into your hand. And Yahweh drove out from before us *all the people, even the Amorites, which dwelt in the land*" (Josh. 24:11, 18). It will therefore be noticed that the narrative in Joshua ignores the late destruction of Shechem by Abimelek, and assumes that this Amorite city between Ebal and Gerizim was taken by Israel at an early stage of the invasion: "And Joshua gathered *all the tribes of Israel to Shechem*, and made a covenant with the people, and set them a statute and a *mishpat* in Shechem" (Josh. 24:1, 25).

Moreover, not content with the earlier, Ephraimite narrative just quoted, the Deuteronomic sections of Joshua make the people go through the literal ceremony of blessing and cursing on Mount Ebal and Mount Gerizim, outside of Shechem, as commanded in Deuteronomy (Josh. 8:33). And then, to make assurance doubly sure, the Deuteronomic sources of Joshua improve still further upon the Ephraimite story by describing in mythical detail how the *entire* Amorite population of Canaan was massacred:

So Joshua left none remaining, *but utterly destroyed all that breathed*, as Yahweh, god of Israel, commanded. They smote them until they left none remaining. Every man they smote with the edge of the sword, until they had destroyed them. Neither left they any that breathed [Josh. 10: 40; 11:9, 11, 14].

Thus the central highlands, in furnishing a proto-Deuteronomic model for Hebrew history and theology, gave at the same time a miniature basis for the generalization of complete conquest.

First clear view of growing Hebrew aristocracy furnished by Gideon.—In the case of Gideon, we see the first clear example of the Hebrew aristocracy which was developing through conquest in the central highlands of Canaan. Gideon is the owner of *slaves*, or *abadim*, out of whose number he is able, on short notice, to select a gang of *ten* (Judg. 6:27). The Hebrew text says, "Gideon took ten men *from* his *abadim*." He is represented, however, as comparatively poor in the house of Joseph: "My clan is poor in Manasseh; and I am the least in my father's family" (Judg. 6:15). This may be taken with a grain of salt; but, even so, if Gideon were among the *less* wealthy proprietors, *then there must already have developed in the Judges period an upper social class in which the majority owned more than ten slaves.* We have, then, to consider what was the origin of this growing slave-class among the Hebrew people.

Ancient Hebrew slavery arose through capture of aliens in war.—Throughout ancient society the chief source of the lower, enslaved class was primarily capture in war. All social groups, on moving up from savagery and barbarism into civilization, accumulate an inferior class which is treated as property, but is not a legal part of the group itself. And when we investigate the conditions and forces leading slowly up to Hebraic nationality under the banner of Yahweh, it is clear that the lower, servile class in Israel evolved according to the tendencies operative in all ancient nations: *"And it came to pass, when Israel was grown strong, that they put the Canaanites to task-work ("the mas") and did not utterly drive them out. The Canaanites dwelt among them and became task-workers. And the hand of the house of Joseph prevailed; so that they became task-workers"* (Judg. 1:28, 30, 35). Nothing is said in this connection about the tribe of Judah as enslaving earlier inhabitants of the land; for no tribe of Judah was in existence at the time of the conquest; and the earlier evolution of Hebrew landholders and slave-owners took its rise in the hills of Ephraim.

Enslavement of Canaanites justified by Genesis legend.— The general idea of an enslaved Canaan had to be explained, or justified, in some way; and this necessity gave birth to an interesting legend, by which the Book of Genesis again comes to our aid in forming conceptions of Hebrew history. The patriarch Noah, we are told, had three sons, by the names of Shem, Ham, and Japheth; and one of these (Ham) was the father of the *Canaanites*. Noah takes up the vocation of husbandry after the flood and plants a vineyard. Imbibing too freely of the wine, he becomes intoxicated and lies exposed in his tent, being observed in this condition by Ham, who reports the state of domestic affairs to his brethren, Japheth and Shem. These two brothers take a garment, and walking respectfully backward, so that they shall not see their father's condition, they carefully cover the sleeping patriarch. Then, after a while, Noah comes to himself; and upon learning about the conduct of Ham, the father of Canaan, he roundly curses the descendants of Ham, saying, *"Cursed be Canaan! A slave of slaves shall he be!"* (Gen. 9:18–27). This legend was supposed to explain and justify the servile state of any and all Canaanites under the yoke of the trium-

phant Hebrew aristocracy. The Canaanites, therefore, had the
alleged misfortune to be descended from the wrong ancestor;
and, according to this logic, they deserved nothing better than
bondage.

Gileadites, east of Jordan, attacked by Ammonites.—Some
time after the fall of Shechem, the Josephites heard that the inhabitants of Gilead, east of Jordan, were attacked by the Ammonites, who lived between Gilead and the desert. The people
of Gilead had rendered no aid to Deborah, Barak, Ehud, or
Gideon, when the house of Joseph needed help; and so far as
this old score was concerned, the people east of Jordan were
hardly in a position to call upon the other side of the river for
assistance. But if the Ammonites overran Gilead, this would
mean the establishment of a hostile state close to the eastern
frontier of Joseph, having the effect of a spearhead pointed at
the heart of the central highlands. The men of Gilead therefore
sent a messenger hurrying westward over Jordan with an appeal
to Ephraim; but, in the meanwhile, before help could arrive, the
Gileadites themselves, led by Jephthah, defeated Ammon "with
a very great slaughter." The militia from Ephraim reached the
scene after the battle; whereupon a misunderstanding arose
which the story exaggerates into the wild and impossible claim
that Jephthah's men slew forty-two thousand Ephraimites. The
tale is very late, coming from a period when older tribal divisions
had vanished, and the name Ephraim had overspread the central highlands. In its present form, as used by the compiler of
Judges, it must have originated long after the days of Gideon
and Abimelek; for in their time the Josephite tribe of *Manasseh*
or Machir lay between Gilead and the Ephraimites, and, if in
existence, would have been called upon by Jephthah as the
nearest neighbor. The tale also involves the assumption, common to the later scribes, that a local hero (in this case Jephthah)
became a ruler, or judge, over "all Israel" (Judg., chap. 11; 12:
1–7).

New power takes form on coastal plain, threatening Ephraim.—In the meanwhile, a greater menace than Ammon was rising gradually on the coastal plain of the Mediterranean, far down below the hills of Ephraim to the southwest, on the way to Egypt. Emigrating from a country known as "Kaphtor," the newcomers were able to establish themselves along the edge of the sea, because the Egyptian empire, which had once controlled this territory, was now in a period of internal weakness. These emigrants built five strong cities, Gath, Ashkelon, Gaza, Ekron, and Ashdod; and, as a people, they were known collectively by the name *Philistines*. Planted squarely across the only practicable trade route coming up from Egypt through Canaan into Mesopotamia, the new power was thus able to levy rich toll on the caravans passing in both directions. The Philistine region, at a *later* period, was the point of entry for the Greeks, who therefore called the entire land of Canaan *Palestine*. The new masters of the coastal plain, securely established in their five cities, looked with great disfavor upon the growing consolidation of the Josephites, or Ephraimites; because the rise of a strong power in central Canaan, even though its main base of operations were in the hill-country, would sooner or later threaten the trade routes, and thus destroy the chief revenue of the Philistines.

Philistines temporarily barred from Ephraim by Danites.—Not only did the geographical formation of Canaan hinder attack upon the central highlands from the coastal plain; but the Philistines were also shut away from the hills by the presence of a half-Israelite community known as *Dan*, which lay wedged in between Ephraim and the Mediterranean. We recall that the inhabitants of this region were named among the "slacker-" groups in the Deborah Song as refusing military help to the house of Joseph against the Amorite host under Sisera. That the possessions of the Danites extended at one time as far as the coast may be inferred from the terms in which Deborah calls attention to their lack of patriotism: *"Why did Dan remain in ships?"* (Judg. 5:17). That the inhabitants of this region were of mixed origin, and not of the pure Jacob-Rachel blood, is proved by the legend which declares them to be sons of the slave-girl *Bilhah* (Gen. 30:4–6). We may suppose them to have been the remnant of a native, non-Hebrew coastal group driven gradually inland by the Philistines.

In the period now under consideration, the Danites had about six hundred men capable of bearing arms (Judg. 18:11); and they did good service to the Hebrew cause by acting as a barrier against the Philistines at a time when the house of Joseph needed to conserve and organize all its power for use in the fateful days to come. The Danites numbered among their fighting men a strongly built hero by the name of *Shimshon*, who is said to have killed a thousand Philistines with the jawbone of an ass (Judg. 15:14 f.). The tales about him are plainly mythical and in the same class with that of *Shamgar*, who is said to have destroyed six hundred Philistines with an ox goad (Judg. 3:31), and *Shammah*, who, single-handed, overcame the Philistines by the help of Yahweh (II Sam. 23:11–12). But such tales may well symbolize the function of the Danites in harassing and blockading the Philistines at this period of Hebrew history.

During the course of operations against the Danites, the Philistines are said to have gone up into the district lying *south* of Jebus, or Jerusalem, which later became known as the "land of Judah." We recall that the Deborah Song does not even mention this part of the country in praise or blame. And now there suddenly appear in the story "three thousand men of Judah" who, if the narrative is to be trusted, are like their predecessors in the time of Deborah, without any feeling of Hebrew patriotism. For instead of aiding the Hebrew cause by *helping* the Danites, they give aid to the Philistines by delivering Samson over to the enemy (Judg. 15:9–13). The story may have become current at a later time, when the Philistines actually held Bethlehem (II Sam. 23:14).

That the village of Bethlehem-Ephrathah, or Bethlehem-Judah, became the headquarters of a pioneering group from Ephraim, in the Judges epoch, seems to be a reasonable deduction from the sources at our disposal; but there is no evidence to support the idea that a full-fledged Hebrew tribe under the name of Judah, numbering three thousand men, existed in the time of Samson.

The original, or Deuteronomic, Book of Judges, which begins at 2:6, comes to an end at the close of chapter 16 with the editorial statement that Samson "judged Israel twenty years." The local Danite hero is thus presented as the final figure in a mythical series of alleged rulers who held sway over an imaginary Hebrew nation before the actual, *historic* nation arose.

"Appendix" to Book of Judges deals with Ephraimite stories.—Appended to the Deuteronomic Book of Judges, which terminates, as we have noted, with chapter 16, are several interesting and highly instructive stories which relate to Ephraimite affairs, but come to us through the editorial work of Judaic, or southern, scribes. If any tales of southern heroes were available, we may be sure that the editor's pride would have given them a place with the others. And therefore, since the appendix, as well as the book itself, deals only with *northern* tales, and since the compilers were nevertheless of Judaic sympathy, we are apparently entitled to assume that *no* stories of Jewish heroes were in circulation with reference to the Judges period, and that only northern matter was in existence. We still find ourselves in the house of Joseph, then, because this part of the land was the true and original starting-point of Israel's history and the real center of Hebrew tradition.

Story of man who lived somewhere in hill-country of Ephraim.—The tale with which the appendix opens is about an Ephraimite called "Micah." This name is a contracted form

of "Micaiah," which in Hebrew means "Who is like Yahweh?"
In the house of Micah was a private chapel, or sanctuary, dedicated to the worship of Yahweh, containing "ephod" and "teraphim," which were molten and graven images made of metal
(Judg. 17:3–5). These objects were in the same category with
the ephod of gold which Gideon placed in the sanctuary at
Ophrah (Judg. 8:24–27; cf. Gen. 31:30 ff.; I Sam. 19:12–16).
The Hebrew religion in the Judges period bore no resemblance
to the complex and elaborate "Mosaic" system which later
Jewish tradition declares to have been supernaturally revealed
in the desert as a monopoly of Aaronic priests. And this fact
comes out even more clearly when we find that Micah installed
over his ecclesiastical establishment a *secular* person, one of his
own sons, who was appointed and consecrated by Micah to be a
priest, or *cohen* (17:5). The work of the priest was to offer sacrifice; but the most important part of his occupation was to "cast
lots" before the ephod image in order to learn, if possible, what
was otherwise unknown about the future or even about the
present. This custom, which arose before the times of written
history, survives today in the practice of shaking dice and flip-
ping coins.

And now some further facts of an equally arresting nature
come before us in connection with the story of Micah the
Ephraimite. Far away in the distance, beyond the frontiers of
Joseph, and among the hills to the south of Amorite Jebus, or
Jerusalem, the little village of Bethlehem-Judah suddenly
emerges into Hebrew history as a place having some ethnic relationship with Ephraim. From this place comes a wandering
descendant of that old *secular* tribe of Levi which was under the
ancient curse of being "divided in Jacob and scattered in Israel"
(Gen. 49:5–7). When the tribe of Levi melted away as a distinct organization, some of its men wandered about and acquired prestige through the casting of lots which happened to
coincide with good fortune, as in the case now coming before us.

The young Levite from Bethlehem-Judah was out of work; and when he appeared at the house of Micah in search of a position, his Levitical prestige resulted in his engagement as a priest, or *cohen*, by the Ephraimite in preference to Micah's own son: "And Micah said, now I know that Yahweh will do me good, seeing that I have a Levite to be my *cohen*" (Judg. 17:13).

In the Mosaic tradition which arose after the Babylonian captivity, the Levite, as such, is only a *temple porter* without priestly functions, who would perish if he dared to approach the altar of Yahweh and officiate as a *cohen;* while the *real* priest is descended only from one special branch of Levi through *Aaron* the brother of Moses. This revised and mythical version of Hebrew history is represented by the symbolic synagogue ritual in which any modern Jew by the name of Cohen acts as the real priest, and any modern Jew by the name of Levi may be an assistant.

Story of Micah merged in story of Danite migration.—The account of Micah's ecclesiastical establishment is followed by, and merged into, an absorbing narrative about the community, or tribe, of Dan, whose increasing population on the far western slope was now uncomfortably crowded between the Philistines on the sea and the Ephraimites in the central highlands. Like the house of Joseph, which said, "The hill-country is not enough for us," the Danites needed more territory; and with this fact in view, they dispatched five of their number as emissaries to spy out the land. Traveling through the hill-country of Ephraim, they passed by the house of Micah, and heard the voice of the Levite priest, with whom they had already become acquainted through his habit of wandering about. So they at once requested that he "ask counsel of divinity" (i.e., cast lots), in order to see what kind of luck they should experience. Having done so, the priest gave the favorable response, "Go in peace! Your way is before Yahweh." Departing, the five Danites went into the far *north* of Canaan, beyond what was then considered to be the frontier of Israel, where they discovered, in the midst of a promising and peaceful region, a city called "Laish," whose inhabitants dwelt in quiet isolation from other people (Judg., chap. 18).

When the spies returned home, they gave such a good report that a large fraction, or all, of the Danite community, numbering six hundred armed men with wives and children, began the northward migration at once. Taking the same route which the spies had followed, the main body of Danites passed by the house of Micah the Ephraimite, nonchalantly appropriating his graven images and kidnapping the Levite who had favored them with good omens. Having thus thriftily stolen a church outfit and a minister, the Danites went on their way, despite the loud protests of Micah, who now felt that the Levite had brought him no luck, and whose feelings found expression, later on, in the saying attributed to Jacob: *"Dan shall be a serpent by the way, an adder in the path"* (Gen. 49:17). Continuing northward, the Danites arrived before the walls of Laish, which they destroyed with fire, and smote the inhabitants with the edge of the sword. Then settling peacefully in their new home, the tribesmen rebuilt the ruined city, calling it by the name *Dan;* while at the same time they erected a sanctuary of Yahweh, in which they established Micah's images and his Levitical priest, whose divination, coinciding with good fortune to the Danites, aided in the further evolution of Levitical prestige.

Editor seeks to change text of Danite story.—As already pointed out, the compilers of the Book of Judges lived at a time far on beyond the epoch with which that book deals; and they were accustomed to the more exalted spiritual ideas which became current in prophetic circles four or five hundred years after the times of the Judges. But since the resources of their day afforded no training in scientific historical exegesis, they could not rightly comprehend the conditions of earlier times; and reasoning, therefore, upon the ground of higher doctrines, *they imagined that the primitive religious customs of the Judges period, as evidenced by these antique tales, were merely the back-sliding of Israel into heathenism.* This was, for many centuries, the official orthodox theory, held alike by Jews and Christians. But the lack of historical insight was not the only occasion for the compilers' belief that the Hebrews of the Judges period had lapsed into paganism. The Jewish writers were the more ready to exploit the supposed shortcomings of early days because the people of that time were Ephraimites and northerners, whose descendants, "the lost tribes of Israel," were discredited by being carried away captive long before Judah went into exile.

A good concrete illustration of this editorial standpoint is found in a statement about the kidnapped Levite, whose name, by the way, was Jonathan (Heb. *Yehonathan*, which means "Yahweh gives"). The conclusion of the Danite story says, "And *Jonathan*, the son of Gershom, the son of *Mosheh*,—he and his sons were *cohanim* to the tribe of Dan until the day of the *captivity* of the land" (Judg. 18:30). Here we see a scribe doing his work *after* the Ephraimite exile; and when we look at the Hebrew text of the passage, we find that it raised a peculiar difficulty for later Jews because it brought the name of *Mosheh* (Moses) into embarrassing complications with the assumed heathenism of the Judges period. The name of Mosheh is spelled in Hebrew with the consonants known as "mem," "shin," and "hay" (*M-SH-H*). And in the passage under consideration the name is daringly changed by a scribe who inserted the Hebrew letter "nun" (or *n*) just *above* the line and *between* the "mem" and the "shin." The word is thus altered from *Mosheh* to *Manasseh*, the latter being, as we already know, a *north-Hebrew* name, designating Joseph's elder son, the brother of Ephraim. But in the days of the valiant scribal adventurer, the text of Judges had become semisacred; and consequently this well-meaning knight of the pen was torn between two loyalties, devotion to Mosaic orthodoxy and reverence for Scripture, which he compromised in the way shown, by putting the letter *n* above the line of letters composing the name of Moses.

The enterprise of this Jewish editor has been carried still further by the doctrinal zeal of modern, orthodox Christian versions of the Bible, which merely give the name as *Manasseh*, without informing the reader about the actual state of the Hebrew text. The American *Revised* Bible, however, is candid enough to put *Moses* into the *main reading text*, while stating in the margin, with somewhat oblique honesty, that "another reading is Manasseh." But the embarrassing passage is handled still differently in the English translation issued at Philadelphia by the Jewish Publication Society of America (1917). This work reproduces in a footnote (p. 318) the actual Hebrew text showing the letter *n* above the line, and adding editorially that this "indicates an earlier reading, *Moses*."

While the scribal interpolator was thus unwilling to change the earlier text *absolutely*, he sought in this awkward manner to accomplish two purposes: first, he wanted to absolve the family of Moses from complication with a paganistic sanctuary of Yahweh; and, second, he wanted to clear the descendants of Moses from a practice which made full-fledged priests out of Levites and thus brought them, as he imagined, into collision with the Mosaic Law, which ordained that only the sons of Aaron could legally act as priests, or *cohanim;* whereas common Levites were only porters of the sanctuary, who could not approach the altar of Yahweh without being struck dead. If the later scribes had known how to do more thorough editorial work, they would have proceeded to change the text further, where it speaks of Jonathan the Levite as being the son of *Gershom*, the son of Moses, etc. (Judg. 18:30). For the *Ephraimite* document actually says that Moses had a son, Gershom (Exod. 18:3); and this name reappears also in the J document (Exod. 2:22). Thus, if the alterations of the text were to be carried through consistently, the name Gershom in Judges ought also to have been changed or wholly stricken out; or it should have been erased from the passages in *Exodus;* and we should have some explanation of the suspicious acceptance of Moses' descendants as *priests* in the Judges period, when the Mosaic Law itself says that only the sons of Aaron may serve at the altar of Yahweh. This case, then, turns out to be very important; and the further we investigate it, the more we are prepared to see that the later scribes, who compiled the Bible for us in its present shape, were very clumsy in their handling of the early Hebrew sources.

Still another important item of historical criticism is yielded by the Danite story, which helps us to realize more fully the nature of Genesis. The city in the far north of Canaan, which the Danites captured and renamed after their supposed ancestor, was called *Laish* by its previous inhabitants: "And they called the name of the city Dan. Howbeit, the name of the city was Laish at the first" (Judg. 18:29). This passage gives a baseline for consideration of a story about the mythical patriarch Abraham, wherein he arms his family slaves and goes with them on a military expedition *"as far as Dan"* (Gen. 14:14). The legends about Abraham deal with a period *more than one thousand years before the times of the Judges;* and yet the narrative in Genesis makes use of the *later* name, Dan, instead of the *earlier* name, Laish; proving along with many other items of evidence, that the Book of Genesis comes to us through the hands and the work of editors living many centuries after the prehistoric, "patriarchal" epoch.

Story of outrage at Gibeah.—The final story in the appendix to Judges begins with chapter 19. It brings to view yet another wandering Levite, this time without a name, who is described as a sojourner on the far slope of Ephraim. He takes a concubine out of the village of Bethlehem-Judah, which thus appears again, but only as before in a brief and casual way. Proceeding northward from Bethlehem with her, the Levite lodges overnight in the hamlet of Gibeah, belonging to the tribe of *Benjamin*, where some village toughs outrage the woman so that she dies before daybreak. Upon finding the lifeless body of his concubine in the morning, the Levite cuts the corpse into twelve pieces, and sends a piece to each of the tribes of Israel (which the editor of the story imagines to be in existence according to the later, orthodox tradition). Then all Israel rises up, assembling together as one man in the neighborhood of Gibeah, and requires the Benjaminites to hand over the culprits who had caused the woman's death. But instead of delivering up the criminals, the Benjaminites, as a tribe, are said to have unanimously protected the village toughs. This precipitates a vast Hebrew civil war, in which the eleven tribes of Israel attack, and nearly wipe out, the tribe of Benjamin.

We need not deny that an outrage of some kind may have served as the occasion for this fantastic tale; but the narrative is loaded with gross exaggerations and improbabilities, and comes from a time far later than the original events—whatever they may have been. Yet the purposes which prompt the story are self-evident: There was always ill feeling between Judah and Benjamin, as witness the aversion of Saul and David for each other, and the legendary spite between Leah, the mother of Judah, and Rachel, the mother of Benjamin. This mutual grudge was heightened in the Deuteronomic period by the Benjaminite prophet Jeremiah, who declared that the sin of Judah was worse than the sin of Ephraim, and who intimated that among all the citizens of Jerusalem not a single righteous man was to be found (Jer. 3:11; 5:1). In return for this vilification a Jewish writer would be glad to publish a story blackening the memory of the entire tribe from which the great insurgent prophet sprang. The striking disposition of the woman's body is modeled upon, and suggested by, the earlier and veritable action of the Benjaminite Saul, at the same village of Gibeah, in

cutting up a yoke of oxen and sending the pieces by the hands of
messengers throughout the country (I Sam. 11:7). The narrative about Saul *seems*, of course, to be later than the fantastic
story about the outrage at Gibeah in the Judges period; but in
reality it is earlier and more primitive. Saul merely hews the
oxen in *pieces*—but not in *twelve* pieces; for in his day the nationalistic evolution had not yet produced the full orthodox
legend of twelve original tribes. The late date of the Judges tale
is also shown by the command of Yahweh that *Judah* shall go
up *first*, ahead of all Israel, to fight the Benjaminites; which has
the same editorial character as the corresponding command in
the prologue that Judah shall go up first against the *Canaanites*
(20:18; cf. 1:2).

**General observations upon period covered by Book of
Judges.**—The appendix to the Deuteronomic Book of Judges
contains the repeated statement, "In those days there was no
king in Israel; every man did what was right in his own eyes"
(Judg. 17:6; 21:25; cf. 18:1; 19:1). This very late observation
is founded upon almost complete misunderstanding of the period, for it grows out of the uncritical idea that human society is
either a unified group ruled by a monarch or else a mere inconsistent aggregate of individual atoms, each having the power to
do as it wills. If the editorial statement were literally correct,
the epoch which marks the beginning of Hebrew history in Canaan was only a time of anarchy. But this is not true. For at no
stage in the history of any people have all individuals had the
power to do as they pleased. The Judges epoch, instead of being given over to mere anarchy, was a turbulent period of tribalism, or provincialism, when *local*, but not individual, interests
held sway. And this is proved by the ancient stories transmitted to us within the "framework" of Judges itself. While individuals in that period were not responsible to a king, they were
answerable to the elders and sheiks of the clans to which they

belonged; while these local communities, in turn, co-operated from time to time in many ways which limited the scope of individual action.

The Judges epoch was a confusing, but inevitable, period begun by the Josephite invasion of the central highlands. The house of Joseph developed the energy to start a nationalistic movement. But it could only go a certain distance along this path. For the rise of a full-fledged oriental kingdom, such as appeared in due time under the house of David, was dependent upon several forces and circumstances which could not be controlled by peasants in the central highlands. A sociologically uniform rural aristocracy of landholders and slave-owners had to grow up, not only in the central hills of Ephraim, *but outside the house of Joseph*, possessing the soil by mishpat tenure in allegiance to the Yahweh cult, and regarding itself as partly or wholly Hebrew; while sooner or later this free upper class had to be brought into accommodation, or adjustment, with the aristocracy in the unconquered Amorite cities which lay beyond the Josephite frontiers, and which never had been destroyed like Jericho, Shechem, and Laish.

Thus, while the Judges period was marked by a great deal of confusion, certain definite tendencies manifested themselves in various ways. A rural upper class with a Hebrew tradition (but not of uniformly pure "Jacob-Joseph-Israel" blood) actually took form in the open country, both within and without the central highlands; and the evolution of this class went straight on through the liquidation of old communities and the rise of new groupings on the basis of kinship or environment. The Yahweh cult was a condition, but not a guaranty, of tribal and national growth, as we can see from the feuds and lack of co-operation between the various groups which were supposed to have that cult in common, but whose connections with it were not always of the same quality.

And meanwhile no definite solution or adjustment was available in the Judges period for the tremendous problem of the unconquered Amorite cities which lay beyond the Josephite frontiers. The last organized effort of the Amorite cities to break the power of Israel was marked by the Deborah-battle; and after that the older inhabitants of Canaan sank back in helpless terror as the rising tide of proto-Deuteronomic revolution, climaxing in the slaughter of the Shechemite aristocracy, swept away the legal rights of baalism throughout the central highlands. Their fears were stirred anew by the Danite conquest of Laish, and again, as we shall see, by a ferocious attack of Saul upon Gibeon (II Sam. 21:1-2 f.). Horrified, as the Amorites inevitably were, by the recurring violence of the new settlers, and scandalized by the frightful economic portent of *mishpat*, the Amorite cities held out stubbornly until the military necessity of the Philistine wars constrained them to make an accommodation with the politic David, under whose dynasty they were absorbed into the structure of the Hebrew nation.

The general state of Canaan during the Judges period, therefore, was one of suspense and unsettlement. The Hebrew nation was as yet unborn, and even its geographical outline had not come into view. The house of Joseph holds fast in the *central highlands* as the main trunk and backbone of the coming kingdom. The *northern limit* of the future monarchy has just been marked out by the newly won district and city of Dan. Between Dan in the north and Joseph in the center we catch fleeting glimpses of groups, or communities, known as Asher, Naphtali, Zebulun, and Issachar; but *Issachar* has already vanished; while east of the Jordan river, the clan, or tribe, of *Reuben* has also disappeared, leaving a vague mass under the name of *Gilead*, connected only in a distant and loose fashion with the groups west of the river. On the other hand, the *southern* district of Canaan is nebulous, being identified thus far with non-Hebrew elements known as Jebusites, Calebites, Jerachmeelites, Kenites, Tamarites, and Adullamites. But, at the same time, two emigrant extensions of Ephraim seem to have taken form: (1) the village of Bethlehem-Judah, or Bethlehem-Ephrathah, below Jebus; and (2) the village of Beersheba, in the far south, on the edge of the desert (see chap. v, pp. 40–42).

Josephite aristocracy growing stronger in times of Samuel and Saul.—Turning away from the Book of Judges and going onward now into the age of Samuel the Ephraimite and Saul the Benjaminite, we find no break in the historical process already begun. The books of Samuel consist mainly of ancient Ephraimite records brought together by Jewish compilers who interject a number of Deuteronomic passages; but in Samuel the old narratives are not inclosed by a rigid framework of recurrent formulas, like the Book of Judges. We find ourselves once more in the familar *hill-country* of Ephraim, where the landed aristocracy is now reckoned through *longer genealogies*. The descent of Samuel brings into view six links, going far back into the earlier Judges period: Samuel ben Elkanah, ben Jeroham, ben Elihu, ben Tohu, ben Zuph (I Sam. 1:1). Elkanah, the father of Samuel, was an Ephraimite *farmer*, living in the village of *Ramah*. His household consisted of two wives, with sons and daughters; and we find a suggestive hint of the family wealth in the offering taken to the sanctuary of Yahweh, which consisted of three bullocks with meal and wine (1:24). The family of Saul, in the nearby district of Benjamin, was in the same social class, and, like that of Samuel, runs back through six names into the Judges period: Saul ben Kish, ben Abiel, ben Zeror, ben Bechorath, ben Aphiah (9:1). The house of Saul possessed a head-slave, or steward, named Ziba, under whom were *twenty slaves* (II Sam. 9:2; 19:17; cf. I Sam. 9:3). The home of the family was in the village of Gibeah; its landholdings were in the open country outside; and the soil was plowed with oxen driven either by the freemen or by the slaves of the establishment (I Sam. 11:4–5). We thus get a sense of the growing peasant aristocracy in the highlands of Joseph—with its homes in little places like Ramah and Gibeah, its tilled estates in the surrounding fields, its lower class of slaves, its cattle and plows and all the equipment of agriculture.

Symbolizing growth of nationalism, ark of Yahweh now first emerges into view.—The house of Joseph, steadily expanding into "a multitude in the midst of the earth," was now developing a sharper and more definite consciousness of itself, exalting the cult of Yahweh into a position of greater prominence as a bond of unity. Symbolic of this growing nationalism, an object called "the ark [or *aron*] of Yahweh" now suddenly appears in a temple at a place called "Shiloh," not mentioned before in Hebrew history. Its priest is named *Eli;* but the origins of priest and sanctuary alike are obscured in the darkness that surrounds the beginnings of Hebrew institutions. Neither the ark, nor the village of Shiloh as its home, appear in the Deuteronomic portion of Judges; and the reference to the ark in the appendix is merely parenthetical, a late gloss, which disturbs the connection and has no logical bearing on the context (Judg. 20:27–28). The hitherto obscure village of Shiloh was not prejudiced or complicated by the loyalties attaching to the older Yahweh shrines in other places; which accounts for the selection of this unknown village as a new and fresh point where the allegiance of the Josephites and others could readily center. The political and military significance of the Shiloh ark is evident because it was carried as a fetish into battle in the times of Eli and of David, and because the latter, when establishing his capital at Jerusalem, placed this Ephraimite cult object in a tent on the hill of Zion (I Sam. 4:3–4; II Sam. 11:11; 6:15–16).

Shiloh ark not legendary ark of Pentateuchal documents.— The late compilers of the books of Samuel believed that the Ephraimite ark was identical with the *legendary* ark of the Pentateuch, which is pictured as the one and only shrine where sacrifice may be offered to Yahweh. The Priestly document locates the ark always at the very *center* of the camp of Israel in the desert, where it is entirely surrounded by the tribes in a certain specified order, and cared for by the priests, or *cohanim*, the sons of Aaron; while the ordinary Levites are porters of the tabernacle, who may not approach the ark without being struck dead. But, on the other hand, the Ephraimite source puts the Tabernacle and ark habitually *without* the camp, and makes the Ephraimite Joshua the minister. These differences, which are too glaring to be reconciled, will be taken up more fully, with references, at a later point in our study; and at present we rest upon the observation that the Pentateuchal ark is a glorified legend suggested by and growing out of the real, historical ark of the house of Joseph.

If the legendary ark of the Pentateuch had been at Shiloh during the entire Judges period, straight along from the invasion to the days of Samuel and Saul, as the only shrine for the legal worship of Yahweh, and managed by an exclusive priesthood counting its descent from Aaron—if such had been the case, why do we not hear of its being taken into the great Deborah-battle,—or of being carried by Ehud and the Ephraimites into the combat with Moab? And why did not Gideon avail himself of it when warring against the Midianites? Moreover, if the tribe of Judah had actually existed at the time of the original invasion, why do we not hear of the ark in the forefront of the campaign, when Judah "went up first," in the van of Israel, to contend with the Canaanites?

Instead of worshiping at an exclusive sanctuary in the Judges period, the Hebrews had altars to Yahweh at many places. Gideon is said to have built a shrine at his native Ophrah by command of Yahweh (Judg. 6:25 f.). The establishment of Micah the Ephraimite was another of the local sacred places; and, according to the story, Micah believed that when he had secured the young Levite as *cohen*, the favor of Yahweh was guaranteed (Judg. 17:13). The same persuasion was held by the Danites when they robbed Micah of his cult equipment and priest for use at still another holy place which they set up in the north.

Not only was the worship of Yahweh carried on at various places during the precise time when the legendary ark is *said* to have been existing in Canaan, but when we turn to the *real*, historical shrine, which emerges abruptly into view at Shiloh, with its ark in charge of the mysterious priest Eli, we find that its constitution has no legitimate basis in a priesthood exercised only by *Aaronites;* for Samuel, who is an *Ephraimite*, becomes a priest, and is consecrated to ecclesiastical office through the vow of his mother Hannah, who dedicates him to Yahweh; and he is accepted in this character by Eli, who therefore becomes a party to it (I Sam. 1:20 f.; chaps 2 and 3). Moreover, the sanctuary is visited by worshipers, not *three* times a year, as commanded by the Torah, or the Law, but only *once* a year: "And the man Elkanah, and all his house, went up to offer unto Yahweh *the yearly sacrifice*" (I Sam. 1:3, 7, 21). And Samuel's mother made him a little coat, "and brought it to him from year to year, when she came up with her husband to offer *the yearly sacrifice*" (2:19).

We find ourselves, therefore, driven to the conclusion that the Shiloh sanctuary, with its ark, or chest, was a logical development of the growing nationalistic sense which became evident in the house of Joseph at this particular stage of Hebrew history. The priest Eli would thus belong to the fraternity of primitive Levitical *cohanim*, who (like Micah's Levite Jonathan) could easily adapt themselves to the new and changing conditions which arose from time to time. The original account of Shiloh, as a Josephite institution, would thus have been abridged and mutilated by the later Jewish compilers, who have clumsily re-worked it from the Deuteronomic and priestly standpoints.

Nationalizing movement forced on by Philistine pressure.— The Philistines rightly perceived that any further growth of nationalism in the highlands would imperil their monopoly of the trade routes across Canaan. And while a source of immediate hostility was removed by the migration of the troublesome Danites, yet the establishment of this aggressive and warlike tribe in the north brought with it a new danger to Philistine domination. For the house of Dan and the house of Joseph thus became two extremes, or outposts, with which the intermediate communities, if not checked, would inevitably merge into a solid, organized mass overlying the commercial highways.

The Philistines accordingly made a sudden march up the Mediterranean coast, and wheeled eastward into the Plain of Esdraelon. The Hebrews, taken by surprise, were only able to collect a raw, untrained levy of militia without competent leadership. And if they imagined that the historic triumph of Deborah and Barak in the same locality was about to be repeated, they were sorely astonished; for the Israelite host was terribly beaten; whereupon the elders of Israel bethought themselves of the ark of Shiloh and sent for it. But in the following battle the Philistines were again victorious, and also captured the ark itself, which they carried away to their chief city, Ashdod.

The compilers then go on to insert a long priestly narrative which recounts, among other details, the sudden and miraculous death of *fifty thousand and seventy* (*50,070*) *Hebrew men* who looked into the ark (I Sam., chaps. 5, 6, 7, 8). The sacred object is alleged to have been the cause of a terrible plague among the Philistines, who are said to have promptly returned it on a cart drawn by two cows; after which "all Israel" underwent a Deuteronomic reformation marked by the "putting away" of heathen gods; being rewarded by the special favor of Yahweh, who "thundered with a great thunder" upon the Philistines, driving them away, "so that they came no more into the coast of Israel; and the hand of Yahweh was against the Philistines all the days of Samuel."

But in the *actual* Hebrew history, as we shall now see, the

Philistines, instead of being expelled from the land of Israel, capitalized their victories promptly.

Philistines advance into central Ephraim, destroy Shiloh, and place garrison in house of Joseph.—Following up their victories in the Plain of Esdraelon, the Philistines advanced into the very heart of Ephraim, and razed the temple at Shiloh to the ground. This new and fresh disaster is not even mentioned in the books of Samuel; but we learn of it from Jeremiah the prophet, who fell out with the Deuteronomists and recorded facts embarrassing to the priestly historians. Speaking in the name of Yahweh to the people of Judah at the Jerusalem temple, this Ephraimite prophet says, "Go ye now unto my place which was in Shiloh, and see what I did to it. . . . . And I will do unto this house [in Jerusalem] which is called by my name, *as I have done to Shiloh.* Then will I make this house like Shiloh" (Jer. 7:12, 14; 26:6, *passim*). Since the Ephraimite sanctuary was the center of a new nationalistic movement, its destruction by the invading Philistines was logical; and as a result of this catastrophe, the priestly family of Eli fled from Shiloh to a place farther south called *Nob*, where we find them a few years later in charge of Ahimelek the priest, the great grandson of Eli, officiating at a new shrine of Yahweh, containing the usual ephod image with an altar and shew-bread (I Sam. 21:1–8; for Ahimelek's descent from Eli, see 22:9; 14:3).

Having destroyed the Shiloh sanctuary, the symbol of growing nationalism, the Philistine conquerors then planted a heavy garrison in the midst of the Josephite hill-country, the presence of which is noticed thirteen times (I Sam. 10:5; 13:3, 4, 16, 17, 23; 14:1, 4, 6, 11, 12, 21). From the camp of the invaders, three different bands of "spoilers" went out in three directions to lay tribute on the Hebrew aristocracy; and thus the house of Joseph groaned under the Philistine yoke (I Sam. 13:17–18).

State of terrorism produced by Philistine occupation.—Extreme terror and confusion resulted from the Philistine seizure of the central highlands. The house of Joseph, by this time, had grown into a population which occupied many hundreds of hill villages, whose farmers and shepherds could look back over a long perspective, beginning with the original invasion, when their ancestors, armed with sword and bow, had wrested the central hill-country "out of the hand of the Amorite." They cherished memories of the Deborah-battle, when the stars in their courses fought against Sisera; they knew the story of Ehud, who defeated Moab; they rehearsed the tale of Gideon, who vanquished the Midianites with the sword of Yahweh; and they remembered the tragic fall of Shechem, when the last of the Amorite baalim in the territory of Joseph were destroyed; so that the law of mishpat was at length triumphant in all Ephraim. But now this hard-won land of liberty was under the Philistine heel, and the Hebrew freemen were sinking into bondage.

Earliest Hebrew prophecy takes form in religious frenzy of Ephraimites.—Amid the prevailing deep distress the religious energy of the Yahweh cult crystallized into a startling phenomenon. Groups of enthusiasts arose with sudden spontaneity, recruited from the most excitable and nervous elements of the population. These fanatical zealots began to travel about through the hill-country, stirring up the discouraged masses on behalf of Yahweh and Israel. Playing upon flutes and harps, and rattling tambourines, they not only aroused the villagers but worked themselves up into frenzy, stripping off their clothes and lying naked upon the ground, uttering inarticulate cries like the Mohammedan dervishes of a later day, and communicating their fury, by a kind of hypnotic suggestion, to innocent bystanders, who would thereupon join the howling groups and follow their example.

These traveling enthusiasts began to be known as *b'nae nebiim*, or "sons of prophets"; but the term *nabi*, or "prophet," did not then signify what it came to mean in later times. Moreover, the wild performances of the sons of prophets were not generally understood at first by all the people; and the movement was looked upon by many with aversion; to such an extent that the term "sons" led to the derisive question, "And who is their *father?*" That is to say, "Who is responsible for them? Who is their leader? And under what auspices do they go about in this fashion?" But those who derided them in that day (like those who fail to understand them now) did not bear in mind that the house of Joseph was constantly under the eye of the Philistine police who stood ready to break up any movement of nationalism that showed itself in the subjugated population. If the new masters of the country had realized the meaning of the excitement caused by the *b'nae nebiim*, and if they had foreseen the outcome of the frenzy now spreading through the highlands, they would have promptly arrested and hung a few of the zealots. But as it was the Philistines were doubtless entertained by this apparently harmless outburst; and they may themselves have started the derisive proverb about the paternity of these wild "sons" who traveled noisily through the hills.

Prophetic movement enlists help of Saul ben Kish.—The spread of the early prophetic movement is made clear by the conversion of a hitherto unknown Benjaminite, Saul the son of a landed proprietor named Kish, in southern Ephraim. Passing along through the country one day, he met a group of the sons of prophets playing upon their musical instruments; and as the Hebrew narrative quaintly says, "The spirit of Yahweh came upon him," so that he was given a new heart and turned into another man; after which he "prophesied among the prophets" (I Sam. 10:5 f.). This expression does not mean that Saul predicted anything, or that he made a speech, but merely that he uttered wild, inarticulate cries. Saul's conversion to the new movement was of such a thoroughgoing nature that he disrobed himself and lay naked for a whole day, "prophesying among the prophets." And all who knew him said, "What is this that is come unto the son of Kish? *Is Saul also among the prophets?*" (*supra* and 19:20–24).

Saul raises militia company and repels Ammonite attack on Gilead.—If those who asked what had come upon Saul were indeed mystified by his conversion, they had not long to wait before its full meaning was demonstrated. The new convert went back to his home at Gibeah; and one day when he was at work in the fields following the oxen, a great commotion arose in the village, where messengers had arrived hastily, asking for help, saying that the *Ammonites*, under their king *Nahash*, were threatening the land of Gilead, east of Jordan. This call for aid would seem to have been rather presumptuous in view of the Gileadites' refusal to assist the Ephraimite highlanders in former days. But a broader spirit of nationalistic unity was now in the air, for conditions were changing; and when Saul came hurriedly from the field to discover the cause of the excitement, his anger was kindled against Nahash the Ammonite, so that he was overpowered by emotion. "The spirit of Yahweh rushed upon him"; and the people were astounded to see him take an ax and fiercely hew a yoke of live oxen in pieces. Putting the bloody fragments into the hands of messengers, he sent them all through the country, saying that if anyone refused to fight against Ammon, *his oxen would suffer likewise!* (I Sam., chap. 11). Saul at this time, it must be remembered, was merely a private person, without any official authority. But the hour called for leadership; the situation was very critical; and therefore the audacious call to arms brought forth a quick response. Leading his militia levy across the Jordan, the volunteer captain attacked and routed the Ammonite force under Nahash.

Saul chosen king at Gilgal.—These events led to the election of Saul as king (or *melek*) by the army. The account of his alleged previous anointing by Samuel is a non-Josephite, southern myth, growing out of the post-Exilic idea that the priesthood was above the monarchy; and it is also intended to magnify the figure of Samuel so as to give divine legitimacy to the later alleged anointing of David the Judean hero. It would, of course, be going too far to say that neither Saul nor David had anything to do with Samuel, who seems to have been connected with the nationalistic movement of crude prophetism and with influences at work under the surface of events. But the narratives in the books of Samuel, as indicated above (p. 110), are compiled from inconsistent sources, giving contrary views of Hebrew politics at that period. The real, historical Samuel was a much less important person than he is made to appear in one series of documents. The compiler is laboring not only to give divine legitimacy to the Hebrew kingdom in general and to the Judaic monarchy in particular; but, in line with this purpose, he also seeks, in vain, to obscure the character of Hebrew nationalism as pivoted upon the house of Joseph. Both David and Saul, as a matter of fact, were enthroned, not by any priesthood, but by secular forces having their center in the hill-country of Ephraim; and when the Josephites eventually withdrew their support, the national authority of the house of David collapsed. The election of Saul to the kingship, therefore, was at the hands of the people (I Sam. 11:15). And it is important to notice that the establishment of the monarchy took place not in the hill-country of Ephraim (which was then held by the Philistines) but far down in the Jordan Valley at *Gilgal*, east of Jericho, where only with the greatest difficulty could the Philistines oppose the nationalistic renaissance.

Saul drives Philistines from central highlands.—By a stroke of good fortune Saul was able to expel the Philistines from the central highlands, but without crushing their main army (I Sam., chap. 14). He was not a conventional king with a fortified city, but rather a magnified "judge," or "deliverer," such as Ehud, Gideon, or Barak; and he remained, from first to last, a village warrior, building up a military organization by a kind of selective draft, consolidating the aristocracy of landholders and slave-owners in the hills of Ephraim under the banner of Yahweh. The extent of his kingdom is not known; but his authority was limited by the still unconquered Amorite cities which lay outside the frontiers of the house of Joseph. These places included, on the south border, Jerusalem, Gibeon, Shaalbim, and other centers of alien life; and on the north, Ibleam, Taanach, Megiddo, Bethshan, and similar Canaanite strongholds. Saul's effective rule, therefore, was confined within the central district; and a reckless impulse to break down this "iron ring" may have driven him to commit one of the most impolitic and atrocious acts of his reign.

Saul makes proto-Deuteronomic attack upon Amorites of Gibeon.—Saul and the people of his day knew that the Josephite conquest of the central highlands was completed by the destruction of Shechem. There had been a treaty, or *berith*, between Israel and the Shechemites; but these older inhabitants of Canaan were nevertheless annihilated by the new settlers. A solemn peace also had been sworn between Israel and the city of *Gibeon*, which was one of the Amorite strongholds lying nearest the home of Saul. If this place could be taken, the frontier of Ephraim would be more secure against Philistine attack from that quarter. We need not be surprised, therefore, to find that in spite of the treaty Saul attacked the Amorites of Gibeon; and while he did not succeed in taking their city, he slew a number of its people and inflamed the rest with a burning desire for vengeance upon Israel (II Sam. 21:1 f.). And just as the destruction of Shechem brought Israel into "bad odor" with the remaining Amorite cities of the land, the same effect was naturally produced by Saul's proto-Deuteronomic attack upon Gibeon. He not only failed to enlarge the territory of Ephraim, but his action tended to renew the old hostility of the Canaanite cities against Israel, *which was exactly what the Philistines wanted,*

*since they desired to keep Israel and the Amorites apart, and thus
prevent the rise of a Hebrew nation with fortified cities.*

**Philistines make new approach west and south of Jerusa-
lem.**—While the expulsion of the enemy from the central highlands by the prowess of Saul was a great accomplishment and
gave the house of Joseph a breathing space in which to recover
their morale and reorganize their forces, it was no solution of
the Philistine problem. For the situation was the same as that
which existed between Rome and Carthage. It was a matter of
life and death, in which one side or the other gained control of
the trade routes. The rise of a Hebrew kingdom including the
Amorite walled cities would bring into play a new power strong
enough to overshadow the masters of the coastal plain and absorb the revenue collected from the rich caravans passing to and
fro between Asia and Africa.

The Philistines, therefore, were compelled, at all costs, to
wage relentless war upon Israel; and with this end in view they
sought to penetrate the highlands by approaching from a new
direction, west and south of the still Amorite city of Jebus or
Jerusalem. Mobilizing their army at a place called Socoh,
where the lower hills break into passes leading up to Bethlehem
and Hebron, they prepared for a new campaign (I Sam., chap.
17). This move called for instant action by Saul, who at once
led the Ephraimite host into a region where they had never
operated before. And now, for the first time, we begin to hear of
men from Bethlehem in the army of Saul. Three sons of Jesse
the Ephrathite—Eliab, Abinadab, and Shammah—belong to a
regiment under a captain (I Sam. 17:12–18). Another man from
the same village, who did not belong to Jesse's family, is mentioned as a hero: *"And Elhanan the son of Jaareoregim the Bethlehemite slew Goliath the Gittite, the staff of whose spear was like a
weaver's beam"* (II Sam. 21:19). The well-known story of
Jesse's youngest son, David, slaying the giant with a sling, is
one of the myths that always grow up around popular favorites.

The narratives about the early relations between David and Saul are hopelessly at variance. Thus David becomes the musician and armor-bearer to Saul (I Sam. 16:14–23). But in the following chapter David kills Goliath, and is then introduced as a stranger to Saul, who asks the name of David's father (17:33–58). Immediately after David's alleged exploit in killing the Philistine, the women of Israel are said to have come forth"from all the cities of Israel, singing and dancing, *to meet king Saul*"; and they greet the monarch with an insult, saying, *"Saul hath slain his thousands; but David his tens of thousands"* (18:6–7). Saul thereupon hates David, and asks, "What more can he have but the kingdom?"

David primarily a southern leader.—The stories magnifying David in his early years are natural enough when considered as legends or symbols reflecting his later achievements; but they can have no other value for the historian. There is no record of any northern exploit in which David figures during the reign of Saul; and we can only understand the career of David when we realize that he was first of all a *southerner*, with southern interests, anxious to keep his native hills free of the enemy from the coastal plain. The Philistines were evidently defeated at Socoh by Saul; but later on they attempted to establish themselves farther south and higher up in the hills, at *Keilah*, a non-Israelite city, with gates and bars, whose men are called *baalim* (I Sam. 23:11–12, *passim*). David now appears as a military leader, operating independently outside of Saul's domain. "And David and his men went to Keilah, and fought with the Philistines, and brought away their cattle, and smote them with a great slaughter. So David saved the inhabitants of Keilah" (23:5). In this character, as a free-lance, he is perfectly understandable; and his ultimate aim to unite the clans of the southern hill-country is revealed by his course after defeating the Amalekites. The spoil taken from these invading Bedouin was carefully sent around through the southern hills to the sheiks of the various

clans with the message, "Behold, a present for you of the spoil
of the enemies of Yahweh" (I Sam. 30:26).

As an independent chieftain, with an army of six hundred,
and with prospects of uniting the scattered clans in that part of
the country, he would be sought as an ally by Saul, and given a
daughter of the Josephite king (chap. 18). But in time the conservatism of the southern clans, and the unlikelihood of their
union with Ephraim under the crown of Joseph, would make the
northern monarch fear the rise of another kingdom so near his
own, and thus alienate Saul from his remarkable son-in-law.
The north and the south were in sharp geographical and sociological contrast; and the differences between them were so pronounced that even the genius of David, at a later time, could
only unite the two sections for a brief period. Thus the alienation between David and Saul would be an early evidence of the
antagonism which ultimately arose in the enlarged Hebrew nation rather than a merely personal matter. Saul's apparently
fratricidal and foolish endeavor to destroy David would then be
explained as a rational course intended to hold back the southern clans from organizing into a group which might lend itself to
Philistine policy against Ephraim. Saul may well have heard
the story in which the men of that region delivered Samson to
the enemy because "the Philistines are rulers over us" (Judg.
15:11). The danger of this possibility is proved by the fact that
after the Philistines failed at Socoh and Keilah, they made another attempt which actually carried them up to Bethlehem,
where they stationed a garrison strong enough to bar David
from his home (II Sam. 23:14-16).

**Nature of religion at this time shown by "teraphim" in
David's house.**—That religion at this time was on a plane far
below the later Judaism of the compiler is interestingly shown
by a story connected with Saul's efforts to destroy David. Hoping to entrap and slay him, Saul sent emissaries to watch David's house. But the princess Michal, daughter of Saul and wife

of David, let her husband down through a window, so that he escaped safely. Then, looking about the house, and seeing the *teraphim*, or family god, she laid it on the couch, placed a pillow under its head, and carefully drew the clothes over it. And when Saul sent messengers to take David, she said to them, "He is sick," thus holding the men off and gaining time for the fugitive, but exciting the royal suspicion. Then Saul sent again, telling his officers to get David and bring him, bed and all, so that he could be slain personally. "And when the messengers were come in, behold, the teraphim was in the bed, with a pillow of goats' hair at the head thereof" (I Sam. 19:16).

That the teraphim was an image in human shape is clear from the manner of its use in the story; and it links the times of David and Saul with the days of Micah, in the Judges period. "The man Micah had a house of gods [*elohim*], and he made an ephod and teraphim" (Judg. 17:5). Another illustration, coming from a time which appears to be earlier still, but is really much later, is found in the JE document reflecting social and religious conditions two hundred years *after* David. In this case, Rachel, the Ephraimite mother, steals the teraphim of her father Laban while he is away at work:

And Laban went to shear his sheep; and Rachel stole the teraphim that belonged to her father. And Laban said to Jacob, wherefore hast thou stolen my *gods?* And Jacob answered, with whomsoever thou findest thy gods, he shall not live; for Jacob knew not that Rachel had stolen them. And Laban went into Jacob's tent, and into Leah's tent, and into the tent of the two women-slaves; but he found them not. And he went out of Leah's tent, and entered into Rachel's tent. Now Rachel had taken the teraphim, and put them in the saddle of the camel, and sat upon them [Gen. 31:19, f., *passim*].

In this instructive story teraphim is equated with "elohim," or "gods." Plural in form, but usually singular in meaning, the word was a common noun for a god, or gods, used in household worship; and thus we find one of these images in the house of David.

Further cause of Saul-David alienation found in Nahash, king of Ammon.—Another possible ground for antipathy between David and Saul is in David's peculiar connection with *Nahash*, king of Ammon, the foe against whom Saul's anger was first kindled into martial action. That there was *hesed*, or kindness, between David and Nahash is claimed in words attributed to David himself: "Nahash shewed *hesed* unto me" (II Sam. 10:2). And later on, a son of Nahash gave much help to David: "And it came to pass, when David was come to Mahanaim, that Shobi, the son of Nahash, ... brought beds, and basons, and wheat [etc.], for David and for the people that were with him" (II Sam. 17:27 f.).

There might be no special significance in these facts by themselves, but they are apparently involved with certain relationships which lead to remarkable conclusions. The term *Nahash* is applied to a local *image-worship* at Jerusalem, which lasted long after David until the reign of Hezekiah; and it also occurs in the family of David, two of whose half-sisters were daughters of a man by the name of Nahash (II Sam. 17:25). The word itself is a Semitic term for *serpent;* while the image-worship at Jerusalem was that of a bronze idol representing a snake, which was called "Nehushtan," derived from the term *nahash*. And three hundred years after David, this idol was at length broken in pieces by King Hezekiah: *"For unto those days did the children of Israel burn incense to it"* (II Kings 18:4). Scandalized by this heathen cult, the Pentateuch sought to explain it as having survived from a time when the Israelites in the wilderness were bitten by serpents, and then cured by looking at a bronze image of a serpent: "And Moses made a *nahash* of brass" (Num. 21:9). Such action, however, would collide with the previously assumed commandment *not* to make any graven image, or any likeness of anything in heaven or earth; and the attempted explanation is an awkward apology for the pagan character of Hebrew religion during early times.

These interesting facts may suggest that the families of David and of Nahash the Ammonite king had subterranean connections of some kind through common adherence to the serpent-cult which was widespread in the ancient Semitic world, and which even the Bible itself does not deny was practiced by the Israelites in Jerusalem from early times. David's religion included the teraphim; and he may also have been a worshiper of the serpent-god Nahash; in which case may be found another possible cause for antipathy between David and Saul. The name Nahash does not occur in Ephraim, and is found only in the south. The circumstances of Ephraimite history had made the people of that region very nationalistic and provincial by the time of Saul. But, on the contrary, the hill district later known as Judah was as yet unorganized; the allegiance of its population was not yet fixed; while even the aristocracy of Bethlehem is not heard of in the army of Israel until the Philistines attack the south. And as for David, all the conditions of his career united to give him a political outlook far more comprehensive than that of Saul the narrow-minded patriot of the central highlands. David took his parents over to Moab, and intrusted them to the king of that country when the campaign against him grew more vigorous; and at length Saul's relentless antagonism drove David to a startling move! Taking with him his force of six hundred men, he deserted to the Philistines, and became a vassal of Achish the king of Gath (I Sam. 27:1-4).

Philistines destroy Saul in battle of Gilboa.—Setting out upon a new campaign, the Philistines passed northward, "by hundreds and by thousands," with David and his regiment of six hundred in the rear. Entering once more into the historic Plain of Esdraelon, they paused while the commanders of the army held a council, reaching the conclusion that it would be dangerous to allow David to take part in the coming battle; and accordingly he was ordered back to the Philistine country. Were the commanders right or wrong? We know that later on David executed nearly all that remained of Saul's family (II Sam. 21: 6–11). Who can say that this non-Ephraimite chieftain from the south would not have co-operated loyally with his new allies against King Saul, who was the mortal enemy of both David and the Philistines? The solution of this riddle is deep in the heart of those forces that rule the destiny of nations, and which frequently operate upon what seem to be the narrowest of margins.

The battle was a great Philistine victory, in which the Josephite forces were driven across the Plain and up into a range of hills, called Mount Gilboa, on the south side of Esdraelon, overlooking the Amorite city of *Beth-shan*. The graphic story of the fight says, "The battle went sore against Saul; and the archers hit him; and he was sore wounded of the archers" (I Sam. 31:3). We catch an echo of the conflict in Genesis: "Joseph is a fruitful bough,—a fruitful bough by a well, whose branches run over the wall. *The archers have sorely grieved him, and shot at him, and hated him*" (Gen. 49:22–23).

Philistines fasten bodies of Saul and three sons upon wall of Amorite Beth-shan.—Finding the king and three sons dead upon the field of battle, the victors took an extraordinary and spectacular course. Carrying the royal corpses down from the hills, and across the valley to the Amorite stronghold of Beth-shan, they fastened, or hung, the bodies to the city wall. This act, speaking more loudly than words, held up to the scorn of the older Amorite inhabitants of Canaan the king who had perfidiously broken the solemn treaty of Israel with the city of Gibeon by attacking that place and slaying some of its people. For not only did the Philistines aim to prevent the growth of nationality in the house of Joseph, *but the conquerors wanted also to widen the breach between Israel and the older population of Canaan*, thus holding the Amorite walled cities on the side of the Philistines against the Hebrew farmers and shepherds who lived in the hill villages. News about the ignominious exposure of Saul's body on the fortifications of Beth-shan would spread all

over the country, serving better than any proclamation to re-
mind the Amorites that the treaty-breaking Hebrews were subjugated and that their king was destroyed.

Hebrew mishpat régime challenged by Philistines.—We
have seen that these implacable enemies of Israel based their
power on five walled cities in the coastal plain, located upon the
pathways of commerce. By their economic situation, therefore,
they represented the *baalistic* idea of property as contrasted
with the simple, mishpat régime of the Hebrew clans. The Philistine city which lay nearest Israel was *Ekron;* and the god of
that city was *Baal-zebub* (II Kings 1:2–3). Accordingly, it is not
strange that the Philistines gave the epic imagination of Israel
a title for the chief adversary of Yahweh, and that the deity of
Ekron, under the name *Beelzebub*, should at length have become
the *prince of devils* in the New Testament (Matt. 12:24). Like
Sisera, who led the hosts of Amorite baalism against Yahweh in
the days of Deborah and Barak, so now, on a grander stage, the
Baal-worshiping Philistines challenged, and sought to destroy
forever, the mishpat régime of Yahweh and Israel.

But still mightier forces were gathering against the conquerors. And when we consider the final outcome of Hebrew evolution, we must have great sympathy for the Deuteronomic and
priestly editors and compilers who, not comprehending the sociological facts, were eager to interpolate into the early documents their tales of miraculous help from heaven, the death-
dealing power of the ark, and the awe-inspiring revelations at
Sinai in the desert. For in a real, psychological sense the miracle
stories of the Bible produce upon the conventional mass mind
the same effect which is left upon the candid investigator after
long study of Hebrew evolution as a purely natural process.
Crude supernaturalism, in other words, is an easy short-cut to
the intellectually more refined position reached through arduous
toil by the scientific historian.

David, as Philistine vassal, forms Kingdom of Hebron, or Judah.—The Philistine village of Ziklag had been given to David as a residence; and upon receiving there the news of Saul's death, David and his force of six hundred men at once went up into the southern hill-country, establishing themselves at the Calebite village of *Hebron*. But in view of the overwhelming triumph at Gilboa, and the status of the Philistines as masters of the Josephite highlands, it would have been suicidal for David to renounce the suzerainty of the victors; and it was therefore as a vassal of the conquerors that he received the allegiance of the clans inhabiting the district later to be known as Judah. The Philistines could easily have crushed him, but they made no move. And thus, to all appearances, the situation justified what we have supposed to be the logic of Saul's opposition to David. The Philistines were now virtually in control of all Canaan; David's hands were tied; *and he was compelled for seven and one-half years to maintain an attitude of watchful waiting at Hebron.*

During this time the remnant of the dead monarch's family was under the charge of Saul's general, Abner, who retired to Gilead, where a weak son of Saul, by the name of *Ishbaal*, was proclaimed king of Israel. But this unlucky son of Saul reigned only as a shadow-king in far-away Gilead; and when he crossed the river into Ephraim, seeking to establish himself west of Jordan in the house of Joseph, *he was driven back by David.* Thus the people of the highlands were now divided against themselves; *while the Philistines could look upon David as their agent in crushing the house of their old enemy Saul* (II Sam., chaps. 2-4).

David consolidates peasant aristocracy in south under name of "Judah."—The name "Judah," as applied to southern Canaan, is clearly the work of David, who formed a little tribe, or kingdom, out of the diverse and alien clans inhabiting that region. The term "Judah" is heard of at first only in connection with Bethlehem, the headquarters of David's family, as the designation of a small district in that neighborhood (see chap. v, pp. 40–41). But the home village of David would not have served as a capital of the new combination which he was creating, for it was too small and was not located centrally enough. So he chose the Calebite village, or town, of Hebron as the base of his operations; and since David was a Judahite, the term "Judah" naturally spread over the entire district which acknowledged his leadership, just as the name "France" gradually extended from the district of Paris and overspread all Gaul.

The work of David at Hebron, then, was to organize the peasant proprietors of south Canaan into a single community under a single name. This new political group formed a landholding, slave-owning aristocracy identical in its nature with the upper social class in the house of Joseph, *but more pastoral and primitive*. A good illustration is found in the case of Nabal the Calebite, who had lands near Hebron, and who owned three thousand sheep and a thousand goats. His complaint was, *"There be many slaves [abadim] that break away now a days, every man from his master"* (I Sam. 25:2–10 f.). Nabal was no doubt wealthier than the average; but his case gives a vivid glimpse into social conditions at the south, where an upper class was coming into existence and exploiting the labor of slaves.

The story of Nabal is related to the career of David in quite an interesting way. The estates of this Calebite landlord were at one time protected by David's men, who did police duty in driving off marauders. But when a tax was laid upon the property of Nabal, to pay for the service, he refused to recognize any obligation. David's men thereupon closed in to enforce collection; and the man's wife Abigail, with great enterprise, paid the tax herself. When this became known to Nabal, he was immediately taken sick; and "Yahweh smote Nabal, so that he died."

But when David heard the news, he said, "Blessed be Yahweh," and made Abigail his wife.

Hebrew evolution based upon two groups of peasant aristocrats, north and south.—Before we go farther, it should now be emphasized (partly by way of review) that Hebrew history is pivoted upon two distinct aristocratic peasant organizations: On the one hand, in the north, was the larger and earlier Josephite group, which took form through the work of Deborah, Barak, Ehud, Gideon, Samuel, and Saul. This community, identified with the hills of Ephraim, was based upon a long-drawn-out "proto-Deuteronomic" conquest, ending with the destruction of Amorite Shechem, which made possible the rise of peasant slave-owners, under a uniform régime of mishpat landholding all through that region. The Yahweh cult in Ephraim was directly in contact with deep-seated Amorite legal usages, and was, therefore, missionary and propagandist in its impulse. The *Ephraimite* source in the Pentateuch regards the worship of Yahweh as the result of conversion from polytheism (Josh. 24: 14); and this document makes Jacob at Bethel put away all "strange gods," burying them in the earth (Gen. 35:1–4).

On the other hand, in the south was the smaller and later-organized group, which took form under the name of "Judah" through the work of David. This group was always more primitive and pastoral than the house of Joseph; and at first it had no connection with the independent Amorite city of Jebus, or Jerusalem, *which lay on middle ground between south and north.* David's work at Hebron, twenty miles to the south of Jerusalem, was that of combining into a single tribe, or kingdom, such non-Hebrew clans as the Calebites, Jerachmeelites, and Kenites— the latter having been adherents of Yahweh in the desert when the early Joseph group was in Goshen. The history of the Yahweh cult in the south of Canaan was unlike its history in Ephraim; for in contrast with the house of Joseph, *the south was more directly in touch with the desert and more shut away from Amorite baalism.* Thus, Yahwism in the south had the character of a native cult; and while the tribe of Judah, as a full-fledged organization, was indeed a late-comer in Israel, yet the sense of Yahweh in the south was older and more intimate than in the house of Joseph. *Thus the tribe of Judah, in its very origin, as well as by its later history, was prepared to take a distinct and unique place in the remarkable evolution slowly unfolding before us.* And, accordingly, the Judaic, or J, document in the Pentateuch looks upon the name and cult of Yahweh as having been recognized in primeval ages among non-Hebrews, just as it was known among the Kenites and other non-Hebraic elements in south Canaan (Gen. 4:26).

But an inconsistency was perceived between the actual historic adoption of the Yahweh cult in the wilderness at a *certain time* and its alleged vogue among Gentiles in *prehistoric* ages. This fact intruded itself more and more upon the consciousness of the editors who combined the Judaic and Ephraimite documents into a single story. And so the very *latest* of the Judaic scribes, in the Babylonian Exile, writing what we call the *Priestly* documents, undertook to smooth out the incongruity: Unable to deny that the *name* "Yahweh" was first current among the Hebrews in the Exodus period, the Priestly document nevertheless claims that Yahweh was only known to the patriarchs as "El Shaddai," but that he was *not* known to them by his name "Yahweh" (Exod. 6:2–3 [P]). Yet we read repeatedly in the J document that Abraham built an altar, "and called by means of [or in the name of] *Yahweh*" (Gen. 12:8[J]; 13:4[J]). And again we read that Isaac built an altar, "and called by means of [or in the name of] Yahweh" (Gen. 26:25[J]). These various documents, however, crystallized into sacred, unchangeable form before they could be ironed out into an absolutely consistent narrative with appropriate theological explanations. And the harmonizing process could not have been pushed forward rigorously without making the text of Scripture unintelligible; because the documents are based upon social, economic, and historical differences between the house of Joseph in the north and the house of Judah in the south, which were necessary to the religious development of Israel.

Hebrew history, indeed, would have been impossible without the evolution of these two groups, which were only combined into a single nation for about eighty years under the house of David, *but were distinct and hostile before and after that brief period*. The conventional treatment of Hebrew history which contemplates the age of Saul as a new epoch, wherein the monarchy of David simply continues that of his royal predecessor, is very inaccurate and misleading. For it throws a camouflage of superficial terms over a process which does not really make a new turning-point in the time of Saul. The real, underlying, and largely ignored process was the organization and solidification of *two distinct peasant aristocracies*, northern and southern, which, through slow stages, developed a Hebrew complex marked by outstanding ideas which are symbolized in the words *Yahweh-Israel-mishpat*, but which never became truly harmonized into a uniform nation, or people. The evolution of these two aristocracies (holding land by mishpat usage, and superimposed upon a lower class of alien slaves, or *abadim*) began with the conquest of the central highlands by the house of Joseph, and reached a period with the completion of David's preliminary rule at Hebron, where he created the house and Kingdom of Judah. These two peasant aristocracies, *divided by neutral territory on which lay the Amorite city of Jebus, or Jerusalem*, were then on the verge of political union under the dynasty of David.

Following death of Saul at Gilboa, conditions gradually become intolerable.—The state of Canaan after the Philistine victory at Gilboa, while pleasing to the conquerors, grew more and more chaotic, and at length became insufferable to the subjugated population, from Beersheba in the extreme south to Dan in the far north. The Philistine power bestrode the whole country like a relentless giant. The inhabitants of the land lay divided and feeble. David was welding the south into unity. The house of Saul, forced over into Gilead, east of Jordan, sought to regain a foothold west of the river, but was repeatedly thrown back by David. The central highlands, without a national head, were dropping into anarchy; while the provinces north of Esdraelon, mixed in blood and always of doubtful Hebrew character, seem to have been disorganized by Philistine occupation (I Sam. 31:7). The time was indeed ripe for change; and a new era of history was about to open.

CHAPTER VIII

AMORITE CITIES ENTER MONARCHY

House of Joseph makes David king of Israel.—After seven years of anarchy, the peasants of north and south sent delegates to Hebron with authority to make David king of *Israel;* and it is clear that in this action the major power was the house of Joseph, without which David could never have become ruler of the enlarged Hebrew nation. The delegates made a covenant with David "before Yahweh" (*liphnae Yahweh*). This term shows that the proceeding was not only a political event, but that it was also a religious transaction which took place at an altar (II Sam. 5:3). One who is accustomed to the modern separation of Church and State finds difficulty in comprehending the vital and intimate connection of religion and politics in the social processes of antiquity. Our investigation of the Judges period has helped us to realize that Hebrew evolution centered around the "Yahweh cult" as originating in tribal obscurity and slowly advancing upon a broader stage; and this principle comes into view still more clearly as we trace the dramatic rise of David.

But while David's accession to the Hebrew throne was indeed a religious event as well as a political transaction, we must be careful to observe that it had no ecclesiastical, or *priestly*, character in the sense imagined by the Judaic editor of Samuel. The later scribes held that the legitimacy of Hebrew kingship was based upon a categorical divine decree, communicated through the medium of Samuel as a *priest*, and validated by the anointing of both Saul and David at the hands of this Ephraimite ecclesiastic (I Sam. 10:1; 16:13). The priestly, or ecclesiastical, version is constructed out of whole cloth, and interpolated by the redactor; while the real, secular history, as a politico-religious evolution, is narrated in the sources describing the choice of Saul at Gilgal by "the people" (I Sam. 11:15), and of David at Hebron by the delegates of the tribes: "So all the elders .... *anointed* David king over Israel" (II Sam. 5:3). David, therefore, not only owed his throne to the house of Joseph, but he became the "anointed" (or *masheah*) not by priestly intervention but through the elders, or *zikanim*.

The choice of David as king of Israel was at once interpreted by the Philistines as an act of rebellion against their authority. But after the seven long years during which David had been a virtual agent of the conquerors in restraining the house of Saul, the Philistines were taken by surprise; they had no idea of the ambition surging in the brain of this remarkable person; and before they could send an army into the highlands, David executed a master-stroke.

David seizes Amorite city of Jebus, or Jerusalem, without destruction or massacre.—One element in the weakness of Saul was his lack of a *walled city* as a base of operations, upon which he could retire when pressed by invaders. His capital was never anything but an open, undefended country village; and he had neither funds nor opportunity for the construction of a great fortress. But in contrast with Saul, David's first act, as king of Israel, was to secure an appropriate stronghold from which to govern the country, and into which he could retreat if attacked by too powerful an enemy. He realized at once that the little town of Hebron, which had served well as a capital for his Kingdom of Judah, could not be headquarters for all Israel. Its location was too far from the center of the new monarchy, and would alienate the jealous, high-spirited house of Joseph, which might easily flare up into rebellion against the south, as it actually did later. Nor could the seat of government be established in the hill-country of Ephraim, for two reasons: first, because the central highlands were full of open villages without any strong city; and, second, because the south might quickly fall into the hands of the Philistines if David located his new headquarters too far from Judah. Moreover, an Ephraimite capital would alienate the *south* as readily as a Jewish capital would estrange the *north*.

Whether all these considerations were clearly present in the mind of David we cannot say. But, in any case, he acted like a true genius in doing what proved to be *essential* under the circumstances. For he hit upon the novel plan of using a hitherto unconquered Amorite stronghold as a capital for the new nation which he was creating. The walled city of Jebus, or Jerusalem, occupied neutral ground between Judah and Ephraim. This place David captured by a ruse, without breaking down the walls or slaughtering the inhabitants. Treating the Jebusites with as much consideration as possible, the king merely occupied a fort on a hill called *Zion*, which dominated the city; and here he took up his residence for the time being. "So David lived in the fort, and called it the City of David" (II Sam. 5:6–9). And here we arrive at the situation depicted by a little fragment of the J, or Yahwistic, source preserved in the Book of Joshua: "As for the Jebusites, the inhabitants of Jerusalem, the children of Judah could not drive them out; *but the Jebusites live with the children of Judah at Jerusalem unto this day*" (Josh. 15:63). This part of the J document was written by a scribe who lived before the assimilation of Israel and the Amorites.

War prestige of Yahweh revived by David.—At last the time had arrived when accounts could be squared with the insolent lords of the coastal cities, under whose yoke the highlanders had lain for more than seven long years. When a primitive social group is defeated in battle, it begins to regard its god with mingled feelings; and when defeat is turned into subjugation, so that the group loses political identity, under a conqueror's heel, its cult naturally dies out, along with the dissolution of its corporate consciousness. What good is a god who cannot defend his worshipers? On this theory, when crops fail in China, the peasants beat the idols which they have placed in the fields to bring fertility. And thus, if the Philistines had succeeded in stamping out the corporate sense which prevailed among the Josephites, reducing them to permanent slavery and selling them as chattels into foreign lands, according to ancient custom, their loss of nationality would have carried the Yahweh cult into oblivion, so far as the house of Joseph was concerned.

These considerations help us to realize how greatly the war prestige of Yahweh had suffered through the conquest of the central highlands by the Philistines, and the death of Saul in the battle of Gilboa. The Josephites had not lost all faith in Yahweh; but in their depressed condition they were no longer able to develop leaders of their *own*, and therefore they accepted the guidance of David, who combined personal ambition with enthusiasm for Yahweh. Calling out the forces of Judah and of Joseph, David met the Philistines in the southern hills, inflicting upon them a terrible defeat, and vindicating the claims of a new and united Israel to the right of nationhood. The remarkable personality of David therefore became the center, or focus, around which the waning prestige of Yahweh revived and the real Hebrew nation of world-history, with its capital at Amorite Jerusalem, came into existence. And thus the house of Judah began to save Israel and take its own, rightful place in the broadening stream of Hebrew consciousness which now began to pass almost imperceptibly into a new psychological era corresponding to the sociological evolution.

Philistine defeat a milestone marking application of Amorite name "Baal" to Yahweh.—Only a meager account has come down to us of the battle in which David avenged Gilboa and lifted the Philistine yoke from the necks of the highlanders. But the action is memorable because it spelled the downfall of the Philistine power, and because it marks the beginning of a new attitude with reference to Yahweh as a divinity of Canaan. The place where the battle occurred is said to have been called by David "Baal-perazim"; but the striking and profound significance of the term, as used here, is not at first apparent in modern versions of the Bible: "And David said, Yahweh has broken [*parats*] mine enemies, like the breach [*perets*] of waters. *Therefore he called the name of that place 'Baal-peratsim'*" (II Sam. 5:20). In other words, Yahweh was conceived as having broken forth upon the Philistines like a flood of waters; and *therefore* David called the place "The Breakings-Forth of Baal." The explicit meaning of the passage is that Hebrew psychology had now reached a point where Yahweh, at first a god of desert mishpat, was being naturalized and acclimated, under the Amorite name "Baal," as a local divinity of Canaan. But nobody in David's time (least of all the king himself) realized the problem which this usage insensibly foretold, and which was one day to overshadow the whole outlook of the Hebrew mind.

David brings Josephite ark of Yahweh from "Baal Judah" to mount Zion.—Further evidence of growing baalistic thought is found in David's course following the Philistine defeat. The Ephraimite "ark of Yahweh," which the Philistines captured in the time of Eli, had lain all these years in an Amorite city called "Kirjath-jearim," under Philistine control (I Sam. 7:1). This cult object, however, was made available to the Hebrews again by the victory of Baal-perazim. But, in the meanwhile, the city of Kirjath-jearim had acquired a new name: "Baalah, which is Kirjath-jearim" (Josh. 15:9 [late document P]). And after defeating the Philistines, David went here to get the ark and bring it up to Jerusalem; so that any prestige connected with it could be capitalized by the new king as legitimate successor of the Josephite Saul. Accordingly we read, "And David arose, and went with all the people that were with him, to Baale-Judah, to bring up from thence the ark" (II Sam. 6:2). Kirjath-jearim clearly got its new name from the ark, symbolizing Yahweh, who was more and more spoken of as a Baal. And under these conditions of compromise with Amorite nomenclature, the ark of Yahweh made its triumphant progress from the old, pre-Hebrew city of Kirjath-jearim to the ancient, pre-Hebrew city of Jerusalem, where it was placed in a tent on the hill of Zion. With his ark resting thus in David's fort, and his military prestige revived by the victory of Baal-perazim, Yahweh could once again be thought of as "a god of hosts, mighty in battle."

David, in contrast with predecessor, follows policy of peace with Amorites.—Jerusalem and other walled cities of Canaan were treated by David, not as conquered territory, but as legal parts of that new, enlarged Hebrew kingdom which was the only guaranty against Philistine supremacy. Not only is this clear from the logic of the situation, which dictated peace and forbade war, between Israel and the Amorites, but positive evidence bears witness to David's reversal of his predecessor's hate policy toward the older population. Saul, as we have seen, attacked and slew people belonging to the Amorite city of Gibeon in defiance of a sworn treaty. And now some striking gesture was needed to heal the breach and assure all the Amorite cities that Israel would act on a policy of good faith and peace. David therefore suddenly arrested seven men of the house of Saul, and gave them over to the Amorites of Gibeon, *who hung them in revenge for Saul's deed* (II Sam. 21:1–10). We do not know what time in David's reign this happened; but it reveals the *attitude* of the king toward the inhabitants of the Amorite walled cities in a highly dramatic way, whose meaning would not be lost upon the older inhabitants of the land. For an impressive transaction of this kind would be at once reported in all the Amorite cities, and help to neutralize the effect of Saul's policy.

Another instructive example of David's attitude is found in his relation to an Amorite citizen of Jerusalem named Araunah. This Jebusite comes before us, long after David's capture of the city, in full and acknowledged possession of his real estate, which the king *buys* of him for fifty shekels of silver (II Sam. 24:18–25). This evidence, together with David's treatment of the Amorites at Gibeon, and the lack of any assertion that he subjugated the walled cities, or took the lands of their inhabitants, proclaim David's departure from the Josephite, "proto-Deuteronomic" policy of "thorough," as exemplified in the complete destruction of Jericho, Bethel, and Shechem, and in Saul's attack on the Gibeonites. The house of Joseph annihilated Jericho, Bethel, and Shechem, and carved out a wide place in the central highlands where mishpat tenure of the soil could be supreme. But we hear of no such conquest by David; and the better his reign is understood, the more clearly we perceive that any subjugation, or extermination, of the remaining Amorite cities and property-holders would have been impossible within the terms of his policy. *"And there was peace between Israel and the Amorites"* (I Sam. 7:14). This notice evidently relates to the period of the united Hebrew monarchy under David. *Peace* between social groups in ancient times was possible only through deliberate and formal sanction, as when Israel took a solemn oath to the Amorites of Gibeon (II Sam. 21:2); and the more extensive peace which now came to prevail between Israel and the Canaanite cities outside the highlands of Ephraim rested upon the same foundation. Thus, while the pre-Hebrew inhabitants of *central* Canaan had been either exterminated or enslaved by the house of Joseph, the upper class in the Amorite cities outside that region were gradually assimilated with the aristocracy of Israel, as in the case of Araunah the Jebusite, who calls David "My lord the King" (II Sam. 24:21).

David's comprehensive policy revealed also by marriage alliances, from south to north.—In contrast with Saul, David entered into marriage alliances linking him with the whole country, from Judah to Dan. We have already noticed that in the south he married the Calebite woman Abigail. He also had another wife, Ahinoam, from the same district (II Sam. 3:2–3). And after capturing Jebus, "He took him yet more concubines and wives out of Jerusalem" (5:13). In the meanwhile, Michal, the daughter of Saul, who had been taken away from David by her father, was given back to him (I Sam. 25:44; II Sam. 3:13–16). These alliances connected the new king with Caleb-Judah, Jerusalem, and Ephraim. But going still farther north, and even before his election as king of all Israel, he had become related by marriage with non-Hebrew elements in the vicinity of Dan, which are mentioned as follows by the J source: "The children of Israel drove not out the Geshurites nor the Maachathites; but the Geshurites and the Maachathites dwell in the midst of Israel until this day" (Josh. 13:13). While still at Hebron, planning for the future, David married into the aristocracy of these foreigners by obtaining "Maacah the daughter of Talmai, king of Geshur" (II Sam. 3:3). This foreign woman is of special interest as mother of the notorious *Absalom*, who gave his father David so much trouble at a later time.

Intermarriage and assimilation take place between Israelites and Amorites.—Based upon the example of David, and following the pattern of the *actual history*, an instructive legend of Genesis makes the mythical patriarch Judah go down to Adullam and become the father of children by his Canaanite wife, Shua, and also by another Canaanite woman, Tamar (Gen., chap. 38). In the present work (see chap. v, p. 41), we have already observed that it was really *David*, and not a legendary forefather, who went down to Adullam and married Canaanite women (I Sam. 22:1; II Sam. 23:13); and the feminine name "Tamar" is found only in David's family (II Sam. 13:1; 14:27). The Canaanite woman Tamar is mentioned with respect in the very late Book of Ruth as one who built the house of Judah (Ruth 4:12); while the Book of Ruth itself tells how a foreign woman out of *Moab*, east of Jordan, married Boaz, a citizen of Bethlehem-Judah, and became the great-grandmother of David. That the tribe of Simeon, like the tribe of Judah, was built up from intermixture with alien blood is revealed by parallel and identical passages in Genesis and Exodus, which refer to

"Shaul the son of a Canaanitish woman" (Gen. 46:10; Exod. 6:15).

David, therefore, based the enlarged Hebrew kingdom not only on the two peasant aristocracies represented by the tribal names Judah and Joseph, but he was also in favor of intermarriage between the Israelite *upper class* in the rural districts and the Amorite *nobility* whose headquarters were in the walled cities of Canaan. During and after the reign of David, then, we at length reach the historical situation implied by the notice in Judges, chapter 3: "*And the children of Israel dwelt among the Canaanites; and they took their daughters to be their wives, and gave their daughters to their sons, and served their gods, ... the Baalim*" (Judg. 3:6, 7). Assimilation on a large scale now set in between the Israelite aristocracy of the open villages and the Amorite aristocracy of the walled cities which, under the administration of the new king, opened their gates and became a part of the newly forming *Hebrew nation*.

Social and cult war impossible in David's time.—No one living in that early age of Hebrew history could foresee the mighty spiritual consequences that were to flow from this gradual amalgamation between the followers of Yahweh (within whose cult was the mishpat impulse toward non-commercial, kindred ownership of the soil) and the native devotees of the Amorite Baalim (whose cults went along with individual property in land on the basis of sale, exchange, and mortgage). For in the days of David, the great problem of the hour was not conflict, but *assimilation;* not avoidance of intermarriage, but *racial friendship and union* between Israel and the Amorites, who were driven together by military necessity through relentless Philistine pressure.

Thus we begin to realize how the crude, partly evolved and heterogeneous nation was as yet very far from the period when the cults of Yahweh and of Baal were to clash in deadly war as the result of property concentration in the right wing of a baal-

ized Hebrew aristocracy. To imagine that anybody in the time
of David had any idea of religious conflict between Yahweh and
Baal—or that the Mosaic Law was already in existence, with its
demand for complete massacre of the Amorite population—is
wholly to misapprehend the nature and course of Hebrew history. The social tension which was to produce the *Law* had not
yet arisen; and instead of warfare between Yahweh and Baal,
the whole tendency of the hour was toward the formation of a
pantheon embracing Yahweh and other gods in a single group,
*and in which, as we have seen, Yahweh tended to lose his earlier
identity under the Amorite name Baal.*

David builds Hebrew empire, and becomes "king of kings."
—At that period of history, a monarch who did not go beyond
his own frontiers, and show his power by subjugating weaker
peoples, would be in constant danger of attack by envious
neighbors. So after David had thoroughly chastised the Philistines, he turned his forces against the Moabites, the Ammonites,
the Syrians, and the Edomites (II Sam. 8:1–14; 10:1–14; 12:
26–31). In fact, this remarkable monarch rose quickly from his
position as king of Israel; for he not only defeated, but also subjugated, neighboring peoples, putting them to tribute, and rising
to political superiority over several kings. Thus David not only
created the Hebrew nation, but made it a small empire, and became a "king of kings."

**Corresponding change in conception of Yahweh as "god of
gods."**—That the evolution of the Yahweh-idea was instru-
mental in the rise toward higher views of Deity, and that the scientific investigator cannot gainsay theistic faith or belief in relation to Hebrew history, are points emphasized in another connection (cf. Preface). The David narrative says that "Yahweh
gave David the victory whithersoever he went" (II Sam. 8:6,
14). But actually the statement should be turned around, to
read that "David gave Yahweh the victory whithersoever he
went"; or that "David's assurance communicated itself to the

army, and helped to bring victory, and led to exaltation of the Yahweh-idea." For the rise of the Hebrew empire, wherein David was "king of kings," brought with it the conditions which put Yahweh on the way toward imperialization as "god of gods."

At the same time, however, this was only one phase of the religious development, and the mere imperialization of Yahweh was nothing *unique* in antiquity. It was not the equivalent of *monotheism;* and considered as a mere process which raised one or another god above the level of competing divinities, it was *crassly materialistic and non-ethical.* Not only so; but without the later work of the insurgent prophets, the Yahweh-idea would have passed into oblivion, like other imperial god-ideas.

David constructed stage for Yahweh-Baal struggle over mishpat.—Although David, as viewed from the standpoint of higher criticism and sociology, is very unlike the David of orthodoxy, he remains a factor of tremendous importance in the evolution of religion. For he not only rescued Yahweh from the low estate into which the Hebrew divinity had been carried by the subjugation of the house of Joseph under the Philistine yoke, but *without realizing the nature of his achievement*, he constructed the stage on which alone was possible the Yahweh-Baal conflict over the problem of mishpat, or social justice. If Hebrew history had remained in the era typified by the house of Joseph, which culminated in the narrow, provincial monarchy of Saul, no upward spiritual evolution would have been possible. For until the time of David, as we have learned, the house of Joseph was only a rural kinship group, which had effected a "proto-Deuteronomic" conquest of central Canaan, culminating in the fall of Shechem and the annihilation of the baalistic régime in the hill-country of Ephraim, resulting in the triumph of mishpat as an unopposed, or *static*, ideal.

But, on the other hand, although David was a "man of blood," he was, at the same time, a tactful politician; and so, in contrast with Saul, he broadened the structure of the Josephite monarchy to include the baalistic Amorites and their walled cities within the framework of the Hebrew nation. His purpose in taking this course was to defeat the Philistines. *Nevertheless, the Davidic policy brought baalism and mishpat face to face within the limits of the same social group, thus gradually creating the conditions of a struggle between two moral codes, which converted the primitive mishpat from a static ideal into a dynamic, evolving spiritual power, compelled to oppose baalism on ethical grounds instead of on the plane of mere physical annihilation.*

Social control transferred from country to city.—In David's childhood, the Israelite element in Canaan was purely pastoral, agricultural, and non-commercial, being identified with open villages in the country. These conditions were scarcely changed in the fifteen-year term of Saul's reign. And yet, within the space of David's lifetime, not only were the village clans organized and consolidated on a wider territorial expanse, *but the political forces of the nation were suddenly focalized within the Amorite city of Jebus, or Jerusalem.* The country shepherd-lad of Bethlehem gradually became an effete, oriental monarch, dwelling within the shelter of stout city walls, influenced by his large harem, and swayed by the counsels of men who were already learning to ignore the social standpoint of kinship groups in the open country. Social transformations are not accomplished quickly; but the reign of David was a kind of "watershed," marking a point where the stream of social force began to flow in a new direction.

Landholding and slave-owning aristocracy under early Davidic monarchy.—A number of illustrations are available showing the status of landed aristocracy under the earlier Davidic monarchy. The first is that of the prince *Absalom*, who emerges abruptly into view as a proprietor in the highlands of Joseph (II Sam. 13, 23–29). His estate was at a place called suggestively *Baal-hazor*, north of Bethel in the hill-country of

Ephraim, where he owned flocks of sheep, which were tended and sheared by slaves, or *abadim* (cf. 14:30, 31, where *abadim* is rendered "servants" three times). Absalom's facilities at Baal-hazor were so extensive that he was able to entertain "all the king's sons" at one time (13:23, 29).

Another example is *Joab ben Zeruiah,* whose early home property was located somewhere in the wilder part of Judah, but who appears later as a landlord in Ephraim, with an estate yielding barley, near that of Absalom at Baal-hazor (I Kings 2:33–34; II Sam. 14:28–31).

Both Joab and Absalom were natives of Judah, not of Ephraim; and they could only have acquired land in the closely settled house of Joseph through disturbance of mishpat claims in the north, whether by purchase, or by some high-handed exercise of the royal power in their behalf. But in any case—and even at this early period—they show the tendency toward formation of a wealthy group on the extreme right wing of the free upper class.

A further view of the aristocracy under the house of David is found in the case of *Shimei ben Gera,* of the tribe of Benjamin. This man's home was at a place called Bahurim (II Sam. 19:16). Removing to Jerusalem, he built there a new house for permanent residence, and thus became an absentee landlord. That he was a slaveholder is interestingly shown by a story about two of his human chattels who ran away into Philistia (I Kings 2:36–40; *abadim* translated "servants" four times [vss. 39, 40]). This case recalls the observation attributed to the Calebite aristocrat Nabal: "There be many *abadim* now a days that run away" (I Sam. 25:10).

Royal authority largely concerned with disposition of land.— That the authority of the king was largely concerned with the disposition of *land* is evident from a remark attributed to Saul when he feared that David would overshadow him: *"Will the son of Jesse give every one of you fields and vineyards?"* (I Sam.

22:7). Sitting as a court of last resort, David ruled that all the land of Saul should belong to the son of his friend Jonathan (II Sam. 9:6–7). Later, he changed his ruling, and gave part of the estate to another person (19:29–30). That the king would have much to do with landed possessions, and not always according to the peasants' idea of mishpat, is claimed in the speech placed in the mouth of Samuel by the Deuteronomist, which is even more significant as an evidence of accomplished fact than it would have been as a mere prediction: "This will be the *mishpat* of the king that shall reign over you. . . . . He will take your fields, and your vineyards, and your olive-yards, even the best of them, and give them to his servants" (I Sam. 8:11, 14). It was doubtless in some such way as this that Absalom and Joab got their landed possessions in Ephraim.

Peasant aristocracy compelled to sue for mishpat in Amorite city.—When the peasant landlords of the new Davidic monarchy had any dispute about mishpat, they found themselves under the inconvenient necessity of taking an appeal to the royal court at Jebus, or Jerusalem, *for final settlement.* That free landlords, who formerly settled all their affairs through local courts composed of elders from the neighborhood, should *now* be compelled to go a long distance for justice was in itself a hardship. Nevertheless, David's prestige as the deliverer of Israel from the Philistine yoke, and as a conqueror shedding glory on the nation, as well as his personal tact, would at first have a tendency to overcome the natural reluctance of the free clansmen to a distant jurisdiction. And so the earlier accounts of the reign say, "David executed *mishpat* and righteousness unto all his people" (II Sam. 8:15).

But, in course of time, the novelty of appealing to a famous leader wore off, while the king's preoccupation with many affairs made access to him increasingly difficult. It would seem to have been well to appoint judges; but the government was not yet fully organized, and apparently no deputies were installed,

or even available, for the delicate function of giving final decisions on appeal. An intolerable situation would arise when provincial freemen could hold cases open against the judgment of
local elders by resorting to the royal court and failing to get the
king's ear *promptly*. Hebrew peasants, from the time of the
original conquest, were marked by reaction against fortified
cities as the strongholds of alien power. The wayfaring Levite
in the Judges period, who passed by the walls of Jerusalem
when the day was "far spent," said to his companions, "We will
not turn aside hither into the city of a stranger that is not of the
B'nae Yisrael" (Judg. 19:12). And it is easy to see why a royal
authority identified with this Amorite citadel should, after a
time, grow vexatious to the clansmen of the open villages, not
merely from the legal standpoint, but also in other ways.

Rebellions against rule of David presage final break.—That
the rebellions which took place in the latter part of David's
reign gave play to the personal feelings of prominent men who
took part in these movements is doubtless true. But such up-
risings never occur without having a popular basis. One of the
leaders heading the first rebellion was a landlord named *Ahitophel*, from the village of Giloh in the hills of Judah. This man
was a member of David's royal council in Jerusalem; and we are
told that his advice *"was as if one had inquired at the oracle of
God"* (II Sam. 15:12; 16:23). Ahitophel, it is true, was the
grandfather of Bath-sheba, whom David had stolen from her
husband, Uriah the Hittite (II Sam. 11:3; 23:34); and he may
have harbored private malice against the king on this account.
But, even so, the personal feelings of a few leaders like Ahitophel
would not be enough to explain a great popular insurrection.
And the same observation applies to one of the other conspira-
tors, Absalom, a son of David, who sought to use the prevailing
social unrest for the purpose of seizing authority in place of his
father. An instructive sense of the situation can be gained from
the narrative relating to Absalom's activities:

And Absalom rose up early, and stood beside the gate. And when any man that had a law-suit came to the king for *mishpat*, then Absalom called unto him, and said, Of what city art thou? And he said, Thy servant is from one of the tribes of Israel. And Absalom said unto him, See! thy case is good and right; *but there is none from the king to hear thee.* And Absalom said, Oh that I were made judge in the land, so that every man which hath a case or *mishpat* might come unto me. And on this manner did Absalom to all Israel that came to the king for *mishpat* [II Sam. 15:2–6, *passim*].

The insurrection led to a great battle wherein Absalom was killed, and which was followed at once by a new outbreak under the Benjaminite landlord, *Sheba ben Bichri*, who roused the hill-country of Ephraim with the cry, "We have no part in David; neither have we inheritance in the son of Jesse: *every man to his tents, O Israel!*" (II Sam. 20:1).

Revolts crushed by standing army of "gibborim."—In illustration of David's growing despotism, it is important to notice that the king's authority was upheld by a regiment of professional mercenaries known as "Cherethites and Pelethites," who formed a standing military force of six hundred at Jerusalem (II Sam. 8:18; 15:18; 20:7). These men were called "strong ones," or *gibborim* (17:8; 20:7, translated "mighty men"). The singular form of the word is *gibbor* (Amos. 2:14; Isa. 3:2). The gibborim were on the side of David in the two revolts that occurred while he was king; and they were the deciding factor on both occasions. The captain of the Cherethites and Pelethites was *Benaiah ben Jehoiada* (II Sam. 8:18; 20:23; 23:20–23). The name of this officer, Benaiah, signifies in Hebrew, "Yahweh has built up"; and we shall see how his activities promoted the fortunes of the house of David in the events that are now to follow.

Upheld by gibborim, Solomon succeeds David on Hebrew throne.—Both David and Saul had been chosen by vote of the peasant aristocracy. But the manner in which the next occupant of the throne became king illustrates the almost inevitable advance of eastern despotism when once a government has been established in a fortified city. The general public was not consulted; the peasantry of the rural villages were ignored. There were a number of possible candidates for the succession; but a palace intrigue revolved around Solomon, the son of David by Bathsheba, the woman whom the king had stolen from her husband. Born and bred in the Amorite city of Jerusalem, this prince had no sympathy with the masses of the people; and his outlook on life was that of the oriental voluptuary.

Upon David's orders, therefore, Benaiah, commander of the gibborim, assembled his force of "Cherethites and Pelethites," and gave military support and prestige to Solomon, who thus became "the anointed of Yahweh" by grace of David and the standing army (I Kings 1:32, 36, 38). But before the new king felt safe on his father's throne, a number of important individuals had to be put out of the way. His procedure in each case was the same, calling for Benaiah and commanding him, "Go, fall on so and so"; whereupon Benaiah would immediately seek the designated person and slay him (I Kings 2:13–25, 28–34, 36–46). In addition to his post as head of the police at the capital, Benaiah was now appointed by Solomon to be commander-in-chief of the Israelite militia whenever it should be mobilized. This office carried with it wide military powers over the inhabitants of the open country.

Amorite walled cities come into view as Hebrew centers during Solomon's reign.—Under Solomon the country was organized into twelve administrative districts for purposes of *taxation* (I Kings 4:7). These divisions, by the way, had nothing to do with any "twelve tribes"; but, on the contrary, the orthodox tribal tradition (which arose *after* Solomon) may have been suggested by the administrative districts themselves. And in any case their significance refers not to the question of tribes but to the levying of taxes, and also to the highly important fact that now, for the first time since the Judges period, an impressive number of Amorite walled cities emerge into view as headquarters for subdivisions of the Hebrew government. We al-

ready know that Jerusalem and Gibeon, with their Amorite inhabitants, had become parts of the nation during the time of
David; but in the reign of Solomon we learn of many other such
places, which appear with abruptness in the character of "Israelite" cities. Thus, in the northwest of Judah, *Beth-shemesh;*
on the southwest of Ephraim, *Shaalbim;* to the north of Ephraim,
in the Plain of Esdraelon, the famous old Canaanite cities *Taanach* and *Megiddo;* while at the eastern end of the Plain was
Beth-shan, where Saul's body had been hung on the wall; and in
the hills to the north of Esdraelon were *Dor* and *Hazor* (I Kings
4:9, 11, 12; 9:15). Several of these places are also mentioned,
along with another Amorite city, *Gezer*, as having been more
strongly fortified by Solomon (I Kings 9:15). To get a clearer
sense of the situation, it is well to review the foregoing names in
the early narratives about unconquered cities (Judg. 1:27, 29,
33, 35; 4:17; 5:19; 19:10–12; I Sam. 12:9; 31:10–12; II Sam.
21:1–2).

Solomon's government uses forced labor on large scale.
—Along with Benaiah ben Jehoiada, commander of the gib-
borim, another very important officer is mentioned as an instru-
ment of royal power, namely, *Adoniram* (or *Adoram*) *ben Abda*
(II Sam. 20:23, 24; I Kings 4:4, 6; 5:14). The function of
Adoniram was to supervise *the forced labor of Israel* (called in
Hebrew "the *mas*"). This term is inaccurately translated "tribute" by the older English Version, and "levy" by the English
Revised and the Jewish Publication Bible. But it is rendered
more intelligibly by the American Revised Version as follows:
"Adoniram the son of Abda was over the men subject to taskwork." This is a "free" translation, which gives a more accurate
sense of the social and economic facts.

The *mas* was instituted in David's reign on a small scale, at-
tracting little attention. But under Solomon the lowest figure of
the forced labor gangs is thirty thousand (30,000 [I Kings
5:13 f.]). The foregoing estimate is the lowest found in the nar-

rative, but much higher statistics are given. And whether legitimate or not, the imposition of regular taskwork on a large scale, in a small nation like Israel, could not fail to have tremendous economic effects and social repercussions. The *mas*, indeed, became one of the most outstanding characteristics of Solomon's rule.

We have illustrated the royal prerogative with reference to the disposition of *land* by quoting from an address which the Deuteronomic editor places in the mouth of Samuel. The speech, as already observed, instead of being a prediction, is really a *post-eventum* summary of what actually occurred under the Hebrew kings; and the passage is worth reading in its entirety as a commentary on the reign of Solomon:

This will be the *mishpat* of the king that shall reign over you: He will take the best of your fields and vineyards, and give them to his servants [i.e., the nobles who surround the throne]. And he will take the tithe [10 per cent tax] of your seed, and of your vineyards, and give to his officers and to his slaves. And he will take your *men-slaves* and *women-slaves*, and your goodliest young men, and your asses, and put them to his work. And he will take the tithe [10 per cent tax] of your flocks. *And ye shall be his slaves* [I Sam. 8:11–17, in part].

Royal power tends to reduce free slaveholders into bondage.—In the interest of clear thought as we go along, it is well to observe closely the real nature of this passage. It assumes, as a matter of course, that the Hebrew nation of those days consisted primarily of an aristocratic *upper class*, based upon landowning and slaveholding, and that the normal Hebrew was not simply a freeman, but one who held slaves and real estate. The grievance which developed among the Hebrew people in the reign of Solomon was not merely that *freemen* tended to be depressed into bondage, but that freemen who were themselves holders of slaves were deprived of their own bondservants, and *then* carried down into the gulf of economic servitude that yawned beneath every nation of antiquity.

Vast program undertaken by Solomon, allied with Phoenicians.—When David became dominant on the trade routes of Canaan, the Hebrew kingdom rose to a point where its friendship was valuable to the great commercial cities of Tyre and Sidon which lay far up on the Mediterranean seaboard, west of the Danites. The king of Tyre sent workmen and building material to David (II Sam. 5:11). Later on the Tyrian ruler made arrangements with Solomon to furnish materials and workmen for building operations in Jerusalem. Cedar trees were cut down in the Lebanon Mountains by Phoenician slaves, and floated along the coast from Tyre to a Hebrew port, and then carried up through the hills to Solomon's capital (I Kings 5:1, 6–11). After this, a group of magnificent structures arose on the highest hills within the city, consisting of a temple for the worship of Yahweh, two royal palaces, a large building known as the "House of the Forest of Lebanon," and a hall for the king's throne, where he sat as chief judge, to render sentence of *mishpat* (I Kings, chaps. 6 and 7).

But the alliance with Tyre was not merely in the realm of building operations; it broadened into another sphere. Uniting their economic resources, the two kings caused an expedition to go down through the land of Edom, which David had conquered; and when they reached the Edomite port of Eloth, on the Red Sea, the Phoenician workmen assisted the laborers of Solomon to build a fleet of ships for trading with the land of "Ophir"; while another fleet went westward through the Mediterranean to "Tarshish" (I Kings 9:26–28; 10:22). Presently came a flood of imports, the like of which the farmers and shepherds of Israel had never seen—spices, garments, armor, silver, jewels, ivory, horses, mules, apes, peacocks, chariots, and, above all, great quantities of *gold* (I Kings 9:28; 10:2, 10, 11, 14, 22, 25, 28, 29). These products were paid for by the exploited labor of the Hebrews and the tribute of such conquered peoples as the Edomites, Moabites, and Ammonites.

Silver falls in value and prices rise with importation of gold.—The sudden outburst of commercial activity in the reign of Solomon had the inevitable effect of causing prices to go up. International exchange was largely effected by the use of gold (I Kings 9:14, 28; 10:10, 14). But, on the other hand, silver, which had been used as a medium of trade all through the times covered by the books of Judges and Samuel, underwent a fall in value. "Silver was nothing accounted of in the days of Solomon; and the king made silver in Jerusalem like stones" (10:21, 27). The price dislocation, which necessarily accompanied the growth of trade and the flow of precious metals into Israel, may be compared to the changes which went along with the Spanish importation of gold and silver from the newly discovered mines of America at the beginning of modern history. The Spanish treasure circulated *all over Europe;* and the universal rise in values played a part among the social forces leading to the Reformation. The corresponding monetary and fiscal changes in Israel were factors (but not, of course, the only ones) which produced the catastrophe that followed the death of Solomon.

Solomon's government a characteristic oriental despotism.—The account of Solomon's reign fills nearly eleven chapters in the book of I Kings (1:11—chap. 12). These chapters are the work of a Deuteronomic writer who compiled a number of *early* narratives, and inserted his own *later* observations, from his own standpoint, reflecting the age of King Josiah, more than three hundred years after Solomon. The longest insertion begins with 8:14, extending to 9:10, and relates to the ceremonies which are *said* to have taken place after the building of the Temple at Jerusalem. This passage makes Yahweh say: "Since the day that I brought forth my people Israel out of Egypt, I chose no city out of all the tribes of Israel to build an house, that my name might be therein; but I chose David to be over my people Israel" (8:16).

The purpose of the Deuteronomic editor becomes clear when

we set the foregoing statement alongside an equally positive declaration credited to Yahweh by the prophet Jeremiah: "But go ye now unto my place which was in Shiloh, *where I set my name at the first*" (Jer. 7:12). And then we recall how Samuel's parents went up to "the house of Yahweh in Shiloh" (I Sam., chap. 1). When saying that there was no *house to the name of Yahweh* before the time of Solomon, the Deuteronomist either ignores the house at Shiloh or else belittles the earlier sanctuary on account of its *Josephite* origin; in which case he passes over Ephraim in silence, and goes, at a single bound, from the exodus to *David*.

The long prayer placed in the mouth of Solomon expresses religious ideas which only became current through the work of the great prophets who arose long after the time of this monarch (8:22–54). The compiler of Kings is not only far astray in his reference to the house of Yahweh, but his estimate of Solomon is purely idealistic; and his view of the importance attaching to the Temple at Jerusalem in the days of Solomon is exaggerated. The Temple was, indeed, the most magnificent of the shrines built for the worship of Yahweh, but it was little more than a royal chapel during many centuries; and even the Deuteronomist is repeatedly compelled to admit that for hundreds of years, down to the time of Josiah, the people sacrificed in the "high places," or *bamoth*, all over Judah, instead of coming up to Jerusalem and worshiping in the central sanctuary (I Kings 14:22–23; 15:14; 22:43, etc.).

Our estimate of Solomon, therefore, must be formed not by the suggestions of the Deuteronomic editor but on the basis of the older material which the compiler uses, and fails to comprehend. Thus, the government of Solomon, from the very first, was an oriental despotism, upheld by such tools as Benaiah, commander of the *gibborim*, and Adoniram, overseer of the taskwork, or *mas*. This view alone is in accord with the real course of Hebrew history.

House of Joseph thrust into obscurity under Solomon.—
The coronation of David as king of all Israel forced the house of
Joseph into the background of the national picture for *seventy-
three years*, until the death of Solomon. The rule of David's
house over the united Hebrew kingdom was based upon the
splendid personality, services, and prestige of its founder: "The
king saved us out of the hand of our enemies; and he delivered
us out of the hand of the Philistines" (II Sam. 19:9). The governmental machinery which David set up was taken over by
Solomon, who used his inheritance to force the nation toward
slavery; and for the time being his régime acquired such momentum that it was irresistible.

But while the house of Joseph was treated with little respect
by the dynasty of David, the highlands of Ephraim nevertheless contained the *bulk* of the Hebrew people. Here was a thick-
ly populated region, filled with primitive clans which continued
to observe the rule of *kindred mishpat*, and whose oldest men
could recall the social conditions of the Judges period. Here
were no Amorite walled cities; for the destruction of *Shechem*
had long ago rounded out the "proto-Deuteronomic" conquest
of the central hill-country, leaving the house of Joseph a solid
mass of uniform clans engaged in shepherding and agriculture, in
small villages which dotted the landscape. Among the peasant
aristocracy of Ephraim were the local elders, or sheiks, who administered communal affairs before the rise of the monarchy,
and who continued in this character, even under Solomon's despotism. Aged men from Ephraim had been a majority of "all
the elders of Israel" that went to Hebron to make David king
(II Sam. 5:3). The word for "elders" in Hebrew is the term
zikanim (from *zakan*, "beard"), and hence could be translated
more picturesquely as "the bearded ones."

Bearing in mind these facts, it is easy to see how the primitive
clans of Ephraim would feel about Solomon, whom they had no
voice in choosing. *His government was allied with the great com-*

mercial city of Tyre, and was administered by a bureaucracy with headquarters in the Amorite city of Jerusalem as well as in other cities of Canaan outside the original frontiers of Ephraim. The house of Joseph in the time of Solomon found itself under the pressure of burdens from which there seemed to be no escape— taxation, forced labor, and a mysterious rise in prices. Comparison with enslavement by the Philistines was natural; but *now* the subjugation was at the hands of masters who had Israelite names. Thus, the clans of Ephraim were taxed by one *Ben Hur* to supply food for Solomon's vast household (I Kings 4:7, 8). The chief overseer of taskwork, *Adoniram ben Abda*, had under him a busy and promising young man, *Jeroboam ben Nebat*, ruler over all the burden of *the house of Joseph* (I Kings 11:26–28). Here we find the historical basis for the legend that *Judah* led the movement which made a slave out of *Joseph* (Gen. 37:26, 27).

CHAPTER IX

MISHPAT STRUGGLE IN EPHRAIM

Stirrings of revolt in house of Joseph.—Jeroboam ben Nebat, the young Ephraimite, was at first engaged in strengthening the fortifications of Jerusalem; and his industry in this work attracted the king's attention so favorably that Solomon, as we have seen, promoted him to be *"ruler over all the burden of the house of Joseph"* (I Kings 11:28). Being now placed over that part of the nation to which he was directly related by kinship, Jeroboam could not fail to hear the complaints of the people; and the ties of blood proved stronger than his loyalty to Solomon; so that "he lifted up his hand against the king" (I Kings 11:26). This means that he entered into a conspiracy, and took an oath against the house of David.

Ephraimite discontent voiced by prophet Ahijah of Shiloh.—The disaffection of the house of Joseph was not merely secular but also religious. For now again, as in the days of Saul, the figure of a prophet, or *nabi*, appears in the foreground, voicing the mind of Ephraim, and speaking in the name of Yahweh. From Shiloh, the former headquarters of Josephite nationalism, the prophet Ahijah came to Jeroboam, whose outer garment Ahijah is said to have torn into twelve pieces, giving Jeroboam *ten* pieces, with the message, "Thus saith Yahweh, the god of Israel, Behold, I will rend the kingdom out of the hand of Solomon, and will give ten tribes to thee" (I Kings 11:29-31). The foregoing is from an old Ephraimite record; but the compiler immediately adds a long Deuteronomic passage making the prophet say, inconsistently, that the house of David shall have only *one* tribe, instead of the two tribes previously remaining after the deduction of ten from twelve; and, in a similar inser-

155

tion, Yahweh himself makes the identical statement to Solomon (I Kings 11:9–13).

The conspiracy became so extensive that it could not be hidden; and when Solomon learned the truth, he sought to arrest the leader of Ephraimite discontent. But Jeroboam eluded the royal police, and fled to *Egypt*, where he remained in safety.

Flaming into rebellion, house of Joseph breaks Hebrew nation into Ephraim and Judah, *ca.* 930 B.C.—Upon the death of Solomon, his son Rehoboam journeyed north to meet the people of Ephraim at Shechem, which now, for the first time since the Judges epoch, reappears in the character of an Israelite city. Solomon had not gone to Shechem at the time of his accession; but his heir doubtless imagined that in view of the Ephraimites' rebellious mood, they would be forced into submission by a show of royal authority in their midst. The masses that gathered at Shechem, however, demanded *reform* as the price of allegiance; to which Rehoboam replied arrogantly: "Whereas, my father did lade you with a heavy yoke, I will add to your yoke. My father hath chastised you with whips; but I will chastise you with scorpions" (I Kings 12:1, 4, 11).

The answer of the house of Joseph was instant: *"What portion have we in David? Neither have we inheritance in the son of Jesse! To your tents, O Israel! Now see to thine own house, David!"* (12:16). Even so, the foolish heir of Solomon, finding that the royal presence did not compel submission, ordered Adoniram ben Abda, the minister of taskwork, to enforce the *mas*. But when this hated official undertook to draft the people, *"all Israel stoned him with stones, that he died"* (vs. 18). Then Rehoboam, in fear for his own life, climbed quickly into his chariot and rode away to Jerusalem. And "there was none that followed the house of David but the tribe of Judah only" (vss. 18–20, *ca.* 930 B.C.). Jeroboam then became king of Ephraim.

Among the narratives of Solomon's reign we find a remarkable

and wholly inaccurate statement that the Amorites and Israelites remained as *contrasted groups*, which did not intermarry or
coalesce; that the Amorites *alone* were subjugated by Solomon;
and that the Israelites were *never* enslaved by him, but were a
distinct race, above the older, Amorite race, and occupying high
positions of military dignity. Thus: "All the people that were
left of the Amorites . . . . upon *them* did Solomon levy bond-
service [*mas obed*] unto this day. But of the children of Israel did
Solomon make no slave [*ebed*]; for they were men of war, and his
abadim [i.e., in a higher sense], and his princes [*sarim*], and his
captains, and rulers of his chariots and of his horsemen" (I
Kings 9:20-22).

Moreover, when we turn to the corresponding passage in the
late, post-Exilic book of Chronicles, whose author is yet more
intensely nationalistic and southern in point of view, even the
foregoing statement is not explicit enough regarding the dignity
of the Israelite race; for this writer copies the verses from Kings,
but completely omits the words "and his abadim," as used in the
higher sense of royal officials. Thus the Chronicler says, "But of
the children of Israel did Solomon make no *abadim* for his work;
but they were men of war and princes [*sarim*], etc." (II Chron.
8:7-9).

These passages are cited here not for the purpose of controversy but in order to show how the Bible was produced by many
writers, of whom some understood the facts better than others.
Thus, if we are to take Hebrew history from the two writers just
quoted, we must ignore the fuller and more concrete sources relating to intermarriage between Israelites and Amorites (Judg.
3:6; Gen., chap. 38, etc.); the king taking the best of their lands
and their slaves, and reducing Israel to slavery (I Sam. 8:11-
17); Solomon's forced labor on the Israelites *themselves* (I Kings
5:13); Jeroboam having charge over the forced labor of the
house of Joseph (11:28); the demand of the Josephites that

their yoke be lightened; and the reply of Rehoboam that whereas his father burdened them with a heavy yoke, he would add to their yoke (12:4, 10, 11).

If these fundamental sources are not the correct ones, then the revolt of the Josephites from Judah was not the beginning of a great moral-religious revolution, but was without valid reason; Jeroboam was a mere demagogue; the prophet Ahijah of Shiloh spoke in vain; while the division of the united Hebrew kingdom into Judah and Ephraim-Joseph was a profound political error, and also a rejection of the one true God, exactly as the Jewish author of Chronicles believes (II Chron. 13:10, 11).

That the interpolators' view of the history survives in our time, however, is curiously shown by the recent publication of a book, *The Status of Labor in Ancient Israel* (1923), by Judge Mayer Sulzberger, of Philadelphia. According to this writer, Jeroboam was impelled by "audacious ambition" (p. 29). It is assumed that King Solomon, instead of reducing the house of Joseph under Jeroboam to forced labor, merely exploited Amorite *subjects* of the Josephites; the Mosaic Law is assumed to have been established in the desert, and to have been the norm of official, public law straight along through Hebrew history; and on the foundation of this premise, Judge Sulzberger declares that slavery in Israel was "essentially different" from slavery among non-Hebrew nations, which is what the cotton-aristocracy of America said regarding their own, peculiar institution before the Civil War (p. 6). That the house of Joseph was enslaved by the house of Judah in Solomon's time, and that the Book of Genesis follows the actual history in making Judah propose to *sell* Joseph into bondage, seems not to have been realized by this writer (Gen. 37:26, 27). He ignores the consideration that whereas David was elected king by the peasantry on the basis of merit, Solomon seized the throne as a dictator; and he overlooks the fact that a new upper class was coming into existence under the house of David through intermarriage between the old Israelite aristocracy of the rural districts and the remaining Amorite nobility of the walled cities.

Ephraim reverts to rule of mishpat and silver money.—The house of Joseph, then, vetoed the principle of a continuous Judaic succession over a united Hebrew state. The revolt against the Davidic dynasty carries us out of Judah's orbit for a time, and fixes our attention once more upon the central highlands, made famous by the earlier heroes of that region. The house of Joseph now emerged from obscurity, and resumed that commanding position in the main current of Hebrew life which it had occupied throughout the long period marked by the names of Joshua, Deborah, Barak, Ehud, Gideon, Samuel, and Saul. *The alliance with the commercial cities of Tyre and Sidon was abrogated;* and the hill-country of Ephraim once more lay under the rule of peasant landowners and slaveholders, headed by village elders, or *zikanim*. The old Amorite cities, beyond the original frontiers of Ephraim, were no longer the seats of an oppressive Solomonic bureaucracy. Adoniram, the minister of taskwork, was dead; and no more could the *gibborim*, or standing police of Judah, venture into the north. Jerusalem, that ancient Amorite capital, which had risen high over the terrified Hebrew imagination, sank now to the level of an alien town, below the southern horizon; and the reaction against city life became so strong that although Jeroboam undertook to fortify the once Amorite Shechem as headquarters, the real capital of Ephraim for the next half-century was the hitherto unknown village of *Tirzah* (I Kings 12:25; 14:17; 15:21; 16:6, 8, 9, 15, 17, 23). The village of Bethel, with its tradition of Jacob, was made the chief royal sanctuary for the worship of Yahweh, a dignity which it retained for many generations, into the time of the prophet Amos (I Kings 12:32–33; Amos 7:10–13). The ideals of this period in Ephraim were non-commercialistic. The importation of gold, cedarwood, ivory, apes, and peacocks was unheard of; and silver again became the medium of local exchange.

Oral traditions of Jacob and Joseph taking more definite form in Ephraim (930–880 B.C.).—The fifty-year period following the rejection of Judahite rule by the house of Joseph was a most important chapter in Hebrew perspective. Reassertion of the primitive régime converted this epoch into a kind of archaic melting pot for traditional ideas in their slow evolution toward forms which they were to assume in the Ephraimite document. The conditions under which that "source" of the Pentateuch and Joshua took final shape did not yet prevail; but separate fascicles were already in circulation. Thus, the story had arisen of Jacob as a *warrior* with sword and bow, taking the hills of *Ephraim* out of the hand of the Amorite (Gen. 48:22 [E]). Becoming a landed aristocrat and cultivator of the soil, he subsisted on bread, lentils, and other produce; and, according to the frankly worded poetry of the time, "his smell was like the smell of a field *that Yahweh had blessed*" (Gen. 27:27). There is no evidence that the Ephraimites at *this* time served the local gods of Canaan with reference to their supposed power as givers of good crops. Early Israel was now conceived as having been a pastoral and farming group in *central Canaan*, originating from a beloved wife, Rachel, but with less important groups arising from a hated wife, Leah, and two slave-girls, Bilhah and Zilpah. The subjection of the house of Joseph to the house of Judah provided material for a legend, as yet inchoate, that the patriarch *Judah* had taken the lead in proposing the sale of Joseph into slavery (Gen. 37:26, 27).

The Josephite redemption of Israel from bondage to the south pointed to the figure of Joseph as the hero and savior of his family; but the concrete occasion of the idea had not receded into the past far enough to liberate it for broader use. Yet suggestions were not lacking: The Josephite leader Jeroboam, fleeing into Egypt at the time of the conspiracy, had been kindly received by King Shishak (I Kings 11:40; 12:2); and presently Shishak invaded Canaan, almost reducing Judah to vassalage (I Kings 14:25, 26). Thus, for the first time since dim antiquity, when the primitive Joseph group was in the pasture lands of Goshen, Egypt now flashes upon the horizon of Hebrew thought in the dramatic hour of Josephite revival.

But thus far the mishpat struggle was only a groping movement, which had not reached a point where it could supply an impulse powerful enough to develop the local Joseph legend upon the background of a truly *national* Hebrew saga, and then to collate the Jacobite and Josephite stories into the "Mosaic" narrative, where they present a superficially harmonious appearance without having internal consistency. A sample of the difficulties awaiting the E and J writers in the centuries *following* the period 930–880 is found in the two pictures of Jacob already emphasized in an earlier connection. The one picture makes him patriarch of a tiny band, fearing lest the treacherous conduct of Simeon and Levi bring him into "bad odor" with the Canaanites, who will rise up in wrath to slay him and his family; while his only protection against the inhabitants of the land is a divine spell, or *"terror of God,"* which holds them back from pursuing him. This picture is in startling contrast with the other, which makes him a fearless warrior, taking the central hills from the Amorites by military force. That these two stories represent serial facts in Hebrew evolution has been already shown. But the compilers of the Mosaic books leave them unresolved without explanation, as relating to the life of an individual *person;* and the same lack of internal coherence will impress itself upon us when we come to consider the origin and compilation of the Pentateuchal documents.

Ephraim drawn into struggle over issue of militarism *v.* pacifism.—The peasantry of Ephraim would have been glad to remain isolated in their unique highlands, far from the swift currents of international affairs. But irresistible forces decreed that the house of Joseph should not be indefinitely shut away from the outside world. Two oriental powers were now becoming greatly concerned about the east-Mediterranean seaboard. The nearest of these was the kingdom of *Damascus*, on the northern frontier of Israel; while the other lay back of Damascus in the Euphrates Valley—the rising empire of Assyria, which loomed as a gigantic portent on the eastern horizon. All the trade of Damascus and Assyria with western countries up to this time had gone through the ports of Tyre and Sidon; and these two Phoenician cities were inhabited by merchants who became wealthy as "middlemen," levying toll on the streams of traffic that went through their hands. Both Damascus and Assyria wanted an outlet, or port, on the Mediterranean, which would enable them to keep more of the profits accruing from their own trade; and in seeking to attain this end, they were preparing to throw armies directly across the hills between Dan and the Plain of Esdraelon, threatening alike the commercial monopoly of the Phoenicians and the independence of Israel.

Accordingly, after four Ephraimite kings had reigned in the village of *Tirzah*, the house of Joseph was convulsed by a great internal struggle. The bulk of the peasant aristocracy, living in their little hamlets, could not grasp the full meaning of the news about world-events which filtered slowly and imperfectly into the highlands. This element in Israel had a vivid memory of the evils resulting from contact with Phoenicia; for thousands of old men were even then living who could recall and picture clearly the conditions which prevailed when the united Hebrew monarchy was allied with Hiram, king of Tyre, and ruled by the despotic Solomon, with his *gibborim*, or standing army under Benaiah, and his taskmasters under Adoniram ben Abda. The house of Joseph had no desire that Israel be involved once more in foreign complications; and the peasant aristocracy of Ephraim was unable to see that their country could not avoid being swept again into the broader stream of world-history. They did not perceive that no nation liveth or dieth unto itself; and while we can see the ultimate futility of their outlook, we can yet sympathize with their provincialism.

But, on the other hand, their opponents were at least awake to the dreadful fact that if Ephraim lay still, it would be subdued, as in the days of the Philistines. Hence large military preparations were needed. The little army, which had been employed in frontier skirmishes ever since the break with Judah, must be reorganized on a broader and more professional basis; and fortifications must be erected without delay. The capital at the village of Tirzah was no more secure against foreign attack than the capital of King Saul at the hamlet of Gibeah; and something should be done at once to impress the imagination of possible foes with the greatness and impregnability of Israel, as in the days when Jerusalem was captured and strengthened by David and Solomon.

That the contrasting tendencies of militarism and pacifism excited violent opposition may be well imagined; nor is it strange that an intestine strife broke out lasting as long as the American Civil War. *"Then were the people of Israel divided into two parts"* (I Kings 16:21a). This quotation is from the royal annals of the house of Joseph; and the compiler of Kings checks up the narrative by indicating that the struggle commenced "in the *twenty and seventh year* of Asa king of Judah" (I Kings 16:15). Half of the people followed a candidate for the throne by the name of Tibni ben Ginath, while the other half were for a certain *Omri*. The struggle took *four years* to reach a decision, when the people who followed Tibni ben Ginath were at length vanquished; and "in the *thirty and first year* of Asa, king of Judah, *began Omri to reign over Israel*" (I Kings 16:23). Under Omri the kingdom of Ephraim was drawn reluctantly out of isolation into the stream of world-events.

Kingdom of Ephraim equipped with new, fortified capital on purchased land.—Not content with the village of Tirzah, which had been headquarters of Ephraim for half a century, the new ruler, Omri, soon projected his design to buy a large, commanding location, and build thereon a strong, fortified city as capital. A magnificent hill in the center of the country caught his attention. It was an agricultural and pastoral property of high value, which had never been built upon as yet, belonging to the family of a certain *Shemer.* Any method of acquiring it would necessarily excite prejudice among the conservative rustic proprietary whose fathers had poured out rivers of blood in winning the central highlands from the grip of Amorite baalism on behalf of the mishpat régime. *"Yahweh forbid it me, that I should sell the inheritance of my fathers unto thee!"* was the exclamation which, at a *later* time, greeted Omri's heir and successor, Ahab, who attempted to buy a much less expensive property from the peasant Naboth (I Kings 21:3). The primary significance of Naboth's refusal to sell, as an outstanding illustration of the old mishpat, has been obscured by his murder through the conspiracy of Queen Jezebel; but aside from the fact of murder, there is a very striking difference between the cases represented by Naboth's vineyard and Shemer's hill. We cannot, of course, know all the details; but there is no record that Shemer *declined,* in the name of Yahweh, to sell his land when approached by Omri, who bought it, without any apparent difficulty, for the high price of two silver *talents,* equaling at least eight hundred pounds in British money, but far exceeding the present worth of that sum (I Kings 16:24). *The two proprietors, Naboth and Shemer, then, were on opposite wings of the Ephraimite landed aristocracy; Naboth being a small peasant on the "left," while Shemer was a wealthy member of the "right."* Nevertheless, the Josephite conquest had been so thorough that even at this late period a proprietor was not yet spoken of as a "baal," but was called an *adon:* "Shemer the *adon* of the hill" (I Kings 16:24 [Hebrew text]).

Having secured a location for his capital, the new king proceeded to erect a city, literally "from the ground up," fortified with almost impregnable walls; and he named the city *Samaria*, after Shemer, who sold him the hill.

Omri was a patriotic and able ruler, who succeeded in holding back the aggressions of Damascus; and if we look at his policy from a purely nationalistic standpoint, it was marked by wisdom. Yet the situation contained the germs of trouble. The erection of Samaria, like the building operations of Solomon, was *costly;* and this expense, along with the outlay for a larger army, involved a growing load of *taxation*.

With such facts in mind, we can easily see how the feelings of the conservative peasantry were outraged, both by the new fiscal burdens and also by the sudden, portentous rise of a *towering capital city*, guarded by a new force of *gibborim*, and founded on a real estate transaction bringing into play the commercial, baalistic usages which put land into the category of sale or exchange, contrary to the cherished customs of old. And thus, only fifty years after escaping the yoke of *Jerusalem*, the house of Joseph passed under the yoke of *Samaria*.

Alliance with Tyre, involving marriage of Omri's son, Ahab, to Jezebel, Phoenician princess.—The alliance of Ephraim with Tyre was necessary if both countries were to withstand the encroachments of Damascus and Assyria. So the Phoenician king, Eth-baal, gave his daughter Jezebel to Ahab the son of Omri; and when Ahab himself became king, he built a temple in the city of Samaria to the Tyrian Baal (I Kings 16:32; II Kings 10:21, 27). This recognition of Jezebel's god was not unusual or peculiar in any way, for it was a practice of antiquity whenever nations entered into alliance. It involved no denial of Yahweh as god of Israel; but eventually, in the minds of conservative Hebrew peasants, all the oppressive aspects of Omri's policy came to be symbolized by the Tyrian Baal. This god, the divinity of a great commercial power, stood for laws and customs contrary to the ideas and ways of the simple farmers who composed the bulk of Ephraim's population; and while the nearer

Amorite cities, which lay around the Plain of Esdraelon, worshiped ancient Canaanite Baals of their own, whose cults were more or less like that of the Tyrian deity, these local gods were not yet influential in the Hebrew pantheon as rivals or competitors of Yahweh. But the *Phoenician* Baal was the god of a great wealthy foreign power; the importation of his worship into the heart of the central highlands produced a very dramatic effect upon the minds of the simple peasants and shepherds who made up the bulk of the community; and the marriage of Ahab with Jezebel of Tyre had a psychological influence like the marriage of Louis XVI of France with Marie Antoinette of Austria, the two queens coming alike to a bloody end.

Developing economic situation typified by treatment of Naboth's land.—Preliminary mention of Naboth's case has prepared us to consider more fully this famous episode. King Ahab, in addition to his royal residence in the city of Samaria, had a new palace in the Plain of Esdraelon at *Jezreel;* and somewhere near his magnificent rural estate was a piece of land which the king wanted for the purpose of completing his garden scheme. The land was owned by a "left wing" member of the peasant aristocracy, who held it as an inheritance from his fathers, according to the mishpat of Yahweh, which forbade alienation of the soil as betrayal of kinship rights. The land was conceived as belonging to the family from an indefinite past into the indefinite future. But the king had been reared in a different social atmosphere. His father Omri had bought the great hill whereon the capital of Ephraim was built; and his wife Jezebel was from the royal family of a mercantile, baalistic nation which had graduated long ago from the stage of mishpat. Ahab's ideas of property, therefore, were unlike those of the primitive peasantry in the farming villages outside his capital; and in seeking to obtain the land of Naboth, he made the owner a straightforward, commercialistic proposition, offering to pay the value of it in *silver*, or to give a better piece of land in *exchange* (I Kings 21:2).

The reply of Naboth, appealing to Yahweh and refusing Ahab, was too energetic to be translated literally into English (vs. 3). The same expression was used by Jonathan the son of Saul, and is rendered, "Far be it from me" (I Sam. 20:9); but it means *"to the profane!"* Met thus by flat refusal, there was nothing which Ahab could do under the old law of mishpat; for Naboth, like the Englishman Hampden, opposed the king, not on the basis of mere personal fancy, but as a matter of ancient constitutional principle, and on even firmer legal grounds than Hampden occupied when denying the fiscal prerogatives of King Charles, who could cite old precedents as convincing as Hampden's; whereas Ahab, unable to fall back on Hebrew antiquity, went back into his palace frustrated and sorely displeased.

When Queen Jezebel heard about the refusal of Naboth to part with his land, she was highly indignant, because in her eyes the customs of mishpat seemed very foolish. And so her active mind set to work secretly to defeat the law, before the king could learn what she was doing. A scheme occurred to her by which Naboth's profanity could be represented, in a special court, as blasphemy of God and the king, constituting the crime of *high treason*, the penalty for which is always death and confiscation of the criminal's property. Accordingly, Jezebel forged Ahab's name on letters to the legal authorities of Naboth's district, ordering them to convene a court session, and cite witnesses against Naboth. Letters were sent not only to the elders, or *zikanim*, but also to the *nobles*, or *horim*, the more "substantial" gentry like Shemer; and when the court was called, the helpless peasant was convicted without delay, being summarily put to death. Jezebel then gave the news to Ahab, telling him to go and confiscate the land of Naboth.

As frequently happens with reference to many historic events, the essential facts of this famous case have been obscured by its dramatic aspects; and thus the story of Naboth has come down through the ages befogged by clouds of misunderstanding. Numerous murders in Hebrew history are passed over by the biblical writers with only slight notice; and *this* case is dwelt upon at some length in the Bible, not primarily because it comes to a climax in murder, but because of its broader implications, which necessarily remain somewhat in the background. The compilers of the Bible seized upon it as exemplifying an economic process which, *with or without murder*, would endow the smaller and wealthier wing of the Hebrew upper class with a private monopoly of the soil, and reduce the bulk of the freemen into the lower social class of slaves, or *abadim*.

Enslavement of the free class illustrated from another standpoint by different case.—The gradual submergence of a large part of the free Hebrew upper class into the lower social stratum was a very complex process, which is illustrated in a different way by the case of a widow whose children were foreclosed upon by a creditor in satisfaction of a debt owed by her late husband: "Now there cried a certain woman of the sons of the prophets [*b'nae nebiim*], ... My husband is dead; and the creditor is come to take unto him my two sons to be bondmen [*abadim*]" (II Kings 4:1). The larger and poorer section of the aristocracy became indebted to the smaller and wealthier element in the community by reason of many causes. The peasantry under the house of Omri were burdened by war service, by taxation, and by inflated prices—which latter comes about under a silver standard, or a gold standard, or any other form of money. These causes of economic depression were complicated by occasional failure of crops through drought or the invasion of locusts. In such cases the poorer peasant was compelled to borrow from a wealthier neighbor—such men as *Naboth*, for instance, applying to such men as *Shemer*. Loans were obtained only by giving the lender a pledge, or mortgage, of land or chattels to secure the debt. The borrowing of money was easy and seductive. But repayment was hard, and oftentimes impossible.

For after the debt was contracted, the conditions that led to it remained as before—taxes, military service, high prices, drought, etc., acting singly or together; and thus the burdens resting on the peasant class were not reduced but were actually augmented by *interest*. The pressure of such conditions always bears more heavily upon the smaller property-owners than upon the larger. The little man, such as Naboth, is taxed more fully in proportion; he is more likely to suffer the disabilities of war service; and he is affected with greater severity by drought, inflated prices, etc. But in the meanwhile, his wealthier neighbor, Shemer, is in possession of a surplus which becomes more valuable as times grow harder. And thus periods of war and economic depression make the poor poorer, while the rich become richer; so that public adversity is coined into private wealth by the fortunate few at the very moment when many are sinking into despair.

If the Hebrew peasant could not liquidate his loan, the question of procedure came up at once: What was to be done? The creditor might foreclose on the peasant's land, thus transferring ancestral soil from the tenure of mishpat into that of commercial baalism. Or, again, the creditor might enslave the *debtor;* so that the poor peasant must leave his family to shift as best they could while he toiled in bondage. But, even so, the taxes on the land must be paid; and his wife and children, struggling on, would soon find themselves unable to manage the ancestral inheritance, which would be confiscated. *Under these or any alternative conditions, the economic forces of territorial society would slowly but inexorably transform all kinship holdings into commercialistic tenures.*

The only procedure satisfactory to the Hebrew *debtor* class in those days would have been for the *creditor* class to write off all mortgages from their books. This course, if made a rule, would indeed have *stopped* the shifting of the economic surplus, through interest payments, etc., from the poor "left" wing of the aristocracy to the wealthy "right" wing. But, on the other hand, the process of making loans without liquidation would have put the surplus property of the *rich* at the disposal of the *poorer* landowners and slaveholders, carrying the economic surplus from right to *left*, instead of from left to *right*. This procedure would have compromised with the mishpat idea of the primitive clan, since it would have given all members of the free upper class a claim on the social surplus; but it would have left the question of the enslaved *alien* class *unsettled*. A similar situation arises whenever the agricultural wing of the property class in *modern* civilization urges readjustment of its own debts regardless of the wage-earning proletariat, in city and country, which, after all, constitutes the bulk of the population.

Economic tension under dynasty of Omri symbolized by issue of "Baal or Yahweh."—Under Omri's dynasty, the colliding usages of territorial civilization and the kinship group reached a crisis wherein the issue *appeared to be very simple and uncomplicated*. The merits of the situation were supposed to be *all* on one side, or *all* on the other, according to the point of view taken. Israel must go back to the ways of the forefathers, and observe the mishpat of Yahweh, uncontaminated by the legality of civilization; or else the nation's future must more and more fall under the hard, commercial, baalistic rules observed by the Amorites before the coming of Israel from the desert and by the Phoenicians of Tyre and Sidon, whose proud Baal was now enthroned at Samaria in the very heart of Ephraim! Mishpat, or *law*, involved relationship with a *deity;* and in the eyes of Hebrew peasants, the tragic fate of Naboth resolved the whole problem into the simple antithesis, "Yahweh or Baal!"

Prophet Elijah comes out of Gilead into Ephraim with proto-Deuteronomic message.—The Naboth case brought into the foreground of Hebrew life the portentous figure of Elijah the prophet, or *nabi*. Looming gigantic amid the shadows of ancient history, and standing out in relief against the background of his time, Elijah marks a crisis in the development of Hebrew religion and a turning-point in the spiritual evolution of mankind. Hailing from Gilead, east of Jordon, where the customs of primitive clan-life were maintained more vigorously than west of the river, this unknown man was impelled by fiery indignation to go up into Ephraim, denounce Ahab, and energize the peasantry of the house of Joseph against the advancing tide of Baalism. *Whether Elijah understood the whole situation in all its complexity, or whether he had a final solution for the problem of his time, does not concern us in the long run; for the fact is that around his figure an ethical process took form and impulse which, with imperfect ideals at the start, was logically bound, by its own momentum, to move onward and upward.*

Ephraimite king denounced not only for murder but for "taking possession."—It is very doubtful whether Elijah made his way into Ahab's presence when the king took possession of Naboth's land, or that he ever confronted the monarch at any time in person. But that he symbolizes a new stage in the progress of Israel toward the Deuteronomic philosophy is absolutely certain. The story which is reproduced from an earlier narrative by the compiler of Kings makes Elijah denounce Ahab, in the name of Yahweh, for taking the life of Naboth; but it also makes Elijah condemn Ahab, in the name of Yahweh, for doing what Naboth objected to at the very *start*, when he refused, with an oath, to sell his land. *The king is arraigned, therefore, not merely for taking the life of an individual, but for depriving a family of the means of subsistence, and thus taking life on a collective scale.*

Moreover, since Ahab had committed murder, and identified himself with a process which was reducing the peasantry to bondage and ruin, the verdict of the prophet against the king is followed by a sentence of death, in the name of Yahweh: "In the place where dogs licked the blood of Naboth shall dogs lick *thy* blood, *even thine!*" (I Kings 21:19). Ahab was not actually

slain in Jezreel, where Naboth died, but over in Gilead, whence
his body was taken to the city of Samaria; after which he was
followed on the throne by his son Ahaziah, and then by his
younger son Joram (I Kings 22:29, 35, 37, 40; II Kings 1:17).
This continued prosperity in the house of Omri was embarrassing
to the compiler; but since he was unable to change the records
without mutilating them beyond recognition, he expanded the
simple prediction of Ahab's retributory death into a long Deuteronomic speech, threatening destruction (after the event) to
the *dynasty* of Ahab (I Kings 21:20, beginning with "because,"
and concluding with vs. 26). But even this passage was not allowed to stand without change, for still another scribe interpolated a *post-eventum* verse threatening *Jezebel* with a violent end
(vs. 23).

**Elijah selects Elisha ben Shaphat as helper and successor in
anti-Baal struggle.**—Knowing that the campaign against the
Baal of Tyre must have native leadership in Ephraim itself,
Elijah selected for this purpose Elisha ben Shaphat, of the village of *Abel-meholah*, in the northeastern part of Ephraim, looking down on Jordan and lying over against far-away Gilead. In
Elisha's family, we get once more a clear view of the upper social
class which, all along, had been identified with the original,
wilderness cult of Yahweh, as brought into the highlands of
Ephraim by the early settlers. The village of Abel-meholah, or
"Dancing Meadow," where Elisha lived, was like thousands of
other hamlets that lay scattered through the house of Joseph.
There were no isolated farms in those days; for the people
dwelt in clan villages of one or two streets, and went forth to
their work in the surrounding fields. The agricultural equipment of Shaphat, the father of Elisha, included twenty-four
oxen, which were harnessed into a single team of twelve yoked
pairs for plowing. An outfit of this magnitude suggests a con-
siderable estate. Elisha was busily at work with the entire team,
in a field outside the village, when Elijah came to Abel-meho-

lah; and the scene recalls the occasion at Gibeah, many generations before, when Saul ben Kish came following the oxen out of
the field, and met the messengers from Gilead in the street of the
village. Elisha and Saul were far apart in time; and their homes
were far apart in space—Gibeah being in the extreme south of
Ephraim, while Abel-meholah was in the north. But their families were typical of the peasant aristocracy that built up the
house of Joseph, the main trunk of the Hebrew nation (I Kings
19:16–21; cf. I Sam. 11:5–7).

Elisha's work seems to have been very active in the district
where the sense of outrage over the Naboth case would naturally be most vivid. His mission frequently took him back and
forth past the village of *Shunem*, which lay near the scene of the
tragedy. In course of time he became acquainted with a Shunem-
ite family which entertained him whenever he passed by; and
they built for him an extra chamber with a table, chair, candlestick, and bed. These new friends of Elisha had land, as usual,
outside the village; and his contact with them gives us yet another glimpse of the upper class in the country districts when the
first great reaction against Baalism was developing among the
Hebrew people. The Shunem illustration has more than the
value of another isolated example; for when Elisha asks what
shall be done to repay this family's kindness, the lady of the
house replies, "*I dwell among my own people.*" In other words,
the family had no need, being in contact with its own kindred
which lived in the village of Shunem and held the soil round
about (II Kings 4:8–18).

**Elisha enlists Jehu, who destroys house of Omri and Phoe-
nician Baalism, and becomes king.**—The movement begun by
the great prophet from Gilead, and continued by his disciple the
son of Shaphat, went forward gradually until at length Elisha,
feeling the time to be at hand for a drastic new step, enlisted the
co-operation of a high military commander, Jehu ben Jehoshaphat ben Nimshi, who was known to be in sympathy with the

anti-Baal propaganda. Thus an army chief comes into the foreground again. But militarism, with its burden of taxes and war service, now had a permanent place in the kingdom of Ephraim, through the unrelenting pressure of Damascus and Assyria. The army officer, Jehu, was a representative member of the Israelite aristocracy; and his name, compounded with that of the national divinity, means "Yahweh is he"; while his father's name, Jehoshaphat, means "Yahweh has judged."

Carrying out the will of the peasant majority, Jehu led a revolution against the reigning dynasty. The entire house of Omri and Ahab went down to destruction in a torrent of blood, carrying with it the hated Jezebel, who, like Marie Antoinette, the Austrian princess in France, died amid the execrations of the populace. And then, having disposed of the royal family, Jehu ordered all the prophets, priests, and worshipers of the Tyrian Baal to gather at the temple of Baal which had been erected by Ahab in the city of Samaria. "And they came into the house of Baal; so that the house was full from one end to another. And Jehu said to the guard and to the captains, Go in and slay them. And they smote them with the edge of the sword" (II Kings, chap. 9; 10:18, 19, 21, 25, 27). Then the temple of Baal was wrecked in a final outburst of religious fanaticism.

Thus Jehu founded a new royal house; and he was urged forward by the accredited prophets of Yahweh, who gave him explicit, proto-Deuteronomic messages in the name of the national divinity (II Kings 9:1–6). Not only so, but Yahweh himself is said to have commanded the prophet Elijah to anoint Jehu king over Israel (I Kings 19:15, 16; II Kings 10:17). And Yahweh himself is quoted as having spoken directly to Jehu as follows: "Because thou hast done well in executing that which is right in mine eyes, and hast done unto the house of Ahab according to all that was in mine heart, thy children of the fourth generation shall sit on the throne of Israel" (II Kings 10:30).

Significance of support given to Jehu by Jehonadab ben Rechab.—A very instructive sociological fact in this connection is the dramatic support given to Jehu by a certain *Jehonadab ben Rechab*, who clasped hands with the revolutionary leader as a formal sign of indorsement, riding with him in his chariot, and going with Jehu into the temple of Baal to witness the massacre (II Kings 10:15, 16, 23). The narrative on its face would lead us only to assume that Jehonadab ben Rechab was a very zealous and influential representative of the pro-Yahweh, anti-Baal party, whom Jehu was anxious to impress. And the compiler of Kings does nothing to show us the real significance of this remarkable passage.

But the Book of Jeremiah, which has afforded us much incidental help, comes to our aid again, and reveals the special importance attaching to Jehonadab's approval of Jehu. The descendants, or disciples, of this man are quoted as declaring, many generations later:

Jehonadab ben Rechab our father commanded us, saying, Ye shall drink no wine, ye, nor your sons forever. Neither shall ye build house, nor sow seed, nor plant vineyard, nor have any. But all your days ye shall dwell in tents, that ye may live many days in the land where ye be sojourners. Thus have we obeyed the voice of Jehonadab ben Rechab our father, in all that he charged us, to drink no wine all our days, we, our wives, our sons, nor our daughters; nor to build houses for us to dwell in. Neither have we vineyard, nor field, nor seed. But we have dwelt in tents, and have obeyed, and done according to all that our father commanded [Jer. 35:1–10].

As by a flash of lightning, we look far back along the course of social development, and behold a clan reverting to the primitive habits of nomadic tent-dwellers in protest against the problem of territorial civilization. The Rechabites, indeed, carried the reaction against Baalism clear over to the extreme "left," *where the bulk of the peasant aristocracy could not follow;* because it was not practicable for the majority of the settled population of

Ephraim to leave their pleasant villages and return to nomadic tent-life. That the people wanted to enjoy the advantages of settled existence was natural; and finding that many evils followed in the train of civilization, the house of Joseph undertook to solve the problem, first, by throwing off the dynasty of David, and then by annihilating the dynasty of Omri, along with Phoenician Baalism. But Jehonadab ben Rechab, not satisfied with such measures, took the apparently more logical step of abandoning private proprietorship in the soil, and thus renouncing the advantages of territorial society. And while he and the Rechabite group indorsed the destructive work of Jehu, they had no suggestions to offer except that of return to nomadism. And consequently, while the Rechabites had the externals of logic on their side, they took up an impossible attitude. For the problem of civilization is to be solved not by running away from it but by grappling with its difficulties.

Significance of Hebrew history begins to become clear in period of Elijah.—All the civilized peoples of the world have traveled by one route or another out of communal nomadism into settled, commercial territorialism; and in the course of this evolution three great political groups have risen up in succession—the *oriental* (including Egypt, Babylonia, Assyria, Phoenicia, and Israel); the *classic* (headed by Greece and Rome); and the *western* (led by modern Europe, America, etc.). And sooner or later the nations of each group have been confronted by problems of land monopoly, poverty, taxation, and war. The ancient oriental civilization went down to decay; while Israel continues to live as a spiritual force, not because it solved the problem of social justice, or constructed a program literally applicable to our own day, *but because it slowly welded the conception of the Divine into the heart of the human struggle for a better world*. The classic civilization took over the Hebrew idea of God without understanding it, and also fell into ruin. Then the spiritual heritage of Israel passed on to the tribes of Europe as they emerged from nomadism into the modern territorial régime. Civilization today is encountering the same social problem which undid the oriental and classic peoples; and while the churches of today cannot advocate concrete programs of political and economic reform, the religious issue of our time is whether organized religion shall be enlisted in defense of a narrow individualism, or in behalf of a social vision which leads men to grapple earnestly with the tremendous problem of our age. That the social impulse was the great dynamic power which underlay the upward evolution of Hebrew religion is the lesson of Hebrew history; and our examination of that history, having reached the period of Elijah the prophet, has now arrived at a point where its economic and sociological factors are coming more and more clearly into view.

Ephraimite struggle against Phoenician Baal involves Judah in more limited contest.—The sanguinary downfall of Tyrian Baalism in Ephraim had an important, but more limited, repercussion in Judah. King Ahaziah, of the Davidic line at Jerusalem, had the misfortune to be a guest of the Ephraimite royal family at the very moment when Jehu set out on his mission to destroy the house of Omri; and when the northern dynasty went down to its bloody fate, the visiting monarch from the south lost his life in the cataclysm (II Kings 9:21, 27). King Ahaziah of Judah was the issue of a state marriage between the house of David and the princess *Athaliah*, daughter of Ahab and perhaps of Jezebel. A temple was built at Jerusalem in honor of the Tyrian Baal; so that Ahaziah of Judah is described as follows by the compiler of Kings: "He walked in the way of the house of Ahab, and did evil in the sight of Yahweh, as did the house of Ahab; for he was the son-in-law of the house of Ahab" (II Kings 8:27).

That Athaliah was a woman of great energy, like Jezebel, is evident from what she did upon hearing the news of her son's death; for she arose and procured the slaughter of the whole house of David at Jerusalem, except one little prince, who was hidden from her fury, after which Athaliah reigned as usurping queen for six years. Then the *priests of Yahweh* brought forth and crowned the hidden prince, *Joash*, of the Davidic line, slew Athaliah, destroyed the temple of Baal, broke the images of Baal in pieces, and killed the Baal priest (II Kings, chap. 11).

With reference to these facts, a highly important consideration must be kept in view. Judah was always more primitive, secluded, and clannish, than Ephraim, having but little commercialism. Hebrew prophecy, *as a pro-mishpat, anti-Baal agitation*, did not originate in the *south*, and was not the dynamic force which overthrew Tyrian Baalism at Jerusalen. Hebrew prophecy originated in *Ephraim* as a political force in the time of Samuel, and as an anti-Baal force in the time of Elijah. *But in Judah the anti-Baal agitation was primarily a priestly movement against the claims of an alien priesthood and in favor of the Davidic dynasty*. This contrast will have to be emphasized when we come to consider the differences between the J and E documents in relation to the process of Hebrew history.

Social conditions worse under Jehu's dynasty, which reigns nevertheless about one hundred years.—Holding the Ephraimite throne for about one hundred years, the dynasty of Jehu was ushered in with bright hopes that were quickly disappointed. No real reform could be achieved under the lead of this demagogic militarist and his descendants. The general state of the world, both within and without Israel, prohibited the realization of any constructive, idealistic program. The whole posture of national and international affairs, during the long rule of the house of Jehu, not only hindered progress in the outward, secular concerns of life, but actually made for deterioration. War and rumors of war; the conscription of simple farmers and shepherds into military service; the burden of taxes; and the increased cost of living—all these conditions were against public welfare and contrary to social progress. Any detailed account of strife and battle would serve no purpose in this narrative; but some reference to the conflict of peoples during the long rule of Jehu's house is necessary to a comprehension of the remarkable development of Hebrew thought which took place in that period.

The outstanding theme is the advance of the *Assyrian empire* toward the Mediterranean coast. This movement was *gradual* and *irregular*. The Assyrians invaded the kingdom of Damascus without overthrowing it, soon after the accession of Jehu. Then civil war and internal weakness prevented the great Mesopotamian power from going westward for *thirty-five years*. Damascus, in the meanwhile, with its hands now free, seized all the territory east of Jordan belonging to Israel (II Kings 10:32, 33). This was followed by an oppression of Ephraim in which, according to the annalist, the people became *"like the dust by threshing"* (II Kings 13:3, 4, 7). But in course of time the Assyrians recovered, coming west again, reducing Damascus, pressing on to the Mediterranean, seizing the whole coast, and subjugating the Phoenicians of Tyre and Sidon. Then, once more, the tables were turned. Assyria was again preoccupied by revolts and internal weakness, being compelled to withdraw from the west for *half a century*. And, in the meanwhile, the kingdom of Damascus, having been trampled upon so mercilessly by the Assyrian war-machine, was now in a reduced condition; so that the house of Jehu regained all the territory which had been lost, and succeeded in restoring the map of Ephraim to its dimensions under the house of David (II Kings 13:25; 14:23–27). *This brilliant restoration of political and military prestige came to a climax in the time of Jehu's great-grandson, Jeroboam II, who reigned forty-one years.*

But the good fortune that came to the house of Joseph in the days of Jeroboam II brought no gain to the mass of the people. For under Jehu's dynasty the bulk of Ephraimite landholders gradually sank into the lower class of slaves, or *abadim;* and, meanwhile, the wealthy men, like *Shemer*, developed into a

small group of magnates, or nobles, who concentrated all economic and political power into their own hands.

**Social conditions under Jeroboam II as reflected in book of
prophet Amos.**—The history of Ephraim under the Jehu-
dynasty is treated in a very brief, disappointing way by the
Book of Kings; but we are fortunate enough to have sources of
more importance relating to this period, one of which is the
little Book of *Amos*, included among the so-called "minor"
prophets of the Hebrew Bible. Amos was not an Ephraimite,
but a *Judean shepherd*, whose home was in the village of *Tekoa*,
on a hill in the wild country ten miles to the *south* of Jerusalem;
and he walked all the way from Tekoa in Judah to the village of
Bethel, in the highlands of Ephraim, for the purpose of delivering a message, in the name of Yahweh, against the house of
Jehu. His prophecy was uttered in the reign of Jeroboam II
(Amos 1:1; 7:9, 10, 11).

To Amos, familiar with the primitive *mishpat* of the back-
woods, the problem of Ephraim is the sale of the *righteous* for
silver, and of the *needy* for a pair of shoes (2:6). In these pic-
turesque terms Amos describes the reduction of poor peasants
into bondage. The "needy," we should observe, are identified
with the "righteous," *who have a just cause*, but are unable to
get any hearing "in the gate," i.e., the law-courts, where the
needy are viewed with contempt, where the just are afflicted,
and where mishpat, instead of being freely dispensed, is turned
into gall and wormwood (Amos 5:7, 10, 12; 6:12). The solution
of the problem, according to Amos, prophesying in the name of
Yahweh, is to restore justice "in the gate"; so that mishpat
shall roll down like waters, and righteousness like a mighty
stream (5:15, 24).

Yahweh cares not for sacrifices offered in the midst of social
injustice; and, as a matter of fact, according to Amos, no system of sacrifice was ever observed by the children of Israel in the
wilderness (5:21-23, 25). This view is identical with that of the

prophet Jeremiah, who says, in the name of Yahweh, "I spoke not unto your fathers, nor commanded them in the time that I brought them out of the land of Egypt, concerning burnt offerings and sacrifices" (Jer. 7:22). *This very simple prophetic view of the pre-Canaanite history is important for us to bear in mind when we consider the origin of the documents entering into the Torah, or Law.* Not only was there no miraculously given régime of sacrifice in the wilderness, but Amos puts the exodus of Israel from Egypt in the same naturalistic category as the migration of the Philistines out of Kaphtor into southwest Canaan, and the removal of the Arameans out of Kir into the region of Damascus (9:7).

In the eyes of Amos, the shortcomings of Ephraim were perfectly symbolized by the great, walled city of Samaria, built by Omri, where dwelt kings and wealthy landed nobles, who lived in *palaces*, and lay upon ivory beds, drinking wine from huge bowls, and singing idle songs to the noise of the viol. *Yahweh hates the palaces of Jacob*, says Amos; and therefore the winter house and the summer house are to be smitten; the houses of ivory shall perish; while the city and all that is therein shall be delivered up to destruction (Amos 3:15; 6:8).

This message, uttered in the streets of Bethel, would of course be heard with satisfaction by any poor country folk who happened to be in town. But Bethel was the seat of an important royal shrine belonging to the *established church of Israel*. For here, in this very place, at the time when the house of David was rejected, the first Jeroboam set up a small *golden bull*, representing Yahweh, who had brought the house of Joseph out of Goshen; and another image of the same kind had been placed in the sanctuary of Dan, far away in the north (I Kings 12:28, 29). The church at Bethel was under the ministry of a clergyman called *Amaziah the cohen*, or priest, who held office by appointment of the king. And when this functionary heard the address by Amos, he at once dispatched a message to Jeroboam

II at Samaria, saying, "Amos hath conspired against thee in the midst of the house of Israel! The land is not able to bear all his words!" Then, without waiting for orders from Samaria, but not daring to arrest the agitator, the priest went out into the street, and cried to Amos: "Go! Flee away into the land of Judah! Prophesy not again any more in Bethel, because it is the king's chapel and a royal sanctuary" (Amos 7:10–13).

Like Jehonadab and the Rechabites, who were also shepherds, Amos represents an extreme protest against the usages of territorial civilization. The views of Amos reflect his native life in Judah, where the population consisted mainly of primitive clans which were first organized into a tribe under David, who afterward took them into the kingdom of Israel. Influenced by the "proto-Deuteronomic," Josephite conquest of the central highlands, and ignoring the Amorite cities outside of Ephraim, Amos extends the scope of conquest over the whole country, in the fashion of the later scribes. He repeatedly calls Israel *Joseph*, and imagines that the Amorites were completely exterminated, *root and branch;* after which all Israel was established in a primitive tribal country shorn of cities (Amos 2:9; 5:6, 15; 6:6). The Amorite word "baal" is not used by Amos in application to men or gods, or in any other way. Thus, the prophet from Tekoa looks upon Israel as a racially pure, "line-bred" nation which, through perversity, has broken away from its early standard of mishpat.

Social conditions under Jeroboam II as reflected in book of prophet Hosea.—The reign of Jeroboam II was also marked by the work of another prophet, *Hosea ben Beeri* (Hos. 1:1). Unlike Amos, who approached Ephraim as an outsider and used the southern phraseology, Hosea lived in the house of Joseph; and his book is wholly steeped in the social conditions of Ephraim. The difference between the two prophets is very instructive. The term "baal" occurs in the Book of Hosea *seven* times, and the term "Ephraim," *thirty-seven* times; whereas Amos employed the term "Joseph" with reference to North Israel (Amos 5:15; 6:6). This prophet's environment, in contrast with Judah, was less primitive and more commercial, being dominated by trade routes and walled cities like Samaria. But Hosea himself stands alongside the village folk who are outraged and helpless amid the "civilization" which is gradually overwhelming them in bondage to the fortunate few. The problem of justice, or mishpat, concerns Hosea no less than Amos. *"Ephraim* is oppressed. He is crushed in *mishpat"* (Hos. 5:11). But in contrast with Amos from the south, Hosea the Ephraimite has a new approach to the subject, and he deals with it in a different way.

Instead of regarding Israel as "line-bred," like Amos, Hosea lays particular stress upon the "melting-pot" in which the descendants of wilderness clans are fused with city populations: *"Ephraim,* he mixeth himself among the peoples, *and is a cake not turned,"* i.e., not cooked into a uniform consistency, but *half-baked* (Hos. 7:8). Trade is looked upon as conducted unjustly; and the old Amorite name "Canaan" is applied in a commercialistic sense to Ephraim: "Canaan! The balances of deceit are in his hand. He loves to defraud. And Ephraim said, I have grown rich. I have found wealth." But because of this very fact—because life is polluted by commercialism—Hosea, like Amos, declares in the name of Yahweh that all the fortresses are to be destroyed, and that Ephraim shall go back to the primitive clan-existence in tents (Hos. 12:7, 8, 9; 10:14). This recalls again the protest of Jehonadab and the Rechabites, and brings to view the original desert mishpat which always lurks implicitly in prophetic thought.

It is only as we understand Hosea's antagonism against commercial civilization that we can rightly interpret his attack on the newly rising Baal cult as incompatible with true worship of Yahweh. The Book of Hosea shows that while the *foreign,* Phoenician Baal cult had, indeed, been destroyed out of Israel by the bloody revolution of Jehu, yet the *local*, native Baal worship, rooted in the older, submerged Amorite life of Canaan, was now reasserting itself as a powerful factor in Hebrew thought and religion. Driven out of Ephraim proper by the vigorous, proto-Deuteronomic conquest of the central hill-country which culminated in the downfall of Shechem; pushed back into such Amorite centers as Ibleam, Taanach, Megiddo, and Beth-shan, which lay beyond the original frontiers of Joseph; and restrained hitherto by the hostile atmosphere of the peasant aristocracy; the Baal cults had always been there, like living roots of some alien growth, waiting the inevitable day when they should spread forth from secret places. And now at length, in the reign of Jeroboam II, when the bulk of the peasantry is falling into helpless bondage, and cannot longer make effective opposition, the local, Amorite Baal cults burst forth into luxurious brilliance, threatening completely to overwhelm the primitive mishpat.

In the light of these considerations, we can see why it is that the Baalim are the central point of Hosea's attack on the problem of his day. The Baalim, regarded from one special standpoint, were no doubt "gods of good crops"; but we cannot begin to grasp the thought of Hosea unless we consider his book as a whole, and also measure him by his later-coming disciple Jeremiah, who practically *ignores* the supposed fertility function of the Canaanite gods, and whose anti-Baal polemic is equated with the struggle for mishpat. *The Baalim, accordingly, stand for the system of commercial civilization which is engulfing Ephraim.* The practice of calling Yahweh by the name "Baal," noticed in the time of David, was reasserting itself strongly in the days of Jeroboam II; but Hosea, speaking in the name of Yahweh, says "Thou shalt call me *Ishi* [my man, or my husband], and shalt no more call me *Baali* [my Baal]; for I will take away the names of the Baalim out of her [Israel's] mouth; and they shall no more be remembered by their name" (Hos. 2:16, 17).

Giving another turn to his denunciation of the Amorite cults, Hosea, for the first time in Hebrew history, equates the word "baal" with the Hebrew term *bosheth*, or "shameful thing" (Hos. 9:10). The name of Baal ought not to be applied to Yahweh, says Hosea, because the use of it obscures the national deity of Israel under a Canaanite name which was not known in the desert. That there was already a practical identification of Yahweh and the Amorite Baalim in certain districts and among certain classes may have been true. But in drawing a clear contrast between Yahweh and Baal, Hosea shows that the original Israelite and Canaanite cults were by no means inseparably confused throughout the entire country, and that the nation as a *whole* had not yet bowed the knee to a triumphant Baalism and completely forgotten the name of Yahweh (Hos. 2:8).

Hosea brilliant example of upward moral evolution in Hebrew history.—We saw that the anti-Baal campaign of Elijah and Elisha was based explicitly upon the supposed command of Yahweh to exterminate the house of Omri (I Kings 19:15, 16, 17; II Kings 9:26, 36; 10:17). The bloody revolution which began with wholesale murder in the valley of *Jezreel* at the country palace of Ahab, and which enthroned the house of Jehu, had the full approval of the insurgent prophets who flourished in those days. But all the prestige of that historic upheaval counts for nothing with Hosea, who declares, at the very beginning of his book, *"Yahweh said, I will avenge the blood of Jezreel upon the house of Jehu, and will cause the kingdom of the house of Israel to cease"* (Hos. 1:4). In this adverse judgment upon the past, we find a higher moral insight beginning to express itself at the heart of the evolutionary process through which the cult of Yahweh rose, by gradual stages, from the level of paganism to the plane of ethical monotheism. *"Let us know,—let us follow on to know Yahweh"* (Hos. 6:3). Hosea's book is, indeed, one of the most powerful writings in the Hebrew Bible.

Baalization of peasant aristocracy.—We saw that Hosea protested against the term *baal* in application to Yahweh, and called, instead, for the use of another term, *ish* (Hos. 2:16). The placing of these words in opposition by the prophet seems to imply an inherent *conflict*, or antithesis, between them; and, as a matter of fact, they bring into relief a tremendously important phase of Hebrew social development which is buried in the Hebrew text of the Bible, hardly appearing on the surface of translations. The Bible was put into modern languages, in the first place, not for the scientific purpose of making Hebrew history intelligible, but for churchly and religious reasons in the conventional sense; and the translators have been embarrassed by many passages which they desired to handle honestly, but whose meanings can be conveyed only through explanations more detailed than the average reader of the Bible will tolerate.

In the case before us, the word *ish* is the most common Hebrew term for "man" as an individual, masculine human being. A woman's husband is called simply "her man [*ish*]"; and there is no ancient Hebrew term corresponding to "husband." This noun, *ish*, is employed in the earliest biblical sources to designate a man of *Israel*, or of a *tribe*, or of a *village*, its plural form being *anashim*. Thus the men of Succoth and Penuel, whom Gideon chastised in Gilead, are called *anashim* seven times (Judg. 8:5, 8, 14, 15, 16, 22).

The case of Succoth and Penuel, in Judges, chapter 8, is chosen out of countless others because it stands in juxtaposition to Judges, chapter 9, where a sharply contrasted example of a different usage occurs with reference to the men of a *non-Hebrew*, *Amorite* city. The Ephraim narrative about the destruction of *Shechem* knows that the citizens of this ancient, Canaanite stronghold were *baalim* (inaccurately rendered "men" fifteen times [Judg. 9:2, 3, 6, 7, 18, 20, etc.]). And, in the same way, the Ephraimite, or E, document is aware that the burgesses of Amorite *Jericho*, destroyed by the house of Joseph at the time of the invasion, were also baalim (Josh. 24:11; incorrectly rendered "men"). Likewise, the non-Hebrew *Uriah the Hittite*, proprietor of a house in the Amorite city of *Jebus*, is called a baal as follows: "And when the wife of Uriah heard that Uriah her *ish* was dead, she mourned for her *baal*" (II Sam. 11:26). This man was a Hittite citizen of Amorite Jerusalem. In similar wise, the men of *Keilah*, a Canaanite city "with gates and bars," are twice called "baalim" by the Hebrew text, but inaccurately "men" by the English versions (I Sam. 23:11, 12; cf. vs. 7).

Thus we see that whereas the peasant aristocracy of Israel proper are designated originally by the term *ish*, the Amorite citizens of non-Hebrew Canaan were known by the Semitic term *baal*. And yet, so far as modern versions go, these terms are translated by the same word, "men," obscuring a sociological problem of major importance which unfolds before us in the phenomena of the Hebrew text.

We are now prepared to understand that the gradual transfer of Israel out of clan society into territorial civilization upon Canaanite soil was accompanied by metamorphosis of *ish* into *baal*, *with reference to the matter of proprietorship in land, houses, cattle, slaves and women*. A preliminary glimpse at this evolution can be had by referring to Israelites of Gilead, not far from Succoth and Penuel, in the village of *Jabesh*. The citizens of that place are designated by the earlier term *ish* in all but the last of the passages following:

Judg. 21:9, *ish*	II Sam. 2:4, 5, *ish*
I Sam. 11:1, 5, 10, *ish*	II Sam. 21:12, BAAL
I Sam. 31:12, *ish*	

This part of Israel was fortified by Solomon and Jeroboam I, at Ramoth-gilead and Penuel, respectively, being brought under the play of political and economic forces operative in the Hebrew kingdom as a whole; and the extreme shock of "civilization" upon the very backward community of Gilead may ex-

plain why the struggle against Baalism was initiated by a prophet from east of Jordan (I Kings 4:13; 12:25; 17:1).

Continuing our survey of the text, we find that an Ephraimite, settled as a proprietor in Gibeah of Benjamin, is twice
called "the man, the baal of the house" (*ha ish, baal ha bayith*
[Judg. 19:22, 23]). An Israelite traveler, with his concubine, is
entertained in this house; a mob surrounds the place, to outrage
the travelers; but in order to placate the besiegers and save the
masculine guest, the men within the house throw out the *woman*
to the mob, since women are chattel property (vs. 25). The victim is abused all night, and expires in the morning; but the
traveler sleeps in safety (vss. 26, 27). The men of the village,
who perpetrated the outrage, are called "the *baalim* of Gibeah"
(Judg. 20:5). This is in the *appendix* to Judges.

Another linguistic phase of the evolution into baalism is introduced by the same Gibeah story. The traveler who took
refuge in the house not only brought with him the woman whom
he threw to the mob outside, but also a *slave;* and he is called the
"lord," or *adon*, of the slave and of the woman (Judg. 19:11, 12,
26, 27). The term *adon*, as indicating ownership of animals, of
the soil and of human beings as chattels, was in the same primitive category as *ish*. Thus, the great Calebite landlord, Nabal,
is an *adon* (I Sam. 25:14). He complains that many slaves
(*abadim*) break away, every one, from his lord, or master (*adon*
[vs. 10]). The master-slave relationship is primarily indicated
by the terms *adon-ebed*, expressed thus in the Judahite Book of
Isaiah: "As with the slave [*ebed*] so with his owner [*adon*]" (Isa.
24:2). Likewise, in the J, or Judahite, source, when Abraham
sends his slave, *ebed*, to get a wife for Isaac, the slave repeatedly
calls Abraham "my *adon*" (Gen. 24:2, 9, 10, 12, etc.); and in the
same connection, Sarah is called the woman of her *adon* (vs. 36).
This usage occurs in the J document fifty times; and while it
seems to have been more characteristic of Judah than of Ephraim, it is also found in the records of the Josephite monarchy,

where it is used with reference to the great landlord *Shemer*, already noticed, who sold his hill at a high price to Omri; the city built thereon being called "after the name of Shemer the owner [*adon*] of the hill" (I Kings 16:24).

On the other hand, we now observe *adon*, like *ish*, passing into the north Canaanite *baal*. Thus, where the Judaic document calls Abraham the *adon* of Sarah (Gen. 24:36), the *Ephraim*-document calls him the *baal* of Sarah. He travels about with her; but fears that some powerful personage, beholding her beauty, may seek his death in order to get Sarah (as David stole the beautiful Bathsheba from her *baal* by procuring the murder of Uriah). Abraham therefore pretends that Sarah is not his wife, but only a sister; so that if any strong man wants her, she can be sacrificed like the woman at Gibeah; while Abraham goes free, leaving Sarah in a harem if necessary. And the story goes on to show that in confirmation of his fear, a certain king sent and took her from Abraham. The purpose of the narrative *itself* is to advance the claims of a higher moral code; and hence, before Sarah is actually taken into the king's *harem*, he is visited in a dream by God, who reveals that the woman is *beulath baal* (Gen. 20:3). This Hebrew phrase is represented in English versions by the words "a man's wife," which, of course, do not give the sense of the original, nor any conception of the problem which we are studying. The Hebrew terms can be translated into English only by the awkward expression "feminine baal of a baal." Precisely the same phrase, *beulath baal*, occurs in the D document, later than E, where it is rendered "a woman married to a husband" (Deut. 22:22). The primitive expression for marrying a woman was merely "he took her" (I Sam. 25:39; Gen. 6:2 [J]; 11:29 [J]; Exod. 2:1 [E]). But the progress of Amorite baalism introduced the competing expression, *ba-al*, as a verb meaning "to marry." The older and newer usages come together in Deuteronomy, where we read, in English, "when a man hath taken a wife and married her"; but the Hebrew text is, "when a man hath taken a wife and *baaled* her" (Deut. 24:1). The latter verb is found separately, e.g., in a late post-Exilic section of Isaiah, where the English reads, "For as a young man *marries* a virgin, so shall thy sons *marry* thee"; but the original text has inflections of *ba-al* for the verb in both cases (Isa. 62:5).

These illustrations take us up to a point where not only the ownership of women but also of real estate and cattle comes into view as designated by the same term. Thus, "the ox knoweth his owner, and the ass the crib of his *baal*" (Isa. 1:3). And, by the same token, a piece of land belonging to a baal is called *beulah land*, because it is "baaled" (Isa. 62:4). Job calls down a penalty upon himself if he has wrongly taken land, or caused the innocent owners (*baalim*) to lose their lives (Job 31:38, 39). That the term "baal" is the proper designation of anyone who has a lawsuit is taken for granted by the Ephraimite, or E, document (Exod. 24:14, inaccurately rendered "man").

Baalistic legalism at length overwhelms primitive mishpat in house of Joseph.—The linguistic transformation thus briefly sketched is the verbal *symbol* of an objective, historic process that overcame the Yahweh revolution which the house of Joseph established in the central Canaanite hill-country. Intermarriage between Israelites and the older population remaining in the land; inclusion of Jerusalem and other pre-Israelite cities within the framework of the new Hebrew kingdom; pressure of militarism, and the burden of taxation; demand for loans by the poorer freemen, and the consequent need of security for debt— all these forces and circumstances carried the Hebrew nation away from primitive clan customs toward the ideas and practices of Amorite civilization. *Thus an aristocracy arose under the name of "baalim," whose "right wing" was identified with ancient Canaanite law and religion, but whose "left wing" clung to the radical "mishpat" of the primitive clans whose ancestors brought the cult of Yahweh from the wilderness The wealthy faction of the property-class worshiped Yahweh as a magnified and powerful*

Baal; but the "poor and needy" element in this class reacted gropingly against the drift of territorial civilization.

The two streams of culture, springing from desert nomadism and settled civilization, flowed along together in the onrushing current of Hebrew history; while the inexorable forces at work in territorial society carried the *government* over toward the "right wing," until the *state* at length reached a position of absolute compromise with baalism. But the sociological pattern of Israel was new in the experience of the world; for never before did a wilderness god become the political symbol of a state which recognized the local deities of a mature civilization. The *rule* was for the already sophisticated god of some such place as Babylon, Rome, Nineveh, or Thebes, to rise above other gods as the outstanding symbol of a nation or empire. But, on the contrary, the capital cities of Judah and Ephraim did not represent a slow process of evolution; *for Jerusalem was abruptly occupied by David; while Samaria was built overnight by Omri;* and, in both cases, a cult of primitive character, whose "unsophisticated" features could not quickly fade from popular memory, was thrust, *per saltum*, into the atmosphere and precincts of "civilization."

All the peoples of antiquity, including Israel, groaned under the burden of social injustice; but among all these peoples, *except* Israel, the gods were sophisticated beings on the side of the wealthy against the impoverished; *and therefore among the Gentiles, any radical revolt against the state was high treason against religion;* so that priestly influence could manipulate even the emotions of the unpropertied mob in suppressing radicalism. But in Israel the unwonted social pattern of the nation *itself* gave the psychological impulse toward political-religious revolt which was lacking among the Gentiles. And thus, Ahijah, the Josephite prophet of Shiloh, instigated Jeroboam I to lead the uprising against the house of David; while Elijah the Gileadite set in motion the forces which annihilated the dynasty of Omri.

The peculiar Hebrew evolution led Israel's thinkers to dramatize divinity on the side of the "poor and needy" against the rich; so that Yahweh became the champion of the "poor," and the leading actor in a story whose villains were the Baalim of Canaan.

But the upheavals which overthrew the dynasties of David and Omri were of no avail. Conditions became so desperate under the house of Jehu that such thinkers as Amos and Hosea lost hope, and gave the nation up to doom. There was no longer any heart or force for political revolts. The existing régime of "state-and-church" was controlled by a small clique of nobles and officeholders on the aristocratic "right wing." And in that epoch the prudent *kept silence* "because it was an evil time" (Amos. 5:13). Hebrew thought was driven back upon itself, and overflowed in the field of literary production, giving rise gradually to compilations of narrative, prophetic and legal matter. Under this head are the books of Amos and Hosea; while in the same category come the tales about Elijah and Elisha, and the material now found in the Ephraimite and Judahite sources, E and J. *But such writings were at first purely private and unofficial; and they retained that character for many centuries before being incorporated in large compilations and received officially as Holy Scripture by the post-Exilic Jews.* Bearing this fact in mind, we turn to a disorderly collection of material which many critics have called the "Covenant Code," but which would better be known as the "Early Mishpat Book."

Utopian proposals for social justice compiled in time of Jehu dynasty.—A collection of legal matter, eventually incorporated into the Ephraimite source, but at first an *independent* production, is now found in Exodus, *beginning at 20:24, and extending as far as 23:20.* This material, which is not arranged according to logical method, does not disclose its real significance until we have examined it carefully. It presupposes an agricultural society *stratified into two rigid classes*, upper and lower, with Hebrew freemen above and *alien* slaves below. The free individual men of the upper class are designated by the old term *ish* twenty-three times; and by the term *adon* seven times; *but by the northern term "baal" twelve times.* The text passes casually from one to the other; and no accurate sense of the Hebrew comes into the conventional modern versions. The lower, enslaved class is referred to by the term *ebed*, or male slave, seven times, and by the term *amah*, or female slave, six times. Moreover, without any warning to the modern reader, the English word "maid" is used for translating *amah* (*supra*) and *betolah*, or young virgin-daughter of a free baal (21:26; cf. 22:16). The freemen constitute an aristocracy which owns and uses the soil for cornland, vineyards, oliveyards, and pasture; while the slaves *normally* contemplated are *non-Hebraic*—a point which has to be held carefully in view to get the full force of the material.

Over against the social background thus depicted are placed a number of rules dealing with situations likely to arise in a community of this kind. An *ish*, or baal, who kills a member of his *own* social class shall be put to death (21:12). But, on the other hand, a baal who beats a slave to death with a rod shall not be executed, but only "punished"—in a manner not specified; and, moreover, if the slave does not die *at once*, but remains alive a day or two before dying, then the baal of the slave shall not be punished at all, *"for he is his money"* (21:20, 21). Thus we find ourselves on a moral plane far below the ethics of present-day Judaism and Christianity.

The underlying preoccupation of the code is with the baalim on the "left wing" of the upper class, in the time of the Jehu dynasty, who are being more and more depressed from their normal status, and forced into the lower class of *abadim*, or enslaved aliens. Thus, if a Hebrew baal buys another free Hebrew as a *slave*, a situation arises which is an outrage to the sense of primitive mishpat. That a free man should become the slave of another free man is abhorrent to the moral feeling of clan brotherhood. Yet the pressure of territorialism, as against the primitive mishpat, has now grown so powerful that a compromise with baalism is deemed necessary. And therefore the wealthy baal who buys a poor baal is forbidden to keep his "brother" in slavery for the rest of his life, as he would in the case of an alien bondservant; and he is directed to set his *Hebrew* slave at liberty after a period of *six years*, that the slave may ascend once more into the full and free status of enfranchised baalism (Exod. 21:2).

If, during the time of his bondage, the Hebrew slave has been given a woman by his master, and she has borne him children, *the mother and her offspring shall not go free with him, but shall remain slaves in the master's house.* On the other hand, if the Hebrew slave were *baal of a woman* (trans., "if he were married") at the time when he was purchased, then his wife shall go free with him. But if he wishes to remain a slave *permanently*, his master shall take him to the door, to *elohim* (i.e., to the family divinity), and shall bore his ear through with an awl (Exod. 21: 2–6).

Again, a Hebrew baal may sell his daughter to be an *amah* (feminine slave); and in such case the baal who *buys* her shall not sell her to a foreign people, but he may resell her to her own family. Nevertheless, if he keeps her and buys another *amah*, he must be careful to treat the *first* feminine slave as well as he does the *new* one; or the first shall be free to go out for nothing (21: 8–11).

Approaching the complex problem of mishpat from still another angle, if a wealthy baal makes a loan of money to a poor and needy baal, the lender shall not charge the borrower any interest whatever (*neshek*). The Hebrew term is translated "usury" by the older English versions, leading some to suppose that this indicates a difference between a lawful and an illegitimate charge for the use of money. But there is no such distinction in the Hebrew text; and, accordingly, the American Revised Bible and the American Jewish Version both translate "interest," because the principle of this idealistic reform code is that the wealthier baals ought to make loans for *nothing* (22: 25).

Moreover, the common baalistic practice of taking a mortgage, or pledge, on landed property is forbidden by implication; and the code assumes that any security, between brethren of the house of Israel, is wrong. But if the lender is determined to require a pledge, let him take his neighbor's *garment* symbolically, *and return it to him by sundown; "for that is his covering, his raiment; and he has nothing else wherein to sleep"* (vss. 26, 27).

Again, the wealthy baal, who owns fields, vineyards, and oliveyards, may cultivate his property and consume the fruit of it for six years; but at the end of every such period, he must let all his property lie *fallow* and bring forth what it will spontaneously, in order that the poor baalim and their families may enter in and enjoy the produce for the entire seventh year (23:11).

The legal situation stressed by Amos with reference to the courts is implied by the command, "Thou shalt not wrest the *mishpat* of the poor in his law suit" (23:6). The code assumes that there cannot be two opposing conceptions of justice, arising out of the clash between primitive clan Yahwism and sophisticated baalism. It takes for granted that mishpat can have only *one*, single, clear meaning; that the poor man's case will always be right; and that the judges ought to be merely referees, who will at once take the side of the poor baal against the rich baal.

But the writers of the code are aware that none of its provisions will be effective as long as Hebrews worship, or take legal oaths in the name of, other gods besides the primitive non-baalistic Yahweh. And in the background of their efforts to deal with this principle, we can plainly see the abiding influence of that bloody uprising against Phoenician Baalism which had swept away the house of Omri in wholesale slaughter by the supposed command of Yahweh. For the rule is laid down cate-

gorically that whoever sacrifices to any god except Yahweh shall
be *utterly destroyed* (22:20). And a solemn injunction is added
that even the *name* of other gods must not be remembered, nor
called to mind, nor heard out of one's mouth (23:13). Thus, the
writers of the code agree with Hosea that Yahweh should not be
called a Baal, and that the *names* of the Amorite Baalim should
be taken out of the mouth of Israel and forgotten (Hos. 2:16,
17). *But Hosea rises above them in his denunciation of the anti-
Baal massacre which enthroned the house of Jehu* (1:4).

That this early Mishpat Book was, in a general way, contem-
poraneous with Hosea and Amos is clear enough. But we cannot
say which came first; and the probability is that the code itself,
instead of being written all at once, was compiled gradually.
The point for emphasis here is not the question of precise dating,
but the fact that Amos, Hosea, and the code are complementary
products of the desperate social conditions which characterized
the long epoch of Jehu's dynasty.

**Mishpat Book voices utopian aspirations of noble souls in
advance of their own day.**—The outstanding provisions of the
Mishpat Book, then, are, non-interest-bearing loans, no mortgage foreclosures, no permanent bondage in the case of Hebrew
baalim, and septennial reversion of large estates to use by "left
wing" baalim for one year. This platform should be judged not
in the light of modern ethical ideas but in view of conditions
existing at the time under consideration. It is the work of noble
souls, distressed by the suffering around them, and compelled
like Amos to remain silent in an evil day; but souls who hope
that some favorable turn of events might give them voice and
influence.

As for the program itself, no group of thrifty proprietors in
that age of the world would accumulate an economic surplus of
money or goods and then make unsecured loans without interest; nor would any large number of peasant aristocrats open
their estates, every seven years, to the inrush of their less for-

tunate neighbors. A code of this kind, if actually put into effect, would shift the social surplus to the "left," encourage parasitism, and penalize all saving. But while the code was utopian and impossible, it proclaims the longing for social justice which animated the age that produced Amos and Hosea.

That the problem of justice in the kingdom of north Israel was insoluble is the view taken by a story about the prophet Elisha, which came into circulation at this time. The tale gets point from the common prevalence of slavery for debt, and puts this literal fact in a setting of myth. A widow's children have been taken by the creditor; and she appeals for help to the prophet Elisha, who, *by a miracle*, increases the widow's oil supply, so that she can sell the oil, pay the debt, and release her children from bondage. This tale bears witness to the conviction that *only by a miracle could social justice be secured* (II Kings 4:1–7).

The social background of the Mishpat Code is, indeed, even more crude and barbarous than already intimated. For not only shall the worshipers of "other gods" be slain without mercy; but "thou shalt not permit a witch to live" (Exod. 22:18). Belief in witchcraft is, of course, mere superstition; and in a state of society where such belief exists, the process of "proving" the alleged crime in the case of an accused person is necessarily cruel beyond words—to say nothing of the resultant execution. Moreover, the crime of mayhem is brought wholly under the *lex talionis*, or law of simple retaliation: "Eye for eye, tooth for tooth, hand for hand, foot for foot, burning for burning, wound for wound, stripe for stripe" (21:24, 25). The code ends with the rule, "Thou shalt not boil a kid in its mother's milk" (23:19).

Mishpat Code supplies material for primitive Judaic, or J., edition of "commandments."—The Ten Commandments are generally thought of as having a definite, unchanging, unitary character, struck out once for all in the same form. But several varying editions of the commandments were issued, no two of which were the same; and the most primitive one was discovered in Exodus, chapter 34, by the German poet Goethe, in what is now called the J, or Judaic, source. The exact number of commands in this document is difficult to make out; but their connection with the Ephraimite Mishpat Code is clear. Thus:

1. Yahweh, whose name is jealous, is a jealous god. No molten gods shall be made (Exod. 34:14, 17; cf. "Mishpat Book," Exod. 22:20 and 23:13).

2. The feast of unleavened bread (*matzoth*) shall be observed; and *matzoth* shall be eaten seven days (Exod. 34:18; cf. Exod. 23:15).

3. Every first-born male belongs to Yahweh (Exod. 34:19, 20; this is found in the Ephraimite Mishpat Book at Exod. 22:29).

4. Six days are for labor; but on the seventh day *sabbath* is to be observed (Exod. 34:21; cf. Exod. 23:12).

5. The feast of weeks is to be observed, the first fruits of the wheat harvest, and of the ingathering at the year's end (Exod. 34:22; cf. Exod. 23:16).

6. Three times in the year shall all men-children appear before the *adon Yahweh, elohae Yisrael* (Exod. 34:23; cf. Exod. 23:17).

7. The blood of the sacrifice is not to be offered with leaven (Exod. 34:25; cf. Exod. 23:18).

8. The sacrifice of Passover (*pesach*) shall not be left over until the morning (Exod. 34:25; cf. Exod. 23:18).

9. A kid shall not be boiled in its mother's milk (Exod. 34:26; cf. Exod. 23:19).

It will be noticed that while the Judahite commandments in Exodus, chapter 34, are clearly *based upon* the Ephraimite Mishpat Book, *they omit all reference to mishpat ethics, and are thus purely ritualistic in character.* This remarkable distinction raises a problem of great importance for Hebrew history. If the southern code is *founded* upon the Ephraimite Mishpat Book, why does it carefully select the ritual demands, and avoid the ethical, social-justice provisions, of the northern document?

No prophetic mishpat struggle in Judah at that time.— The commandments of the J source do not emphasize mishpat ethics, because, *during the period when the J and E documents were beginning to take form,* no ethical-prophetic struggle was going forward in Judah like that which had convulsed Ephraim. The southern kingdom, as already pointed out, was economically and socially more primitive than the northern kingdom. Thus, while Ephraim overlay the trade routes of oriental civilization, Judah rose higher above sea-level, and was an isolated province whose lower extreme southern frontier section, the Negeb, lay entirely open to the Arabian wilderness. The clans of Judah were accordingly more primitive, and adhered more tenaciously to mishpat than did the population of Ephraim.

The inhabitants of Judah heard only dim, far-away echoes of the mighty struggle under Elijah and Elisha during the period of Omri's dynasty; and they could have only a remote interest in the conflict. Not only so; but when the struggle between Yahweh and Baal *first* invaded the south, it assumed the form of a non-prophetic, priestly revolution in Jerusalem, which repudiated the granddaughter of Omri and restored the Davidic line (p. 178; II Kings, chap. 11). *These considerations help us to see why the commandments of the J source in Exodus, chapter 34, have a ritualistic, non-ethical atmosphere.* The contrast, or distinction, between J and E, therefore, is not because Judah was less moral than Ephraim, or less interested in mishpat than the house of Joseph, but simply because Judah was more *primitive,* and was more slowly swept into the mishpat struggle.

Ephraimite form of Ten Commandments less ritualistic and more ethical than foregoing Judaic version.—A much better-known form of the commandments, with a more ethical atmosphere—but still not the *final* edition—is found in the Ephraimite document at Exodus, chapter 20, just before the Mishpat Book. This version, as distinguished from the Judaic one in Exodus, chapter 34, denounces concentration of property through covetousness, but recognizes the existence of human slavery.

1. I am Yahweh thy god, which have brought thee out of the land of Egypt, out of the house of slaves [*abadim*]. Thou shalt have no other gods before me [Exod. 20:2, 3].

2. Thou shalt not make unto thee any graven image, etc. [vs. 4].

3. Thou shalt not take the name of Yahweh thy god *in vain*, etc. [vs. 7].

4. Remember the sabbath day, to keep it holy [*kadosh*, i.e., separate from other days]. Six days shalt thou labor, and do all thy work. But the seventh day is the sabbath of Yahweh thy god. Thou shalt not do any work, thou, nor thy son, nor thy daughter, thy male slave [*ebed*], nor thy female slave [*amah*], etc. [vss. 8–10].

5. Honor thy father and thy mother, etc. [vs. 12].

6. Thou shalt not kill [vs. 13].

7. Thou shalt not commit adultery [vs. 14].

8. Thou shalt not steal [vs. 15].

9. Thou shalt not bear false witness against thy neighbor [as happened, for instance, in the Naboth case] [vs. 16].

10. Thou shalt not covet thy neighbor's *house*, nor thy neighbor's *wife*, nor his male slave [*ebed*], nor his female slave [*amah*], etc. [vs. 17].

In the tenth and last commandment, the *order* of the forbidden categories of covetousness calls for special notice; because in the *final* edition, which we shall study later on, these categories are sharply reversed, and a new one is added; while the ethical tone is higher still. But of this, more presently.

The two early editions of the commandments flank the Mishpat Book on either side; the Ephraimite compilation, in Exodus, chapter 20, coming *before*, and the more primitive Judahite version, in Exodus, chapter 34, coming *after*. An inconsistent explanation of the difference is given by the redactors of the Book of Exodus, who allege that the more familiar Ephraimite commandments, just quoted, were given to Moses on two tablets of stone; that Moses broke these tablets in anger when he saw the children of Israel worshiping a golden god made by Aaron; and that other stones were then prepared, on which the greatly differing, and more primitive, Judahite version was inscribed. But, as a matter of fact, neither set of commands was final, as we shall discover in connection with the history of Judah after the house of Ephraim has vanished; for the Torah itself gives a third and more finished edition of the commandments, arranged in a different order, and expressed in still other Hebrew terms.

Ephraimite legends in time of Jehu dynasty recognize Elijah as first great leader of mishpat struggle.—The same epoch that produced the Early Mishpat Book, the two early forms of the commandments and the writings of Amos and Hosea, gave rise also to legends and miracle stories about Elijah and Elisha, committed to writing by anonymous authors who were part of that great but silent literary awakening which took place in the evil times of the Jehu dynasty. The prophet Elijah was the first outstanding leader of the mishpat struggle; he belonged, not to Judah, but to the kingdom of Ephraim; and we need to remember always that he was first among the new type of prophets which characterize the Hebrew people. The religious leaders of Israel prior to his day were of a different kind; for during the entire pre-Elijah period there was no economic and social conflict *within* Israel itself which brought into play a cult-war between Yahweh and other gods. Thus, the earlier prophet *Ahijah of Shiloh*, for instance, was promoter of Jeroboam I in the revolt against the house of David; the still earlier prophet *Samuel* was identified with the establishment of monarchy in Ephraim as a defense against the Philistine foe; and, in a remoter past, the prophetess *Deborah* rallied the house of Joseph against the Canaanite host of Sisera. And thus, before the time of Elijah, Hebrew prophecy was *political*, having to do with the formation of the *state;* and in those earlier times, by the very nature of the case, there could be no domestic issue as between Yahweh and Baal. But with Elijah, the course of prophecy began to enter that new stage which has lifted Hebrew history to spiritual distinction in the world; and accordingly the special work of this prophet is recognized by the grandeur of the legends and myths that gathered around his memory.

Set apart, then, from all his predecessors, Elijah is unique; and his picture is painted upon a broad canvas by the epic imagination of Israel, working in troublous times: He is fed by the birds of the air and by angels from heaven; multiplies the widow's oil and meal; withholds rain; causes fire to fall from the sky; raises the dead to life; talks with Yahweh on Mount Horeb; divides the waters of Jordan, passing over dryshod; and at length ascends in a chariot of fire to heaven without death (I Kings, chaps. 17–19; II Kings, chap. 2). The great proto-Deuteronomic hero of Ephraim is, indeed, historically the founder of Hebrew monotheism; and his thaumaturgic powers are equaled only by the attributes which legend ascribes to the founder of Christianity.

That Elijah began the movement which resulted in Jehu's bloody expulsion of Tyrian Baalism from Israel is the sober testimony of history. And the legendary narratives confer direct personal credit upon him for the massacre that blotted out from Israel the devotees of Tyrian Baal. Thus, in I Kings, Elijah, on Mount Carmel, says, "Take the prophets of Baal. *Let not one of them escape.* And they took them; and Elijah slew them" (I Kings 18:40). But there is a very different account in II Kings, which we have already considered in part:

And Jehu said, Call all the prophets of Baal, all his servants, and all his priests. *Let none be wanting.* And all the worshippers of Baal came; so that there was not a man that came not. And they came into the house of Baal; and the house of Baal was full from one end to another. And Jehu went, and Jehonadab the son of Rechab, into the house of Baal. And Jehu said to the guard and to the captains, Go in and slay them. Let none come forth. And they smote them with the edge of the sword. *Thus Jehu destroyed Baal out of Israel* [II Kings 10:18, 19, 21, 23, 25, 28].

The actual destruction of Tyrian Baalism was by Jehu, long after Elijah's disappearance; and the claim that Elijah in person slew the devotees of the Tyrian god is part of the well-known story in which he calls down supernatural fire from heaven upon Mount Carmel. The executioner was *Jehu*, not Elijah.

Ephraimite patriarch Joseph depicted as land reformer.— Contrasted with Elijah, who champions the peasantry when their lands fall into the grip of the wealthy baalim, is another Ephraimite figure, moving entirely in the atmosphere of myth, and approaching the same problem of the *land* from a different angle. The picture of Joseph was added to the gallery of Israel's heroes at a time when concentrated ownership of the soil was becoming chronic. The wealthy few, as Amos declared, were not grieved for the *affliction of Joseph*, whereby the kingdom of Ephraim was to be carried into slavery by foreigners (Amos 6:6, 7). The Ephraimites, at an earlier time, had been sorely afflicted by their own brethren of Israel under the Davidic dynasty, when King Solomon appointed the young Jeroboam to be in charge "over the *burden* of the house of Joseph" (I Kings 11: 28). And in all subsequent years, this outrage at the hands of Judah had never been forgotten or forgiven. Ephraim had fared poorly under the rule of kings, and now needed to have before it the ideal of a righteous ruler, who should save the nation.

Brief reference to the Joseph myth has been made at an earlier point (see chap. ix, p. 160). A portion of the narrative relating to this patriarch is found in the northern, or Ephraimite, document of the Pentateuch; but a great deal of it comes to us through the Judaic, or J, source; while sections of it are blended so closely that the two documents cannot be distinguished (EJ or JE). The J source, because of its more *primitive* atmosphere, has been wrongly taken to be earlier than E. This undoubted contrast, however, is not chronological but sociological. Thus, the ritual commandments of J, in Exodus, chapter 34, follow in the wake of priestly revolution against Omrid influence at Jerusalem; and while this J decalogue is more primitive than that of E, in Exodus, chapter 20, nevertheless the Ephraimite com-

mandments reflect the rise of social prophetism in the house of
Joseph, and are earlier than the Judahite decalogue. The main
body of Hebrew tradition originated in *Ephraim;* and any departure of J from E is the result of manipulation in the interest
of southern prestige by a school of writers focalized at Hebron
in central Judah.

The question of documentary chronology will come before us
again; and it is adverted to here because the subject arises
naturally in relation to Joseph, the definitive ancestor of Ephraim. The most characteristic delineation of him as a wise and
righteous ruler occurs in the Judaic document at a point which
nevertheless reflects the social problem of *Ephraim.* The story
of Joseph is a challenge to the great nobles who were seizing the
soil under the forms of baalistic law, and exploiting the masses
of the once-free Josephite peasantry. But we must bear in mind
that the picture of Joseph, as a reformer, was painted at a time
when social agitators like Amos were denied a public hearing.
For the party in power considered that all discussion of the social problem was dangerous and "anarchistic." And so the story
of Joseph naturally evolved itself through the pressure of the
times. Anonymous authors imagined an ideal administrator
who provided against the age-old exploitation of oriental peasantry. The actual workers on the soil—the "dirt farmers"—
retain 80 per cent of their produce, while paying to the crown a
tax of 20 per cent on the land as a national estate; the king himself being the trustee of the community, and not the figurehead
of corrupt ringsters who add house to house and field to field
(Gen. 47:12-27).

While the program of "Joseph" has technical defects when
viewed from the standpoint of modern economic science, it was
the most revolutionary and far-reaching proposal of social reform ever before made in human history. Its authors labored
under the political and psychological disadvantages that confronted the book of "Revelations," under the Roman Empire,

whose writers dare not openly allude to conditions in their own day, but who apparently transfer the center of attention to "Babylon." Thus, the story of the Ephraimite hero is located in *Egypt*, and not in Israel; *but its application is domestic; and it is the fine flower of the primitive mishpat re-expressed in terms of settled civilization.* Joseph nourishes "his father and his brethren and all his father's house with *bread*, according to their families"; and each holder of land is entitled to four-fifths of the produce yielded by the soil. This ideal program of reform is addressed wholly to the needs and problems of a landowning community, whose main food is bread, and not the milk and dates of the nomad; yet it is pervaded by the brotherly spirit of the wandering clan, all of whose individuals have a right to subsistence as members of a kinship group.

That Egypt should be selected as the scene of a "planned economy" under a broad-minded ruler is not strange. It was the nearest great nation to Israel; and its hithermost province of Goshen had been a refuge for ancestors of the house of Joseph in dim antiquity. Moreover, in times just preceding the rise of the E and J documents, Egypt had again emerged as a factor in Hebrew life. Its king, Shishak, had entertained for some years the *founder* of the new Josephite monarchy, Jeroboam I, who had fled from the wrath of Solomon; and a few years later the same Pharoah had reduced the kingdom of *Judah* to temporary vassalage and subjection. "Shishak, king of Egypt, came up against Jerusalem; and he took away the treasures of the house of Yahweh, and the treasures of the king's house. He even took away all. And he took all the shields of gold which Solomon had made. And king Rehoboam made in their stead brazen shields" (I Kings 14:25, 26, 27; cf. 11:40).

The author of the Joseph story, in writing a prophetic homily for the edification of his contemporaries and later ages, had abundant historic material to stimulate his imagination. There was the comparatively recent enslavement of the house of Joseph by the Judaic dynasty. And farther back in time, the house of Joseph, almost alone, had fought the Deborah-battle without the help of Reuben, Dan, Asher, and Gilead; while again the Josephites had redeemed Israel from the despotism of Rehoboam. No investigator has ever found any trace of a Hebrew dictatorship in Egypt; and while the story of Joseph is mythical, it deals with authentic materials drawn from the nation's experience, and combined into a program which anonymous writers thought applicable to the *desperate* situation of the house of Joseph under the dynasty of Jehu.

The Joseph legend itself, as we now have it in the Book of Genesis, lacks harmony and self-consistence, being built up out of two earlier, contradictory narratives. Thus, in one tale Joseph is sold into slavery on the advice of *Judah*, the southern patriarch, and is bought by traveling *Ishmaelites* for twenty pieces of silver. But, according to the other tale, Joseph is merely placed in a pit, on the advice of *Reuben*, the northern patriarch; and then, in the *absence of his brethren*, Joseph is taken out secretly, not by Ishmaelites, but by *Midianites*, who carry the lad into Egypt, and sell him to Potiphar. Meanwhile, Reuben goes *alone* to the pit, finds it empty, to his great consternation; then returns to his brothers, and reports the case to them (see Appendix, "The Two Stories of the Sale of Joseph"). There was also another story, not much noticed, wherein Joseph's trouble, instead of being with *all* his brethren, was only with the sons of the two *slave-girls:* "And the lad was with the sons of Bilhah and with the sons of Zilpah, his father's wives; *and Joseph brought an evil report of them unto his father*" (Gen. 37:2). Again, after Joseph tells his dream about the sun, moon, and eleven stars doing obeisance to him, his father says, "Shall I and thy mother and thy brethren come to bow down to thee?" (Gen. 37:5-11 [E document]). But Jacob's question here is not in point, because *Rachel*, the mother of Joseph, had already passed away two chapters earlier (35:16-20 [JE]). These and many other indications reveal that the Joseph legend, as it now stands, is a combination of earlier materials, joined together with ragged edges by subsequent writers.

E and J documents an ethical prehistory of Israel, emphasizing claims of mishpat.—The documents called E and J by modern critics are the *basis* of the Torah, or Law, *viewed as a preamble to Hebrew history before the Israelite settlement of Canaan.* Thus, while the Torah seems to be the earliest part of the Bible, placed as we now find it in the very forefront of Scripture, it was produced later than the history recorded in Judges, Samuel, and Kings; and, accordingly, the Torah follows the pattern of Hebrew evolution after the house of Joseph established its power in the central highlands of Canaan. The compilers of these documents are, in reality, preaching a *sermon;* and the Torah gives a legendary introduction to Hebrew history *in accordance with the ideals of the prophetic, reforming party in the epoch of Elijah.*

Compilers of prehistory therefore seek amalgamation of "Joseph" and "Jacob" legends.—The main trunk of Hebrew history, as we have seen many times, is rooted in the highlands of Ephraim, in the house of Joseph; but the historic nation of Israel eventually broadened out beyond the frontiers of Ephraim, so as to include other tribes upon a larger map of Palestine. And therefore, if the compilers of the "prehistory" were to avoid a provincial Ephraimite outlook, and make use of a *national* perspective as the background of their documents, they must unite the legends which had already grown up around the figure of "Joseph," as an Ephraimite patriarch, and the legends referring to "Jacob," as the father of all the communities, or tribes, which ultimately came to be parts of the actual, historic, Hebrew nation.

Accordingly, Jacob is represented as an individual Aramean emigrant, who comes into Canaan from the northeast, with a small company, consisting of two wives, two concubines, eleven sons (Benjamin being as yet unborn), one daughter, and some slaves (Gen. chap. 32). Encamping near the Amorite city of *Shechem,* Jacob enters into a covenant with the citizens of that place. But Simeon and Levi, two sons by the hated wife Leah, massacre the Shechemites, bringing upon themselves the reproach of Jacob, who declares, "Ye have brought me into bad odor among the inhabitants of the land, among the Canaanites; and I, *being few in number,* they shall gather themselves together against me and slay me; and I shall be destroyed, I and my family" (Gen. 34:30).

In course of time, *Judah,* one of the sons of Leah, makes his proposal to sell *Joseph,* the eldest son of Rachel, into slavery (Gen. 37:26, 27). Upon being sold to traveling merchants, Joseph is carried into Egypt, where he eventually becomes dictator. Then follows a time of great famine, which results in the migration of *Jacob* and his group into the Egyptian province of *Goshen* (Gen. 46:28, 34; 47:1, 4, 6, 27). The tradition thus far makes Jacob an emigrant from Aramea, with a small entourage, driven about by fate from one country to another; and this picture of him, as we find it in the J and E documents, is later on taken up into the Deuteronomic ritual, where the Israelite worshiper of later days is bidden to come before the altar of Yahweh, and say, "A nomadic *Aramean* was my father; and he went down to Egypt *few in number* " (Deut. 26:5).

But now the background of the narrative begins to assume a different aspect. Joseph brings his two sons, Manasseh the elder and Ephraim the younger, into the presence of the national patriarch Jacob, who gives the greater blessing, not to Manasseh, but to *Ephraim,* the younger son; and after doing so, Jacob turns to *Joseph,* and says, "I have given thee one portion above thy brethren, *which I took out of the hand of the Amorite with my sword and with my bow*" (Gen. 48:20-22). In other words, where Jacob was presented by the foregoing sources in the character of an emigrant with a small band, "few in number," traveling about in terror of his life, the narrative is carried on by reproducing a passage from a wholly different source, wherein Jacob is transformed into a powerful conqueror, who has *already* taken the central highlands of Canaan out of the hand of the Amorite by military means, leaving this part of the country as the inheritance of the house of *Joseph*, in which the tribe of Ephraim has *already* outshone Manasseh, and stamped its name on the northern kingdom of Israel.

Having changed from one character into another, by a transformation more startling than that of Dr. Jekyl into Mr. Hyde, the patriarch then reverts to his rôle as an individual; and the story is continued from another source, wherein Jacob calls his twelve sons together so that he can make his last will and testament (Gen., chap. 49). But here, again, the alleged references of Jacob to the different "sons," or "tribes," is fashioned on the pattern of Hebrew history in Canaan, hundreds of years after the time when the prehistoric, ancestral group was in Egypt. The "Testament of Jacob" in Genesis, chapter 49, assumes that the house of Joseph is in possession of central Palestine; and the only tribe on which the patriarch ventures to confer *land* is that of *Zebulun*, which, as a matter of historic reality, conquered its own possessions by assisting the house of Joseph in the Deborah-battle (Gen. 49:13; cf. Judg. 5:18).

While these glaring discrepancies prove that the compilers are not reliable historians in the modern sense, we must bear in mind constantly that it is not as *historians*, but as *moral teachers*, that they are to be judged. They may fail as historians; but they were the harbingers of success in the greatest ethical production of all time—the Bible.

The compilers' evident failure to articulate the Joseph-Jacob material throws us back once more upon the outstanding consideration that the main trunk of Hebrew history is *Josephite*. The kingdom of Saul, in the hills of Ephraim, preceded the larger kingdom of David, which overlay Canaan as a whole; and, likewise, Joseph is primarily in Egypt, and is afterward followed by Jacob with his family. The need for a comprehensive Hebrew ancestor was felt when the nation expanded from its Josephite beginnings in the central hill-country, and absorbed the non-Ephraimite groups to the north and south; after which a *common father* was naturally required for all the members of the coalition. Hence, the figure of Jacob, with his beloved Ephraimite wife Rachel, his hated wife Leah, the mother of Judah, and the less honored slave-wives, Bilhah and Zilpah, whose sons were of more diluted Hebrew blood. The real "Testament of Jacob," therefore, is not in Genesis, chapter 49, where *all* the "sons" are mentioned, but in the Ephraimite document quoted in Gen. 48:20–22, where Jacob, having conquered the central hill-country by war, gives this region to Joseph; while, on the other hand, the larger "Testament," in Genesis, chapter 49, gives land only to *Zebulun*, which helped the house of Joseph in the Deborah-battle; and, likewise, the "Blessing" attributed to Moses in Deuteronomy, chapter 33, gives land only to *Naphtali*, which also co-operated with Joseph in the historic fight (Gen. 49:13; Deut. 33:23; Judg. 5:18).

No conquest occurred in Judah, which was an amalgamation of primitive clans, brought into the Hebrew community by David after the death of Saul; and, therefore, the "sword and bow" of Jacob, which conquered the central hill-country, are in fact identical with the weapons of Joseph. The collocation of these two instruments of war in the same phrase is *Ephraimite* (Gen. 48:22; Josh. 24:12; I Sam. 18:4; II Kings 6:22; Hos. 2:18). We therefore come back to the original trunk line of Hebrew evolution. The house of Joseph inherits the hills of Ephraim, not from "Jacob," but from *itself*. The patriarchs Jacob and Joseph are differentiations of the same ancestral group figure, symbolizing the nomad clan, *"few in number,"* which entered the pastures of Goshen during a famine era; increasing by natural multiplication and by the adherence of a "mixed multitude" (Exod. 12:38 [J]; Num. 11:4 [JE]); thence re-entering the wilderness and locating at "En-Mishpat"; passing around eastward into Gilead; continuing to increase; and at length crossing Jordan into the central highlands.

Josephite "escape psychology" expressed in story of release from Egyptian bondage.—The compilers of Genesis, after attempting to articulate the Joseph and Jacob legends, then leaped over a vast, empty, chronological gulf—an unrecorded hiatus of centuries—passing on to the emergence of Israel from Egypt. Accordingly, Genesis, the first, but not the earliest, book of the Bible, stands apart from the next following book, Exodus, *by about four hundred years;* and the compilers have no material with which to fill in the gap. The story of emergence from Egypt is crowded with impressive miracle tales, and gives voice to Josephite slave mentality during the prophetic upheaval under the dynasties of Omri and Jehu, when the E and J documents of the Torah began to take form. The contrast between the vague references to "Pharaoh" all through this narrative, and the specific mention of *individual* Pharaohs by their *personal* names in the really historical books of the Bible is noteworthy. Jeroboam is befriended by Pharoah *Shishak,* who subjugates the Kingdom of Judah; King Josiah is killed in battle by Pharaoh *Necho;* while the prophet Jeremiah, in the time of the Babylonian Exile, denounces Pharoah *Hophra* (I Kings 11:40; 14:25; II Kings 23:29, 33, 34; Jere. 44:30; 46:2). But the story of the exodus knows none of the Egyptian kings by *name,* and refers to them constantly by the formal title "Pharaoh," moving freely in the realm of the imagination.

Historical kernel of exodus includes help to Josephite nucleus by gentile tribe of Kenites.—That the historical books of Judges, Samuel, and Kings make repeated mention of help given to Israel in the wilderness by a friendly non-Hebrew tribe called *Kenites* has been observed earlier in our study. The Kenite woman, Jael, slew Sisera, the arch-enemy of Israel (Judg. 5: 24 f.). King Saul recognizes that the Kenite clan showed *hesed,*

or kindness, to Israel in connection with the exodus from Egypt
(I Sam. 15:6). Gifts are sent to them by David (I Sam. 30:29).
And there is some indication that Jehonadab ben Rechab, who
strongly supported the prophetic party against Baalism on behalf of primitive clan life, was also a Kenite (I Chron. 2:55).
The foregoing references are mainly in Ephraimite records. But
in the Judaic preface to the Ephraimite Book of Judges, the
tribe of Judah is alleged to have participated in the exodus, and
to have been accompanied by "children of the Kenite, Moses'
relative by marriage," in passing around Edom to Gilead, across
Jordan to Jericho, and up into the wilderness of Judah (Judg.
1:16). This passage, however, simply takes the Kenites, by a
long, circuitous journey, from a point of *departure* in the south
which is also their point of *arrival* at the end of a useless march.
But since the tribe of Judah was not formed until David's day,
our only inference can be that the Kenites were in the south all
the time, and that a few, such as Heber the Kenite, may have
journeyed with the house of Joseph into central Canaan. The
Judaic editor is correct in associating the Kenites mainly with
Judah; but he wrongly projects the situation of his own day
back into the exodus period. And not only so; but he seeks to
link the figure of Moses with *Judah* more closely than with
Ephraim.

Moses intermediary between Kenites and house of Joseph.
—In studying the latter part of the Judges period, we saw that
a certain *Levite* came up into Ephraim out of Bethlehem-Judah;
that he was installed as priest, or *cohen*, in the house of an
Ephraimite called Micah; that he was kidnaped, or stolen, by
the tribe of Dan as they migrated from the Philistine frontier
into the north of Canaan; that this man, *"Jonathan, the son of
Gershom, the son of Moses,"* founded a line of *cohanim* which
ministered in the Danite sanctuary of Yahweh until the Ephraimites were carried into captivity; and that a subsequent Jewish
editor unsuccessfully tried to conceal the Mosaic ancestry of

this Levite by changing the name "Moses" into "Manasseh" (see chap. vii, p. 99). Thus, one Jewish editor seeks to obscure the connection with Moses, and another lays emphasis on it.

In the case of this Mosaic Danite priest, there were *possibly* four reasons why a late Jewish editor should seek to obscure the connection with Moses. In the first place, according to the orthodox view of the "Priestly" document in the Torah, no mere Levite could have any legal claim to serve as a priest, or *cohen*, of Yahweh; for only a certain *branch* of Levi, the descendants of *Aaron*, the brother of Moses, could be priests; while the Levites who were *not* descended from Aaron could only be *porters* of the sanctuary, and might not approach the altar and perform the priestly office without being struck dead (Num. 4:15). In the second place, while this Jonathan was, indeed, a Levite, his descent was not from Aaron, *but went back through Gershom to Moses, who was not a priest.* In the third place, while Jonathan's father Gershom was, indeed, the son of Moses, yet Gershom's *mother* was not a Hebrewess, but a gentile woman from the non-Hebrew tribe of *Kenites*, into which Moses married. This tribe, according to the J document, was a shepherd community of the desert, in "the land of Midian"; and they came into relation with Moses when he left Egypt: "Now the priest of Midian had seven daughters. . . . . And Moses was content to dwell with the man; and he gave Moses his daughter *Zipporah;* and she bare a son; and he called his name *Gershom*" (Exod. 2:16–22 [J document]). In the fourth place, to fill the cup of these irregularities to overflowing, the J source even implies that Moses neglected to perform the rite of circumcision upon his son by the gentile woman.

To rectify the case, an early form of J tradition undertook to make a readjustment of matters in a very striking and crude fashion; which, however, only satisfies *one* of the four objections to Jonathan as a priest. A ritual procedure was imagined whereby *Yahweh in person* should intervene and cause the circumcision of Jonathan's father Gershom the son of Moses. The tale is extraordinary; and it stands in the primitive J source like a geologic fossil imbedded in some prehistoric stratum of rock. Speaking of Yahweh and Moses, this fragment of mythic anthropology begins: *"And it came to pass, by the way at the hostelry, that Yahweh met him and made as if to kill him."* Many readers of the Bible have wondered why Yahweh should threaten death to such a person as Moses. But we must bear in mind that "Yahweh" is a hypostatization of the evolving religious consciousness; and that a great many attempts were made, by various interests, *to capture the corporate prestige attaching to this name.* We have seen, for example, that the name was used by Elijah the prophet as a warrant for extinction of Omri's dynasty; but that a few generations later the prophet Hosea, with equal sincerity, quoted Yahweh as opposed to the method of blood by which the anti-Baal party effected their purpose. These attempts to monopolize the prestige of the name resulted in success or failure according to the merits of a given case. The tendency, in the long run, was for the best interpretation to win and at length to become *official.* But, in the meanwhile, the literary development which produced the Bible was like a river bearing diverse objects along in its current, and finally entering a colder climate where the stream and its contents are crystallized in frigid form. One of the unsuccessful attempts to capture the prestige of the name "Yahweh" is found in this remarkable tale about Moses at the lodging-place in the desert; but it was carried along in the swelling current of Hebrew literature, and at length crystallized in Scripture before it could be stricken out. The story goes on to relate that only by the quick action of *Zipporah*, the Kenite woman, was Moses rescued from death at the hands of Yahweh: *"Then Zipporah took a stone knife, and excised the foreskin of her son, and made it touch his feet. And she said, Thou art, indeed, a bridegroom of blood to me. So he* [*Yah-*

weh] let him [Moses] alone. Then she said, a bridegroom of blood in regard to the circumcision" (Exod. 4:24–26).

But while this extraordinary intervention guaranteed the ritual correctness of Moses' descendants at the sanctuary of Dan, *as originating from Hebraic circumcision*, it was not convincing to the post-Exilic scribes who made the final edition of Judges; because by that time *another* current in the stream of tradition had successfully manipulated the prestige of Yahweh so as to confer priesthood upon the descendants of Aaron *alone*, degrading all other Levites to the level of porters in the sanctuary. And yet, in the meanwhile, the text of Judges, at first private and unofficial, had crystallized by the process of sanctification; and the timid scribe could only venture to change the name of Moses to Manasseh by such a clumsy device that his effort failed; while the story of Moses and Yahweh at the lodging-place, being crystallized into the *Torah* (which is even more sacred than Judges), escaped the ritualistic solicitude of the editor entirely.

Moses authentic figure, but magnified to proportions of Elijah as champion of mishpat.—That the non-Hebrew Kenites assisted the Josephites at the exodus period cannot be denied; nor can we impugn the historicity of Moses, or Mosheh, as a factor in the situation. Yet we must observe (1) that the oldest, or Ephraimite, strand in the Pentateuch makes use of Moses primarily as an *agent*, or go-between, to receive the Ephraimite version of the commandments and the "Early Mishpat Book"; the latter being strongly tinged, as we have seen, with baalistic terminology; while both are dominated by the "prophetic" interest. But on the other hand (2) immediately after getting this material, Moses finds, according to the E document, that in his absence his brother Aaron has taken the "golden earrings" of the people and made a small image of a bull, called in derision, because of its diminutive size, a *calf* (Exod. 32:2–4 [E]). The Ephraimite source makes Aaron follow the example of two leaders in the house of Joseph (Gideon and Jeroboam I), the former of which took "golden earrings" and made an image; while the latter made small golden bulls (likewise called calves) for the shrines of Bethel and Dan, saying, "Behold thy *elohim*, O Israel, which brought thee up out of the land of Egypt" (I Kings 12:28; cf. Judg. 8:24 f.). Aaron accordingly is made to declare, "These be thy *elohim*, O Israel, which brought thee up out of the land of Egypt" (Exod. 32:2-4). The spectacle of image-worship excites the anger of Moses, who breaks the stone tablets on which the commandments are engraved. The compiler then shifts back to the J document; Moses calls for volunteers to *"slay every man his brother, and every man his companion, and every man his neighbor"*; and there is quick response from the *Levites*, who kill about three thousand men (Exod. 32:25-29 [J]). *The narratives are taking form upon the sanguinary legend of Elijah and the actual massacre ordered by Jehu.* And after the example of Elijah, who went into the desert, and stood at the "entering in of the cave" on Mount Horeb, when Yahweh passed by, the compiler now shifts to still another document, the object of which is to give a picture of Moses in a relation to divinity even closer than that experienced by Elijah. And, accordingly, Moses now asks to *see* Yahweh; but while his request is partially denied, he is told that he may have a *glimpse*, thus: "And Yahweh said, I will put thee in a cleft of the rock, and will cover thee with my hand while I pass by; and I will take away my hand, and thou shalt see my back parts; but my face shall not be seen" (Exod. 33:18, 20-23, part of redactional insertion, vss. 12-23). The compiler again shifts to the J document; and Moses is told to prepare tables of stone as before, and return to the mount, which is always called "Sinai" in J, but "Horeb" in E. Then, having ascended the mount, Moses obtains the promised glimpse of Yahweh; but instead of the *ethical, prophetic, Ephraimite code*, which was on the former tables, he now receives the *Judaic, primitive, ritual commandments*, concluding with the injunction,

"Thou shalt not boil a kid in its mother's milk" (Exod. 34:1–26 [mostly J, but with non-Ephraimite redactional insertions]).

These considerations make it even more clear that the E source is *northern* and mainly prophetic; while the J source is mainly ritual and *southern*. The characteristics of J are made evident, not merely by the code substituted for the Ephraimite commandments, but by the ritual interest of J at other points, e.g., the attempt of Yahweh to slay Moses for neglecting to circumcise Gershom (Exod. 4:24–26); massacre of golden-calf worshipers by Levites (32:25–29); removal of shoes on account of "holy ground" (3:5); demand upon Pharaoh for "sacrifices and burnt offerings, that we may sacrifice unto Yahweh our god" (11:25 and *passim*); first mention of Hebrew *priests* (19:22), etc.; all in agreement with priestly revolt against Athaliah at Jerusalem in middle of the ninth century B.C.

The meaning of this distinction between J and E, and the significance attaching to the composite figure of "Moses," will become clear only as we recall that the Bible, in its *present* form, is *not* the work of Ephraimite scribes, but is the product of Jewish compilers *who have allowed the prophetic, Ephraimite material to stand.* In other words, the primitive "Judaic" document in the Pentateuch, is already seeking to do what is later accomplished more fully by the Deuteronomic redactors, and later still by the Priestly writers in the Babylonian Exile, namely, *to take the prophetic emphasis on "mishpat," which first arose in Ephraim, and guard it within a defensive wall of priestly ritual, as the sole means of transmitting the message of prophecy through the storm and stress of historic evolution.*

The figure of Moses, therefore, begins to appear in the light of its true purpose. Built upon the fact of a real person who is now lost amid the shadows of an early age, his picture is that of a northern prophet, or *nabi*, created by the Ephraimite imagination upon the model of Elijah, who is really Moses' *predecessor*, and not his disciple. Accordingly, the E document makes Moses say, "Would *elohim* that all the people of Yahweh were *proph-ets*" (Num. 11:29 [E]). This fact stands out so clearly that some unknown scribe attached a note at the very end of the Torah, saying, "And there arose not since in Israel such a *nabi* as Moses" (Deut. 34:10).

Prophetic interest of E source discredits Aaron by golden-calf incident.—By the same token that Moses the prophet of mishpat is exalted as the leading hero of "prehistory," Aaron the priest is discredited and left under a cloud. The priests of actual history were always opposed by the great insurgent prophets like Amos, who denounced the reactionary Amaziah, priest of the golden calf at Bethel. The entire ministry of Hebrew priests, from the entrance of Israel into Canaan, is condemned by the prophet Jeremiah in the following words, which he ascribes to Yahweh: "I brought you into a plentiful country, to eat the fruit thereof. But when ye entered in, ye defiled my land, and made my heritage an abomination. *The priests said not, Where is Yahweh?*" (Jer. 2:7–8). Accordingly, the picture of the first priest of Israel as leading the people to worship a golden calf is allowed to stand by the post-Exilic Jewish compilers of the Torah, who *themselves* added the priestly, or P, sections of the Law. *No more striking evidence could be found that the Hebrew Bible in its completed form, including all the elaborate priestly elements, is the work of scribes faithful to the prophetic ideal.*

In the golden calf of Aaron, then, we are looking simply at the actual, historic golden calf of Jeroboam at Bethel, and, in the further distance, at the image made by Gideon from the golden earrings of his followers; while the reactionary Amaziah, priest of Bethel, is the prototype of Aaron. And in view of our unpayable debt to the later scribes of Judah, we should not begrudge them the satisfaction which they naturally felt in emphasizing these examples of *Josephite* image-worship.

Aaron is a shadowy figure, even at best, as we see, for instance, in the two stories of his death. He dies and is buried

first at a place called Moseroth, or Moserah: "And the children
of Israel took their journey from Beeroth to *Moserah*. There
Aaron died, and there he was buried. From thence they journeyed unto Gudgodah, and from thence to Jotbah" (Deut.10:6–
7 [E]). But in the Priestly narrative, the spot where Aaron is
already said to have expired in the E document proves to be
exactly seven stopping-places away from Mount Hor, which the
later source declares to have been the place of his death (Num.
33:30–38). In this document Aaron is taken up to *Mount Hor*,
by direct command of Yahweh; and there, after being stripped
of his priestly garments, he expires, and is mourned thirty days
by all the house of Israel (Num. 20:22–29).

It has been suggested, indeed, that the name "Aaron," which
in Hebrew is *Aharon*, arose by inclusion of the letter *h* in the
same way that "Abraham" originated through insertion of *h*
in the earlier "Abram." The term for the priestly ark in Hebrew is *aron;* and thus the priests, being "sons of the ark," were
in time thought of as descended from a literal Aron, or Aharon.
The Hebrew term "son," or *ben*, is often used figuratively, as in
the statement that "Noah was a son of six hundred years,"
which is translated into prosaic English, "Noah was six hundred
years old" (Gen. 7:6). By the same quaint usage, it is said that
"Joseph died a son of one hundred and ten years" (Gen. 50:26).

**Release from social injustice, and escape from foreign
domination, symbolized by myth of Red Sea crossing.**—
Ephraimite sources, both historic and mythic, were at hand for
suggestions toward the well-known story of Israel's passage
through the Red Sea. The tradition of Elijah makes him smite
the waters of Jordan with his mantle, and pass over dry-shod
(II Kings 2:7–8). The story of the Deborah-battle depicts the
chariots of Sisera floundering in the suddenly risen waters of
Kishon (Judg. 5:21–22). And when we place the *Ephraimite
document* over against the background of social injustice and
foreign domination prevailing under the Jehu dynasty, we can-

not avoid recognizing it as an example of "escape psychology" on a grand scale—combining in a single picture the two motives of emancipation from *slavery* and release from the grip of a heartless *foreign power* by passing through a sea of trouble to safety on the shores beyond.

E and J narratives private and unofficial in origin.—Although the E and J sources are impressively *official in form*, ascribing moral commands, ritual rules, and marching orders directly to Yahweh, the fact is no ground for assuming that these documents, when first composed, had any official character, or any standing in the eyes of any Hebrew government. Precisely the same form is taken by the Exilic Book of *Ezekiel*, which, in the name of Yahweh, gives elaborate rules for the reestablishment of the Jews after the return from captivity. But the code of Ezekiel was never carried out by the returned exiles at Jerusalem. Nevertheless, the book *itself* became so popular that it was finally received as *authoritative Scripture*. But the Jewish rabbis had a terrible time with it, because they could see plainly that its code was impracticable and had never been put into operation. The Book of Ezekiel is a good example of the Hebrew tendency to give impressive, official *form* to a proposed law which is in the non-authoritative stage. And the only difference between Ezekiel and the JE narrative is that since the prophet of the Exile threw his laws into the *future*, they could be compared with the actual course of history; whereas the JE narratives and laws (and also, in due time, the other documents of the Pentateuch) were thrown far back into the *distant past*, and could not be verified by the witness of contemporary facts. The J and E documents, then, were private and unofficial in origin, like Ezekiel. The same consideration, of course, applies to *Amos* and all the prophets, whose books today are *Bible*, but were at first only private, unofficial writings.

The relation of the JE narratives to the "prehistoric" age came under the scrutiny of Jewish investigators hundreds of years ago. Thus, Rabbi Ben Ezra, of Spain, as far back as the twelfth century A.D., hinted that the Pentateuch was written by unknown scribes long after the Israelite invasion and settlement of Canaan. The same position was taken, even more decidedly, by Baruch Spinoza, of Holland, in the seventeenth century; and these Jewish thinkers prepared the way for modern historical criticism of the Bible.

Ephraimite kingdom finally destroyed by Assyrians, giving rise to tradition of "lost tribes."—In the latter part of the eighth century B.C. the Assyrian empire again revived, and threw a powerful army into Palestine. A huge tax of one thousand silver talents was laid upon the kingdom of Ephraim. This amount, calculated at three thousand shekels to each talent, would come to *three million* shekels; and it was divided among the landholding baalim at fifty shekels per head; the figures, if correct, indicating a total of sixty thousand proprietors. A tax imposed in this way, at a flat rate, was very unjust; because the poorer baals, already in debt, would have to borrow from the wealthier baals, and thus fall even deeper into poverty; so that the economic process of concentration, which made the poor poorer and the rich richer, would be accelerated. The situation is obscured by the older English text at this point, where it says that the money was paid by "all the mighty men of wealth," which gives an exaggerated sense of the average baal's financial ability (II Kings 15:20). The Hebrew text merely says that the money was taken from each *gibbor hayil*, i.e., every landholder who, in time of war, would be liable to military service.

The heavy tribute was given to the Assyrian king in the hope that Ephraim would be let alone. But the invaders imposed a regular annual tax; and when this was not forthcoming, they laid siege to Samaria, the capital, which Omri had built. The walls of the city were strong, and resisted the besiegers three years. Then the fortifications were crushed; the city was laid waste; and the Assyrians carried half the free population of

Ephraim into exile. Many thousands of alien colonists were brought in by the conquerors; and the assimilation of these foreigners with the remaining Ephraimite element gave rise to the "Samaritans." Thus perished the northern Hebrew kingdom, the so-called "lost tribes of Israel."

Ephraimite kingdom a heathen state.—The house of Joseph, in its official character as an oriental kingdom, deserved all that the prophets Amos and Hosea said about it; and only as we recognize that Ephraim was a heathen community, from its beginnings in the Judges era, straight on through to the fall of Samaria, can we understand the place of north Israel in Hebrew evolution. *"Yahweh abhorred the tent of Joseph, and chose not the tribe of Ephraim,"* declares the post-Exilic psalmist with essential historic truth (Ps. 78:65–68). For although Ephraim was the scene of that great prophetic movement which took shape around Elijah, such prophecy was unofficial and without real effect upon the "established" religion of the state; and even though the government was in the *name* of Yahweh, as "god of Israel," the kingdom was nevertheless pagan.

The terms "heathen" and "pagan" refer not simply to the worship of more than one god but rather to that common aspect of primitive cults wherein a god is expected to imitate the pattern of a human chief or king, and fight on the side of his followers against their enemies *under all conditions whatsoever.* This dogma, in its Hebrew application, simply means that Yahweh, *being the god of Israel*, is bound to save his people from their enemies under all circumstances, *whether justice prevails or injustice rules.* And such is the *real* essence of heathenism.

Contrary view taken by insurgent prophets under lead of Elijah.—On the other hand, in opposition to the kings of north Israel, the prophetic movement led by Elijah took the view that Yahweh, instead of defending Israel under all circumstances, would become hostile and permit them to be destroyed by their foes *if social injustice were allowed to prevail.* Such prophets were what we now call "defeatists." But since they were always for "mishpat," they gained the sympathy of poorer baalim on *ethical* grounds. And yet, at the same time, what they gained by standing for social justice they tended to lose by their defeatism. Thus, when the prophetic movement of Elijah and Elisha put the house of Jehu into power, *and yet failed to deliver mishpat*, the masses of the people naturally became confused; and the defeatism of such prophets overshadowed their popularity; so that only the clearest thinkers, like Amos and Hosea, could perceive the merits of the situation. Amos was in the line of succession from Elijah; but when he predicted the defeat of Jeroboam II, and was driven away from Bethel by Amaziah, priest of the golden calf at that place, he seems to have had no active popular support in his arraignment of the "established religion." Amaziah called him a prophet, or *nabi;* and yet Amos was quick to to deny the term, because the majority of Yahweh prophets in Ephraim had always taken ground contrary to Elijah, and had steadily supported the heathen view of Yahweh as a god of success (Amos 7:9–14).

Elijah type of prophecy outweighed in Ephraim by nationalistic prophetism.—The heathen view of Yahweh, as a god of success, not only had continuous governmental sanction; but it was upheld by nationalistic prophets, like the arrogant *Zedekiah ben Chenaanah* who, at the head of a great company of *nebiim*, predicted success in battle for King Ahab: "And Zedekiah ben Chenaanah made him horns of iron; and he said, *Thus saith Yahweh*, With these shalt thou push the Syrians until thou have consumed them" (I Kings 22:11). This prediction was opposed with equal confidence, in the name of Yahweh, by another prophet, *Micaiah ben Imlah*. But Micaiah, who foresaw *defeat*, was put in prison; so that Zedekiah and his great company of prophets who looked for success were the "official" spokesmen of the Josephite monarchy. And even though Micaiah, the prophet of disaster, was justified by events, yet the defeatist prophets of Ephraim were overshadowed by the narrow optimism which always upholds a "khaki" government.

But no matter how prevalent the heathen, optimistic idea of religion may have been, at any one period or in any community, its practical outcome was that when a tribe or nation met permanent defeat, everyone drew the inference that the god of the vanquished group was powerless to save his worshipers from their enemies; whereupon his cult fell into neglect, and people ceased calling upon his name. Thus ancient history is everywhere strewn with the remains of heathen gods.

Thus Ephraim, although indispensable to Hebrew evolution, disappears from stage of history.—The whole burden of Hebrew nationalism was carried by the house of Joseph during the Judges period and the reign of Saul, when the tribe of Judah was yet unborn. A great deal of the matter contained in the Bible is Ephraimite, or Josephite. Insurgent prophecy arose in Ephraim, giving direction to the social forces which destroyed the house of Omri and established the house of Jehu. But the Elijah prophets were discredited by the failure of Jehu's dynasty to bring social justice, and by their own defeatist view of Yahweh; whereupon the lower, nationalistic type of prophecy came into vogue; and the successors of Elijah were overshadowed; Amos was driven away from Bethel; the entire work of Hosea was private; while the "Ephraimite" document was both anonymous and unofficial. So the fall of Ephraim left only *Judah* to continue the struggle for emancipation of religion from heathenism.

"Ephraim is joined to idols! Let him alone" (Hos. 4:17).

CHAPTER X

MISHPAT IN JUDAH

Hebrew history forced into Jewish channel by destruction of Ephraim.—The sudden collapse of north Israel, then, put the whole burden of Hebrew evolution upon the little Jewish kingdom which was to stand as an isolated remnant in southern Palestine for a century and a quarter, and then to suffer the same fate which had overtaken Ephraim. But while the fate of Jerusalem bears objective resemblance to that of Samaria, it has a profoundly different character, *since the doctrine of Ephraimite insurgent prophecy was eventually taken over by Judah, and, through the great Deuteronomic revolution under Josiah, became the official platform of a government for the first time in human history.* The house of Judah, therefore, was just as indispensable to Hebrew evolution as the house of Joseph; and we get the Bible, not through Ephraimites, but through the creative work of Judaic scribes, who project into a dim, prehistoric past the functional character acquired by southern Israel after the fall of Ephraim. In the light of Judah's final position, therefore, the psalmist whom we have already quoted gives a correct symbolic outline of Hebrew history: *"Yahweh awaked, as one out of sleep. He abhorred the tent of Joseph, and chose not the tribe of Ephraim, but chose the tribe of Judah,—mount Zion which he loved"* (Ps. 78:65 f.).

Judah more primitive than Ephraim, and more tenacious in adherence to clan-mishpat.—The central mountain range of Judah, running north and south, is higher than any other part of Palestine, rising three thousand feet above sea-level at some places. Eastern Judah is a wilderness, falling through rugged slopes to the Dead Sea. Western Judah goes down more gradually through the "Shephelah," or lower hills, to the Mediterranean, where, in biblical times, the frontier was barred by the Philistines. Northern Judah was defended by the fortress of Jerusalem. Southern Judah, at the opposite extreme, descends through the "Negeb" into the desert of Arabia. There has always been far less arable soil in Judah than in the north; and the region as a whole is better adapted for the raising of sheep and goats than for agriculture. South Israel, then, had a wilder environment than Ephraim; it was relatively more secluded from the outer world; and, accordingly, the main currents of oriental commerce ran past it and not *through* it. These facts help us to see how Judah was naturally more fitted than Ephraim to be the home of primitive clans, and how its inhabitants clung to the archaic "mishpat" even more tenaciously than did the house of Joseph. That Judah was not so "civilized" as Ephraim was to its advantage and not to its discredit.

Contrast between Judah and Ephraim heightened by different relative location of capitals.—The great physical and social contrast between Judah and Ephraim was emphasized by a remarkable difference in the location of their capital cities. King Omri built Samaria in the very *center* of Ephraim, where it influenced and corrupted the house of Joseph at the heart; whereas Jerusalem lay *almost* on the northern frontier of Judah, and therefore had less opportunity than Samaria to dominate and control the kingdom of which it was the political head. The true capital of Judah was the little town of Hebron, located more centrally and more in keeping with the primitive nature of the southern population. Here David established himself when he created the tribe of Judah out of the diverse clans in south Canaan; and here he reigned more than seven years before he took up the task of creating the united Hebrew monarchy. The city of Jerusalem was chosen by David for political reasons; because, in fact, it was not Judean, and stood on the border between south and north. The clans of Judah, then, could oppose the policy of Jerusalem with more ease and effect than if their capital had been located, like Samaria, in the center of population.

Judah isolated from world-affairs after separation from house of Joseph.—For the space of nearly two hundred years after the house of Joseph swung off into its own orbit, we have only a small amount of historic matter concerning Judah. Isolated and primitive, it remained apart from the current of world-affairs, while on the northern frontier Jerusalem had fallen from its imperial glory to the level of a courthouse town. The people of the land, "the *am ha arets*," worshiped Yahweh at "high places," *bamoth*, or village churches, all over the country. These local shrines were at Beersheba, Hebron, Bethlehem, and elsewhere (Amos 8:14; I Sam. 20:6; II Sam. 5:1, 3; 15:7). The Temple of Jerusalem was little more than a royal sanctuary, or king's chapel; and the local shrines were the chief seats of popular worship. The complaints against them as illegal, which we find scattered along throughout Kings, are by the editors who collate the narrative out of earlier books, and who intersperse their own *post-eventum* observations from the standpoint of the Deuteronomic reform under King Josiah.

Mishpat retains hold over Judah for generations.—Certain events in the southern kingdom, after the disruption of the united monarchy, have been spoken of briefly. The invasion by Pharaoh Shishak, during the reign of Rehoboam, confined itself to Jerusalem, and had no permanent effect upon the country at large. The revolt against Phoenician Baal-worship, following entanglement with the house of Omri, had the character of a priestly upheaval among the nobility at the capital, and was not accompanied by far-reaching social and economic phenomena such as were displayed by the anti-Baal revolution in Ephraim. The clan-life of Judah flowed quietly in the old paths, and the southern monarchs were more hospitable to the mishpat of the country population than were the kings of Ephraim. This contrast is revealed by a narrative in which two Hebrew kings—one from the south and the other from the north—ask advice from the prophet Elisha, who shows high respect for Jehoshaphat of Judah, but great contempt for the ruler of Ephraim, to whom he declares, "Were it not that I regard the presence of Jehoshaphat the king of Judah, I would not look toward thee nor see thee" (II Kings 3:14). Friendly relations between the government at Jerusalem and "the people of the land" are implied by several sources quoted in Kings: "And all the people of Judah took Azariah, who was sixteen years old, and made him king. . . . . And Jotham the king's son was over the house, judging the *am ha arets*" (II Kings 14:21; 15:5).

Judah becomes vassal of Assyria as Ephraim hastens to destruction.—During the reign of *Ahaz*, king of Judah, the house of Joseph, moving rapidly toward its fall, embarked upon a desperate scheme to block the westward advance of Assyria. Confronted by the looming Mesopotamian peril, Ephraim actually entered into alliance with its old foe Damascus; and these powers now sought to make Judah unite with them against Assyria. But King Ahaz took a different view of the situation, and would not become a party to the plan. So Damascus and Ephraim prepared to attack Jerusalem, with the object of ousting Ahaz, and enthroning one who would be an instrument of their policy. Ahaz, overcome by terror, was approached by the prophet Isaiah, who advised him to have faith in Yahweh and do nothing. But this counsel was disregarded by the king of Judah, who hastily gathered all the gold and silver that he could find in the temple, sending it by the hands of speedy messengers to the king of Assyria, requesting help. And, accordingly, when the armies of Damascus and Ephraim opened war on Judah, the Assyrians moved on Damascus, *compelling the allies to abandon the siege of Jerusalem.*

But the help given by Assyria was obtained only at the cost of becoming a dependency of that colossal power; and thus the little Kingdom of Judah was forced into the obligation to pay annual tribute, *which involved a heavy increase of taxation upon the "am ha arets," or country proprietors*. King Ahaz was followed by his son *Hezekiah*, who continued the annual payments to Assyria, and who beheld, with mingled feelings, the long siege of Samaria and the final destruction of Ephraim. But in spite of this dreadful object lesson, the landed proprietors of Judah became so restive under the new burden of taxation that Hezekiah was forced into rebellion against paying further tribute; whereupon the Assyrians once more invaded the land.

That the enemy would not be able to take Jerusalem was declared by the prophet Isaiah (37:21 f.). But whatever cause or consideration may have preserved the capital *itself*, the whole country outside of Jerusalem was ground under the conqueror's heel, as we read in the "Prism Inscription" of the Assyrian emperor Sennacherib and in two different scriptural narratives: "Now in the fourteenth year of king Hezekiah did Sennacherib king of Assyria come up against all the fortified cities of Judah, and took them" (II Kings 18:13; Isa. 36:1). Not only was the kingdom occupied, but a new and heavier burden of taxation was imposed upon Judah, and accepted by the king in Jerusalem as a condition that the enemy depart: "And Hezekiah sent to the king of Assyria, saying, I have offended. Return from me. That which thou layest on me I will pay. *And the king of Assyria charged upon Hezekiah king of Judah three hundred talents of silver and thirty gold talents*" (II Kings 18:14).

Prophet Isaiah, seeming to abandon "defeatist" platform, did not do so in fact.—Isaiah stands in the line of succession from Elijah; but by proclaiming the impregnability of Jerusalem he seems, at first glance, to abandon the "defeatist" platform, which declares that if social injustice were allowed to prevail in Israel, then Yahweh, instead of protecting his people, will forsake his worshipers and let them fall into the hands of the enemy. But it should be observed that in spite of his dogma concerning Jerusalem, Isaiah says nothing about immunity for Judah *as a whole;* nor does he anywhere say that Yahweh will not punish for lack of social justice.

The preservation of the capital itself, in the mind of Isaiah, was either consciously or intuitively correlated with the fact that if the government and capital city of Judah, *at that particular time,* were to suffer the fate of Samaria, the last remnant of the Hebrew people would succumb *without having officially adopted the platform of ethical prophecy.* For even yet the doctrine of the defeatist, or insurgent, prophets was unofficial and private; the radical code of Deuteronomy had not been accepted by the government; and therefore the Kingdom of Judah was *legally* heathen, as Ephraim had been at the time of its fall. The ruin of Jerusalem in Isaiah's day would have entailed the same result which followed the destruction of Samaria; for Judah, like Ephraim, would have been cast adrift without the psychological and spiritual anchor of a publicly received *Law Book,* and could not have remained Hebrew in the vast flood of ancient paganism. And so, by all means, Jerusalem and the Davidic dynasty must remain standing as the indispensable framework of a living people until the physical machinery of the state could be identified with a higher purpose. *Insurgent prophecy, therefore, was in a desperate race with time; and upon the narrow margin between Judah and annihilation stood the figure of Isaiah.*

Social position of Isaiah differentiated from that of other insurgent prophets.—Hebrew insurgent prophecy was based on the reaction of the social periphery against the center of the social mass; and it therefore expressed the psychology of the village as contrasted with the mental atmosphere of the fortified city. The insurgent prophets' defeatism was correlated with the countryman's ancient prejudice against metropolitan life. But, on the other hand, the *older* Israelite prophecy, which arose in the earlier days of Deborah and Saul, as the mouthpiece of military success, now took on the character of an archaic survival.

outlasting its primary function. The "success-prophets," therefore, should not be dismissed as merely "false." They simply
stood for the persistence of a crude, primitive type of thought
in the midst of new conditions; and they consequently took the
centralized, conservative standpoint in opposition to the higher
moral claims of the defeatist, or insurgent, prophets.

The prophet Isaiah, in this complicated sociological situation,
agreed with the demand for mishpat, or justice; but at the same
time he made a partial, but not absolute, compromise with conservatism, *and backed the government against the Assyrian foe.*
Here again, without any disparagement of Isaiah, we may find
some explanation of his attitude in the fact that instead of being
a *rural* prophet, like Amos, he was a resident of Jerusalem, and
had personal contact with the "right wing" of the baal class, and
not with its poorer "left wing." The remarkable personality
which takes form before us in the Book of Isaiah carries no suggestion of the humbler freeman who, in the sweat of his face,
toils upon the land of his ancestral heritage, like Elisha ben
Shaphat and Saul ben Kish, who drove ox-teams; or like the
Ephraimite settler in Gibeah, who came from his work out of
the field at even (Judg. 19:16; I Sam. 11:5; I Kings 19:19).
Isaiah had a residence inside the walls of Jerusalem, with a wife
and children; and such an establishment, isolated from the primary sources of economic production, with leisure for literary
work, implies inherited social position with an assured income
(Isa. 7:3; 8:3). This prophet was, indeed, of such high standing
that he could not only summon the chief priest as witness to a
document, but could approach royalty with assurance of a hearing (7:3 f., 8:2–3). Without seeking too close a parallel, we may
compare Isaiah to a British peer who champions the cause of
labor. Acquiring prestige among the common people, he nevertheless won the favor of his own class through his powerful in-
sistence upon the impregnability of Jerusalem; and therefore his
agreement with reaction, *at this point*, outweighed his radical-

ism. Isaiah's denunciation of the wealthy baalim, after all, was not coupled (like that of the other insurgent prophets) with a demand for political revolution.

Use of term "baal" in Isaiah contrasted with language of other Judean prophets.—We have already seen that in the Hebrew Bible the term "baal," as applied to human beings, is used at first with reference to the Amorites of Shechem, Jericho, and Keilah, and also of the Hittite Uriah in Jerusalem, who is called the "baal" of his wife Bathsheba (see chap. ix, p. 186 f.). But when the earlier clan-life merged into settled civilization, and the problem of justice became pressing, the Hebrew proprietary classes in the house of Joseph began to be known more and more by this term, borrowed from pre-Israelite Canaan. As for *Judah*, however, the south continued to be so primitive that the word "baal" does not appear at all in the books of the *rural* prophets *Amos* and *Micah*. But at the same time, their colleague Isaiah, in Jerusalem on the northern edge of Judah, takes the common noun "baal" for granted as designating the *proprietary* class, both urban and rural. For in the opening chapter of his prophecy he calls heaven and earth to witness that while the ass knows the stall of his owner, or *baal*, the people of Israel do not know their god Yahweh (Isa. 1:3). This term, then, which describes the Jerusalem citizen, Uriah the Hittite, in relation to his wife, is also used by the prophet Isaiah to indicate proprietorship with relation to an animal.

The capital of Judah, indeed, was the center of operation for those baalistic forces which, by slow stages, against powerful protest by the insurgent prophets and the *am ha arets*, finally overwhelmed the mishpat of the village clans. That the city was Amorite in the Judges period we have already learned (Judg. 19:10–12). It was not destroyed like Shechem, but merely *occupied* by David, who did not massacre its inhabitants (II Sam. 5:6 f.). And consequently we read that "as for the Jebusites of Jerusalem, the children of Judah could not dispossess them; but the Jebusites abide with the children of Judah at Jerusalem unto this day" (Josh. 15:63 [J document]). The capital of Judah, in truth, was Amorite, Hittite, and alien at every period of Hebrew history; and as the medium which corrupted south Israel, its true character is recognized by the prophet Ezekiel when he writes, "Thus saith Yahweh unto Jerusalem: *Thine origin and thy birth is of the land of Canaan,—thy father being an Amorite and thy mother an Hittite*" (Ezek. 16:1–3, 45).

In the midst of this environment, Isaiah beheld the steady advance of baalistic legalism, seizing upon the pillars of state and society at the capital. Among these pillars he lists the *elders*, *counselors*, and *wise men*, who shape governmental policy; the conventional *prophet*, or "nabi," who sides with them, in the name of Yahweh; the *judge*, who administers the law which the politicians have decided upon, and which the success-*nabi* supports; and, not least of all, Isaiah mentions the *warrior*, the *captain of fifty and the strong man*, the *"gibbor,"* who are instruments for carrying out the measures by which Amorite law is brought to bear upon the people of the villages. And in spite of his dogma concerning the impregnability of Zion, Isaiah's essential "defeatism" comes into view when he declares that Yahweh will take away from Jerusalem and from Judah the whole support of bread and water (3:1–15).

Heavy taxation, caused by Assyrian tribute, brings mishpat problem into foreground.—The annual Assyrian tribute, beginning in the reign of Ahaz, was the economic force which, more than anything else, transformed the face of Judean society; and although it was an evil to the kingdom as a *whole*, slowly draining the life-blood of the country, it promoted the wealth of the few aristocrats while dispossessing the poorer baalim, and forcing them down into slavery as *abadim*. This phenomenon, as we have learned in connection with our study of Ephraim, was rooted in the necessity which drove the poor to borrow from their wealthier neighbors.

Defaulting debtors might lose a portion of their crops and live stock through distraint, or they might have to relinquish part or all of their ancestral heritage. The circumstances in any given case could vary within wide limits, but the general tendency was to impoverish the poor and enrich the more fortunate. And this inexorable economic transformation collided with the static rigidity of primitive mishpat by liquidating land as an item of sale and exchange under the terms of baalistic law. While many abuses no doubt occurred, the victims of the process naturally and humanly took the view that the more fortunate Israelite "brother" should always quash loans which were doubtful or impossible of repayment. But the baal of larger substance inevitably took the opposite view—that he had *some* legal rights. And yet this difference of standpoint would never have emerged from the obscurity of private argument unless the debtors, in course of time, had not come to be the majority of the nation, while the creditors remained a small group alienated from the *am ha arets*.

We are now prepared to see why it was that Judah tended to move more decisively than Ephraim toward the "left." It was more primitive in social constitution, and more closely in touch with desert clans on the south. The ethics of desert nomads permit a wandering tribe to enslave the inhabitants of an oasis, and then exact for themselves a share of the annual harvest which leaves the actual cultivators just enough to remain alive and raise another crop. *But the tribe which enslaves the dwellers of the oasis will divide the spoil among themselves with approximate equality.* In other words, the nomad believes in *tribal-socialism*, founded, where possible, upon alien bondage. The men of the tribe are all "brothers," and are entitled, as such, to an equal share of any good fortune that falls to the lot of the *group*. This illustration gives us, in the simplest possible terms, the Judaic point of departure for criticizing the wealthier baalim. Substituting *Palestine* for the desert oasis, and assuming the tribal mishpat philosophy as the foundation of argument, the orthodox conception of Israel takes form as that of clan-brethren who conquer Canaan, reducing the earlier inhabitants to slavery; while the invaders become a free upper class. These members of the upper class are gradually transformed into *baalim* through the pressure of territorial civilization; and yet, when differences of economic fortune arise between "brethren," or "neighbors," the claims of mishpat are advanced as a check upon baalistic evolution. Human slavery, therefore, is regarded as ethical *if aliens alone are kept in bondage;* but the amassing of surplus goods or land in one section of the aristocracy must be neutralized by a leveling process based upon abolition of interest on loans and cancellation of debts.

Mishpat philosophy not clear-cut formula of right and wrong.—In the light of these considerations, the criticism which the insurgent prophets raise against their own age does not exhaust the merits of the case. The issue between absolute "right" and absolute "wrong" in social problems is never so clear as, for example, the writings of Isaiah imply: "Yahweh will enter into mishpat with the *elders* of his people, and the *nobles* thereof. It is ye that have consumed the vineyard! The spoil of the *poor* is in your houses! To what end are you crushing my people and grinding the faces of the poor?" (Isa. 3:14, 15). In this passage the "poor" are the freemen on the "left wing" of the aristocracy; while the "elders" and "nobles" constitute the more substantial "right wing." The arraignment itself is good poetry, and is also authentic evidence that land-ownership is concentrating in the hands of the few. Its ethical quality, however, would have to be considered from a great many standpoints. The history of each case would have to be taken up on its own concrete merits. But far more than this— above and beyond the prophetic arraignment itself—is the implied view that private property in slaves and land is morally valid, *while the accumulation of such property in a few hands is ethically wrong.*

Private ownership in the soil has obtained among all nations; but, at the same time, it has always gravitated into the hands of the few. The problem was attacked in vain by Greece and Rome through readjustment of debts and interest. France guillotined her landed nobles, and reapportioned her soil among the peasantry. Russia's landed nobility was expropriated in the Red Terror. America more recently has undertaken to stay the concentration of land by legal moratoria and national guaranty of mortgage bonds. The mass of Great Britain's population was long ago swept off the soil into overcrowded centers, where the productive capital of the middle class pays ground rent, and also carries a mounting burden of direct taxation. Since modern society has not thus far discriminated the moral and economic factors of its collective problem, we cannot, with fairness, go back twenty-eight hundred years into the past and blame the prophets of Israel for not opposing the institution of human slavery; nor should we pick flaws when they assail the concentration of private landownership among a small clique of nobles, while ignoring the deeper question of individual proprietorship in the earth as a moral issue.

The nomad clan at least believes that the group, as a whole, should benefit from the natural resources which fall to its lot. And yet when such a group moves out of nomadic life into the régime of territorial society, *land socialism is impracticable.* Hence, every nation thus far, when passing from tribal equality into settled existence, has gone toward the opposite extreme under the forms of "baalism" or "fee simple"; wherein land may remain vacant indefinitely, on the assumption of its non-social character, to be held pending the increase of population until a monopoly price can be exacted for it; the monopoly charge, in turn, being capitalized as ground rent, which then becomes a liability upon productive business in addition to taxes and rates. It is this very problem, in its ancient setting, that comes to view as we read Isaiah's famous denunciation of those who lay field to field until there is no room (Isa. 5:8). The insurgent prophets were virtually compelled to accept the major premise of baalism, while at the same time denouncing the effects which flow from baalism everywhere, in all societies. One of the greatest problems which ultimately confront all nations is that of recognizing the social character of land, while simultaneously guaranteeing secure and absolute private possession; so that the benefits of personal enterprise and work may accrue to the individual. But this problem has never been solved by any nation at any time during the course of history.

The insurgent prophets did not grasp the economic elements of this question; and they left us no concrete scheme of social reform applicable to modern circumstances. But such considerations do not in any way lessen the spiritual and moral significance of Hebrew prophecy.

Significance of Israel found in social tension which divorced idea of Yahweh from heathenism.—When the light of sociology is turned upon ancient Israel, we find a historical process taking place which lends itself to elucidation within purely naturalistic terms of cause and effect. These terms come clearly into view as we grasp the peculiar characteristic of Hebrew evolution, whereby a wilderness divinity was enthroned with comparative *abruptness* over the sophisticated gods of a territorial society. And the significance of Israel is found in the social tension between mishpat and baalism, *which divorced the cult of Yahweh from the primitive group dogma of unfailing supernatural protection against alien groups, and lifted the idea of God above this heathen level into a higher altitude where failure to observe the broader scope of the moral law entails absolutely certain defeat, since God refuses to uphold a nation founded upon social injustice.*

Insurgent Hebrew prophecy, then, had no final scheme of so-

cial reform applicable to every nation and every age. But the
prophets of defeatism put God on the side of the struggle for a
better world; and they expressed themselves within the terms
of that peculiar social and economic evolution which places Hebrew history in a class by itself. An ethical development, which
reveals a rising perception of moral values, comes before us in
the prophetic writings, the narrative books of Judges, Samuel,
and Kings, and the various "documents" of the Pentateuch, or
Law. Thus Elijah, in the name of Yahweh, commands the
slaughter of the house of Omri; but in the following century
Hosea, speaking also in the name of Yahweh, condemns that
very massacre. And likewise the editions of the "Decalogue"
show increasing refinement of the moral sense; while the Hebrew
Bible, as a whole, records an ascending standard of sex relations
and a growth in the spirit of humanitarianism. The real successors of the insurgent prophets, then, are not those who claim
that religion was once for all delivered as unchanging dogma,
but those who seek the deepening of moral insight.

Isaiah promulgates doctrine of "divine holiness."—Isaiah's
distinction as a prophet is not found in his doctrine of Zion's
physical impregnability; nor yet in his emphasis upon mishpat,
which is common to *all* insurgent Hebrew prophecy. But his
peculiar contribution to religious thought is found in the remarkable synthesis which he discovered, or deduced, between
mishpat and another very important Hebrew term, *kadosh*—
which English translations render by the word "holy," without
pausing by the way to explain the technical history back of this
word.

The term *kadosh* is from a root, *k-d-sh*, which has the sense of
being *physically* set apart from common affairs. Thus, the Phoenicians, whose language was akin to Hebrew, applied the term
to their divinities, calling them the "holy" gods, in the sense of
mere *distinction* from humanity. And, in the same sense, a
woman connected with a heathen cult or temple, and *set apart*
from her own sex for the purpose of ritual prostitution, was

called in Hebrew a "holy woman" (*kedeshah*). The term stands
in the text of Genesis, with exactly this physical, non-moral
meaning, in the story of Judah and Tamar. "And he asked the
men of that place, Where is the *kedeshah* that was by the side of
the way? And they answered, There was no *kedeshah* here"
(Gen. 38:21). This word is rendered by the older English versions "harlot"; but the American Revised has "prostitute," and
puts a transliteration of the Hebrew in the margin. The same
term occurs in the prophecy of Hosea, where complaint is made
that the men of Ephraim "sacrifice with prostitutes," or *kedeshoth* (pl. Hos. 4:14).

Now the prophet Isaiah takes this archaic, materialistic, non-
moral, heathen term, and makes a new and impressive application of it, in such a way as profoundly to affect the Jewish and
Christian idea of God. Setting out from the merely *physical*
conception of "holiness," *in the sense of being separate or distinct*,
but without characteristic moral quality, Isaiah perceives that
the logic of Hebrew history makes Yahweh *kadosh* (distinct, or
separate) in relation to *mishpat*. The great struggle for social
justice developed a sense of Yahweh as *distinct* from the ordinary Baalim, or gods, of territorial civilization; and inevitably
this new sense of the divine sought appropriate formulation in
speech and writing, which was first given, clearly and persistently,
by the prophet Isaiah, although perhaps not without suggestions
from earlier sources (cf., e.g., Ephraimite "Mishpat Book"
[Exod. 22:31]). Accordingly, we read, "Yahweh of hosts is exalted in *mishpat;* and the *kadosh* divinity makes himself *kadosh*
in righteousness" (Isa. 5:16). This passage, even if it were inserted by some redactor, would be an authentic interpretation
of Isaiah, who repeatedly calls Yahweh *"kadosh Israel,"* rendered "the Holy One of Israel" (5:19; 10:20, etc.).

**Demand of Micah for mishpat shows countryman's preju-
dice against walled city.**—Like the Judaic prophet Amos of
Tekoa, Micah was a villager among the *am ha arets*, or "people
of the land." But his part of the country was more fertile than

the region around the home of Amos; for he lived in the "Shephelah," the lower hills of *western Judah*, which fall down from the high central range to the Mediterranean. Denouncing wealthy aristocrats, he says, "They covet *fields*, and seize them, and *houses*, and take them away; and they oppress a man and his house, even a man and his heritage" (Mic. 2:2). They are able to do this "because it is in the power of their hand" (2:1). In other words, they can make use of the strong men, or *gibborim*, in carrying out legal distraints and foreclosures.

According to Micah, the social problem was very simple: The law courts ought always to assume the standpoint of the "poor and needy," adjusting every suit on the ground of brotherhood mishpat. All the merits of each case were on one side; and all the demerit was on the other. Thus the idealist is always finding a perfectly sharp antithesis between absolute right and wrong on the surface of life. The standpoint of insurgent prophecy was at first assumed without question by modern biblical critics, who, having dispensed with a miraculous Pentateuch, fell back upon Amos, Micah, Isaiah, and the rest as having pronounced the final word. For example, Professor A. F. Kirkpatrick, of Cambridge University, England, wrote as follows, about thirty-five years ago (italics mine):

No doubt there were not a few among the wealthy nobles of Micah's day who prided themselves on not being guilty of injustice. Yes! Perhaps they were *entirely within their legal rights* when they seized the land of some poor neighbor who, through bad seasons and misfortune and pressure of heavy taxes, had fallen into their power. *But was conduct like that brotherly?* [Kirkpatrick, *The Doctrine of the Prophets* (London, 1901), pp. 225–26].

Nevertheless, the ethical merits of Hebrew history cannot be condensed into a simple question like the foregoing; because if one is to admit that the wealthier baalim were perhaps "entirely within their legal rights," then one has to recognize that the older clan-mishpat was in process of modification toward the legal usages of territorial society, wherein the ethical standpoint of nomadism was challenged by the necessity for another form of landholding. The sociological and economic facts of Hebrew history are not completely accounted for by the insurgent prophets, nor by modern scholars who echo their verdicts.

Older, heathen view of Yahweh, as non-ethical protector, held up to scorn by Micah.—The heathen view of Yahweh, as protecting his worshipers, regardless of moral principle, is brought into vivid relief by Micah in one of his finest passages: "Hear this, ye heads of Jacob and rulers of the house of Israel, *who abhor mishpat and pervert all right.* They build up Zion with blood, and Jerusalem with iniquity. The heads thereof judge for reward; and the priests thereof teach for hire; and the *prophets* thereof divine for money. *Yet they lean upon Yahweh, and say, Is not Yahweh in the midst of us? No evil can come upon us!*" (Mic. 3:9–11).

The whole attitude of primitive religion is here expressed in a few cutting sentences. A god must be the invariable divine champion of the *social group* which worships in his name. This view, of course, found its earliest Hebrew expression in that older prophecy, or nabiism, which arose during the time of Saul, who was "among the *nebiim.*" The original impulse of Hebrew prophecy was to inspire the house of Joseph against the Philistines and other external foes. There was, at that time, no internal problem of rich and poor, involving opposition between Yahweh and Baal. The prophets at that time were a consistent, united fraternity, animated by simple patriotism; and it was this earlier form of prophecy, lasting over into the conditions of a later age, that gave rise to the nationalistic success-prophets denounced by Micah.

Prophetic "defeatism" of Micah remains living memory in Judah.—In opposition to the "100 per cent" patriotic type of prophecy, Micah raised the cry of defeatism; and although he did not induce the "heads of Jacob" to change their ways, he spoke with such force and effect that his words remained a living recollection among the *am ha arets* into the time when Deuteronomy was written. For the last prophecy of Micah dealt with destruction at the hands of alien foes: "Thus saith Yahweh concerning the *prophets* that make my people err; that bite with their teeth, and proclaim 'Peace!' . . . . *Therefore shall Zion, for your sake, be plowed like an open field, and Jerusalem shall become rubbish*" (Mic. 3:5, 12).

This is perhaps the most explicit illustration of "defeatism" to be found among the literary prophets. Contrasting strongly with Isaiah's tenderness for Jerusalem, the country prophet Micah reflects the grievance of the *am ha arets* against the capital; so that his prophecy of destruction was remembered and quoted seventy-five years later by the elders, or *zikanim*, who represented "the people of the land" (Jer. 26:17 f.).

Pressure of social problem increases during reign of Manasseh ben Hezekiah.—It was well that Micah's vigorous prophecy was uttered in a form powerful enough to be remembered; for Judah was on the verge of a period like that which Ephraim had experienced under the house of Jehu, when the unofficial "Ephraimite" document was composed by the somber enthusiasm of unknown scribes in the house of Joseph, and when the prophet Amos, venturing into the north, declared the times to be so evil as to demand silence on the part of wise men (Amos 5:13; cf. 7:12). All the tendencies now came to a head which, during the reigns of Ahaz and Hezekiah, had been breaking down the clan-mishpat, impoverishing the poorer peasantry, enriching the wealthier proprietary, spreading the régime of baalistic legalism, and insinuating Baal-worship into the religion of Judah. One of the blackest periods of Hebrew history is marked by the long reign of *Manasseh*, who occupied the throne of south Israel for more than fifty years (II Kings, chap. 21). Judah continued as vassal of Assyria, compelled to pay annual tribute, entailing heavy taxation which put the small village aristocracy more and more into the grasp of rich nobles at Jerusalem.

That the religious and economic influence of the vanished northern kingdom spread into the south at this time is clear. The king's name was that of Joseph's elder son (Gen. 41:51). The conditions for an influx of poor and needy Ephraimite elements had been already provided in the reign of Manasseh's father, Hezekiah, through the partial depopulation of Judah by Sennacherib when he took the fenced cities of the land (II Kings 18:13 f. and Sennacherib's "Prism Inscription"). Moreover, the ravaging of the country districts at the very time when Jerusalem was left unscathed had the effect of increasing the capital's economic advantage over the peasantry; and this condition would only reinforce the other influences which were coming to a head in the dark reign of Manasseh.

As in the case of Ephraim, crushed under the rule of its capital, Samaria, so Judah was oppressed by forces controlling the government at Jerusalem. This ancient stronghold, indeed, was always an Amorite city; and the worst allegation against Manasseh is that he did wickedly "above all that the *Amorites* did which were before him" (II Kings 21:11). The old, pre-Hebrew population of Jerusalem had always been there in spirit, straight on through Hebrew history, its blood mingled with Israel's blood, its ancient baalism under the surface, ready to burst forth under favoring conditions.

Altars for Baal were built by Manasseh (II Kings 21:3). And, moreover, Yahweh was worshiped under the name of Baal, as having the character of an Amorite god, authenticating the baalistic laws of property. And along with increasing concentration of economic power came looseness of morals. Professional cult-prostitutes, or "holy women" (*kedeshoth*), multiplied in Jerusalem; while masculine perverts, consecrated to horrible vice, "holy men" (*kedeshim*), were also a part of the heathen system which now issued from the hidden recesses of life and reared its head in the capital. These persons carried on their trade *inside* the temple, where they had regular apartments (II

Kings 23:7. The older English Version translates wrongly *"by the house of"* Yahweh; but the English and American Revised Bibles, and the new Jewish Bible, translate correctly *"in* the house of"). The most horrible feature of Manasseh's reign was child-sacrifice and the shedding of "innocent blood very much, until Jerusalem was filled from one end to another" (21:6, 16). The immolation of children was an extreme ritual act, prompted by despair, as when the king of Edom, in a time of great national peril, offered up the crown prince for a burnt-offering to the god Chemosh (II Kings 3:26, 27). The long reign of Manasseh was, indeed, a reign of terror.

Country people still hoping for social justice, or mishpat.— But while Jerusalem, on the northern edge of Judah, fell more and more under the grip of Baal-worship; and while the term *baal*, as a designation of proprietorship, was gaining ground; yet the villagers of the open country were still swayed by the deep desire for social justice, or mishpat, already expressed by the insurgent prophet Elijah, the upheaval against Omri's dynasty, the "Ephraimite" document, and the books of Amos, Hosea, Isaiah, and Micah. The crux of their problem was the necessity, to which they were forced, of giving *land* in pledge for a debt, when, at the same time, they rebelled against the logic which resulted in *foreclosure.* Thus, the small baalim, the *am ha arets*, wanted loans from the wealthier baalim; and they could only get loans by pledging the "inheritance of their fathers." Yet they felt that interest on money was wrong, and they objected to losing their lands by legal process when the loan became "frozen," as we now say.

The situation was, of course, impossible. *But its very impossibility generated the impulses which lifted the primitive cult of Yahweh above the level of surrounding heathenism, and sent the faiths of Judaism and Christianity in search of a better world.* Looking back, then, over the course of Hebrew history, from the desert period up to the end of Manasseh's dark reign, we can see the difficult situation of Israel in Palestine coming to its inevitable head. Hebrew history thus far had given rise to a mass of private, unofficial documents in the name of Yahweh; but the essence of this earlier literature, culled out and *improved* upon as the Book of Deuteronomy, was now to be made the official constitution of Judah.

Noble families in background of Manasseh's reign, destined for prominence in Deuteronomic period.—Before turning to Josiah and the great revolution, it is instructive to linger a while in the moral and religious gloom of Manasseh's reign, and observe how, during that very epoch, a number of noble families existed whose representatives were to be prominent in the Deuteronomic era. First of all, we notice *Meshullam* and his son *Azaliah*. While of course no absolute conclusion is deducible from these names, yet a certain importance attaches to their meaning in Hebrew when we consider (1) that the men who bore them were ancestors of Josian reformers, (2) that they lived in a troubled age when their names were highly appropriate, and (3) that other equally fitting names, presently to be mentioned, were contemporary with them. We know that expressive names were given to Hebrew children by their parents, and also that the activities of mature life resulted in a *change* of name (Isa. 8:1-4; I Sam. 1:20; Hos. 1:4, 6, 9; Judg. 6:32; 7:1). The two men cited above, *Meshullam* and *Azaliah* (father and son), were immediate ancestors of *Shaphan*, the royal secretary under King Josiah (II Kings 22:3). The word "meshullam" probably means "one who is kept in safety, or in peace [*shalom*]"; while "azaliah" means "one who has been set apart by Yahweh." Such terms would be appropriate, in the dark and horrible reign of Manasseh, as names for men whose families were looking forward to a better day. Another name equally fitting is that of *Tikvah* ("hope"). A man of this designation lived in Manasseh's period; and his son *Shallum*, "peace," was appointed royal chamberlain to King Josiah and was also husband of *Huldah* the prophetess, whose backing promoted the Deuteronomic reformation ((II Kings 22:14). Still another name, remarkable but more commonly found, is that of *Michaiah* ("Who is like Yahweh?"), applied to the father of *Achbor*, one of Josiah's counselors (II Kings 22:12). Two other persons of importance in Manasseh's time were *Amariah*, "Yahweh has spoken," and *Gedaliah*, "Yahweh is great." These men, father and son, were in the immediate ancestry of *Zephaniah*, a minor prophet in the reign of King Josiah (Zeph. 1:1). The accomplished *Baruch*, secretary to the prophet Jeremiah, was the son of *Neriah*, "Yahweh is light," whose father, unknown to history, must have lived in the dark days of Manasseh, and who perhaps bestowed the name in anticipation of brighter times (Jer. 36:3–4). While this canvass of the pre-Josian age raises many questions, it seems to give us a fleeting glimpse at a period when, in spite of difficulty, faith was carrying the remnant of Israel on toward some high mission.

Josiah placed on throne at age of eight by uprising of "am ha arets."—Josiah was made king by an uprising of the country people. A mob invaded Jerusalem, and slew many of the royal counselors who had served Manasseh and his son Amon (II Kings 21:23, 24). Josiah's mother was a country girl from the village of Bozkath in the lowlands; and *her* father's name was Adaiah, "Yahweh advances" or perhaps "Yahweh adorns" (II Kings 22:1). The new monarch was only eight years of age when crowned; and since the royal counselors of the preceding, Baalistic era were slain by the mob, the way was now open for a better government by the nobles whose lineage we have sketched in the preceding section (II Kings 22:3, 12, 14). The tables were now turned; and where the higher prophetic party had been silenced under the bloody rule of Manasseh, the pro-Baal nobles were terrorized by the death of their leading politicians in the sanguinary uprising of the *am ha arets*.

There are three direct biblical sources for the reign of Josiah:

(1) the account in II Kings; (2) a brief but pointed reference in Jeremiah; and (3) the Book of Deuteronomy itself. These three sources must be examined in relation to each other, and in view of Hebrew history as a whole.

Reign of Josiah considered from different standpoints by Jeremiah and Kings.—The first eighteen years of this reign are left *absolutely blank* by the Deuteronomic editor of Kings. He first quotes from an earlier source telling how the country people slew the politicians of Manasseh (II Kings 21:23–24). Then, after adding comments of his own, he leaps *completely* over the eighteen-year space, and quotes again from the earlier source, which tells how a little roll, or book, of law was "found" in the temple by Hilkiah the *cohen*, and immediately put into force by the government (II Kings 22:3–15; 23:1–24). The account in II Kings, however, merely describes an *ecclesiastical*, ritualistic reformation, whereby the country churches all over Judah were suppressed, and the worship of Yahweh centralized in the Temple at Jerusalem, which was purged of Baal altars and the *asherah*, or wooden image; while the "sacred" prostitutes of both sexes (*kedeshoth* and *kedeshim*) were summarily evicted from their apartments. These measures correspond with the ritualistic requirements of Deuteronomy in all but one respect. The centralization of the cultus at *one place* will deprive the village priests of clerical standing and income unless provision is made for them to minister at the capital city (Deut. 18:6 f.). The lawbook has in mind such priests as the Levite of Bethlehem and Dan, and the Levite of Ephraim (Judg. 17:7; 18:30; 19:1). Such men are now to come and serve as full priests in the temple of Yahweh. But the Josian reform itself commenced the degradation of Levites by taking the professional ground from under their feet, since we read in Kings, "The *cohanim* of the high places did *not* come up to the altar of Yahweh at Jerusalem; but they ate *matzoth* among their brethren" (II Kings 23:9). Later on we shall trace the emergence of the Levites, as mere porters, distinct from *cohanim*, in the post-Exilic document P.

So far as the compiler of Kings is concerned, this is all that we discover about the great Josian reformation! The "people of the land," as we learn from Isaiah and Micah, have been oppressed by the concentration of real estate in the hands of the few. They have cried out for mishpat, or social justice, during the reigns of Ahaz, Hezekiah, Manasseh, and Amon. They now rise up, slay the Baalistic politicians at the capital, and enthrone Josiah. Then the people quiet down into silence for the space of eighteen long years. Then a lawbook is "found" in the temple, according to which the government suddenly "disestablishes" all village churches; unfrocks the Levites who had been priests at the local sanctuaries; provides that all worship shall be at one place, the Temple of Yahweh at Jerusalem; requires the people to cease labor three times a year, and make the journey from all over Judah to the capital, paying dues and fees to a small group of priests who monopolize the cultus. There is no word here about the great, characteristic mishpat problem; but, instead, the compiler of Kings tells us, with deep satisfaction, that Josiah "did right [*yashar*] in the eyes of Yahweh" (II Kings 22:2 [Deuteronomic framework]). We could study the reign of Josiah in the Book of Kings (as it is actually studied in countless church schools and Sunday schools), and learn absolutely nothing about the essence of the situation!

But, on the other hand, in startling contrast with Kings, we get a wholly different sense of Josiah from Jeremiah the prophet, without whose book we should be unable to check up the history. This remarkable prophet lived through a large part of Josiah's reign and into a later time when the reformer king had been long dead, and when the old evils of Baalism had returned in full force. Looking back on the days of Josiah from the standpoint of his evil son Jehoiakim's reign, Jeremiah says, "Thy father [Josiah] did *mishpat*. Then it was well with him. He judged the law cases of the *poor and needy*. Then the times were good. Was not this to know me? saith Yahweh" (Jer. 22:15–16). The phrase "poor and needy" in Hebrew does not have the meaning which the modern translation seems to convey; but, as we have already emphasized, it refers to the smaller baalim, on the left wing of the property class, who composed the "people of the land," i.e., the *am ha arets*. And thus, under the lead of Jeremiah, we can see that the Deuteronomic reformation had to do with *social justice*, and was more than a change in the cultus—important and worthy as that change proved to be in the evolution of monotheism. And, moreover, although Deuteronomy itself lays down cultus regulations like the ones carried out by Josiah, this transcendently important, strategic book in the Hebrew Bible agrees with Jeremiah also in emphasis upon mishpat.

Deuteronomy expresses "defeatist" reaction against horrible reign of Manasseh.—The platform upon which the Josianic revolution was based, then, is found in the book known to Gentiles as "Deuteronomy," but which the Jews call *D'barim* (i.e., "words"), from the opening sentence, "These are the words, etc." (1:1). Much of the material now in Deuteronomy, however, was added by expansion and revision before the book had become unalterable Holy Scripture; but this added matter has been carefully distinguished by critical investigation. The book stands for a "defeatist" reaction against the horrible reign of Manasseh; and we cannot assume that it was discovered *only* by accident in the eighteenth year of Josiah. Its fundamental ideas were already present in such unofficial writings as the E document, the J document, the Elijah stories, and the books of Hosea, Amos, Micah, and Isaiah. Thus, Deuteronomy summarizes and improves upon the earlier literature.

Double revolution of cultus and mishpat raises problem not usually considered.—Deuteronomy, as we must ever bear in mind, stands for a movement which has *two phases:* (1) revolution in the *cultus*, as described in Kings and (2) reformation of *mishpat*, as described in Jeremiah. Hebrew historians have scarcely recognized the problem raised by these plain facts. To take for granted that the mishpat feature of the Josian policy was postponed eighteen years in the face of great social distress *would be to assume that the horrible conditions of Manasseh's time were prolonged through much the larger part of Josiah's reign, and then only dealt with on the authority of a hitherto unknown booklet.* Yet this is the assumption which, whether deliberate or tacit, has been constantly made.

But, on the other hand, it is more consistent with experience to take for granted that in the earlier part of Josiah's reign a readjustment was *already going on* with relation to landed property, interest on loans, the status of debts, and the emancipation of "left-wing" baalim from slavery. Such a movement would be promoted by the polemic of Zephaniah, who called for destruction of Baalism to the last vestige, branding the princes of Jerusalem as "roaring lions" and the judges "evening wolves" (Zeph. 1:4; 3:1–3). Only against great obstacles do economic and social reforms make their slow, uncertain headway; and with Baal-worship yet awaiting destruction through the law-booklet, the sins of Judah would not seem to have been expiated when Jeremiah, in the thirteenth year of Josiah's reign, uttered his prophecies about the foe from the north as the instrument of Yahweh's anger against the kingdom. That the sins of Manasseh were not wiped out, even by the revolution of Josiah as a *whole*, and that the exile of Judah in Babylon was the penalty paid by Jerusalem for the lasting influence of Manasseh, is indeed a fixed idea of the Deuteronomist (II Kings 21:9–15; 23:26; 24:3–4; cf. 17:19–20).

If, in the field of mishpat reform, the new government were already demonstrating good faith, even against opposition, it would find easier the task of uprooting ancient cult-habits, abolishing the village churches, and centralizing all worship at

Jerusalem. From this point of view, then, the Deuteronomic reformation would not begin with the advent of the little book; but, on the contrary, the government would slowly build up a structure of prestige firm enough to support the proclamation of the written code in the eighteenth year of Josiah; after which the course of reform would be smoother.

Adoption of Deuteronomic law by government enthrones "defeatism" officially in Hebrew religion.—The enthronement of defeatism at the heart of Israel's religion became *official* for the first time in Hebrew history by the Deuteronomic reformation under King Josiah; whereas, prior to this epoch, defeatism was only a tenet of private individuals, without the validating stamp of the government. The *earlier*, success-prophecy, as we have seen, came into vogue when there was no mishpat problem, and when the struggle between alien social groups was not complicated by antagonism between social classes *within* groups. It was founded upon the universal postulate of primitive religion, that the bond between a people and its divinity was absolute and *unconditional;* so that the god of every nation was expected, as a matter of course, to champion the cause of his worshipers, and bring victory to his own social group against all others. Arising out of the purely physical, non-ethical sense of *group integrity*, this idea survived into the epoch of the mishpat problem, when it solidified as a *heathen dogma*, contrary to the new claim, raised by the insurgent prophets, that Yahweh would become a *foe* to his own people, and bring enemies upon Israel to defeat them if his worshipers did not follow mishpat (Deut. 28:25; 4:25, 26). The success-prophets, therefore, cannot be described as bad or wicked men; because, in last analysis, they were only a belated survival from an earlier phase of social evolution. And while they took the part of the nobility who exploited the poor baalim on the aristocratic left wing, they had a psychological advantage of tremendous weight; for one who proclaims *victory* is always more popular than one who harps on *destruction.* And when we take all the circumstances into account, then, it is not strange that the newer and higher prophets maintained their doctrine at the peril of their lives *against the organized force of the state.*

But now, after two hundred and fifty years of struggle, defeatism was at length accredited, sanctioned, authorized, and validated by a Hebrew government as the official formula of the relationship existing between Yahweh and Israel (II Kings 23:1–3). The adoption of the Deuteronomic platform, of course, did not instantly sweep away the older, primitive, heathen idea of an *unconditional* bond between a social group and its god. But by the solemn covenant of king and people, the new ideas were all at once raised out of unofficial ambiguity, and impressed upon the social psychology of Judah. And even though later Jewish authorities neglected part or all of the Josian revolution, the Book of Deuteronomy never was repealed but continued as definitive Jewish law, *forming the literary point of attachment around which the Hebrew and Christian Bibles developed.* The original, brief edition of Josiah's lawbook, then, was the *first* Hebrew Bible; and at the time of its promulgation, all the other documents and writings now in the Old Testament, and which *we* think of as "Bible," were still the private property of scribes, or were yet to be composed.

Deuteronomic code takes chattel slavery for granted as basis of social group.—We shall presently notice how the Deuteronomic code, with its amended version of the Ten Commandments, improves upon the earlier Decalogue, and upon the Mishpat Code found in Exodus. But first we should observe that the Book of Deuteronomy, like the rest of the Bible, takes for granted, as normal and right, the existence of two social classes, composed of masters, or *baalim*, above, and *non-Hebrew*, alien slaves, or *abadim*, below. The abstract idea of human freedom was practically unthinkable at that stage of social evolution; and we ought not to look for it anywhere among the peoples of antiquity. There is no point in the doubtful claim, put forward by some orthodox gentile scholars, that slavery in ancient Israel was "more genial and kindly than among other peoples." This claim was also made about American slavery. And whether true in one case or in both, it is an admission that chattel slavery existed in denial of human liberty as a principle. We have quoted elsewhere the complaint of the slaveholder *Nabal*, in central Judah, who said, "There be many slaves [*abadim*] now a days that escape every man from his master" (I Sam. 25:10). And we have also noticed the case of the Benjaminite landlord in Jerusalem, whose *abadim* escaped (I Kings 2:36–40). Such fugitives, no doubt, felt that the institution of slavery was not "genial."

But it is precisely this institution that is taken for granted as legal and ethical by the Ephraimite Decalogue and the Deuteronomic version of the Ten Commandments. Thus, the earlier Decalogue says, "Thou shalt not covet thy neighbor's man-slave [*ebed*], nor his woman-slave [*amah*]" (Exod. 20:17). And the Deuteronomic treatment of this item is exactly the same (Deut. 5:21). The modern translation "manservant" and "maidservant" obscures the sense of the Hebrew text; for if such persons were merely free servants, working for wages, there could be nothing wrong in desiring their services enough to offer them better compensation. It is their legal status as chattel property, like the horse and the ox, that makes it wrong, from the standpoint of the codes, to "covet" them.

Deuteronomic program seeks rescue of poorer baalim from lower, enslaved class.—Neither code (the Ephraimite nor the Deuteronomic) is preoccupied with slavery as an institution, but with the very different problem of keeping "poor and needy" baalim *out of* the lower, non-Israelite, enslaved class, and of *rescuing* such persons, if, through misfortune, they have sunk into slavery. And since the forfeiture of personal freedom was nearly always connected with loss of *land* through foreclosure of unpaid, or "frozen," mortgages, the Deuteronomic code has four provisions which its authors hoped would meet the difficulty.

First of all, a new ordinance is laid down whereby every *creditor* is commanded to release, or cancel, any loan at the end of seven years. Not only do we see in this law a difference of economic standpoint as compared with the Ephraimite document, but we notice a new term for "creditor" as contrasted with usage in II Kings, where the moneylender, who enslaves the children of his debtor, is called *nosheh* (II Kings 4:1). For in Deuteronomy the creditor is called simply a *baal*. Thus, "At the end of seven years thou shalt make a release. Every *baal* that lendeth anything to his neighbor shall release the debt, and shall not require it of his neighbor or his brother" (Deut. 15:1–2). The moneylender in question is a wealthy baal on the right wing of the Hebrew aristocracy; and the debtor is a "poor and needy" baal on the left wing.

Another stipulation repeats, and enlarges upon, the command of the earlier code with reference to interest on money, and says that there shall be no lending upon *interest* either of money, or of supplies, or of anything that is loaned (Deut. 23:19–20; cf. Exod. 22:25). The term is translated "usury" by the King James Version; but the American Revised and the American Jewish Bibles render the Hebrew in today's English as "interest." And this, of course, was the meaning of "usury" when the earlier English Bible was published; but, in the meanwhile, usury has come to signify an exorbitant charge for the use of money; and so the later versions are changed accordingly. What the Hebrew text means is that no interest *whatever* is to be charged for any kind of loan between Hebrews. But the text adds, that "unto a stranger [i.e., a foreigner] thou mayest lend upon interest" (Deut. 23:20).

A third prominent feature of the Deuteronomic platform is the injunction against removal of *landmarks*, which always went along with foreclosure of mortgages: "Thou shalt not take away thy neighbor's landmark which they of earlier times have set in thine inheritance" (Deut. 19:14). This command is given again as part of a public ritual to be recited about things cursed (Deut. 27:17). A landmark was the sign of ownership, and raised a legal presumption that the designated field or lot was the property of the person whose name or sign was on the stone; so that a creditor, on foreclosing his claim, would naturally want the ancient mark taken away. But if the stone could *not* legally be removed, then a mortgage could not be liquidated so easily; and there would be one more obstacle in the path of richer baalim who sought to "add house to house and field to field."

A fourth point in the Deuteronomic treatment of the land problem is revealed in the contrast between the earlier, Ephraimite version of the tenth commandment and the new phrasing of this item in the final, or Josian, version of the Decalogue. The *older* formula merely says, "Thou shalt not covet thy neighbor's *house*"; and there is nothing further about the question of real estate in the early code (Exod. 20:17 [E source]). But, in the meanwhile, the polemic of Isaiah and Micah had given this commandment a more definite expression. For, as we have already seen, Isaiah pronounces woe upon those who "add *house to house*, and *field to field*"; while Micah says, "They covet *fields*, and seize them, and houses, and take them" (Isa. 5:8; Mic. 2:2). Accordingly, the *new* tenth commandment not only quotes the former injunction, "Thou shalt not covet thy neighbor's *house*," but it goes on, and adds explicitly, "his *field*" (Deut. 5:21). Comparison of the two codes will show the term "field" in the Deuteronomic version *only*. Recitation of the Decalogue in a public service has value of its own; but ritualistic repetition also has the disadvantage of obscuring the social stress in the background of the Ten Commandments, and making the mind impervious to the history which they symbolize.

Thus we see that four concrete provisions aim to check the

fall of "poor and needy" baalim into the lower class of alien slaves. How far these features of the *present* Book of Deuteronomy agree with *Josiah's* little book of law we do not know. But considering the economic aspects of Hebrew evolution, and remembering the categorical declaration of Jeremiah that King Josiah "did mishpat, and judged the law cases of the poor and needy," the conclusion is irresistible that *some* program of reform was attempted and put into effect. That it was more or less utopian and impossible in the long run does not detract from its ethical significance; nor is its ultimate spiritual value diminished because its immediate results were swept away in a few years by the tragic onrush of events. For when we consider the tremendous difficulties which even today block the course of social readjustment, the wonder is that far back in the darkness of an ignorant age (twenty-five hundred years ago), the Deuteronomic reformation accomplished what it did, and made its powerful mark on world-history.

Looking at the situation objectively, the government of Josiah could, without any doubt whatever, do a great deal in restoring land to the *am ha arets*, who had been deprived of ancestral holdings by foreclosure. But, at the same time, only a miracle would have induced the more well-to-do baalim, on the right wing of the aristocracy, to loan surplus funds or goods to the less fortunate proprietors, without any interest or security, and in view of the certain prospect that such debts would legally be canceled at the end of seven years. And while the government, then, could have done much to break up large estates, the campaign to prevent *reconcentration* of property by laws requiring cancellation of loans, prohibiting interest on money, forbidding removal of landmarks, and banning even the "desire" for one's neighbor's field in security for debt—such ordinances and commandments were clearly too great a strain upon human nature. And, moreover, even if they had been put into general effect, they would have resulted in the steady transfer of economic surplus toward the left wing of the aristocracy while frustrating the incentive to thrift.

Deuteronomy seeks higher social status for woman.—The Ephraimite code, it will be recalled, stipulates that a poor Hebrew baal, held in slavery, shall be released at the end of six years; but that if his master has given him a wife, and she has borne children, the mother and her offspring shall *not* be set free, to go out with the father (Exod. 21:2, 4). But in contrast with this law, the later-coming code of Deuteronomy provides that enslaved women of Israel be liberated *equally with men.* "If thy brother, an Hebrew man, *or an Hebrew woman*, be sold unto thee, thou shalt let them go free in the seventh year" (Deut. 15:12). In the light of this change, it is highly instructive to notice a corresponding modification of the Decalogue with reference to the status of woman. The *Ephraimite* version of the tenth commandment begins, as we have already seen, with a prohibition against coveting one's neighbor's *house.* This item is given a sentence by itself, which constitutes the *opening clause.* And then, after disposing of the real estate question, the commandment goes on to schedule *other* items which must not be coveted, putting the neighbor's wife into the same category with slaves and cattle (Exod. 20:17 [E document]). Deuteronomy, on the other hand, in accordance with its more liberal provision for emancipation of Hebrew women-slaves, makes a wholly different approach to the tenth commandment. Postponing the real estate question, it places woman *first*, in a class by herself, beginning, "Thou shalt not desire thy neighbor's *wife.*" Then come the house and field; and, last of all, the slaves and cattle (Deut. 5:21). In other words, the Deuteronomic law is not only defeatist, but *feminist.*

Withdrawal of religious ratification for permanent slavery of Hebrews.—The earlier, Ephraimite code prescribed a religious formality in the case of once-free Israelites who, after being slaves for six years, desired to remain in the master's household.

A temporarily enslaved Hebrew baal, in the *earlier* code, who did not care to take advantage of the six-year emancipation law, was to be brought unto the *elohim*, unto the door of the house, unto the doorpost, or *mezuzah*, where his ear should be bored through with an awl. (Exod. 21:2, 5, 6 [E document]). The term *elohim* (usually translated "God") points to a religious rite; and the doorpost, or *mezuzah*, has always been sacred in Hebrew thought, as a place to which divine writings may be attached (Deut. 6:9). But in sharp contrast with the earlier authentication of permanent slavery by a religious rite, the code of Deuteronomy stipulates that when the enslaved Hebrew desires to remain *always* with his Hebrew purchaser, the ear-ceremony is to be performed *without reference to "elohim" or "mezuzah."* The slave simply goes to the *door;* and the awl is thrust through his ear *into the door itself* (Deut. 15:17, with omission of *elohim* and *mezuzah*). The reason for this remarkable change *appears* to be that since all religious rites are centralized in Jerusalem by Deuteronomy, no sacred service may *now* be conducted in the home. But, at the same time, no direction is given that the rite may be conducted at the temple *if desired.* History, therefore, had reached a point where the permanent slavery of a Hebrew had become a *private* matter between the slave and his master, *since Yahweh no longer sanctions perpetual bondage for a son of Israel.* The logical result of this position will come before us in the yet later "Holiness Code."

Deuteronomic monotheism implicit platform of progressive universal justice.—That Deuteronomy is the *official* beginning and foundation of Hebrew Scripture becomes increasingly evident as we examine the book. Amending the earlier codes, it leaves an open path for still further progress; and it is therefore an *evolutionary* work. Its idea of God is not static, or final, but dynamic and progressive. Instead of shackling religion to the *past,* it unlocks the door to a broadening future. These considerations are the basis of Deuteronomic theology: *"Hear Is-*

rael: Yahweh our God is One" (Deut. 6:4). The unitary principle implies that the law of justice in human society is like the
laws which govern the physical universe—of uniform and im-
partial application, relating equally to all classes and peoples,
without special privilege or favor. Hence, the ideal of monotheism leads onward beyond anything yet realized: "The servant
of Yahweh shall bring forth *mishpat* to the nations. He shall not
fail nor be crushed until he has put *mishpat* in the earth; and far
countries shall wait for his teaching" (Exilic Isa., chap. 42,
passim). "They shall beat their swords into plowshares and their
spears into pruning hooks. Nation shall not raise up sword
against nation; and they shall not learn war any more" (Isa.
2:4; Mic. 4:3). Biblical monotheism points to universal justice, within and between all nations, as the only cure for war.

**Framework of Deuteronomy patterned upon Ephraimite
conquest of central highlands.**—That the history of the house
of Joseph in central Canaan furnished a *model* for the Deuteronomic philosophy has been pointed out above. Historical critics
rightly demonstrate that the conquest of Canaan, as a whole,
was incomplete; but the original *Josephite* conquest amounted
virtually to extermination of the landholding Amorites, or
baalim, in the central district. The baalim of *Jericho* were slain
and their city laid waste; *Bethel* was reduced; and, finally,
Shechem and its baalim were destroyed. Thus, the Ephraimite
hill-country became the original "inheritance" of Yahweh; the
custom of mishpat landholding took the place of baalistic law;
and the Amorite cults were suppressed in central Canaan.

This thorough process, carried out locally by the house of Joseph, culminating in the fall of Shechem, was the archetype,
idealized by the Deuteronomist, who felt that it should have
been followed out from the very start and extended all over the
country, from Beersheba to Dan. Accordingly, he *imagines* a
command as having been laid upon Israel to exterminate completely the *entire* population of Canaan: "Thou shalt not save

alive *anything* that breatheth" (Deut. 20:16, 17). Their altars
are to be overthrown; their stone pillars (*mazzeboth*) broken;
their cult-poles (*asherim*) burned with fire; and the images of
their gods hewn down (Deut. 12:3). And likewise, after this
thorough conquest, if an *Israelite* city is ever found worshiping
other gods beside Yahweh, it must be totally destroyed with all
its inhabitants (13:12 f.). And also, to the same effect, if an
individual Hebrew is found serving other gods, he must be slain
"without pity," even if he should be a close relative (13:6–10).
The completion of the conquest is to be followed by a ceremony
of "blessing and cursing" upon the two mountains, Ebal and
Gerizim, outside of Shechem, where the *actual*, Josephite conquest reached its climax (Deut. 11:29; 27:4, 12, 13). While
Deuteronomy registers ethical advance in some notable respects, yet its bloodthirsty ideal is a reversion to sanguinary
measures already condemned by the prophet Hosea in the name
of Yahweh (Hos. 1:4).

**Deuteronomy labors in vain to settle issue between oppos-
ing schools of prophecy.**—Seeking the official victory of "defeatism," the Deuteronomist is very sensitive about the issue
between prophetic "schools." Being a diligent investigator of
Ephraimite history, he is much impressed by the dramatic scene
wherein Micaiah ben Imlah accurately predicted the defeat of
Ahab, while the conventional prophets wrongly foretold success.
And so he says that Israel must not follow a prophet whose pre-
dictions fail (Deut. 18:21, 22). This, however, does not go to
the heart of the issue; and elsewhere in the same book it is con-
ceded that *any* prophet may utter an accurate prediction; but,
in such case, if he speaks in the name of "other gods," he must
not be trusted, even though his words come true. Prediction as
a test of prophecy is thus *eliminated;* and the whole question is
left in the air (Deut. 13:1–5).

Deuteronomy not a "pious fraud."—It is wholly beside the
merits of the case to ask whether any conscious deceit, or

fraud, was involved in the writing, or "finding," of the little book of law in the temple. The author was either an insurgent prophet or a prophetically minded scribe; and since all shades of Hebrew opinion were sincerely expressed in the name of Yahweh, the *literary* production of the book raises no problem whatever. The *am ha arets* were already strong for *mishpat;* and so the economic reorganization of Judah could proceed without any lawbook, by appeal to tradition. But after the good faith of Josiah's government had been demonstrated over a long period by "judging the law cases of the poor and needy," the force of public opinion would concentrate behind the king; and then the purely *cult-phase* of social institutions could be altered by means of a definitive, written code, centralizing all religious and legal machinery at Jerusalem, where the government could more effectively control the state.

King Josiah was only eight years old at the time of his accession. But this was nothing new in the history of Judah; for one of his predecessors, *Joash*, whose ministers deposed Queen Athaliah, was an infant of six; and the notorious *Manasseh* was a boy of twelve at the beginning of his dark reign (II Kings 11:2, 3; 21:1). King Josiah was in the power of the royal council; and his government was able to manipulate the prestige of the crown because public opinion, for the time being, was thoroughly aroused against the pro-Baal party, the Tory politicians of Manasseh having been slain by the mob.

Whether or not Josiah was a party to the "finding" of the lawbook, we are unable to deduce from the narrative. In either case, the *royal council* was dominant; for if the king had no knowledge of the book until it was brought to him by *Shaphan*, the secretary of state, his instant acquiescence and co-operation prove that he was completely in the power of his ministers; while, on the other hand, if Josiah were taken by surprise, the sequel also proves that the *council*, and not the king, was the real force in the government. The reformation, from beginning

to end, moves on like clockwork: The booklet, having straight-
way received royal assent, is taken by a group of nobles, including Shaphan and his son *Ahikam*, to the prophetess *Huldah*,
who promptly sanctions it. But Huldah is the wife of the royal
chamberlain, *Shallum;* and so the whole process of authentication takes place within the closed circle of ministerial counselors.
Then the government brings into play the *am ha arets*, headed
by their elders, the *zikanim* of Judah; and a huge convocation
of the people, "both small and great," is gathered in Jerusalem.
The pro-Baal party meanwhile, deprived of its foremost politicians, and completely terrorized for the time being, shrinks
helplessly in the background; while an excited multitude over-
runs Jerusalem; and the whole movement comes to a climax
with ratification of the Deuteronomic lawbook by king and assembly (II Kings 22:3–15; 23:1 f.)

Decline of Assyrian empire help to Josian reform.—During
the Deuteronomic period, the Assyrian empire, which had oppressed the oriental world for many generations, began to go
steadily into decay. Attacked by other powers, and preoccupied
with its own weakness arising from economic ruin of the common people, the Assyrians were no longer able to collect the
tribute which they had been gathering from conquered nations.
Thus, the Judean *am ha arets* benefited both from reduction of
taxes and from the "doing of mishpat" by the government of
Josiah. And yet the international situation, which thus promoted the Deuteronomic movement, had repercussions of another sort upon Hebrew history. The decline of Assyria roused
the avarice of Egypt, whose ruler at this time, *Pharaoh Necho*,
undertook to seize for himself a part of the disintegrating Mesopotamian empire; and with this aim in view, he prepared to
throw his army northward across Palestine to the Euphrates
River.

**Egyptian passage across Palestine opposed by small Jewish
force under Josiah.**—When the authorities at Jerusalem heard
of the proposed Egyptian move, they regarded it with alarm as

a threat against all Palestine. The huge expedition from the
Nile country went slowly up the Mediterranean coast, avoiding
the hills of Judah, and passing through the Plain of Sharon, along
the course followed by the Philistine armies in the far-off days of
King Saul. But, in the meanwhile, Josiah and his counselors had
been active; and now a Jewish force moved rapidly north toward the Plain of Esdraelon, into which the Egyptian army
would soon be turning.

That a small force like Josiah's would fling itself against a
powerful military host, such as the one coming up from Egypt,
seems incredible. Yet this was exactly what the Jewish king
and his counselors were proposing! Did they trust in the promise of Deuteronomy that if Israel obeyed the lawbook, every foe
should fall in battle before the Hebrews? Did the early edition
of Deuteronomy contain such a promise? The *final* one has the
following: "When thou goest out against thine enemies, and
seest horses and chariots, more than thou, be not afraid. For
Yahweh thy god is with thee, which brought thee up out of the
land of Egypt. He shall cause thine enemies to be smitten before
thy face. They shall come out against thee by *one* way, and
shall flee before thee *seven* ways" (Deut. 20:1; 28:7). We may
rightly suspect that these very words were in the Josian edition
of the lawbook, and that the reference to *Egypt*, in particular,
may have been conclusive and exciting, as if it were actually a
prediction of what was now coming to pass.

The little Jewish army soon reached a point in the Ephraimite hills overlooking the Plain of Esdraelon where "the stars
in their courses" had sided with Deborah against the Amorite
general Sisera, whose chariots and horsemen, caught in the
sudden downpour of heavy rain, were swept away *by the waters
of Megiddo.* And it would have been strange if Josiah did not
recall that battle, hoping for a like intervention from heaven as
he beheld the huge, glittering host of Egypt advancing along the
plain, with its bright spears, polished armor, and shining chariots.
Then, without waiting longer, the tiny Jewish force descended from

*the hills and hurled itself to inevitable destruction. "And the
servants of Josiah carried him in a chariot dead from Megiddo,
and brought him to Jerusalem"* (II Kings 23:29, 30).

Josiah's defeat, although a foregone conclusion, was wholly
unexpected; and the death of the king, like the death of Lincoln,
is one of the most pathetic events in history. The Kingdom of
Judah was filled with sorrow and alarm; but, in spite of dismay,
the *am ha arets* took Prince Jehoahaz, or Shallum, and anointed
him to succeed his father (II Kings 23:30). The mourning for
Josiah continued some time (Jer. 22:10).

**Egyptians dethrone people's choice; make Jehoiakim vas-
sal-king.**—Pharaoh Necho had not made any declaration of
war against the house of David; and his expedition across Palestine was wholly outside of Jewish territory; so that the issue
was really forced by Josiah; and the result threw the politics of
Judah into confusion. The king of Egypt, returning trium-
phantly from the Euphrates, arrested Jehoahaz, whom "the people of the land" had anointed to rule over them; while in his place,
another son of Josiah, by the name of *Eliakim*, was crowned *as a
vassal of Egypt*. And moreover, the Egyptian king, to show his
own power, changed the name of this new and inglorious ruler
from Eliakim to *Jehoiakim* (II Kings 23:33, 34).

But this was only the beginning of trouble; for now, in place
of the Assyrian tribute, *"Pharaoh Necho assessed upon the land
one hundred talents of silver and a talent of gold. And Jehoiakim
took the silver and the gold from the am ha arets, from every man
according to his taxation, to give it unto Pharaoh Necho"* (II Kings
23:33, 35).

Judah once more falls into grip of Baalism.—King Josiah's
tragic death, and the sudden vassalage of Judah to Egypt, gave
the pro-Baal party at Jerusalem an opening which they were
quick to seize. They could point to the national misfortune as
proof that the insurgent school of prophecy was wrong in its
claim that the rejection of Deuteronomy would cause defeat;

for the exact opposite *appeared* to be true; and the observance of the lawbook was actually followed by defeat in battle, the death of the king, subjection to Egypt, and a new tax burden Insurgent prophecy, for the time being, had no obvious dramatic answer which could make headway, in the popular mind, against the force of these tremendous facts. The Deuteronomic school had made religious fidelity a guaranty of success in battle to such effect that a combination of unfortunate circumstances, like those including the death of Josiah, would greatly embarrass the insurgent prophets, and give the opposing faction of "heathen" politicians an opportunity to make unanswerable charges. Thus, the higher prophecy was thrust into the background by the misfortunes of Judah; while the government again fell into the hands of the pro-Baal party, as in the dark times of Manasseh.

Central-altar law of Josiah maintained, but rest of Deuteronomy ignored.—The Josian lawbook had been put into official force by a parliament of king and people; and if it were to be formally repealed, its rejection would have to be accomplished in the same way. For since the break-up of the *united* Hebrew monarchy, the house of David had been shorn of its despotism, and measurably democratized, in comparison with the rule of Solomon and the Ephraimite kings. And even though Jehoiakim, the son of Josiah, were unfriendly to the reforms of his father, he and his pro-Baal counselors would not dare convoke a popular assembly for the outright purpose of destroying the reformation. And not only so, but there was one outstanding phase of the Deuteronomic law which even the most reactionary elements in Jerusalem did not wish to see repealed—the law of the central altar, which abolished the country churches, and gave a monopoly of position and income to a small sacerdotal clique at Jerusalem, forcing the multitudes to visit the temple, pay temple dues, and patronize the city markets. Since Deuteronomy brought business to the capital, this consideration alone was enough to save it from oblivion. And thus the ordinance relating to the one central sanctuary was maintained.

But, on the other hand, the *mishpat* legislation was allowed to become a dead letter, as it must have *tended* to become, even in the reign of Josiah himself. A government friendly to the rural population could do much toward breaking up large estates, redistributing the soil among the smaller proprietors, and the checking of drastic mortgage foreclosures. But *no* administration, however well disposed it might be toward the *am ha arets*, could compel the more fortunate proprietors, who had an economic surplus, to loan their excess money or goods without interest, and then write off such debts at the end of seven years. And where Josiah was necessarily weak, his son Jehoiakim, the vassal of Egypt, had no motive whatever to cherish the ideals of his father. So the heavy tribute, which Pharaoh Necho demanded, was imposed upon the *am ha arets*, "to every man according to his taxation"; and the small proprietors had to make whatever terms they could with tax-collectors and money lenders.

Problems of mishpat and Baalism viewed as identical by Jeremiah.—The insurgent prophet Jeremiah has been quoted and referred to so frequently in this book that his general position ought now to be clear. This remarkable man, who was in many ways the greatest of Hebrew prophets, outlived the unfortunate Josiah and continued to preach until the downfall of the Jewish kingdom. He was not a Judahite, but an *Ephraimite*, whose birthplace was at the country village of Anathoth, in the district called by the name of an imaginary patriarch *Benjamin*, traditionally the younger son of Rachel and brother of Joseph (Jer. 1:1). Contrasted with the Judean prophets Amos and Micah, who did not employ the term "baal," Jeremiah makes frequent and impressive use of this old Amorite, or Canaanite, word which expressed the standpoint of Semitic territorial civilization. Jeremiah was influenced very strongly by

Hosea; but he never joins this Ephraimite prophet in making Israel say, "I will go after my lovers, the Baalim, who give me my bread, water, wool, oil, etc." Hosea's approach to the Baal question was concrete, personal, and biological, growing out of his unfortunate relations with the woman Gomer. His emphasis on the Baal question is true in a limited sense; yet the well-merited prestige of Hosea has tended to obscure the sociological and economic factors at the basis of Hebrew religious evolution. But with Jeremiah, on the other hand, Baalism, instead of being treated from ritualistic and biological points of approach, is viewed as a divergence from the mishpat of primitive clans which went after Yahweh "in the wilderness, in a land *not sown*" (Jer. 2:2). To Jeremiah, as to Deuteronomy, the worship of "other gods" is not to be treated as a question of *idolatry*, distinct and apart from social ethics; because the Baal-and-mishpat problems are fundamentally the same; and if one takes a legal oath in the name of Baal, *or in the name of a Baalized Yahweh*, he follows legal precedents contrary to the ancient mishpat of the *am ha arets* and their nomadic forefathers.

Heathen dogma of unconditional bond between deity and social group reasserted.—The reign of Jehoiakim was marked by recrudescence of the primitive, heathen dogma that a god and the social group which worships him are united by an absolute, unconditional bond; so that a people's deity *must* fight for the group that follows him, and be their champion in battle regardless of ethical conditions within the group itself. And this dogma, in post-Josian times, could be reformulated anew in peculiar terms: The one legitimate sanctuary of Yahweh at Jerusalem had been forsaken by the house of Joseph when they rebelled under Jeroboam I against the house of David. And therefore Ephraim had been carried into captivity for this great sin of refusing to worship at the Hebrew capital; while *Judah*, on the other hand, had been preserved, and would always be upheld by the power of Yahweh, whose *temple* was the guaranty of national integrity forever. That no Book of Deuteronomy was in existence when Jeroboam headed the revolt of Ephraim against the house of David, and that when the kingdom broke apart there had long been altars of Yahweh at many places in Judah and Ephraim alike, would have no force against this new phrasing of heathen self-sufficiency because the pro-Baal faction was now discovering that the central sanctuary law had possibilities which could be turned to account by their own party. The claim could now be made with some force that if the Ephraimites had remained faithful to the house of David, they would have been saved from destruction, just as David himself was always upheld against his enemies. *And therefore Yahweh must always defend his holy city and his temple.* This pious logic is a good concrete illustration of the countless arguments which take shape in reactionary minds for the purpose of upholding the *status quo* at any given period.

Jeremiah tried for high treason in reasserting defeatist view of Yahweh.—But upon the crystal-clear mind of Jeremiah, the argument about an indestructible sanctuary had no convincing effect; and against this newly devised form of Jewish-heathen dogmatism, the Ephraimite prophet set his face. In opposing it he went and stood in the court of the temple itself, on a holy day when, according to the Deuteronomic statute of centralization, people from all over Judah were coming into Jerusalem to offer sacrifice. And here, at this public place, Jeremiah lifted up his voice in the following prophecy:

Thus saith Yahweh, If ye rigorously do *mishpat* between man and man, I will cause you to dwell here. But put no trust in lying words, *The temple of Yahweh! The temple of Yahweh!* For this house, which is called by my name, has become a den of *robbers.* But go ye to my place which was in *Shiloh,* and see what I did to it for the wickedness of my people Israel. And likewise will I do unto this house wherein ye have confidence; for I will cast you out of my sight, as I have cast out all your brethren, the whole seed of Ephraim [Jer., chap. 7].

These words, when viewed from the conventional, reactionary, heathen standpoint, were nothing less than high treason against the Kingdom of Judah; and as soon as the full import of Jeremiah's prophecy became evident, he was arrested and brought for trial at a place called the "New Gate," where legal sessions were held. His accusers and prosecutors were the priests and the "success-prophets." The charge against him was *high treason;* and the penalty demanded was *death.* The judges in the case were the *princes of Judah,* who had been gathered in advance at the royal palace, and who now *came up* from King Jehoiakim's residence to the New Gate, where they sat as a court of last resort (Jer., chap. 26).

The scene was one of the most momentous in Hebrew history, and, indeed, in the world's history. The case was argued back and forth for a long time in the presence of an excited multitude. The prosecutors loudly emphasized their points, trying artfully to work on the feelings of the judges and the audience. But before a verdict was reached, the attention of the court was requested by certain "elders of the land" (*ziknae ha arets*), or counselors from the rural districts, who wanted to cite a precedent. These men pointed out that long ago, in the reign of Hezekiah, there was a certain defeatist prophet by the name of Micah, who predicted the destruction of Jerusalem, *and was not put to death.* Micah, to be sure, was never brought to trial; and therefore, from a legal point of view, there was no exact parallel between his case and that of Jeremiah; but the citation was useful in forming a precedent. The stormy session was at length brought to a close when the judges, with the concurrence of all the people, gave the following purely technical and noncommittal verdict regarding Jeremiah: "This man is not worthy of death, *because he has spoken to us in the name of Yahweh our god.*"

Occurring in the midst of a great political and economic reaction, this case is highly significant. The intractable Ephraimite prophet was vindicated by the highest court of Judah; while his prophetic and priestly accusers were given a backset. Jeremiah was gaining prestige. *The endless economic misery of the people gave defeatist prophecy ever new occasion for warfare against Amorite Baalism.*

Jeremiah supported by house of Shaphan, active in Josian reform.—Not only was Jeremiah favored by the plain people at his trial, but he was also upheld by a powerful house of Jewish nobles, which had been active in the Deuteronomic movement. King Josiah's prime minister, or secretary of state, was the scribe *Shaphan*, the son of Azaliah the son of Meshullam, whose known lineage therefore went back into the dark reign of Manasseh. Shaphan the scribe and Hilkiah the priest were the persons through whom the lawbook first came into notice; and Shaphan, together with his son *Ahikam*, were in the forefront of the reformation. This house remained faithful to the cause of "mishpat," notwithstanding Josiah's death and the great Baalistic reaction; for in the trial at the New Gate of the temple, *"the hand of Ahikam the son of Shaphan was with Jeremiah"* (Jer. 26:24). Just *how* Ahikam supported the prophet we cannot learn. He may have been one of the judges; he may have suggested the citation of Micah by the *zikanim;* or he may have been present with a band of *gibborim*, or strong-arm men; for the narrative says pointedly that Ahikam's influence was operating to save Jeremiah from death at the hand of executioners. This is not the only evidence we have regarding the house of Shaphan in the post-Deuteronomic period; and we shall now find other members of that remarkable family coming to the aid of Jeremiah at a juncture hardly less important than the trial itself.

Upheld by house of Shaphan, Jeremiah seeks new reformation through own book.—A few years after his trial, Jeremiah once more took advantage of the centralized cultus to stir up all Judah when the country people were gathered in Jerusalem on a holy day. Calling upon Baruch the scribe, the son of Neriah, an adherent whom he had found among the literary classes, he dictated, in the name of Yahweh, a little roll, or book, which agreed in principle with the mishpat section of Deuteronomy, and which predicted the fall of Jerusalem in case it were not obeyed (Jer., chap. 36). When the book was finished, Jeremiah requested Baruch to go into the temple and read it aloud in the ears of the multitude—his object being to force the hand of the government and start a new reformation. Baruch therefore carried the book to the sanctuary, and went up into a room above the New Gate, overlooking the "higher court." This room was the office of *Gemariah the scribe, the son of Shaphan.* But Gemariah himself was not there at the moment, being in a session of the *princes* at the royal palace, where he later comes into view and plays his part. Everything was clearly prearranged, moving forward with an automatic precision which recalls the finding of Deuteronomy. Gemariah the scribe, then, was not in his office; but his son *Michaiah* was there awaiting Baruch the scribe, who immediately went to the window looking down on the multitude in the court, and read the little book of Jeremiah's prophecy in a loud voice while Michaiah, the son of Gemariah, stood listening.

When this part of the program was completed, *Baruch* remained in the office with his little book, while the zealous Michaiah hurried away to the king's house, where "all the princes" were sitting. Then this worthy grandson of Shaphan proceeded to repeat the substance of Jeremiah's book, which Baruch had read in the ears of the people; whereupon the princes, without delay, sent a messenger to Gemariah's office requesting Baruch to come and read the book to them. Baruch at once complied; and when he had finished reading the prophecy, the princes turned in fear to each other, saying, "We will surely tell the king about all these words."

The next phase of the process involved more difficulty; because King Jehoiakim was hostile, and would not permit Baruch, the disciple of Jeremiah, to enter the royal presence. And, accordingly, the princes, before going farther, said to Baruch, *"Go, hide thee, thou and Jeremiah; and let no man know where ye are."* Then, leaving the book in the council chamber, they went to the royal court and recited in the king's ears the substance of the prophecy; whereupon Jehoiakim commanded that the roll of parchment be brought and read aloud. The king, in the meanwhile, sat by a *hearth,* on which a fire was burning; and after the book had been read through to him, he took a knife, cut up the manuscript, and was about to throw the pieces into the flames, when the minority faction of the council, *identified with Gemariah the son of Shaphan,* made intercession with the king not to destroy the parchment. But the king knew that his own father Josiah had been slain in battle after accepting a book from Shaphan, the father of Gemariah; and he was not much impressed by this new literary demonstration. So he cast the book into the fire, and ordered the arrest of Jeremiah and Baruch. But these two had already secreted themselves; while their *accomplices,* or co-operators, in the royal council itself were of such high position that the king dare not proceed against them.

This affair gives us another significant view behind the scenes. The royal council consisted of two parties, or factions. On the one hand was the *pro-Baal faction,* headed by King Jehoiakim, who was kept in power by Pharaoh Necho, king of Egypt. On the other hand was the *pro-Yahweh faction,* which included the house of Shaphan, formerly among the ministers of Josiah; and this group had enough influence to secure the acquittal of Jeremiah from the charge of treason, while keeping its policies before the public and shaking the inner circles of government.

Pharaoh Necho defeated by Nebuchadnezzar of Babylon, to whom Jehoiakim transfers allegiance.—About the time when Jeremiah and his party were trying to start their new reformation, the field of international politics underwent another catastrophic change. The Assyrian empire was at last broken up, and its capital city, *Nineveh*, was destroyed. This great power, in its origin, was an offshoot of *Babylon*, farther south in the Tigro-Euphrates region: "The beginning of his kingdom was *Babel;* and out of that land went *Asshur*, and built *Nineveh*" (Gen. 10:10, 11 [J document]). The fall of Assyria made possible the re-emergence of Babylon upon the field of oriental history; and the city rose to new greatness under a line of kings among whom the most famous was *Nebuchadrezzar*, or, as his name is misspelled in some biblical passages, "Nebuchadnezzar." The army of Babylon attacked, and severely defeated, the forces of Egypt at a place on the Euphrates River known as *Carchemish* (Jer. 46:2). The battle of Carchemish, one of the most important in history, compelled Pharaoh Necho to give up his claim on Mesopotamia. "And the king of Egypt came no more out of his land, because the king of Babylon had taken from the river of Egypt unto the river Euphrates" (II Kings 24:7). Having thus made himself the imperial overlord of Palestine, the Babylonian king demanded the allegiance of Jehoiakim. "In his days, Nechuchadnezzar king of Babylon came up; *and Jehoiakim became his servant*" (II Kings 24:1). In other words, the annual tribute, formerly paid to Assyria, and then to Egypt, was now to be collected for the account of *Babylon*.

Jehoiakim rebels; and Nebuchadnezzar makes preliminary deportation of Judah to Babylon.—After making annual payments to Nebuchadnezzar during a term of three years, Jehoiakim *rebelled;* which means that he refused longer to pay tribute. And this, in the eyes of the new overlord, meant that Judah was probably falling back into alliance with Egypt, and strengthening Pharaoh Necho against Nebuchadnezzar, who must therefore send his army westward again to deal with Palestine. When the Babylonian host arrived at Jerusalem, King Jehoiakim had passed away; and his son *Jehoiachin* was on the throne. The ancient capital of David was at once besieged, and would have been destroyed; but the new king surrendered without a struggle; so that Nebuchadnezzar found himself able to pursue a rather lenient policy. He left the *am ha arets*, or main body of the population, upon the soil; and instead of demolishing Jerusalem, he destroyed the *government*, preparatory to setting up a new administration. All articles of silver and gold in the royal palace and the temple were seized as booty; and a large part of the city's inhabitants, consisting of the king, the princes, and the wealthy burghers, with all their slaves and craftsmen, were sent in chains to Babylon.

Nebuchadnezzar appoints Mattaniah king of Judah; changes name to Zedekiah.—After these drastic measures, Nebuchadnezzar appointed as king another son of the lamented Josiah, whose name was "Mattaniah." But, like Pharaoh Necho, who changed the name of Eliakim to Jehoiakim, the Babylonian monarch wanted to show his power and authority by doing likewise; and so he gave his new vassal the name *Zedekiah*. This prince of the Davidic line owed his regal position entirely to Nebuchadnezzar; and he took a solemn oath of allegiance, promising faithfulness to the Babylonian emperor, who now departed once more to his own land.

King Zedekiah proved to be a very weak, vacillating ruler, unsatisfactory to all classes. He was at once confronted by a double task. New government officials must be appointed; and some disposition must be made of lands forfeited, through treason to Babylon, by wealthy baalim now in exile. One can imagine this Davidic prince, elevated from obscurity to the seat of power, and besieged by a horde of sycophants clamoring for offices and favors. That he showed no statesmanship is proved by the quick rise of a new *Tammany machine* at Jerusalem, which was denounced by Jeremiah more fiercely than he had condemned the preceding administration. The princes of the dead king Jehoiakim, as we have seen, included the house of Shaphan with its allies in the royal council; and these men, viewed against the background of exile and suffering, were spoken of by the prophet as *good figs*, in contrast with "Zedekiah the king of Judah and his princes and the residue of Jerusalem," who were called *bad figs* (Jer. chap. 24). These newly rich grandees had stepped into the shoes of the exiled baalim, and said, "Unto US is the land given as a possession" (Ezek. 11:15).

The government of Zedekiah found itself confronted by the old problem of taxes for two separate accounts—foreign tribute and home affairs. Inexorable economic forces, therefore, continued to weigh upon the mass of poor baalim on the aristocratic "left wing," pushing them down from the upper, free social stratum into the enslaved class below (Jer. 34:9, 14, 17). The redistribution of land, which we assume to have taken place in Josiah's time, would have no abiding effect if the wealthier baalim, on the "right wing," were not prepared to lend surplus goods and money to poor neighbors without interest, and write off such debts at the end of every six years. And from all that we can learn about the new group of nobles, judges, tax-gatherers, etc., who had charge of public business in Zedekiah's reign, these "bad figs" were not swayed by altruistic motives of any kind.

After nine years of tribute-paying, Zedekiah rebels against Nebuchadnezzar.—The new aristocracy, indeed, became so inflated with arrogance and pride as to imagine that Yahweh would soon destroy Nebuchadnezzar, lift the foreign yoke from the neck of Judah, and restore the gold and silver which the Babylonians had carried away from Jerusalem. This was the old, "patriotic" group sociology once more; and it spurred Jeremiah into one of his most dramatic prophecies. Constructing a *wooden yoke* to wear about his neck, he appeared on the streets, exhorting Zedekiah and all the people to remain subjects of Babylon, *lest they die and the Kingdom of Judah be destroyed* (Jer., chap. 27).

But the growth of patriotic nationalism went on apace; and the conventional type of heathen "success-prophets" now undertook to destroy the influence of Jeremiah. His outstanding opponent at this time was *Hananiah ben Azur*, a native of ancient *Gibeon*—one of the Amorite cities which Israel had not conquered, and which assimilated with the newcomers from the wilderness to produce the Hebrew kingdom (Jer., chap. 28). The Gibeonite prophet was in good repute as a "man of elohim"; and even the Book of Jeremiah calls him a *nabi* (28:5, 12). The two prophets clashed one day in the presence of a large multitude gathered at the temple. Jeremiah was wearing his clumsy wooden collar, when suddenly Hananiah stepped up, lifted the yoke from his neck, and shattered it on the pavement. Then Hananiah proclaimed loudly, "Thus saith Yahweh, Even so will I break the yoke of Nebuchadnezzar king of Babylon from the neck of all nations *within the space of two full years;* and within two full years will I bring again all the vessels of Yahweh's house that Nebuchadnezzar king of Babylon took away from this place" (Jer. 28:10, 11, 3).

The violent opposition between such prophets made it very difficult for the plain masses of the Hebrew people to reach definite opinions, one way or the other; and in last analysis the antagonism between the two schools of prophecy came to the same practical issue as the differences between modern political parties. Thus, while the masses of the people were friendly to Jeremiah's gospel of *mishpat*, they were naturally cool to his "defeatism" and correspondingly favorable to the "success-prophecy" of Hananiah. Hence, the politicians and patriots who controlled the king made him forget his oath to Nebuchadnezzar; and, accordingly, in the ninth year of Zedekiah, *Judah rebelled against Babylon.*

Babylonian army again marches to Palestine, and begins final siege of Jerusalem.—Once more the army of Nebuchadnezzar marched into Palestine. Its plan this time was to destroy Jerusalem, and wipe out the Kingdom of Judah. The enemy therefore completely encompassed the ancient stronghold of David, and began systematic operations to reduce the city. A number of measures were always taken during a siege. High towers were built, overlooking the walls; and within these elevated structures were expert bowmen, who shot arrows into the city. Great mounds were cast up; and upon them were placed engines with powerful springs, which threw flaming javelins. And still more dreadful were the *battering-rams*, which pounded upon the walls endlessly.

That the revolt would only bring the Babylonians into Judah once more was clear to the mind of Jeremiah. But the cheap little politicians around King Zedekiah were blind in their pride and arrogance. Yet when the host of Nebuchadnezzar actually appeared before the walls of Jerusalem, the king and his princes were stricken with terror. The excitement was intense; and amid the fall of arrows and flaming darts and the dreadful crash of battering-rams, we are now to observe a tragi-comedy which was enacted within the capital.

Princes try to gain favor of Yahweh by emancipating "left wing" baalim.—Seized by panic, and fearing lest they were doomed, the rulers of Jerusalem sought to gain the favor of Yahweh by suddenly putting into effect the mishpat ordinance of Deuteronomy which commands the release of poor baalim from slavery after a period of six years, "that every man should let his man-slave and his woman-slave, *being an Hebrew or an Hebrewess*, go free; that no man should be served by them,—*a Jew of his brother*" (Jer. 34:8, 9; cf. Deut. 15:12). This measure, we must bear in mind, was not directed against human slavery in *general*, but against the bondage of Hebrews to persons of their own race.

And the result of emancipation seemed to be miraculous! For after the Hebrew slaves had been liberated, the arrows and flaming javelins no longer fell upon Jerusalem; the battering-rams were silent; the siege was raised; *and the Babylonian army vanished!* Great was the astonishment of the people when, upon cautiously mounting the walls, they discovered that the host of Nebuchadnezzar had melted away. Only one explanation seemed possible under the circumstances: Jerusalem had been saved by the mighty power of Yahweh!

Wealthy princes again reduce emancipated Hebrews into slavery.—But the utter lack of good faith which led to emancipation is proved by the fact that when the Babylonians vanished, the princes decided there was nothing more to worry about, and again reduced their former Hebrew slaves into bondage. They "caused the men-slaves and women-slaves, whom they had let go, to return; and brought them into subjection" (Jer. 34:11).

This act was bitterly denounced by Jeremiah, who cried, "Thus saith Yahweh, Ye have not hearkened unto me, in proclaiming liberty, every one to his brother and to his neighbor. *Behold, saith Yahweh, I proclaim a liberty for you, to the sword, to pestilence, and to famine; and I will make you to be removed into all the kingdoms of the earth*" (Jer. 34:17).

Presently, the reason was discovered why the besiegers had vanished with such mysterious abruptness: An army from Egypt was approaching to relieve Jerusalem; and since the Babylonians did not care to fight Egyptians and Jews at the same time, the host of Nebuchadnezzar had withdrawn to engage Pharaoh's forces at a great distance from the Jewish capital.

Jeremiah, seeking to leave city, arrested and imprisoned.—The temporary lifting of the siege gave the city a welcome chance to replenish its food supply; and certain gates were thrown open. Jeremiah then rose up to visit his home at the village of Anathoth in the land of Benjamin. But upon going to the north side of the city, and passing through the "gate of Benjamin," he was observed by an officer called "the *baal* of the ward," who laid hold of Jeremiah, charging falsely that the prophet was deserting to the Chaldeans, i.e., the Babylonians. The officer then took Jeremiah to the princes, who smote him and put him in prison, "in the house of Jonathan the scribe" (Jer. 37:11–15).

The divided counsels of the government are clearly shown by the way Jeremiah's case was handled. He remained in prison for a long time in the house of Jonathan the scribe; and one night King Zedekiah sent men who carried the prophet away secretly, and brought him to the royal palace. When taken into the king's presence, he was asked by Zedekiah, *"Is there any word from Yahweh?"* To which the answer of the fearless Jeremiah was, "Thou shalt be delivered to the king of Babylon." Then the prophet changed the subject, and asked in scorn, *"Where now are thy prophets which declared unto you, saying, the king of Babylon shall not come against you, nor against this land?* And wherein have I offended against thee, or against this people, that ye have put me in prison?" The king's replies, if any, are not given; but when Jeremiah requested that he be not sent back to the house of Jonathan the scribe, lest he die there, the king ordered that he be detained in "the court of the guard," where he should have daily a loaf of bread "from the street of the bakers" (Jer. 37:16–21).

When the princes heard that Jeremiah had been placed in a better prison, they went angrily to the king, saying, "Let this prophet be executed; *because he weakeneth the hands of the men of war*"; whereupon the vacillating monarch replied, "Behold, he is in your power; for the king is not one who can oppose you." Then the nobles gave orders that Jeremiah should be placed in a certain terrible prison *below ground*, where there was no water, but only mire; and so the prophet was carried thither, and let down with cords into the dungeon, where he sank in the mire.

The prisoner would now have quickly perished in oblivion, amid the excitement of the times, if help had not arrived from a wholly unexpected source. An *Ethiopian*, by the name of Ebed-melek, who was an officer of the king, had been attracted in some way by Jeremiah's preaching; and when he heard of the princes' latest move, he at once went to Zedekiah with a vigorous protest. Then the king secretly ordered the Ethiopian to take men with him, and remove Jeremiah from the dark hole. So Ebed-melek and his helpers went to the dungeon, carrying cords with a bundle of old rags, which they let down, telling Jeremiah to place the rags under his arms as a protection from the cords while he was being drawn up. Thus the prophet was rescued and placed again in the "court of the guard," where he remained until the city was taken (Jer. 38:1–28).

Babylonians return; crush walls; execute princes; and give Jerusalem to flames.—In the meanwhile, the Babylonians defeated the Egyptian army, and, returning to Jerusalem, pressed on the siege with still more vigor. The battering-rams kept up their horrible din by day and night, until the *north* wall was crashed; and when the besiegers made their way into the city, they found that the king had already fled through the *southern* gate with a band of his warriors. But the fugitives were captured and brought into the presence of Nebuchadnezzar, where the sons of Zedekiah were put to death before his eyes; the king himself was deprived of sight and bound in chains, while the perfidious *nobles* were executed. But the fate of Jeremiah was different. Finding that he was in prison, in the court of the guard, Nebuchadnezzar said, "Take him, and look to his welfare, and harm him not; but do as he shall say." Then the enemy turned their attention to Jerusalem and its inhabitants. The walls were broken down all around the city; the houses and public buildings were destroyed; while the people were bound in fetters of iron, and sent away to join the earlier colony of captives *by the rivers of Babylon* (Jer., chap. 39).

Nebuchadnezzar attempts to maintain Jewish state under house of Shaphan.—The Babylonian overlord now desired to reconstitute the state of Judah under a governor, without royalty, hoping to maintain a faithful population in Palestine. The mass of the Jewish country people were still peacefully at work on their farms and in their pastures, with less to fear at the hand of the conqueror than from Hebrew exploiters and grafters who arose in their midst. A new economic deal was begun by redistributing the land more fairly among the *am ha arets*. But where could a proper man be found who would rule over them justly? The house of David was impossible, because two of its kings had rebelled against Babylon. Yet Nebuchadnezzar did not wish to put a foreigner over the Jewish people, because an alien would offend their national sentiment. But he knew something of Hebrew history; and in rejecting the Davidic line, he turned to the liberal house of *Shaphan*, which had come into prominence as upholders of the Deuteronomic reform, and which, as we have seen, had remained on the side of Jeremiah ever since. From this remarkable family Nebuchadnezzar chose *Gedaliah the son of Ahikam the son of Shaphan*, making him governor of Judah, and putting him in personal charge over Jeremiah, to take care of the aged prophet (II Kings 25:22; Jer. 39:10–14).

Gedaliah forms new government, but is assassinated by member of Davidic family.—In the light of events, the hopeful effort of Gedaliah to rebuild his nation is almost as pathetic as the story of Josiah and the earlier movement of reform. The new administration was located in a rustic village by the name of *Mizpah*, which lay a few miles north from the ruins of Jerusalem; and here the kindly grandson of Shaphan, in company with Jeremiah the prophet, organized a new government. Many Jews in foreign lands, attracted by the cheerful state of affairs, and having confidence in the house of Shaphan, came back to join the *am ha arets* under Gedaliah's banner. "All the Jews returned out of all places where they were driven, and came to the land of Judah, to Gedaliah" (Jer. 40:12). This was a fore-shadowing of the Zionist movement.

But soon darkness fell over the new enterprise; for a jealous descendant of David, resentful that public authority should be lodged in the hands of another Jewish house, conspired against the governor. That anyone was planning to slay him, Gedaliah would not believe, and went calmly on with his work. But about three months after the fall of Jerusalem, a conspirator, "Ishmael the son of Nethaniah the son of Elishama, *of the seed royal,*" appeared in Mizpah; whereupon the governor, to show good faith, invited Ishmael to be a guest at his table. The treacherous descendant of David had scarcely seated himself when he arose, drawing a sword from his garment, and slew Gedaliah, whom Nebuchadnezzar had made governor of Judah (Jer. 41:1–2).

Last remnant of Hebrew state vanishes.—The murder threw the whole community into a panic, fearing what the Babylonians would do; and, after a few days, a large number of the Jews fled away into Egypt, carrying Jeremiah with them, against his will and in spite of his energetic protest. Thus disappeared the greatest of Israel's prophets, who was never heard of again; and while an inconspicuous remnant still clung to the soil of Judah, the hope of the future now lay with the exiles in far-away Babylon.

CHAPTER XI

MISHPAT AND PRIESTHOOD

Defeatist prophets vindicated by march of history.—Nothing save the visible downfall of both Hebrew kingdoms, Judah and Ephraim, together with the destruction of both capitals, Jerusalem and Samaria, could ever have led up to the final triumph of defeatist prophecy with its doctrine of *ethical monotheism*. The two lines of prophets, culminating in the rival figures of Jeremiah ben Hilkiah and Hananiah ben Azur, might have continued their arguments forever if the march of history had not silenced the one and vindicated the other. Jeremiah and his predecessors labored under the heavy psychological disadvantage of appearing to be unpatriotic in the eyes of the multitude. But, on the other hand, the forces arrayed with Hananiah and his type of prophecy were based on the powerful sense of *group integrity*—"my country, right or wrong"—regardless of social ethics; and these forces could never have been overcome on the merits of the case by mere *logic*.

Moreover, in spite of Jerusalem's dramatic ruin, the establishment of monotheism was not *instantly* achieved, but was even yet resisted by popular inertia and superstitition. The blind forces of conservatism, which operate alike in gentile and Hebrew society, were so unyielding and obstinate among the Jews that even when the first band of exiles had been carried away to Babylon, the success-prophet Hananiah, as we have seen, could oppose Jeremiah with a strident prediction that Yahweh would bring the rule of Nebuchadnezzar to an end in two full years; and at the very time when Babylonian battering-rams were shaking the walls of Jerusalem, the government could imprison Jeremiah in a foul dungeon. The same spirit of disbelief was

manifested by the first band of exiles, deported while Jerusalem
was yet standing; for these unhappy prisoners, anxious to return
home without delay, would not credit the words of their fellow-
captive, *Ezekiel ben Buzi,* who foretold the destruction of the
city (Ezek., chaps. 4, 5, 6, 7; 33:30–33). They preferred to believe the optimistic *opponents* of Ezekiel, namely, *Zedekiah ben
Maaseiah* and *Ahab ben Kolaiah* (Jer. 29:21–22). Likewise, the
fugitives who took Jeremiah into Egypt were not convinced of
his vindication by the fall of Jerusalem; for they withstood him
to his face, declaring that their misfortunes were due, not to the
anger of Yahweh, but to the wrath of the goddess Ishtar, the
so-called *queen of heaven:* "When we burned incense to the
queen of heaven, we had plenty of food, and were well, and saw
no evil. But since we left off burning incense to her, we have
needed all things, and have been consumed by the sword and by
the famine" (Jer. 44:17, 18).

Thus we can see that although history vindicated the prophets
of defeatism, yet the downfall of Jerusalem did not *promptly*
transform the Jews into ethical monotheists. This consumma-
tion was to be reached only when the exiles acquired a longer
perspective.

"Holiness Code" gives new and higher version of mishpat.
—Among the more thoughtful and higher-minded exiles, who
had absorbed the spirit of ethical prophecy, a new platform was
unofficially worked out, in the name of Yahweh, for the reestablishment of Israel in Palestine; and the authors who prepared this code hoped that it would some day get official recognition, by governmental authority, as public law. Conceived in
a spirit of humanitarian idealism which gives it a unique place,
the new *"Holiness Code"* is an improvement upon the "Deuteronomic Code" which came before it, and the still earlier
"Mishpat Code" of Ephraim.

The new system is imbedded in the Book of *Leviticus* (chaps.
17–27); and its date is interestingly shown by reference to the

"fallow year" provision of the old Ephraimite code, which contemplated absolute rest, *every seventh year*, for all fields, in order that the spontaneous, unsown crops, which came up of themselves, might be food for the poor and needy baalim (Exod. 23:10–11). That this rule had *not* been observed ever since Israel came into Palestine is implied by the Deuteronomic Code, which *omits* the fallow-year law, and instead of it provides that in every harvest the prosperous farmer shall not return to his field in search of a *forgotten sheaf* (Deut. 24:19 f.). But the new, exilian code proceeds to re-enact the Ephraimite fallow-year law, and then goes on to observe that when Israel is taken away from Palestine into captivity, the empty land shall enjoy its overdue rest, which it did not have when Israel was living there —"even then shall the land rest. . . . . As long as it lieth desolate it shall have rest,—*even the rest which it had not . . . . when ye dwelt upon it*" (Lev. 26:34, 35, 43; 25:1–7).

These words are, of course, placed in the mouth of Yahweh, as if spoken during the wilderness period, before the Israelite invasion of Canaan; and if they stood by themselves, out of relation to context, they would not be decisive as to date. But when examined in their context, we find them to be part of a new system which makes up for the shortcomings of the earlier codes, and anticipates the return of Israel from captivity into the homeland. Thus, the law of the "forgotten sheaf," by which Deuteronomy sought to compensate for non-observance of the fallow-year, is amplified in the new Holiness Code by making public property of the *corners of all fields*, whereon a portion of the crop is always to be for the "poor and needy" (Lev. 19:9–10; 23:22). But the differences thus far cited are only by way of introduction to still more conclusive evidence.

Permanent slavery of Hebrews abolished by exilian code.— The code of Ephraim not only made legal for six years the slavery of one Hebrew baal to another, but in case the slave desired to remain in bondage forever, it provided a religious rite,

in connection with "God and doorpost" (*Elohim* and *mezuzah*).
A step in advance upon this rule was made, as we have seen, by
the next, or Deuteronomic Code, wherein the sanction of religion for permanent slavery was *withdrawn;* the reference to
Elohim and *mezuzah* was omitted; and the awl ceremony was
made a private affair between master and slave, by having the
instrument driven through the slave's ear into the door itself
(*deleth*). But now the *latest* code moves forward onto still higher
ground, providing that when a poor baal has lost his landed
possession through debt, and has been purchased by a wealthier
baal, *he shall not have the legal status of slavery, but shall be treated
as a hired servant who is legally a free man* (Lev. 25:39–42).

**"Holiness Code" links personal freedom with land ques-
tion.**—But the creators of the new system went *still farther*
beyond preceding codes, because they caught sight of the fact
that permanent release from slavery cannot be accomplished
without correlative *land legislation*. For example, if the members of a given community are personally *free*, while at the same
time a small minority of them possess all the land, the so-called
"free" majority are not *really* free, but must conform to the
rules of the monopolist landlords, as did the peasantry of Europe during the Middle Ages. The authors of the new system
began to perceive that the emancipation of a Hebrew slave, at
the end of six years' bondage as provided by the *earlier* codes,
would not really give him personal freedom *if he had no land*.
The earlier codes, in fact, were prepared with so little grasp of
the economic situation that they never asked, *What becomes of
a debtor's "inheritance" when he loses it through foreclosure?* In
attacking the problem of the landless freeman, the Ephraimite
code merely proposed the septennial "fallow-year" law; while the
later-coming code of Deuteronomy recognized the non-observance of this law, and laid down the rule of the "forgotten sheaf" as
applying to *every harvest*. But the authors of these pioneer systems
never addressed themselves to the question of land monopoly *as*

such. The nearest pre-Exilic approach to the general problem is afforded, as we saw, by the tale of *Joseph*, wherein the land belongs to the king, as representing the nation; while the peasantry on the soil *retain four-fifths* of their produce and pay 20 per cent in taxes. The fundamental principle of the Joseph tale reappears in the new, exilian code, which, after abolishing Hebrew slavery, proposes economic legislation of a radical nature, going far beyond the Ephraimite and the Deuteronomic systems. That the contemplated measure was impossible and utopian should not confuse or distract us; because the real significance of it lies not in the objective world of practical things but in the realm of idealism.

Land theoretically released from grip of commercialistic baalism by new code.—Seeking to break up land monopoly at its root, an amendment is inserted in the code providing that land shall not be sold or exchanged according to the rule of absolute, baalistic, private ownership which prevailed among the Amorites of Canaan: *The land shall not be sold with perpetual title; because the soil belongs to Yahweh as the guarantor and patron of mishpat* (Lev. 25:23). Following the lines of the Joseph story, the Holiness Code substitutes Yahweh for Pharaoh as the supreme landlord; and it also copies the Joseph narrative with reference to landed endowments of the *priesthood*, as we read in Genesis, "The priests of Egypt had an inheritance given them by Pharaoh; *wherefore they did not sell their lands*" (Gen. 47:22 [J document, adapted from E]). Accordingly, the Levites (not as yet degraded from the priesthood) are given complete ownership in their lands: "The field of the suburbs of their cities shall not be sold; *because it is their perpetual possession*" (Lev. 25:34).

But the injunction against baalistic treatment of land is only one approach to the general problem; for at the same time a legal rule is formulated whereby the peasant who has been deprived of ownership, through sale or foreclosure, may return to his property. This is furnished by the utopian law of the *Jubi-*

lee, according to which a trumpet is to be blown throughout Israel, *once in fifty years,* proclaiming liberty to all Hebrews; whereupon every man shall return to his kindred and his "possession" (Lev. 25:9–10). This ordinance did not exist before the Babylonian captivity, and it was not observed at any period after the return of the Jews to Palestine.

Holiness Code based on Isaiah's ethical conception, "Holy One of Israel."—When examining the relation of *Isaiah* to Hebrew history, we saw that he was the first prophet who took the common Semitic term "holy" and pressed it into the service of ethics. The original idea of "holiness" in Semitic religion, as we have seen, is that of *separateness,* through the mere physical setting-apart of a thing or person, which thereby acquires a character of distinction. Thus, a woman dedicated to ritual prostitution in a heathen temple is "holy" on account of being set apart from other women. She is therefore called *kedeshah,* this term being derived from the root *k-d-sh,* which contains the idea of separation or exclusiveness. But Isaiah declared that while Yahweh, indeed, was distinct, separate, or *kadosh,* this distinction, instead of being *mere* exclusiveness, or physical separateness, arose from the fact that Yahweh championed social justice, or *mishpat,* as against the Baalim and other territorial gods. Thus, by fusing into a single concept the two ideas of separation and mishpat, Isaiah elevated the term *kadosh,* or "holy," into the ethical and spiritual realm, and actually gave it a new meaning. Yahweh shall be exalted in *mishpat;* and the Holy One (*Ha Kadosh*) makes himself holy (*nikdash*) in righteousness (cf. Isa. 5:16).

This higher conception is taken over by the new, Exilic "Holiness Code," wherein the key-thought is that the children of Israel shall be "holy ones" (*kedeshim*) because their divinity, Yahweh, is a "Holy One"—*kadosh* (cf. Lev. 19:2). Accordingly, the expression "I am Yahweh" occurs in the Holiness Code *forty-three times* as a kind of signature, following various ordinances of social justice and moral purity. Thus, "Ye shall do no wrong in *mishpat*, in weight or measure; but ye shall have just balances, just weights, etc. *I am Yahweh*" (Lev. 19:35, 36).

Holiness Code commands love of "neighbor" and "stranger" equal to love of self.—Ascending still higher in the realm of idealism, the exilian Holiness Code puts forward a requirement which, as yet, has been scarcely followed by any religion or nation, Jewish or Gentile: "Thou shalt love thy *neighbor* as thyself—*I am Yahweh*" (Lev. 19:18). And as if this were not sufficiently exacting, another admonition is laid down, which collides even more sharply with the universal shortcomings of mankind, and which, if observed, would stop all wars forthwith: "Thou shalt love the *stranger* as thyself.—*I am Yahweh*" (Lev. 19:34). Not only is the signature "I am Yahweh" a literary peculiarity of the "Holiness Code," as compared with all the other Hebrew codes; but it occurs more frequently in *Leviticus, chapter 19*, than elsewhere in the code itself; and this chapter deserves independent reading and study. The code as a whole repeats much that is in the earlier legislation—for example, the command against interest on loans; but Leviticus presents the old material in a broader perspective, more in harmony with the international outlook of the Exile. It reaches the highest level of the Hebrew codes, and is to be appraised, not with reference to practicality, but from the standpoint of idealism, as one would think of a torch raised up in darkness.

Human freedom still viewed as pertaining to kindred social group.—In the interest of scientific accuracy, however, we should observe that while the principles of justice, liberty, and love are extended by the Holiness Code beyond all previous application, yet this latest reform program is to be judged in view of its context. The Book of Leviticus is the product of many writers; and, accordingly, some glossator, fearing that the progress of social and economic radicalism would be too speedy, has

added the following paragraph about slavery by way of qualifi-
cation, or interpretation:

> As for thy male and female slaves, which thou shalt own: Of the na-
> tions round about you, of *them* shall ye buy slaves. And of the children of
> strangers among you, of *them* shall ye buy. And they shall be your posses-
> sion; and ye shall appoint them to be an inheritance for your children
> after you, to hold for a possession. Of them shall ye take your slaves *for-
> ever*. But over your brethren, the children of Israel, ye shall not rule with
> rigor [Lev. 25:44–46, in part].

The context of the Holiness Code, then, shows that the mishpat idea begins with, and always tends to be limited by, the
principle of *clan-aristocracy* (cf. Deut. 15:12; Jer. 34:8–15). On
this ground, all the members of a kindred social group are
normally and rightfully *free;* while, at the same time, a lower
class, of *alien* origin, may rightfully exist in a condition of permanent bondage. Another illustration is found in America before the Civil War, when it was regarded as "right" for negroes
to be slaves but "wrong" for white persons to be bought and
sold as property.

**Literary practice of giving official form to private codes illus-
trated by Ezekiel.**—We have already cited Ezekiel, the prophet of the Babylonian captivity, as illustrating the common Hebrew usage whereby *private* codes were invested with an imposing *official* form in the name of Yahweh (p. 220). Giving the
clearest and most unquestionable instance of this practice in all
Hebrew literature, Ezekiel put forth a rigid, complicated, ecclesiastical utopia as the basis of a *restored Israel* in Palestine.
With the formal sanction of Yahweh, a divine "blue print" is
given, whereby the twelve tribes are to be settled in designated
strips of territory, running *east and west* between the river Jordan and the Mediterranean Sea; the entire plan centering
around minute directions, giving actual cubit measures, for a
new *temple*, an exact *ritual*, and a fully organized *priesthood*
(chaps. 40 ff.).

Ezekiel's program, being thrown into the *future*, was brought to the deadly critical test of comparison with *events after the Exile;* and, being impossible of realization, and therefore never followed out, it hung in the air, giving rabbinical commentators much embarrassed perplexity. But, on the other hand, the codes which are ascribed, under the same official and authoritative form, to *Moses* were all thrown into the *distant past* by their anonymous authors, where they could not be subjected to the test of *contemporary* criticism. That they were produced long after the Israelite settlement in Canaan was only realized for the first time by Rabbi Ben Ezra in the twelfth century of the Christian Era and then by the Jewish philosopher Baruch Spinoza in the seventeenth century—both of whom laid the foundations of modern literary and historical criticism of the Bible. But with *Ezekiel*, however, the case was different. His remarkable and well-written book held the attention of the Jews, who persisted in reading and liking it after the return from Babylon, even though its utopia was not realized. That it narrowly missed being left out of the Bible seems to be suggested by the legend that Rabbi Ben Hiskiah took three hundred measures of lamp-oil to his chamber, and finally announced that the prophecy of Ezekiel was worthy of inclusion among the sacred writings.

Ezekiel true to spirit of defeatist prophets in emphasis upon mishpat.—One of the considerations which made the Book of Ezekiel popular, and very hard to exclude from the Bible, is its faithfulness to the demands of the insurgent, or defeatist, prophets for mishpat, or social justice. In fact, his entire "blueprint" program is intended to secure the union of Israel and Yahweh in a theocratic state *guaranteeing the permanent reign of social justice.* The priests are not only to be ministers of the ritual, but are to be judges who see that the *mishpat* of Yahweh is observed (44:24). And at the same time, the civil rulers, or princes, of restored Israel are to execute mishpat, being especially admonished "not to take the people's inheritance by oppression, to throw them out of their possessions" (45:9; 46:18). To do mishpat is, among other things, to make loans without interest, and not to seize the debtor's house and land (18:7–17; 22:12). Jerusalem, being of *Amorite* origin, transformed the mishpat of Yahweh into wickedness (16:3; 5:5–6). And instead of doing the mishpat of Yahweh, the house of Israel walked in the mishpat of the Gentiles, or *goyim* (11:12).

Ezekiel's demand for mishpat is interwoven so thoroughly with his denunciation of "other gods" that he makes heathen worship the *symbol* of social injustice; and he declares that, in the neglect of mishpat, one's eyes are "after idols" (18:12, 15, 17; 20:24). Bowing down to the Amorite Baalim, therefore, was not simply worshiping "gods of good crops." Ezekiel, then, stresses mishpat like a prophet, while emphasizing *ritualism* like a priest, or *cohen*. He was, in fact, of priestly descent—"Ezekiel the *cohen*, the son of *Buzi*, in the land of the Chaldeans [i.e., Babylonians], by the river Chebar, among the captives" (1:1, 3).

Ezekiel proposes demotion of Levitical majority to menial rank as porters.—Another consideration which gives peculiar character to the Book of Ezekiel is its new doctrine that the majority of Levites, having served as priests at the local "high places" (*bamoth*), be now reduced from the rank of priests, or *cohanim;* and that they become only ecclesiastical porters, doing the menial work of the sanctuary. In advancing this novel proposition Ezekiel based himself upon the logic of the Josian reform, which (rightly or not) viewed the local shrines as *heathen*, whose odium communicated itself to the village priests. This was, indeed, unfair to history, through its correlative assumption that the Temple at Jerusalem had been always of higher ethical standing than the local altars. The exact *opposite* was, in fact, the case; because the Temple, being headquarters of royal worship, had been always open to the contamination of municipal and international politics. But the period intervening between Josiah's reform and the Exile had given Jerusalem a new spiritual importance, which would only be heightened in the retrospect of the captivity; so that Ezekiel and his followers could throw this prestige back into earlier times, to the disadvantage of the priests who had served the village parishes.

We know that in Josiah's reign the country Levites did *not* come up to the Jerusalem sanctuary and serve as priests (II Kings 23:9). But the real cause of their exclusion was, of course, the house of *Zadok*, which had ministered at the royal shrine ever since the days of David, and which now desired to have an ecclesiastical monopoly. Ezekiel, therefore, sought to base the demotion of the Levites upon their "iniquity" as priests of the village altars.

Because they ministered unto them before their idols, and caused the house of Israel to fall into iniquity. Therefore have I lifted up my hand against them, saith Yahweh; and they shall bear their iniquity. And they shall not approach near unto me, to do the office of a *priest* unto me, nor to come near to any of my holy things in the most holy place. But they shall bear their shame, and their abominations which they have committed. *But I will make them keepers of the charge of the house, for all the service thereof, and for all that shall be done therein* [44:12-14].

Mass of Levites accordingly given menial work in exilic "Priestly" document.—The ecclesiastical, or "Priestly," source in the Hebrew Bible now claims our attention. This document, or series of writings, grew up among the Jews in the Babylonian captivity after the time of Ezekiel. Its real nature does not become clear upon cursory perusal; but a closer examination reveals that it is the most pro-Jewish element in the Bible. In the first place, following out the bias of Ezekiel, the Priestly source denies all ministerial rank to the bulk of Levi's descendants, the *Gershonites* and *Merarites*, who are appointed to be mere porters, or carriers, of the "Tabernacle," or sacred tent, in the wilderness, during the alleged "forty years' wandering." Under their charge are the *external* appurtenances of the nomadic sanctuary, i.e., the tent-covering, door-hangings, curtains, boards, bars, pillars, cords, etc. (Num. 3:21–26, 33–37). Another branch of Levi, the *Kohathites*, while debarred likewise from the priesthood, is put in charge of the internal equipment of the Tabernacle, i.e., the ark of Yahweh, the altars, the candlestick, the vessels, etc. (Num. 3:27–31). But even *these* Levites, who carry the most holy apparatus of worship, must not *see*, or come into immediate physical contact with, the sacred objects in their custody, *lest they be struck dead* (Num. 4:15). All these meticulous rules for keeping the bulk of the Levites in their menial position lead up to the central ordinance regarding the higher personnel of the priesthood.

Sons of Aaron designated by code as absolutely exclusive priesthood.—Actual ministration before the altar is to be done by Aaron and his sons *alone*. They *only* are priests, or *cohanim;* while the remainder of the Levites are not to be considered as priests in any sense whatever. The Aaronites *alone* may enter the holy place where the ark rests; they alone may offer sacrifice; and when the children of Israel move onward from one point in the wilderness to another, the house of Aaron must carefully wrap and pack the internal, holiest equipment of the sanctuary before it may be picked up and carried by the ordinary Levites (Num. 4:5–15; 18:1, 7).

According to the Priestly code, Moses was a Levite and brother of Aaron; but only Aaron was a priest; while Moses had no right or authority to offer sacrifice. Such being the case, we can see why it is that the later scribes were so embarrassed by the narrative in Judges about the Levite who was a grandson of Moses, who served as a *cohen*, and who founded a permanent line of priests at the northernmost Hebrew city, *Dan* (p. 99 f., *supra*).

Israel pictured encamped around Tabernacle in wilderness, with Judah in place of honor.—The Priestly writings describe the Tabernacle in the desert as being *surrounded* by the Levites, *with Moses and Aaron and the sons of Aaron located on the east, or* *front, side of the sanctuary* (Num. 1:53; 3:38). The holy tent, thus protected, is *then* pictured as being *further* surrounded by all the tribes of Israel in a *hollow square*, facing east, west, north, and south, and having *three tribes* on each side of the square. The tribe of *Judah* is in the nearest position to Aaron and Moses, on the center of the east side, "toward the rising of the sun," *and therefore occupying the most honorable place held by any of the non-priestly, or secular tribes* (Num. 2:3).

But, on the other hand, the house of *Joseph*, consisting of Manasseh, Ephraim, and Benjamin, is located on the *opposite* face of the square—at the west, or *back side*, of the camp, in the *least honorable* position (Num. 2:18–24).

Priestly document imagines other points of Jewish distinction in the wilderness.—Having thus discovered the anti-Josephite, pro-Jewish character of the Priestly writing, we are prepared to find the tribe of Judah also pictured as foremost in construction of the Tabernacle by direct appointment of Yahweh. Thus, the chief architect is Bezaleel the Judahite, who is a cunning craftsman in gold, silver, brass, timber, and all kinds of workmanship (Exod. 31:1 f. [P document]). And with more significance than at first appears, this *Jewish* constructor is given charge over a workman from the tribe of *Dan;* so that these two shall be chiefs and organizers of all that were "wisehearted" in Israel for the work of building the sanctuary in the desert (Exod. 31:6; 36:1–2). We saw that the tribe of Dan was located *originally* southwest of Ephraim in central Canaan, wedged between the Philistines and the house of Joseph, during the time of Samson in the Judges epoch; that the Danites at length migrated to the extreme *north* of Israel; that the tribe of Judah, in the *south*, was first organized by David; and, consequently, the expression "from Dan to Beersheba" did not come into use until the time of the monarchy. Hence, the Priestly writer, when imagining workmen chosen from the *extremes* of Israel, had before his mind's eye the map of Palestine as fixed by the monarchy, and expressed in the saying, "from Beersheba to Dan."

Continuing to give Judah pre-eminence in the wilderness, the Priestly account says that after completion of the Tabernacle, a call was made upon the princes of all Israel to bring offerings of gold, silver, etc., for use in the sanctuary; whereupon, the *first* who came with a contribution was a prince of the tribe of Judah (Num. 7:1–12).

Again, the Priestly document is very careful to say that when Israel broke camp in the wilderness and went forward on the line of march, the advancing host was *always* led, not by Reuben, the first-born, but by Judah; while, on the other hand, in the *rear* of the procession came the house of *Joseph*, consisting of Manasseh, Ephraim, and Benjamin, descendants of the beloved wife Rachel, trailing along with Dan, Asher, and Naphtali, descended from the slave-girls Bilhah and Zilpah (Num. 10:14–27).

Tabernacle in "Priestly" document compared with Tabernacle in "Ephraimite" document.—The character of the Priestly document is thus revealed as distinctly pro-Jewish; with Judah foremost in the construction of the Tabernacle; foremost in offering gold, silver, etc., for the service of the sanctuary; foremost in the line of march through the desert; and also holding the position of highest honor in the protective hollow square which was *always* formed about the Tabernacle when the marching tribes came to a temporary halt. Bearing in mind the picture of the uniform, unvarying hollow square, with the portable tent set up in the midst of the tribes, let us read with careful attention certain passages in the *Ephraimite* source, presenting a different view, which diverges widely from the Judahite picture:

Moses was accustomed to take the Tent, and set it up *outside* the camp, *far away* from the camp; and he named it the Tent of Meeting [*Ohel Moedh*]. And every one who sought Yahweh *went out* unto the Tent of

Meeting, which was *outside* the camp. And when Moses *went out* unto the Tent, all the people rose up, and stood, every man at the door of his tent, and looked after Moses until he was gone into the Tent. And when Moses entered into the Tabernacle, the pillar of cloud descended, and stood at the door of the Tent; . . . . and [Yahweh] spoke unto Moses face to face, as a man speaketh to his friend. And he would then *return into* the camp. *But his minister, Joshua ben Nun, departed not out of the Tent.* . . . . And Yahweh said unto Moses, Gather me seventy men of the elders of Israel, and bring them unto the *Ohel Moedh;* and I will take of the spirit which is upon thee, and will put it upon them; and they shall bear the burden of the people with thee. And Yahweh came down in a cloud, and gave the spirit unto the seventy elders; and when the spirit rested upon them, they *prophesied.* But there stayed two men *in the camp.* The name of the one was Eldad, and the name of the other was Medad; and the spirit rested upon them. And they were of those that were called; but *went not out* unto the Tent; and they prophesied *in the camp.* And a young man went and told Moses, and said, Eldad and Medad do prophesy *in the camp.* And Moses said unto him, *Would that all the people of Yahweh were prophets!* And Moses withdrew *into the camp*, he and the elders of Israel. . . . . And Yahweh suddenly spake unto Moses and Aaron and Miriam, *Come out,* ye three, unto the *Ohel Moedh.* And they three *came out.* . . . . And Miriam was *shut out* from the camp seven days [Exod. 33:7–11; Num. 11:16–17, 25–30; 12:4, 15, etc., in part].

These highly significant passages, from the Ephraimite source, present a view of the Tabernacle which differs in a startling way from the rigid, legalistic picture given by the Priestly document. The Hebrew verb takes the form known as "frequentative," showing that the position of the tent outside the camp was *customary.* Not only so, but other differences are equally arresting. Yahweh is revealed not within the Tabernacle to the *priesthood* but at the *door,* in a pillar of cloud; and the emphasis of the narrative is not upon ritualism but upon *prophecy,* the desire being expressed that all the people of Yahweh could be prophets. And, accordingly, the tent is not in charge of priests from the tribe of Levi, but under the care of Joshua the son of Nun, who was an *Ephraimite,* and was afterward buried in the highlands of Ephraim (Josh. 24:29–30 [E source]; Judg. 2:8–9). In this document also priestly functions are performed by "young men of the children of Israel"; while Moses himself, acting as a priest, takes the sacrificial blood, and sprinkles it on the altar (Exod. 24:5–8). It is this Ephraimite narrative, indeed, which connects with the story in Judges about the grandson of Moses officiating as a priest. Another point of difference is, that while the Priestly document leaves the Ark *inside* the Tabernacle when Israel is on the march, the Ephraimite narrative sends the Ark on *ahead* of the host, as a pioneer: "And the Ark of the covenant of Yahweh went *before* them, to seek out a resting place for them; and when the Ark set forward, Moses said, Rise up Yahweh, and let thine enemies be scattered; and let them that hate thee flee before thee" (Num. 10:33–36).

Of these two documents, the Priestly is by far the *later*, being removed at least *seven hundred years* from the scenes which it professes to describe; while, on the other hand, the *Ephraimite* narrative is about *four* hundred years distant from the wilderness period. And although it cannot be taken as authority for happenings in the *desert*, its outlook is far more *primitive* than that of the Priestly source, corresponding to some extent with conditions in Ephraim about the time of Samuel, when an "ark of Yahweh" rests in the hill-country at Shiloh (I Sam. 1:3).

The ark known by Samuel is in the house of *Joseph;* and it has no connection with any Levites, or with *Judah*, which has not yet emerged upon the stage of Hebrew history as a tribe. The house of God at Shiloh is visited by Ephraimite worshipers, not *three* times per annum, as contemplated by the later-coming "Law," but only *once* a year (I Sam. 1:7, 21). Samuel himself is not a Levite, but, like Joshua the son of Nun in the E source, he is an *Ephraimite;* and, like Joshua, he has charge of the sanctuary. Moreover, Samuel is consecrated to the service of Yahweh not by priestly descent but by the vow of his mother, Hannah (vss. 11, 27, 28). That the Shiloh ark had any connection with the wilderness period, there is not the slightest evidence.

It suddenly rises out of the mist, at the close of the Judges period, as an emblem of the Josephite desire for national *unity*, expressed also at this time by the new movement of the "sons of the prophets" (*b'nae nebiim*), in relation to Saul, the first king. It is captured by the Philistines, and recovered years later by David, who makes use of it as a political relic, symbolizing Hebrew unity on a broader platform. The last we hear of this ark is through the Ephraimite prophet Jeremiah, who, as a defeatist, would naturally have little respect for an ancient piece of ecclesiastical furniture, identified in its origin with success-prophecy. "They shall no more say, The ark of the covenant of Yahweh. Neither shall it come to mind. Neither shall they remember it. Neither shall they visit it" (Jer. 3:16). He could not have realized that this venerable souvenir stood for a *nationalistic movement* without which neither he nor his prophetic rivals would have had any footing.

The actual, historic Josephite sanctuary was the pattern upon which the Ephraimite source built its narrative of the *Ohel Moedh* in the desert, which differs to such a startling degree from the Priestly Tabernacle in the wilderness. But the real ark of Samuel's time, and the imaginary *Ohel Moehd* of the Ephraimite document, were *both* pushed into obscurity and overshadowed by the mythic tabernacle in a hollow square amid the camp of Israel, in charge of Levitical porters and Aaronic priests, and furnishing a dramatic background for the exaltation of Judah over the house of Joseph.

Priestly document, in promoting Judah, follows pattern of Hebrew history.—We have seen that the legends of Genesis are based upon actual Hebrew history in Canaan, *projected into the past;* and, accordingly, we have made large use of Genesis considered as a source for the study of Israel's evolution. *The same principle was at work in the Priestly document.* The group calling itself "Judah" became self-conscious as the only surviving fragment of the older Israel, compelled to bear the burden of ethical monotheism alone, shedding the light of true religion amid the darkness of a world sunk in heathenism; and this thought loomed larger and larger upon the mental horizon of the Babylonian captives, until finally, in their own eyes, the Judaic remnant of Israel began to overshadow the earlier mass of the nation.

Thus the Priestly document evolved in a wholly new atmosphere, at a time when the missionary function was literally being forced upon the remnant of Israel in exile; *and, accordingly, the new character of Judah, as champion of Yahweh, was projected back into the wilderness period, before the Israelite invasion of Canaan.* Very complex, then, were the circumstances under which the books identified with Moses were brought into the form which they *now* display at the forefront of the Bible. The Josephite material could not be thrust aside, or too seriously mutilated, since it was indispensable as a background against which the house of Judah might shine. The Exilic scribes were unable to take from the house of Joseph the prestige of organizing and establishing the Hebrew nation in the central highlands north of Jerusalem, when Judah was not yet in the perspective; nor could they omit the legends about Joseph as the favorite son of Jacob by his favorite wife Rachel; nor yet the tales presenting the patriarch Joseph in a better light than the patriarch Judah. But by throwing into the distant *past* the function which was devolved upon Judah at a late period of history the Priestly document was able to do a measure of justice to Judah in its new character, and also to afford a retrospective triumph as contrasted with the imperishable glory of Joseph. Originating like other Hebrew literature as a private, unofficial production, the books of the Law awaited the future for validation through some official decree, like that by which the reforming government of Josiah had placed the national imprimatur upon Deuteronomy.

Priestly document a "framework" inclosing mishpat material of Bible.—Any appraisal of the Jewish priestly document on the ground of its apparently exclusive interest in the ritual of worship and cognate themes is beside the main question. The priestly writings took form, in first place, as an *independent* work, apart from the Ephraimite, Judaic, Deuteronomic, and Holiness documents; and there is no evidence that the priestly scribes were obsessed by an *exclusive* concern for the matters which their document covers. That is to say, we have no reason for limiting their outlook to the ritualistic and legalistic phases of history alone. And, in the second place, even if the priestly writers themselves were as narrow as this, we have absolutely no evidence that the books of the "Law," as they *now* stand in the Bible, were compiled by the same persons who wrote the original Priestly documents.

On the contrary, everything indicates that the Law was compiled by editors who, while they had priestly interests, were also motivated by other forces, and were thus *eclectic* rather than priestly in a narrow sense. And, moreover, we have no proof that the term "Jew," applied to the Babylonian scribes and their fellow-exiles, had the restricted sense which the word now seems to convey. For the territory of Judah was a channel through which various Hebrew, or Canaanite, elements passed, especially after the political disruption of Ephraim. We know that Jeremiah, the outstanding prophet of Judah in the generation before the Exile, was an Ephraimite; that men from Shechem, Shiloh, and Samaria came into Judah after the fall of Jerusalem; and that the deportations of Sennacherib from Judah left room for an influx of colonists out of the Josephite mass remaining in the north after the monarchy of Ephraim had been destroyed (Jer. 1:1; 37:12; 41:5). The term "Jew," or "Jewish," as an ethnic designation, either before or after the Babylonish Exile, is purely formal. And thus, the compilers of the

Law were not only non-priestly, but they were were Hebrew, or Canaanite, rather than Jewish in the provincial sense too frequently understood of this term.

These considerations help us to see that the Law is no product of narrow-minded scribes, but was compiled by editors having wide cultural interests. The anonymous compilers made use of the Priestly document as a "framework," and put the ritual of worship into outstanding prominence; *but they also included within that framework all the mishpat material bearing upon the problem of social justice; and they viewed the priestly regulations as rules guaranteeing the corporate integrity of the Jewish people on the long, difficult way upward from heathenism toward ethical monotheism.* A section of the P document stands at the very portals of Scripture, with the majestic words, "In the beginning God created the heavens and the earth" (Gen. 1:1—2:4). The same source elsewhere puts emphasis upon the early patriarchs, Enoch, Noah, and Abraham, as men who "walked with God." The P document, viewing creation as the outcome of Moral Purpose, is not the work of a mere ecclesiastic.

In spite of disagreements and inconsistencies, therefore, the underlying logic of Hebrew history held the writers and compilers of the Jewish Bible true to one, fundamental theme, from first to last; and all the documents and codes derive their force and meaning, directly or indirectly, from the impact of the primitive mishpat ideal of the desert and the open country upon the commercialistic baalism whose headquarters were in the walled cities of Canaan.

The compilers and editors did not know that they were producing what later ages would view as a single, unitary book; nor did they realize that posterity would one day receive their work as "Holy Scripture" and look upon it as "infallible." For, laboring as they did, across the flight of unknown generations, they could never hold a round-table conference to achieve absolute consistency; and while some of them, at one time or another, sought to manipulate the narratives into harmony, such work was not the result of any concerted action; and thus, in the long run, the documents congealed into sanctity on the ground of a liquid and fluctuating tradition, with their discrepancies uncorrected. Representing different stages of ethical evolution, they culminate in the Priestly document, which embraces the *Holiness Code*, commanding love to one's neighbor and also to the alien stranger. Thus, beginning in the realm of pagan provincialism, the evolution of Israel moves upward, step by step, here a little and there a little, until at length unknown seers look over the edge of nationalism and catch the vision of humanity.

CHAPTER XII

CONCLUDING OBSERVATIONS ON BIBLICAL MONOTHEISM

Judaism an evolving religion based on pre-Exilic Hebrew history.—The successive codes imbedded in the Law prove that the ethical monotheism of the Bible is a development, or evolution, of ideas relating to social justice and personal morality. The Deuteronomic code is the foundation of Jewish thought: "Hear Israel! The Lord our God is one Lord. And thou shalt love the Lord thy God with all thine heart, and with all thy soul, and with all thy might" (Deut. 6:4–5). Although Deuteronomy now stands as the final book of the Law, we have seen that it was the *first* book to become *official Bible* through the sanction of Hebrew public authority. Another principle of Judaism, second only to the foregoing, is the command embodied in the "Holiness Code," which became official Scripture after the Exile: "Thou shalt love thy neighbor as thyself" (Lev. 19:18). This principle follows from the first; while both constitute the platform of biblical monotheism, and can be interpreted only in the light of the great Hebrew struggle for mishpat, not as mere static propositions, but as *evolving ideals*.

Orthodox Jewish theology a *post-eventum* explanation of Hebrew history.—Judaism after the Babylonian Exile was in possession of the same literary materials which we now find in the Hebrew Bible; but there had not yet developed any *science* by which this material could be explained in terms of natural cause and effect. The post-Exilic Jews knew that their forefathers had been polytheists and Baal-worshipers, and that the Babylonian captivity somehow marked the victory of ethical, defeatist monotheism. But since they were unable to interpret this tremendous result in modern evolutionary terms, they took the only possible alternative at that stage of human experience, and called it a miracle, or wonder, produced by direct supernatural intervention. And thus orthodoxy was born as a *post-eventum* explanation of *pre-Exilic* Hebrew history.

Jewish orthodoxy not an abstraction but a concrete historical movement.—The complex body of thought known as "Jewish orthodoxy" is not a cut-and-dried abstraction, as it appears to be in the eyes of non-sympathetic onlookers. It stands for an intensely vital movement of thought which turns around the wonderful fact of Israel's evolution out of heathenism into monotheism. Rooting itself in the great insurgent prophets, who labored before the Babylonian Exile and were vindicated by the fall of the Hebrew kingdoms, orthodoxy was created by unknown scribes who wrote the documents of the Law (E, J, D, H, P, etc.); and it was further built up through the labors of a multitude of rabbins whose thought crystallized in the "Talmud." Jewish orthodoxy, then, is an evolving body of thought; and in modern times it tends to pass into new forms of doctrine and practice which aim to preserve the moral and intellectual values of Hebrew prophecy.

Orthodoxy views Israel as "witness bearer" engulfed in heathen world.—The real nature and purpose of Jewish orthodoxy can be understood only as we grasp the historical significance of Israel's own evolution out of heathenism, and then the appalling spectacle of the Jewish remnant engulfed in heathen antiquity, hard pressed from all sides by alien paganism which tended to overflow and annihilate the first monotheistic people. The fundamental aims of orthodoxy, therefore, were two: first, it sought to explain pre-Exilic Hebrew history in a form intelligible to oncoming Jewish generations at an epoch when there was no modern science; and, second, it sought to promote the missionary function of Israel as a "witness bearer" for ethical monotheism in the midst of the vast heathen flood which threatened the very existence of the Jews.

The ancient scribes and rabbins, therefore, undertook to build up and keep alive a corporate community which would conform as nearly as possible to the prophetic ideal, and thus bear witness for God, by personal martyrdom if necessary, until such time as the Kingdom of Heaven should be established on earth.

In view of these considerations, Judaism should be judged with reference to its evolutionary character, its environment of inexorable pagan hostility, and its form as a mechanism of defense.

Judaism viewed from standpoint of struggle for existence.— The gradual reconstitution of Israel in Palestine after the Babylonian Exile was marked by the rise of a new spirit of charity and humanitarianism. And wholly aside from the question of social reform as required by various codes of the Law, the Jewish leaders faced the complex task of educating the restored community in monotheistic worship and at the same time repressing pagan habits of thought—an enterprise which required centuries for its accomplishment.

The nature of historic evolution, as already set forth, shows us why no fundamental reform of society could be expected of post-Babylonian Israel in Palestine. There was no knowledge about the real facts of society anywhere in the world at that period; and there has been controversy in all nations down to the present regarding the exact nature of social justice, to such an extent that neither Jews nor Gentiles have been able thus far to arrive at a solution of this mighty problem.

We have pointed out the utopian character of the provisions in Deuteronomy relating to interest on loans and the release of debts. These requirements were found very embarrassing by the post-Exilic Jews, who nevertheless received as divine the books of the Law. The building-up of monotheism was difficult enough in the sphere of psychology; but, on the other hand, when we turn to the domain of economics, we find that no "baal" with a surplus of goods or cash was likely to compromise the immediate interests of his family and himself, amid the vicissitudes of an uncertain world, by making loans without security or interest, and writing off such debts at the end of every seven years. So the Deuteronomic financial injunctions were nullified by an instrument executed in court, known as the "Prosbul," which at length was put into standard form by the great rabbinical authority *Hillel*, in the first century before the Christian Era.

If the central economic demands of insurgent prophecy were thus evaded by post-Exilic Jews, it seems at first glance, as if the whole vast movement leading out of heathenism into ethical monotheism were somehow void and ineffectual. But we have attempted to show at every point that the Hebrew struggle for monotheism gets meaning, not through any concrete economic program which it puts forward, *but in the unique fact that it raises the social problem and unites the idea of God with the struggle for social readjustment.* If, as claimed by orthodox Jews and Christians, the Law were literally the product of supernatural divine decree, upon a flaming mountain, there might then be some force in the assumption that it should give us an infallible charter of social reform. But the significance of the history which gave rise to the Law is to be found not in the sphere of perfection but in its upward evolutionary progress, through circumstances which were neither more nor less than fallible, imperfect, and human.

Not only were the central economic demands of Hebrew prophecy evaded, but post-Babylonian Jews, like Israel before the captivity, continued to hold gentile slaves and also slaves of Jewish birth. Human bondage in the Old Testament and in Judaism, however, must be considered in relation to the persistence of chattel slavery among Christian peoples for many centuries, and also in view of the fact that it is taken for granted by the New Testament: "Slaves, obey in all things them that are your lords according to the flesh" (Col. 3:22). "Let as many as are slaves under the yoke count their masters worthy of all honor" (I Tim. 6:1). In these and other passages, the newer versions recognize that the Greek text is to be rendered "slave" or "bondservant"; but the older versions translate "servant," which, in its contemporary meaning, does not give the sense of the New Testament text. All Christian nations have held slaves at various periods; and even in America, up to the Civil War, the institution of slavery was defended by the churches, not merely in the South but in the North as well, being justified by quotations from the Old and New Testaments; while, at the same time, the Abolition movement was composed of radical extremists who made their way without religious or ecclesiastical sanction. Christianity, then, did not depart from Judaism on this important count.

Hebrew basis claimed for Christianity in New Testament.— When we turn to the earliest and briefest of the Christian gospels (the Book of *Mark*), we read that the question was put to Jesus, "Which is the first commandment of all?" And the answer is taken from the Deuteronomic code: "Hear Israel. The Lord our God is one Lord. And thou shalt love the Lord thy God with all thy heart, and with all thy soul, and with all thy mind, and with all thy strength" (Mark 12:28–30; cf. Deut. 6:4–5). Following this commandment, another is quoted from the "Holiness Code" in Leviticus: "Thou shalt love thy neighbor as thyself" (Lev. 19:18). Jesus then goes on to say, "*There is no other commandment greater than these*" (Mark 12:31).

That the original gospel, as interpreted by Jesus, did not have a "Christological" character is clear from a number of indications. Thus, in the same source referred to above, we read, "And there came one and kneeled to him, and asked him, Good master, what shall I do that I may inherit eternal life?" (Mark

10:17.) But before proceeding to answer this question, Jesus takes up a matter which is raised by the inquirer's personal attitude toward him. "Why callest thou me good?" he asks; and then goes on to say, "There is none good but *one*, that is, *God*" (vs. 18). The distinction between Jesus and the Deity is here drawn in clear terms; and it also appears in another New Testament book, which was written even before Mark, i.e., *I Corinthians*. In this book the apostle Paul declares that God gave Jesus a certain work to do, and that after the work is accomplished, Jesus is to be subjected to God, "*that God may be all in all*" (I Cor. 15:28).

These New Testament sources are cited here not for the purpose of theological argument but simply to show that Christianity, like Judaism, strikes its roots deep into the soil of that ancient religious evolution which took place in *Hebrew history*, long before the rise of synagogue or church. The earlier parts of the New Testament bear the same kind of relation to the later and more theological Christian writings that the Hebrew prophets bear to the Exilic "Priestly" document. In other words, Christianity, like Judaism, was an *evolution*, although it evolved in another way and under very different circumstances.

Christology obscures, but does not abolish, Hebrew foundations of monotheism.—The Jew, as we have seen, gets his monotheistic faith by contact with his own race and by acquaintance with ideas and cult-usages peculiar to Hebrew history. In other words, Judaism is primarily based not on abstract, philosophic discussion but on a concrete, national experience, the memory of which is perpetuated in certain concrete ways within a given race-group. The nature of Judaism, as being at once doctrinal and racial, is not realized by Christians in general; and, in the same way, most Jews thus far have not understood historic Christianity as a movement springing from the soil of Hebraism. Since Gentiles are non-Jews, they are psychologically unable to acquire ethical monotheism by looking back, as a Jew does, along the path of national Hebrew experience. But at the same time the masses of Gentiles, like the Jews themselves, have not been able to absorb monotheistic religion as *abstract unitarianism*.

Hence, when the religion of one God spread from Palestine into the gentile world, its interest began to revolve more and more about concrete ideas regarding the life and person of Jesus. The unitarian campaign of Paul broke down at Athens, the intellectual and cultural center of Greece; and he went from Athens to Corinth, with the firm idea to preach nothing but Jesus as the Anointed, or Christ; and not merely so, but to preach him as crucified (I Cor. 2:2; cf. Acts, chap. 17). Although Paul, as we have seen, continued to be a Jewish monotheist, he helped to lay the foundations of *Christology*, which, after his death, took on its "orthodox" form.

Thus, Christian orthodoxy, like Jewish orthodoxy, grew out of the natural desire to interpret, or explain, *something earlier than itself*. The doctrine of the person of Jesus has undoubtedly tended to obscure the Hebraic foundations of monotheism as expressed in the Gospel of Mark and as rooted in the Hebrew struggle for mishpat, or social justice. But from the standpoint of the gentile world, this obscuration, for the time being, was necessary and inevitable. Scientific investigators thus far have not fully realized the social value and meaning of the gentile conversion from licentious polytheism to the worship of Jesus. A purely individual gospel was the first need of the ancient non-Jewish world; and a monotheism based on outright demand for social justice could not have been propagated in the Roman Empire and medieval Europe. That Christianity rests back upon Hebrew foundations, however, was perceived by the rabbis of the Middle Ages, who said, "Christians are not idolators. They make mention of Jesus; but their thought is toward the Maker of heaven and earth" (Abrahams, *Jewish Life in the Middle Ages* [1917], p. 41).

Judaism and Christianity alike founded upon pre-Exilic Hebraism.—Going back through the "orthodoxies" which envelop the Old and New Testaments, we find that Christianity is not an outgrowth of Judaism, but that the synagogue and the church are both founded upon pre-Exilic *Hebraism*. In other words, the faith of Jew and Christian alike is rooted in the great warfare for mishpat, or struggle for social justice, through which the concept of ethical monotheism projected itself above the spiritual horizon of mankind. The social process of Hebrew history took place within the terms of imperfect human life, moving slowly upward through stages of increasing refinement; and its value for modern religion is found not in any concrete program of social reconstruction but in its welding of the God-concept into the struggle for a better world. Nor do these considerations exhaust the meaning of the social process.

Social justice functional in value, but not ultimate purpose of history.—Only in a slow, gradual way can social justice be secured; and therefore countless millions must necessarily perish before the goal is won. And even if the complete renewal of society is at length achieved, the ultimate beneficiaries will pass quickly off the stage of life. Thus, the study of history carries with it an intimation that social justice ought *not* to be estimated simply as a physical, objective scheme of reform which guarantees welfare and happiness to late-comers in the human drama. The fleeting nature of history points to the conclusion that social justice, while immeasurably important, cannot, in itself, be the final object of human life. While the conception of God is intimately related to the social process, yet when religion is identified with sociology, it resolves itself into materialism. But, by the same token, the struggle for justice has functional meaning as a discipline with transcendental implications, in a universe dominated by an unfolding moral purpose which cannot be fulfilled in Time and which therefore projects itself into Eternity.

APPENDIX

I. THE TWO ACCOUNTS OF CREATION

Of the two creation-stories in the Bible, the narrative in the left-hand column below is by far the older and more primitive. It is from the J document, employing the personal name "Jehovah," or "Yahweh," in connection with "Elohim." Reading the left column first, we notice (1) the use of the term "Yahweh Elohim." This is rendered "LORD God" in the older English Bibles and in the Jewish English Bible (Philadelphia), but "Jehovah God" in the American Revision; (2) the *order* of events, beginning with (*a*) creation of "earth and heaven," then (*b*) creation of Man as a masculine being *without a feminine consort*, then (*c*) creation of vegetable and animal life, and *finally* (*d*) creation of Woman *from* Man. This narrative emphasizes the creation of vegetable and animal life as intervening *between* that of Man, as a purely masculine being, and that of Woman as originating *from* the body of Man.

But, in sharp contrast, the narrative in the right-hand column is taken from a very much later and more sophisticated source, the P, or Priestly, document. Here we note (1) that creation is the work of "Elohim" (rendered "God"), and (2) that the *order* of events is very different from that of the J account, as follows: (*a*) creation of "heaven and earth"—not "earth and heaven," (*b*) vegetable and animal life, (*c*) and, finally, human species, male and female, *at the same time*. In this account there is no intervening creation of vegetable and animal life *between* the creation of Man as a masculine being and a subsequent creation of Woman *from* Man. In other words, the unfolding of creation is more like that envisaged by modern science, i.e., first, the physical universe; then vegetable life; then animal life; and, last of all, human life as the climax of the creative process, the two sexes originating *concomitantly*.

315

EARLIER ACCOUNT

J DOCUMENT

"In the day that Yahweh Elohim made earth and heaven .... Yahweh Elohim formed Man from the dust of the ground, and breathed into his nostrils the breath of life; and Man became a living soul. .... And from the ground Yahweh Elohim made to grow every tree which is pleasant to the sight and good for food. .... And from the ground Yahweh Elohim formed every beast of the field and every fowl of the air. .... And Yahweh Elohim caused Man to sleep; and he took one of his ribs. And the rib, which Yahweh Elohim had taken from Man, made he a Woman."

[The compiler of Genesis begins to use the J document at Gen. 2:4b, commencing with "In the day that Yahweh Elohim," etc. The J account of creation is then followed to the *end* of chap. 2. We have reproduced only the essential part of this material; but the reader will find it instructive to underline with a red crayon the entire passage (Gen. 2:4b,

LATER ACCOUNT

P DOCUMENT

"In the beginning Elohim created the heaven and the earth. .... And Elohim said, Let the earth bring forth grass, the herbs yielding seed, the fruit trees bearing fruit. .... And Elohim said, Let the waters bring forth abundantly swarms of creatures that have life, and fowl .... and cattle, and creeping things and beasts of the earth. And it was so. .... And Elohim said, Let us make Man in our image, after our likeness. .... So Elohim created Man in his image; in the image of Elohim created he him; male and female created he them. .... Thus the heaven and the earth were finished, and all their host. .... These are the generations of the heaven and of the earth when they were created."

[The compiler of Genesis begins to use the P, or Priestly, narrative at Gen. 1:1; and the Priestly account of creation is followed through Gen., chap. 1, up to and *including* the first clause of Gen. 2:4, "These are the generations of the heaven

EARLIER ACCOUNT

J DOCUMENT

LATER ACCOUNT

P DOCUMENT

to and including vs. 25), await-ing further direction for under-lining the Priestly narrative.]

and of the earth when they were created," *at which point, in the middle of vs. 4, the com-piler ceases, for the time being, to use the P document, and be-gins to use the older, or J ac-count, which we have already quoted in the left column here-with.* The differences between the two documents are found not only in the sharp contrast between the *order* of events in the two sources, and the name "Elohim" in P and "Yahweh Elohim" in J, but there are other stylistic and verbal vari-ations which need not be taken up here. The contrast in the divine names, therefore, is only one feature of the case; and the reader may bring the P document into relief by un-derlining with a blue crayon Gen. 1:1 to and including the first clause of Gen. 2:4, ending *with* the word "created."]

II. THE TWO STORIES OF THE FLOOD

The J and P documents again come into sharp contrast with reference to the "Flood."

In the J source, the divine name "Yahweh" is used as before, but this time without the Elohim-suffix; Noah is commanded to take *seven* males and females out of all "clean" beasts and out of the fowls of the air, and *two* males and females out of all "unclean" beasts; the rain lasts *forty days;* after which the earth dries off in *two weeks;* and Noah comes out of the ark at the end of a *fifty-four day sojourn* in the vessel.

But, on the other hand, in the "Priestly" document, the divine name "Elohim" *only* is used, as in the P account of creation; no distinction is made between beasts that are "clean" and beasts that are "unclean"; Noah is merely commanded to take *two* males and females out of *every* kind of living flesh; the flood begins in the six-hundredth year of Noah's life, the *second* month, and the *seventeenth day* of the month; while the rain, instead of lasting *forty* days, continues for *one hundred and fifty days, or approximately five months*, after which the windows of heaven are closed; and in the *seventh* month, upon the *seventeenth* day of that month, the keel of Noah's ark rests upon the invisible summits of "the mountains of Ararat," which are *even yet* below the surface of the water, *because the flood still prevails everywhere upon earth*. But the waters then begin to dry off, *gradually decreasing for many weeks*, until the *tops* of the mountains emerge on the first of the *tenth* month. Yet a huge body of water still remains, *and the drying process goes on during a further long space of three additional months*, until the beginning of the six hundred and first year of Noah's life, when the flood is at length dried up from off the earth. But although the *waters* are now evaporated, the ground itself is *a vast mass of mud*,

which requires another month and twenty-seven days to harden; so
that by the end of this time the *earth* is dry; after which Noah
comes out of the ark, having thus, according to the "Priestly"
document, inhabited his marine home *exactly one year and ten
days*, whereas, the J narrative confines him in the ark only
fifty-four days.

The two contrasted accounts of the Flood follow, omitting
non-essential details:

EARLIER ACCOUNT
J DOCUMENT

"And Yahweh said unto
Noah, Come thou and all thy
house into the ark. . . . . Of
every *clean* beast thou shalt
take to thee by *sevens*, the
male and female; and of beasts
that are *not* clean by *two*.
. . . . Of fowls also of the air
by *sevens*. . . . . And I will
cause it to rain upon the earth
forty days. . . . . And Yahweh
shut him in. And the flood
was *forty days* upon the earth;
and the waters increased, and
bare up the ark, and it was
lifted up above the earth.
. . . . And it came to pass, at
the end of *forty days*, that Noah opened the window of the
ark. . . . . And he sent out a
dove. . . . . But the dove found
no rest. . . . . And she returned. . . . . And he stayed

LATER ACCOUNT
P DOCUMENT

"And Noah was six hundred
years old when the flood of
waters was upon the earth.
And Noah, and his sons, and
his wife, and his sons' wives
with him, entered into the
ark. . . . . Of *clean* beasts, and
of beasts *not* clean, and of
fowls, and of *everything* that
creepeth upon the earth, there
went in *two and two* unto Noah
into the ark, the male and the
female, as Elohim had commanded Noah. In the *six hun-
dredth year* of Noah's life, the
second month, the *seventeenth
day* of the month, the same
day, all the fountains of the
great deep were broken up,
and the windows of heaven
were opened. . . . . And the
waters prevailed and were increased greatly upon the earth.

EARLIER ACCOUNT

J DOCUMENT

LATER ACCOUNT

P DOCUMENT

yet other seven days, and again he sent out the dove. . . . . And the dove came in to him in the evening; and in her mouth was an olive leaf plucked off. . . . . And he stayed yet other seven days, and sent forth the dove, which returned not again. . . . . And Noah removed the covering of the ark, and looked, and behold the face of the ground was dry. . . . . And Noah built an altar unto Yahweh, and took of every clean beast, and of every clean fowl, and offered burnt offerings on the altar. . . . . And the sons of Noah that went out of the ark were Shem, and Ham, and Japheth. . . . ."

[A red crayon should be used, as before, in underlining the J narrative. Begin with Gen. *7:1*, continuing on through the following verses, to and including vs. *5*; then pass to, and underline, vs. *10* (which we did not quote); then pass to, and underline, vs. *12;* then go on to, and underline, *the last four words* of vs. *16;*

. . . . And the mountains were covered. . . . . *And the waters prevailed upon the earth an hundred and fifty days.* . . . . And Elohim made a wind to pass over the earth, and the waters subsided. . . . . *And after the end of the hundred and fifty days* the waters were *abated.* And the ark rested, in the *seventh* month, on the *seventeenth day* of the month, upon the mountains of Ararat. And the waters went down continually until the *tenth* month. In the *tenth* month, on the *first* of the month, were the *tops* of the mountains seen. And it came to pass, in the *six hundred and first year* [of Noah's life], in the *first* month, the *first* of the month, the *waters* were dried up from the earth. And in the *second* month, on the *twenty-seventh day* of the month, was the *earth* dried. And Elohim spake unto Noah, saying, Go out from the ark, etc."

[A blue crayon should be used in underlining the P narrative, as before. Begin with Gen. *7:6 through* vs. *9;* then

then vs. *17*, complete; then vss. *22 and 23*, entire; then pass to chap. *8*, and underline *the last seven words* in vs. *2*, and the first *nine* words of vs. *3;* then pass to, and underline, vss. *6 through 12;* then pass to, and underline, the *last* part of vs. *13*, beginning with the words "and Noah"; then pass to, and underline, vss. *20 through 22;* then pass to chap. *9*, and underline vs. *18*.

All the matter thus underscored may then be read seriatim, practically as we have quoted it above, including certain unimportant details which we have omitted. A great deal of the J document in the vicinity of the Flood narrative is not brought out by this underscoring, since we consider *here* only that part of it which relates directly to the Flood.]

vs. *11;* then vss. *13 through 16;* then vss. *18 through 21;* then vs. *24;* then *8:1*, and the first *sentence* of vs. *2*, ending with the word "stopped"; then vs. *3*, beginning with the words "and after," and going on *through* vss. *4 and 5;* then vs. *13*, through the word "earth"; then vss. *14 through 19*.

All the matter thus indicated may be read seriatim, practically as reproduced above, including some non-essential matter omitted from our quotation, as in the case of the J document. A great deal of the P narrative in the vicinity of the Flood-story is not brought out by this underscoring, since we consider *here* only that part of the P document relating directly to the Flood.

The P source puts in the ark *two* each of "clean" and "unclean" animals; and it mentions no sacrifice at an altar by Noah after the Flood; *because the Priestly writer believed that no ritual distinctions were made, and no sacrifices*

LATER ACCOUNT

P DOCUMENT

ordained, until many centuries later, at the time when the "Mosaic system" was alleged to have been established.

The J and P accounts of the Flood have been pieced together by the compiler of Genesis more intimately than the two accounts of creation, which stand apart more independently in the text. Yet the two stories of the Flood are, in the main, easily distinguishable in the Hebrew text of Genesis and in the translation. That a Hebrew scribe should have pieced them together in this manner seems at first incredible to a modern reader. But there was no sense of literary property in ancient times, as there is today; and the famous Arabic historians also compose their works in exactly this way, omitting credit to earlier books.]

III. THE TWO STORIES ABOUT THE SALE OF JOSEPH

The stories about the sale of Joseph differ from each other in several very important particulars. Thus, according to the Judaic, J, or *southern*, document, the leader of the brethren is *Judah*. The brethren are in a field, when they see a company of *Ishmeelites* drawing near; whereupon Judah (reflecting the enslavement of the house of Joseph by the Davidic dynasty) proposes to sell Joseph as a slave into the hands of these Ishmeelites. The brethren proceed to carry out this plan, selling the boy to the Ishmeelites for twenty pieces of silver. The Ishmeelites then carry Joseph down to Egypt, and resell him to an Egyptian.

But, on the other hand, in the *northern*, Ephraimite, or E, story, the leader of the brethren is *Reuben*, the northern patriarch. Knowing the evil intentions of his brethren, Reuben plans to deceive them; and he therefore induces the brothers to place Joseph in a *pit* in the wilderness, where there was neither food nor water, intending *himself* to return secretly, take Joseph out of the pit, and restore him to his father Jacob. Accordingly, the brethren, without suspecting that they are to be tricked, follow out Reuben's plan, casting Joseph into the pit, and then going away to eat their meal. Then there passes by a company of *Midianites* (not Ishmeelites); and, seeing Joseph in the pit, they (the Midianites) draw him out, unobserved by the brethren, and carry him down to Egypt, where they sell him to Potiphar, an officer of the guard. But in the meanwhile, *Reuben*, secretly holding to his plan of deliverance, goes back to the pit, and makes the horrible discovery that Joseph is gone! He then returns with the news to his brethren, exclaiming, "The child is not! And as for me, whither shall I go?"

J DOCUMENT

"And they lifted up their eyes and looked, and, behold, a company of Ishmeelites came from Gilead with their camels, bearing spices and balm and myrrh, going to carry down to Egypt. And Judah said to his brethren, What profit if we slay our brother and conceal his blood? Come, and let us sell him to the Ishmeelites, and let not our hand be upon him; for he is our brother and our flesh. And his brethren . . . . sold Joseph to the Ishmeelites for twenty pieces of silver. And Joseph was brought down to Egypt; and an Egyptian purchased him from the Ishmeelites."

[Using a red crayon, as before in the case of J, begin underlining with the *second* "and" in Gen. *37:25*, underscoring onward to and including vs. *27;* pass thence to the middle of vs. *28*, and begin underlining with the words "and sold," continuing *through* the word "silver"; pass thence to *39:1*, beginning to underline with the words "And Joseph," continuing through the next

E DOCUMENT

"And Reuben said unto them, Shed no blood. Cast him into this pit that is in the wilderness, lay no hand upon him; that he might save him out of their hands, to deliver him to their father again. And it came to pass, when Joseph was come unto his brethren, that . . . . they took him, and cast him into a pit; and the pit was empty—no water in it. And they sat down to eat bread. Then there passed by Midianites, traders; and they [the Midianites] drew and lifted up Joseph out of the pit; and they brought Joseph into Egypt. And Reuben returned unto the pit; and, behold, Joseph was not in the pit; and he [Reuben] rent his clothes. And he returned unto his brethren, and said, The child is not; and as for me, whither shall I go? And the Midianites sold him [Joseph] into Egypt, unto Potiphar."

[For the E document, take an *orange* crayon. Begin underlining with Gen. *37:22*, continuing to underline straight onward through the next two

J DOCUMENT

"and"; omit the next *nine* words *after* this "and"; beginning to underline again with the words "an Egyptian," continuing through to the end of that verse.]

E DOCUMENT

verses and the first sentence of vs. *25*, ending with the word "bread"; then go to vs. *28*, and begin underlining with the word "Then," and ending with the word "pit"; beginning again in the *same verse* with "and they," and continuing straight on thence through vss. *29, 30*, and *36*. This does not include all of the E material in question, but it brings out enough to serve the purpose. The compiler of Genesis has united the J and E stories about the sale of Joseph quite intimately, but not so closely as to conceal the sources.]

IV. "ADON" AND "BAAL" IN THE SOURCES

The distribution of the terms *adon* and *baal* in the Hebrew text of the Old Testament is of importance comparable to that of the terms *Elohim* and *Yahweh*. The Josephite conquest of Ephraim (i.e., the central highlands north of Jerusalem and south of Esdraelon) was drastic in character, exterminating the Amorite proprietors, or *baalim*, of Bethel, Shechem, and elsewhere in the highlands, and of Jericho in the Jordan Valley. And consequently, for several generations in Ephraim, the term *baal*, as applied to men of property, went largely out of use, along with the cults of the local Amorite gods, or Baalim. Sporadic instances of its use occur in the Josephite aristocracy, as, for example, the alternative name "Jerub-baal" for Gideon (Judg. 6:32; 7:1). This is deliberately altered by a later scribe to "Jerub-besheth" (II Sam. 11:21)—the term "besheth," or rather "bosheth," meaning "shame." But as a common noun indicating proprietorship, the term *baal* was displaced for a long time in the central highlands. Thus, as late as the reign of Omri in Ephraim, the proprietor of the land purchased by Omri for his capital, in contravention of mishpat-usage, is called "the *adon*" [owner] (I Kings 16:24). The same term is used in the *south*, in the more primitive region later known as Judah, where Nabal complains that slaves break away, every man from his *adon* (I Sam. 25:10). David is called *adon*, or lord, thirteen times by Abigail the wife of Nabal (I Sam. 25:24, etc.). As part of compound proper names, this word occurs only in Judah, where David's minister of labor is "Adoni-ram" (my lord is high); while one of David's sons bears the name "Adoni-jah" (my lord is Yahweh). Thus, for the Judean prophet Amos, Yahweh is usually *"Adon* Yahweh" (Amos. 1:8; 3:7, 8, 11, 13).

The proprietors of Samaria (like Shemer) are not "baalim," but *adonim* (Amos 4:1).

It seems clear that the term *adon* tended to displace *baal* in the central highlands north of Jerusalem for several generations after the Josephite conquest; that it is older than *baal;* and that it persisted longer in the highlands of Judah. Accordingly, upon turning to the Judaic, or J, source in the Torah, we find that Abraham is the *adon* of his wife Sarah (Gen. 18:12). Yahweh is also called by the same term five times (Gen. 18:3, 27, 30, 31, 32; *adon*, rendered "Lord" in contrast with the rendering "the LORD," which is the older English usage for "Yahweh"). The angels that appear to Lot in the gate of Sodom are *adonim* (19:2). All of these examples are in J. The same document also gives many instances of the same usage when describing the journey of Abraham's chief slave in search of a wife for Isaac. In this connection the slave refers to Abraham twenty-one times as "my *adon*" (Gen. 24:9, 10, 12, 27, etc.; translated "my master"). In the J narrative also, Jacob, when seeking to curry favor with his offended brother Esau, calls him "my *adon*" seven times (Gen. 32:4, 5, 18; 33:13, 14, 15). In Genesis, chapter 39, the Egyptian owner of Joseph is called *adon* seven times (rendered "master" six times and "lord" once [vss. 3, 7, 8, 16, 19, 20]). In 43:20, *adon* is rendered "sir," and in chapter 44 "lord" thirteen times; in chapter 47, "lord" twice. All the foregoing examples are from the Judaic source.

But upon turning to the northern, or Ephraimite, source (E), the term *adon* is found less commonly, and the growing influence of Canaanite territorialism north of Jerusalem appears in the more frequent use of *baal*. Thus, in Gen. 20:3 (E), Sarah is called *beulath baal* (i.e., "feminine baal of a baal"). The English translators, however, obscure the facts by rendering the phrase "a man's wife." Abraham, therefore, having been the *adon* of his slaves and of Sarah in the J document, is now transformed into a *baal* by the northern source. In the same document Joseph is called "*baal* of dreams," the linguistic situation being once more obscured by the translators, who simply render the phrase "dreamer" (Gen. 37:19 [E]). Again, the Ephraimite source implies that a lawsuit can be initiated only by a *baal*, a member of the upper social class, the situation being hopelessly hidden under the rendering "any man" (Exod. 24:14).

The growing prevalence of the term *baal* in Ephraim is illustrated with special force by that portion of the E document which we have called "the Early Mishpat Book" (Exod., chaps. 21, 22, etc.), wherein *baal* occurs thirteen times and *adon* but seven times. Thus, Exod. 21:3, "if he be *baal* of a woman," translated "if he be married"; verses 4, 5, 6, 8, *adon* six times rendered "master"; verse 22, *baal*, rendered "husband"; verse 28, *baal*, rendered "owner"; verse 29, *baal*, twice, rendered "owner"; verse 32, *adon*, rendered "master"; verse 34, *baal*, twice, rendered "owner"; verse 36, *baal*, rendered "owner"; 22:8, *baal-ha-bayith*, translated "master of the house"; verses 11, 12, 14, 15, *baal*, four times, "owner." The *Ephraimite* prophet Hosea condemns the application of the term *baal* to Yahweh (Hos. 2:16). He describes Baal-worship as *bosheth*, "shameful" (9:10). Likewise, the Ephraimite prophet Jeremiah declares that the people of Israel forgot the name of Yahweh "*in Baal*" (Jer. 23:27). And following the example of Hosea, he calls Baal-worship *bosheth* (11:13). This is why the later scribes undertake to change the baal-suffix in Ephraimite aristocratic names to *bosheth* or *besheth;* but the documents hardened into sanctity before the transformation could be completely carried through, giving still another example of attempts by posterity to re-edit the earlier sources. Hosea's demand that Israel cease calling Yahweh a *baal* would undoubtedly have been indorsed in principle by Jeremiah. But the latter's Ephraimite habits of thought made this impossible; for in the Hebrew text of Jeremiah's book, Yahweh requires backsliding Israel to return unto him because he is in a *baal-relationship* with them (3:14; 31:32).

These passages greatly embarrass the translators; the English versions make Yahweh a "husband," or "married," to Israel; while the Jewish-English Bible uses the term "lord" in each case.

The earlier Hebrew documents do not use the term *baal* to indicate the domestic relationship of man and woman; and a study of the sources with reference to *adon* and *baal* helps to show how the territorial, or Amorite, side of the nation's ancestry almost overwhelmed the primitive ideas and institutions inherited from the nomadic forefathers who came into Canaan from the desert, or *midbar*, of Arabia. Only the tremendous cataclysm of political downfall and exile wrenched the term *baal* from use in connection with Yahweh; so that in post-Exilic times the Jews reverted to the earlier *adon*, which is always pronounced in repeating the "Shema."

V. THE SOURCES FOR HEBREW HISTORY

Hero-stories, legends, and primitive poems accumulated here and there—in Ephraim at first, and then later in the south, after David created the kingdom and tribe of Judah. The "Song of Deborah" is Ephraimite, and is probably the earliest composition in Hebrew literature; its occasion being a battle of scattered highland clans with Baal-worshiping Amorites in the valley of Esdraelon.

The earliest sources were very simple and concrete, centering about prominent personalities. A collection of such material was made under the suggestive title, *The Book of the Wars of Yahweh* (Num. 21:14), another took form as *The Book of Yashar* (Josh. 10:13). These writings and others (all of which have disappeared) furnished matter for our *present* books of *Judges* and *I Samuel*, dealing with village clans in the hill-country, at a time when the nomadic and seminomadic population of Canaan was taking character as "Israel," and before these elements were brought into political connection with the older Amorite walled cities outside the highlands of Ephraim. The period of the "Judges" not only covers the time contemplated by the book of that name, but also runs through the days of Samuel and Saul, overlapping the earlier part of David's career.

The sources for the earliest period of Hebrew history in Canaan are admirably treated by Professor George F. Moore in a volume entitled *A Critical and Exegetical Commentary on Judges*, and by Professor Henry Preserved Smith in *A Critical and Exegetical Commentary on the Books of Samuel*. The ground is well covered also by Professor Karl Budde in *Die Bücher Richter und Samuel*.

In the reign of David we first hear of an official secretary, or

keeper of records, Jehoshaphat ben Ahilud, the *mazkir* (II Sam.
8:16). There is a reference to *The Book of the Acts of Solomon*
(I Kings 11:41). And after the division of the kingdom into
Israel and Judah, there were two lines of state histories, known
respectively as *The Book of the Matters of the Days of the Kings of
Israel* and *The Book of the Matters of the Days of the Kings of
Judah* (I Kings 14:19, 29). These writings are frequently re-
ferred to by the compilers of our present, or biblical, books of
Kings. A good brief treatment of Kings is given by Professor
John Skinner, *Kings*, and a more extensive consideration by
Professor Rudolf Kittel in *Die Bücher der Könige übersetzt und
erklärt.*

It is now a commonplace of scholarship that Hebrew history,
in the times referred to by Judges, Samuel, and Kings, went on
without reference to, or knowledge of, the so-called "books of
Moses," which were not compiled in their present form until
after the Hebrew nation was destroyed by Mesopotamian conquerors. Some hints leading to this conclusion were thrown out
by the Spanish rabbi, Ben Ezra, in the Middle Ages, and by the
Dutch Jew, Baruch Spinoza, in the seventeenth century. The
analysis of the documents into J, E, etc., was commenced in a
primitive and partial way, about the middle of the eighteenth
century, by the Frenchman, Jean Astruc, who published his
findings in 1753. The documentary method was carried farther,
and the term "higher criticism" was first applied to Hebrew
literature by Professor J. G. Eichhorn in his *Introduction to the
Old Testament*, issued in 1780. The foregoing literary analysis
led to a further step, taken by Wilhelm de Wette, who published
a dissertation on Deuteronomy (1805), pointing out that this
book was first known only near the end of old Hebrew history in
the reign of Josiah, when already the kingdom of Ephraim had
been dissolved by the Assyrians, and soon the kingdom of Judah
was to be annihilated by the Babylonians.

Following in the path blazed by De Wette came a number of

powerful scholars. Foremost among these were W. Vatke, whose *Biblical Theology* was published in 1835; A. Kuenen, whose *Origin and Collection of the Books of the Old Testament* was issued from 1861 to 1865; and K. H. Graf, whose volume, *The Historical Books of the Old Testament*, appeared in 1866; after which came two other important treatises by Professor A. Kuenen, *The Religion of Israel* (1870) and *Prophets and Prophecy in Israel* (1874). Research had, by that time, brought into shape the modern higher critical view, according to which, along with the rise of defeatist prophetism, *between 850 B.C. and 750 B.C.*, the J and E documents of the "Mosaic" books came into private circulation; while the D, or Deuteronomic, document, was prepared about a century later in Judah; and the P, or Priestly, document was written last of all, after the Babylonian Exile of Judah. Investigation, beginning as *literary* criticism, had therefore passed into a *historical* stage; the completed "Law," which appears in the forefront of the Bible, being *transposed* from the beginning of Hebrew history in Canaan to the beginning of post-Exilic Judaism; the advance of Israel from polytheistic religion to monotheism being an evolution of *some kind*, which was promoted *in some way, by the higher, or "true," prophets in opposition to the lower, or "false," prophets.*

The entire critical movement, with its new "source theory" and its evolutionary perspective, was brought to a focus by Professor J. Wellhausen, whose epoch-making *Geschichte Israels* ("History of Israel") was issued in 1878; and thenceforward the critical view of Hebrew history was almost identified as "Wellhausenism." Outstanding scholars in Germany, Holland, France, Great Britain, and the United States gave in their adherence to the new views during the generation following the appearance of Wellhausen's work; so that, by the beginning of the *present* century, most universities and theological seminaries were detached from traditional "orthodoxy." The best study of the documents entering into the compilation of the "Mosaic

Law" available in English is *The Composition of the Hexateuch* by the Oxford authorities Carpenter and Harford, and the separate volumes of the *International Critical Commentary* by Skinner, Driver, and Gray. For the prophets (Amos, Hosea, etc.) consult the volumes of the same *Commentary* as far as it has gone; also Professor George Adam Smith in *The Expositor's Bible;* W. R. Smith, *The Prophets of Israel;* and L. W. Batten, *The Hebrew Prophets.*

Nevertheless, higher criticism of the Hebrew sources had not really solved the problem before it, and biblical scholarship entered upon a rather confused march in the early part of the twentieth century. A frontal attack on the Wellhausen position was ventured in 1906 by Professor James Orr, of the United Free Church College, Glasgow, Scotland, in his book, *The Problem of the Old Testament.* This was the last respectable assault on the new position; but Orr's concessions to the claims of criticism weakened the force of his own argument, so that critics and anticritics alike were not satisfied with his work. Professor Francis Brown, of Union Theological Seminary, New York, although himself an advanced critic, proclaimed in 1908 that the central problem of criticism (its relation to the idea of God) had not been liquidated (*Old Testament and Semitic Studies in Honor of William Rainey Harper,* p. xxx); and the same admission was made by Wellhausen himself in 1909 (*Kultur der Gegenwart* [Berlin], Teil I, p. 15). Moreover, the original title of his book as *"History"* was premature; and he had already substituted for it in later editions the term *"Prolegomena,"* which more accurately describes the work of biblical higher criticism up to the twentieth century as dealing with a new "source theory" rather than as furnishing a rounded interpretation of the facts before it.

In the meanwhile, from 1902 to 1911, a number of articles were published in journals of the University of Chicago under the following titles: "The Capitalization of Social Development," "Sociological Significance of the Bible," "Sociology and Theism," "Professor James Orr and Higher Criticism," "Biblical Sociology." These articles, in the *American Journal of Sociology* and the *American Journal of Theology*, were in preparation for *Sociological Study of the Bible*, issued in 1912, the sequel to which is the present volume, *God and the Social Process* (1934).

VI. NOTE ON HEBREW PROPHECY

Both schools of *nebiim* were undoubtedly sincere; they were psychologically *intense* in their concern with public questions; and there is no reason to gainsay the honesty of their claims to be in special touch with Yahweh. Nothing is more instructive than the standing which both types acquired in the popular mind, and the way in which both are treated by various Hebrew sources.

The subject is well raised by the conflict between Hananiah ben Azur the "success-*nabi*" and Jeremiah the "defeatist-*nabi*" (Jer., chap. 28). The opposed claims of such men would appear to inspire the belief of *each* that the other is a false prophet; and, as a matter of fact, *Jeremiah* declares that his opponent was not sent by Yahweh, and that he made the people to trust in a lie (vs. 15); while, at the same time, *Hananiah* would seem, by the logic of his own position, to have held the same uncomplimentary opinion of Jeremiah.

And yet the merits of the question are not settled so easily. That any prophet of either school may conceivably foretell the truth is admitted by the Book of Deuteronomy, which, therefore, seeks to do away with prediction as a test of prophecy. This book undertakes to condemn in advance any prophet who speaks in the name of any *other* god than Yahweh (Deut. 13: 1–5). The view of Deuteronomy seems to be shared by Jeremiah when he declares that his opponents prophesy in the name of *Baal* (Jer. 2:8; 23:13).

But this would not cover a case like that of Hananiah, who prophesied *in the name of Yahweh*. To meet such a contingency, the Deuteronomic author falls back once more upon the principle of prediction, and says that if the words uttered by a *nabi* in

the name of Yahweh fail to come true, then the man is a false
prophet (18:21, 22).

Furthermore, the conflict between the two schools of *nebiim* is
thrust into a region of still greater darkness and uncertainty by
the claim that false prophets themselves are, after all, in actual
touch with Yahweh, but are themselves deceived by a "lying
spirit," sent out from heaven by Yahweh (I Kings 22:20–23).
This view is also taken by the prophet Ezekiel (14:9). And even
the author of Deuteronomy asserts that Yahweh *himself* is the
inspiring force in the words of the false prophet, seeking to
"prove" Israel (Deut. 13:3). The same idea emerges in the repeated claim of the Pentateuchal documents that Yahweh
"hardened" Pharaoh's heart (Exod. 9:12; 10:1, 20; 11: 10).

When the literary sources thus reveal so many possibilities
for doubt and argument with reference to Hebrew prophecy, it
is easy to perceive that the masses of the Hebrew people were
necessarily at sea on the merits of the long controversy between the two lines of prophets. Since the documents themselves contemplate the agency of Yahweh in *both* types of
prophecy, and since many of the prophets prophesied in the name
of the Baalim, who were imagined as real beings, the conclusion is irresistible that *all the nebiim of both schools* were commonly held to be in touch with *demonic powers*. And therefore
any view or prejudice which acquired vogue at any time, and
which was expressed by a so-called *nabi*, was thought to have
some kind of superhuman standing or status. Hence, the issues
remained unsettled until the battering-rams of Nebuchadnezzar
crushed the walls of Jerusalem and vindicated the insurgent, or
"defeatist," line of prophets.

VII. THE LAW AS REFLECTING INSURGENT PROPHECY

The dependence of the Torah, or Law, upon insurgent, or "left-wing," prophecy is bound to become clearer in the degree that the prophets of "defeatism" are understood in their true character. These prophets, in imagination, could *see* the history of Israel as a transparently clear process of guidance by the hand of Yahweh; and they assumed that "the people" ought to share and act on this view. But, as we have seen, the real, objective Israel before the Exile was not a conventionalized, uniform *nation:* it was a congeries of ethnic groups and social classes, necessarily devoid of harmonious and consistent outlook upon the past, and representing various currents of thought and custom.

Thus, Isaiah sees Yahweh "nourishing and bringing up" Israel, as if the nation had all the characteristics of an integrated personality (Isa. 1:2–3). He is therefore scandalized because Israel does not follow Yahweh with even the low intelligence of a dumb beast, which knows enough to enter the stall of its owner. Likewise, Jeremiah clearly sees Yahweh bringing Israel out of Egypt, through the desert, into a plentiful country; and in view of this dramatic history, he wonders how the people can possibly bow down to the Baals and other gods (Jer. 2:5–8).

Not only did the nation as a whole fail to share the standpoint of this prophetic school, but we must bear in mind that there was a rival group of prophets, equally vociferous, whose "vision" was authoritative and influential throughout large areas of the community. While the pre-Exilic Hebrew people worshiped Yahweh as the symbol of nationality, they showed much reluctance to accept the special view of Yahweh advocated by the left-wing prophets. Thus, Amos envisages Yahweh as causing drought, blasting of olive gardens and fig trees by insects, the

337

slaughter of Israel's men and horses in war, and the havoc of earthquake. The prophet could "see" these manifestations of calamity as the direct work of Yahweh; and he wonders naïvely why it is that in spite of all this the people have not "returned unto Yahweh" (Amos, chap. 4).

The type of prophecy represented by Elijah and his successors grew more and more insistent in depicting the people of Israel *as receiving clear proofs and signs of Yahweh's intervention, while remaining obdurate.* This idea, in fact, is one of the structural conceptions entering into documents E and J. The psychology revealed by the fourth of Amos is typical: Yahweh's complaint that the people have not "returned" to him is equal in force to the passage where he says, "How long will it be before this people believe on me, *for all the miracles which I have done among them? I will smite them with the pestilence*" (Num. 14:11 [JE]). Having before their eyes the undeniable fact of Israel's heathenism after settling in the land of Canaan, the writers of the Torah documents project the contemporary situation back into the pre-Canaanite epoch, describing the Israel of that early period as unbelieving and "stiff-necked," although deluged by a flood of miracles in Egypt and in the desert. Thus, the Law is an *ex parte* condemnation of Israel, reflecting the standpoint of defeatist prophecy before the Babylonian Exile.

VIII. THE SOCIAL PROBLEM IN ISRAEL AND IN OTHER NATIONS

In essential features, the social and economic problem of ancient Israel was the same as in other countries. All nations are overtaken, sooner or later, by the double pressure of heavy taxes and concentrated landownership. But among gentile peoples this problem has been expressed in secular phraseology; whereas, in ancient Israel the problem clothed itself in religious terms, owing to the peculiar course of social development among the Hebrews. No other national evolution has enthroned a cult of desert origin over cities representing a previously rooted commercialism. This peculiar structural fact in Hebrew history made it possible to formulate reactions between the nomadic and the territorial points of view in terms of cult-rivalry. And thus, while the social and economic problem of ancient Israel was the same as in other parts of the world, there is a difference in the forms of expression, whereby the God-idea was uniquely welded into the process which at length gave rise to Judaism and Christianity.

IX. NOTE ON THE NAME "YAHWEH"

The first half of the name occurs, by itself, in Ps. 68:4, as follows: "His name is Yah." It also occurs as the final syllable of the well-known Hebrew expression "Hallelujah," which is an exhortation to praise Yah. The full name is found in the Hebrew Bible, thousands of times, where it stood, like other Hebrew words, *without* vowels, for many centuries, in the form *Y-H-W-H*. But finally the vowels of the Hebrew term *adonai*, "my adon (lord)" were inserted arbitrarily among the foregoing consonants, thus making Y'howah, Y'hovah, or J'hovah—a name unknown to the ancient Hebrews, and etymologically impossible. The form *Yahweh* appears in the present work, in accordance with the usage of most scholars, because it is the most plausible modern transliteration of the Hebrew. The primary syllable, Yah, may at first have been merely expletive in character; and any early concrete significance, attaching to the entire word, has been overlaid and obscured by projecting back into it the abstract theological and philosophical concepts which took shape as late products of Hebrew religious evolution toward metaphysical monotheism. Thus, there is no point in manipulating the root-stem, *H-W-H*, to give the abstract meaning of "existence"; or in the assumption that it is in some way a causative, or "hiphil," form. Accordingly, the French translation, "the Eternal," and the interpretations given in Exod. 3:14, are *post-eventum*, and without scientific basis.

X. PARTIAL SUMMARY OF OUTSTANDING POINTS, NOT FULLY REPRESENTING TREATMENT

"*Proto*-Deuteronomic" conquest of central Canaanite highlands made by elements later known as "house of Joseph," or "Ephraim," and more vaguely as "Israel." Conquest of central Canaan begins with destruction of Amorite *Jericho* and its *baalim* (E document), ending with fall of Amorite *Shechem* and its *baalim* (pre-E material in Judges).

Thorough nature of Josephite conquest gives part of inspiration for later-coming Book of *Deuteronomy*, with curse and blessing on two hills outside of Shechem. Deuteronomy, based on sanguinary example of Josephite conquest, reproduces and re-edits Ephraimite *mishpatim* (Exod. chaps. 21 f.) and Ephraimite "Decalogue" (Exod., chap. 20, in part). "Orthodox" idea of *complete* conquest of Canaan correct with reference to house of Joseph, but mythical when extended to entire land, as in Deuteronomic element of Joshua.

Josephite conquest clears territory north of Jerusalem and south of Esdraelon (highlands of Ephraim), where mishpat land-holding (anticommercialistic tenure) is established by kindred clan-groups, forming *Israelite aristocracy* resting upon lower class of alien slaves (*abadim*). This aristocracy dominated by clan-group, formerly in Egyptian province of Goshen, which encamped at oasis of "En-Mishpat," acquired worship of Yahweh by conjunction with alien Kenites, and made way into Canaan from east through Gilead.

Growing nationalistic movement in Ephraim during later Judges period gives rise to "Ark of Yahweh" at Shiloh, representing ideal of *group-unity*. Primitive Hebrew prophecy gives expression to conflict between social groups, per se, and not to antagonism between classes *within* groups. Early Hebrew

341

prophets therefore "success-*nebiim*" (Deborah, Samuel; Saul "among nebiim" also).

Adhesion of non-Ephraimite clans to Joseph nucleus gives rise to tradition of Joseph as favorite and superior son of shadowy patriarch (Jacob-Israel) through *beloved wife*, Rachel; other children being born from *slave-girls*, Bilhah and Zilpah, and *hated wife*, Leah. These legends, however, fluid, fluctuating, and inconsistent; making Jacob primarily a warlike differentiation from Joseph, conquering highlands of Ephraim "*with sword and bow*" from the Amorites (Gen. 48:22; real "Blessing of Jacob" in 48:14–22 and not in Gen., chap. 49).

Wider Israelite, or Hebrew, kingdom formed on *contra*-Deuteronomic basis by David, who creates tribe of Judah. Amorite walled cities, located south, west, and north of original Ephraim frontiers, now included in Israel *without* destructive, or "Deuteronomic," military conquest such as took place at Jericho, Bethel, and Shechem (i.e., Jerusalem, Gibeonite confederacy, Megiddo, Bethshan, etc.). Alliance made with Phoenician Baal-worshipers. *New Judaic dynasty enslaves house of Joseph.*

Under inspiration of prophet Ahijah, from old nationalistic center Shiloh, Josephites begin mishpat struggle by conspiring against dynasty of Judah. Future Josephite king, Jeroboam, flees into *Egypt*, and is befriended by Pharaoh Shishak. New fascicles of Israel epic take form: *Judah proposes to sell Joseph into slavery*. Ephraimites continue secluded in central highlands fifty years after casting off Judah. Important period of Hebrew history.

Ephraim taken into world-politics by *Omri*, who founds dynasty, builds capital on land purchased for money, *in contravention of mishpat*, from Shemer, the *adon*, or owner. New alliance with Baal-worshiping Phoenicia. Omri's policy of land purchase continued by his son Ahab, who encounters resistance from Naboth: "*Yahweh forbid!*" Murder of Naboth, followed by seizure

of land, kindles flame of revolt among peasant aristocracy. Hebrew prophecy now bifurcates. Original "success-*nebiim*," surviving from Judges period, champion government (e.g., Zedekiah ben Chenanah). New group, or school, of "defeatist-
nebiim" oppose concentration of landed property and predict
fall of state (Elijah, Elisha, Micaiah ben Imlah).

Jehu, supported by defeatist *nebiim*, annihilates house of
Omri, founds new dynasty, and repudiates alliance with Phoenician Baalism. But concentration of land goes on, according to
baalistic, anti-mishpat usage of territorial society. House of
Jehu, on throne a century, fails to deliver mishpat as desired by
left-wing faction of proprietary class. Defeatist prophecy
forced into background by war, militarism, and foreign oppression. E document slowly takes form. Term "baal" comes into
use, in competition with "adon." Ephraimite "Mishpat Code"
proposes compromise with territorial usage by conceding slavery
of left-wing baalim six years. Joseph emerges into legend as prehistoric land reformer, guaranteeing possession of soil to the
peasantry. Prophet Amos silenced by priest at sanctuary of
golden calf in Bethel: "An evil time, wherein to keep silence."
Hosea demands retraction of term "baal" as applied to Yahweh, with reversion to "ish." Defeatist prophecy, as represented by Amos, Hosea, and Ephraimite document, under ban of
state. Ephraim, continuing as heathen power, is destroyed:
"Joined to idols. Let him alone!"

Mishpat struggle slowly develops in Judah. Southern kingdom gradually baalized. Platform of defeatist prophecy at
length becomes official through Deuteronomic reformation.
Book of Deuteronomy based upon Ephraimite military model
and E Mishpat Code, with improvements; its inspiration being
northern, its composition southern. Reaction follows tragic
death of Josiah. Ephraimite prophet Jeremiah utters final curse
of Yahweh upon Judah for failure to emancipate left-wing baal-

im. Priestly document in Babylonian Exile seeks to redress balance of Hebrew history in favor of Judah as ultimate witness to monotheism.

Social tension within baalistic aristocracy the evolving force which differentiates monotheistic Judaism from primitive, pagan Hebraism. Constant approximation to social justice needed, but not fundamental purpose of human life. Implications of history transcendental.

INDEX OF SUBJECTS

Yahweh: evolution of idea of, not explained by critics, x f.; originally one among many deities, xii, 5; cult of, acquired in Arabian desert, 53; worship of, regarded from different standpoints by E, J, and P, 53; fluctuating tradition of, 55; tends to become powerful Canaanite Baal, 55 f.; desert cult not priestly system, 56; a god of Mishpat, 64; v. Baal, in Judges period, 74; cult older in southern Canaan than in Ephraim, 128; P and J on antiquity of worship, 128; prestige suffers in Philistine conquest, but restored by David, 133, 134; called "Baal" at Perazim, 135; v. Baal issue, ignored in David's reign, 139; "god of gods," 140; v. Baal, stage for later struggle constructed by David, 141; v. Baal, under Omrid kings, 170; worshiped as magnified Baal, 190; champion of "poor and needy," according to defeatist prophets, 192; invoked to validate Mosaic priests, 214; "chose not Ephraim," 222, 225; note on name, 340

Zedekiah: made king by Nebuchadnezzar, 274; and new Jerusalem Tammany, 274; rebels against Nebuchadnezzar, 275 f.; consults Jeremiah during siege, 279; punished, 280

Zikanim, elders, 153

Zionism, foreshadowed, 281 f.

Zipporah, Kenite wife of Moses, 213 f.

[PRINTED IN U·S·A·]